American Plays of the New Woman

American Plays
of the
New Woman

Edited with an Introduction by
KEITH NEWLIN

Ivan R. Dee, Chicago

AMERICAN PLAYS OF THE NEW WOMAN. Copyright © 2000 by Keith Newlin.
All rights reserved, including the right to reproduce this book or portions thereof in
any form. For information, address: Ivan R. Dee, Publisher, 1332 North Halsted
Street, Chicago 60622. Manufactured in the United States of America and printed on
acid-free paper.

The Great Divide was originally published by Macmillan, New York, 1909. *A Man's
World* was originally published by Richard G. Badger, Boston, 1915. *As a Man Thinks*
was originally published by Duffield & Co., New York, 1911. *Overtones* was originally
published by Doubleday, Page & Co., Garden City, N.Y., 1916. *The Outside* was
originally published by Small, Maynard & Co., Boston, 1916. *Why Marry?* was
originally published by Charles Scribner's Sons as *"And So They Were Married,"* New
York, 1914.

Library of Congress Cataloging-in-Publication Data:
American plays of the new woman / edited with an introduction by Keith Newlin.
      p. cm
   Includes bibliographical references.
   Contents: The great divide / William Vaughn Moody—A man's world / Rachel
Crothers—As a man thinks / Augustus Thomas—Overtones / Alice Gerstenberg—
The outside / Susan Glaspell—Why marry? / Jesse Lynch Williams.
   ISBN 1-56663-286-2 (alk. paper)—ISBN 1-56663-299-4 (pbk.: alk. paper)
   1. American drama—20th century.   2. Sex role—United States—Drama.   3.
Women—Social conditions—United States—Drama.   4. Feminism—United
States—Drama.   I. Newlin, Keith
PS338.F48 A44 2000
812'.5209352042—dc21

                                                              99-054225

For my sister Susan,
a bit of a New Woman herself

Contents

Introduction   1

Bibliography   33

A Note on the Texts   37

The Great Divide by WILLIAM VAUGHN MOODY   39

A Man's World by RACHEL CROTHERS   86

As a Man Thinks by AUGUSTUS THOMAS   140

Overtones by ALICE GERSTENBERG   207

The Outside by SUSAN GLASPELL   218

Why Marry? by JESSE LYNCH WILLIAMS   227

Introduction

WHILE IT WAS not the only subject of plays produced in the early years of the twentieth century, the New Woman was certainly the dominant theme of many of the more interesting dramas that still claim the modern reader's attention. Surveying the recent offerings of the stage in 1914, one critic observed, "Every play produced on the American stage, with perhaps a few negligible exceptions, has its say on the feminist question. Until sex ceases to be the main preoccupation of drama, this must necessarily be so."[1]

The "feminist question" was actually comprised of a host of questions, issues, and concerns, brought on by the increasing role of women in the workforce. During the nineteenth century women had served principally as supportive wives and nurturing mothers; now the demands of a growing economy pushed many out of the home and into colleges, factories, and the professions. From 1900 to 1920 the enrollment of women increased 1000 percent in public universities and colleges and 482 percent in private ones, while the number of women entering such professions as the ministry, law, medicine, nursing, photography, teaching, and journalism grew from 6.4 percent in 1870 to 10 percent in 1900 and 13.3 percent in 1920. Similarly, women employed in clerical and sales positions increased from 0.8 percent in 1870 to 9.1 percent in 1910 to 25.6 percent in 1920.[2]

This increased visibility of women in the workforce prompted both men and women to reexamine their assumptions about the role of women in society and especially their expectations of "proper" public behavior for women. The questions and problems created by an expanding female workforce dominated newspapers, novels, serial fiction, and the theater. Gender was "in the air," and most dramatists responded to its presence. Of course the conflict between the sexes has always been central to drama, as one exasperated chronicler remarked in 1925 about one of the plays in this anthology: "*A Man's World* sounds very old-fashioned at this date, as indeed it was when it was written. Everything the author says about the life of her woman novelist . . . seems now trite not because it is fifteen years old but because it is thousands of years old."[3]

The six plays included in this collection focus on what was popularly called the "woman problem"—that is, the debate over the "proper" role of women in a rapidly changing and increasingly industrialized society. As illustrated by these plays, the conflict most commonly occurred over such issues as the double standard, the advent of the New Woman and turn-of-the-century feminism, and the conflict between a woman's desire to work and her role in marriage. William Vaughn Moody's *The Great Divide* (1906) offers an early exploration of conventional expectations of women's moral "superiority," couched in mythic symbols of Eastern and Western contrast, which other playwrights would shortly question. Rachel Crothers's *A Man's World* (1910), for example, critiques male expectations of women, morality, and marriage while offering a still trenchant exposé of the double standard. Augustus Thomas's *As a Man Thinks* (1911) is the conservative (and more commercially successful) reply to Crothers's play.

The early twentieth century was also a time of dramatic experiment, and this collection offers two examples of innovations in dramatic structure in plays written for the noncommercial theater. Alice Gerstenberg's *Overtones* (1913) reveals the impact of Freudian psychology in the play's depiction of the id and the ego as the "shadow selves" that haunt two conventionally decorous women. And Susan Glaspell's *The Outside* (1917) suggests through highly developed symbols the ebb and flow of the life force as two women come to terms with the loss of their husbands. The final play in the collection, Jesse Lynch Williams's *Why Marry?* (1917), won the first Pulitzer Prize for drama. This witty, Shavian discussion play offers a most controversial critique of marriage—and it remains a delightfully zesty comedy.

I

AT THE TURN OF THE CENTURY the American theater was dominated by "combination companies," theatrical troupes organized to perform a single play for the season. They would continue to produce the play until audiences stopped coming to see it. Audiences went to the theater not so much to see the play as to see a star display the range of his or her particular talents. These star players often became the managers of their companies as well as maintaining control over the business of casting, staging, and arranging for performances. Both the stars and their managers were continually looking for material that would enable them to present thrilling performances and thus to maintain the cult of personality upon which their livelihood depended. Dramatists responded by trying to write plays that would showcase the star's particular talents.

These companies often tried out their plays in the major cities surrounding New York, testing the play's appeal and rewriting scenes until the manager felt the play would "draw." It would then open in New York and be puffed in the papers. When attendance began to fall off, the company would take the play "on the road" for a series of "one-night stands" throughout the country until audiences became saturated. Then the process would start anew. Arranging bookings for the many traveling companies became complicated—but profitable. In 1896 an organization called simply the Theatrical Syndicate was formed by the businessmen A. L. Erlanger and Marc Klaw, the producer Charles Frohman, and other theater owners, ostensibly to manage bookings for these traveling companies but in effect to control all bookings in theaters it owned. By 1903 the Syndicate held a virtual monopoly in nearly every major city in America. According to one historian of the theater, in 1904 "the Syndicate controlled over five hundred theaters," including "all but two or three first-class houses in New York City and all but one each in Boston and Chicago"; other major cities "were completely in its hands." In 1905 the Shubert Brothers, with David Belasco, Harrison Grey Fiske, and Minnie Maddern Fiske, formed a rival organization to counter the stranglehold imposed by the Syndicate and embarked on an ambitious program of theater construction. By 1906 the Shubert organization controlled more than fifty theaters, and by the next year the number of theaters was so large that both organizations were encountering difficulties in filling them.[4]

Because the economics of this booking system demanded that managers maintain full houses to ensure their profit, play selection and production methods soon became conservative. Managers took few chances with controversial or challenging plays, preferring instead the reliable draw of melodrama, farce, social comedy, and musicals. With so much money at stake, producers naturally wanted reliable assurance that their investment would reap a profitable return, so they gravitated to proven actors and proven plots—just as today Hollywood relies upon the proven success of the buddy movie, the teen sexploitation film, and the dramatized best-seller. Dramatists often wrote their plays with specific actors and actresses in mind for the starring role, developing scenes that would enable the chosen actor to shine. Today's ensemble acting was virtually unheard of, for the star dominated almost every scene. Often the star would demand that the playwright revise a scene if he or she was not getting enough stage time. Few dramatists could resist such economic pressures, as William Vaughn Moody was to learn when he set out to stage *The Great Divide*.

II

BORN IN Spencer, Indiana, on July 8, 1869, William Vaughn Moody was graduated from Harvard in 1893 and the next year returned to take a master's degree. While teaching English as an instructor and then as an assistant professor at the University of Chicago from 1895 to 1902, Moody gained a reputation as a poet of tremendous promise whose career was cut short by his early death in 1910 at the age of forty-one. Fusing elements of romanticism, realism, symbolism, and a fondness for sensory imagery, Moody's lyrical poetry has been described by one scholar as anticipating that of Robert Frost "in its psychological insight, realism, and colloquial idiom and rhythm."[5]

Although Moody was revered as a teacher and scholar, he did not like what he viewed as the onerous duties of correcting student papers, and he contrived a series of contracts that would enable him to teach part-time so that he could devote more time to his poetry. The publication and financial success of *A History of English Literature* in 1902, co-authored with Robert Morss Lovett, enabled him to resign from teaching. In 1901 Moody's *Poems* had appeared. He also envisioned a trilogy of philosophical verse dramas. *The Masque of Judgment*, published in 1900, examines God's purpose in creating good and evil and man's place in the world. In 1904 *The Fire Bringer*, based on the story of Prometheus, appeared. A third play, *The Death of Eve*, about the reconciliation of God and man through Eve, was to have completed the trilogy, but Moody died before finishing it. He extended these themes to two prose dramas, *The Great Divide* (1906) and *The Faith Healer* (1909), which established his reputation. Moody's achievement as a poet was recognized in 1905 with his election to the National Institute of Arts and Letters.

Moody's reputation today largely rests on a single prose play, *The Great Divide*, first produced on April 12, 1906, under the title *A Sabine Woman* at Chicago's Garrick Theater. Employing the mythic contrast between an enervated Eastern gentility and the more life-nurturing Western frontier spirit, the play has been widely praised for its synthesis of theme and action, its realistic portrayal of character conflict, its lyricism and symbolism, and its employment of contemporary cultural myths.

The play opens in an Arizona cabin where a refined Eastern girl, Ruth Jordan, has been left alone one night while her brother, Philip, her sister-in-law, and her suitor have left for town on an errand. Three drunken louts break into the cabin and attack her. Ruth pleads with one, Stephen Ghent, to spare her the ignomiy of gang rape, in return promising, "I will pay you—with my life." Ghent pays one, a "Mexican," to leave Ruth alone. The other he wounds in a duel. The first act closes with

Ruth sentimentally kissing a picture of her mother after hastily writing an explanation of a fictitious elopement. She then departs with Ghent for his mining claim.

After this sensational opening, the second and third acts explore the consequences of Ruth's bargain. Consumed with bitterness over the memory of her abduction, the humiliation of having been sold to the highest bidder, and troubled by her sexual involvement with Ghent despite a hastily arranged marriage, Ruth is determined to salvage her self-respect by earning back her bride price. After she accumulates the money, however, Ghent refuses to grant her freedom, explaining that her "price has risen" because he has grown to love her. When Ruth pleads for pity and reveals that she is pregnant, Ghent becomes even more resolute, thundering that Ruth is "Mine by almighty Nature whether you like it or not!" Philip then enters to take her back to their New England home while remaining ignorant of the circumstances of her marriage to Ghent.

As the scholar Lois Gottlieb points out, Moody does not portray Philip as the rescuing hero of melodrama because his action does not restore Ruth to moral equilibrium. Rather, Ruth becomes increasingly "depressed, withdrawn, indifferent to both her child and her own life."[6] Moody's point in the play is not to fashion a melodramatic tale of virtue tainted and then reclaimed but to explore the clash of two American cultures—Eastern gentility and Western "barbarism"—with the aim of demonstrating the superiority of the Western mythos.

Ghent is the embodiment of the Western archetypal hero: rude and unrefined, but with a strength absent in the more patrician Ruth. And Ruth recognizes and responds to what Moody depicts as Ghent's rough but essential wholesomeness. She tells her sister-in-law Polly that she wants a husband who "isn't finished . . . the man I sometimes see in my dreams is . . . well, like this country out here. . . . I am talking of a sublime abstraction—of the glorious unfulfilled—of the West—the Desert." Ghent is the latent embodiment of her fantasy, and she clearly sees herself as the agent of his moral refinement. Despite their ignominious beginning, she grows to love him—or, more properly, the romance that he represents—until his lust spoils her ideal. As she explains to him:

> That night, when we rode away from the justice's office at San Jacinto, and the sky began to brighten over the desert—the ice that had gathered here—[*she touches her heart*]—began to melt in spite of me. And when the next night and the next day passed, and the next, and still you spared me and treated me with beautiful rough chivalry, I said to myself, "He has heard my prayer to him. He knows what a girl's heart is." . . . And then—and then—I woke, and saw you standing in my tent-door in the

starlight! I knew before you spoke that we were lost. You hadn't had the strength to save us!

To redeem himself from his actions (what Ruth refers to as those of "the human beast, that goes to its horrible pleasure as not even a wild animal will go—*in pack, in pack!*"), Ghent must first undergo a morally cleansing process of self-torture to repay his wrong. Ironically it is Ruth who suffers because her Puritan upbringing prevents her from recognizing Ghent's spiritual growth. As Gottlieb explains, Ruth "comes to realize that the conflict is not between her and Ghent, but between two poles of her self: her physical desire for Ghent in conflict with her need to suffer for enjoying the pleasures of the flesh."[7] While Ghent has become morally regenerated through his suffering, Ruth still anguishes over her divided allegiance to Eastern gentility and the social codes it represents, and Western barbarism and the *joie de vivre* it represents. Also ironic is that while Ruth has sought to "finish" Ghent's moral education, the play closes with Ghent completing Ruth's education by teaching her the need to live in the present, not the past, for the life that is to come (embodied physically in their child) and not the life that was. As he explains to her,

> What have we to do with suffering and sacrifice? That may be the law for some, and I've tried hard to see it as our law, and thought I had succeeded. But I haven't. Our law is joy, and selfishness; the curve of your shoulder and the light on your hair as you sit there says that as plain as preaching.

Discouraged by Ruth's scripture-quoting denunciations, in a quite lengthy speech Ghent gives up his claim to Ruth and admits, "You belong here, and I belong out yonder—beyond the Rockies, beyond—the Great Divide!" Ruth responds to Ghent's impassioned speech, recognizing his primeval strength and her own enervation. She tells him, "You have taken the good of our life and grown strong. I have taken the evil and grown weak, weak unto death. Teach me to live as you do!" The poles of her divided self are united, and the play closes with the lovers in a symbolic embrace.

Moody's achievement in *The Great Divide* was to explore various cultural myths of the first part of the twentieth century and to graft those myths onto a melodramatic plot while avoiding the simplistic characterization typical of melodrama. The melodramatic pattern is evident: Ghent is the licentious, grasping villain (especially in the first act); Philip is the ranting wronged man when he rails against Ghent's villainy; and Ruth tries to rise to the conventional expectation that, as a despoiled woman, she has a duty to kill herself—but she cannot bring herself to do so because, as she tells Ghent, she loves life too much: "I ought to die. I have a right to die. But I cannot, I cannot! I love my life, I must live. In torment, in darkness, it doesn't matter." But the "Great Divide" of the title extends to their characters as well, as Moody explained in a 1906 letter to his fiancée, Harriet Brainard:

> I have found for her [Ruth], I believe, the "dissolving word," by which she brings her struggle and the man's refusal to see any need for anything but whole-hearted acceptance of their fate into a common focus, showing them both to have been forms of the "expiation" her nature demanded: hers traditional, negative, self-conscious, gloomily purgatorial; his natural, positive, spontaneous, and cleansing through joy and life instead of through grief and refusal to live.[8]

While scholars have praised *The Great Divide* for its evocation of myth and its acknowledgment of female sexuality, the play ironically closes with a reaffirmation of culturally designated gender roles. Chief among these is the designation of women as responsible for the moral education of men. Ghent specifically attributes his regeneration to Ruth's moral superiority: "That's the one thing you can't throw back at me—the man you've man of me, the life and meaning of life you've showed me the way to!" Modern readers may be troubled by Moody's apparent acceptance of gender-coded cultural myths: that women are attracted to and fall in love with primitive, brutish men, even those who design to commit rape, abduct, and corrupt; that women need to be "won"; that in marriage women "sell" themselves. As Ghent explains to Ruth: "Does it rankle in your mind that I took you when I could get you, by main strength and fraud? I guess most women are taken that way, if they only knew it. Don't you want to be paid for? I guess every wife is paid for in some good coin or other."

The Great Divide underwent a summer of intense revision to meet the demands of its two stars, the temperamental Margaret Anglin (as Ruth), who was known for her "expressive emotionalism," and Henry Miller (as Ghent), who also produced the play. It opened on October 3, 1906, in New York's Princess Theater, and proved to be a sensational popular and critical success, running for 238 performances, with tickets put on sale three months in advance. Critics applauded its characterizations, its use of Western setting, and the acting of the two experienced stars. Maurice Brown, Moody's biographer, points out that the play succeeded because it was "not a startling break with theatrical tradition. It represented a new treatment of that tradition and so was acceptably new."[9] The *New York Times* review suggests that the audience responded to the play's infusion of character development into a largely melodramatic conflict—thus melding the new with the old:

> As a whole . . . the play rises far above [melodrama]. Its characterizations are splendidly real, there is an undercurrent of subtle thought, its human contrasts are bold, strong, powerful, and convincing, and with the exception of an occasional maundering of the interest necessary for the manipulation of the characters, it moves forward with a steady, insistent, and absorbing grip upon the attention and the sympathy.[10]

Even while the play was packing the Princess Theater, its producer was considering assembling another company to take it on the road, and a parody quickly appeared in the burlesque theaters entitled *The Great Decide*—a certain indication of the play's popular appeal.[11]

III

WHILE MOODY EXPLORED the mythic symbolism occasioned by expanding gender roles, Rachel Crothers devoted most of her plays to examining the status of women in a patriarchal society. Her dramas tend to be "social problem plays," works that examine such issues as the double standard, the conflict between traditional notions of motherhood and meaningful work, the search for personal freedom in a man's world, and the effect of liberation on romantic relationships. Crothers herself resisted the explicit identification of her work with feminist ideology. Looking back on her work in 1941, she remarked, "I've been told that my plays are a long procession reflecting the changing attitude of the world toward women. If they are, that was completely unconscious on my part. Any change like that, that gets on to the stage, has already happened in life."[12]

Born on December 12, 1878, Crothers was the most successful and prolific woman dramatist writing in the first part of the twentieth century. In a career spanning thirty-eight years, she saw twenty-four full-length plays produced on the commercial stage, beginning in 1899 with a series of one-act plays in what we would now call off-Broadway houses and concluding in 1937 with the prize-winning *Susan and God*. Crothers's interest in drama began at an early age. By the time she was twelve or thirteen she had written and acted in her first play; and she took part in high school dramatics, graduating in 1891 at the age of thirteen. She then moved to Boston to study elocution at the New England School of Dramatic Instruction, where she received a certificate in 1892, after one term. During 1896–1897 she enrolled in the Stanhope-Wheatcroft School of Acting in New York City. After completing one term she was asked to become an instructor, a position she held for the next four years.

During this time she wrote a number of one-act plays for her students, and in these plays she served her apprenticeship, seeing to details of directing, casting, costuming, and the like. She saw a number of her one-act plays produced in the older theaters, and she received her first public recognition in 1902 when *The Rector* was reviewed by the *New York Times*. Crothers's professional stage debut came in 1897 when she joined E. H. Sothern's company, where she acted in a variety of supporting roles.

The Three of Us became her first commercial success in 1906 when it appeared at the Madison Square Theater for 227 performances before going to London with Ethel Barrymore as its star. This play set the pattern for many of Crothers's early dramas. Rhy MacChesney is a "forceful and fearless" New Woman who is supporting herself and two younger brothers through ownership of a Nevada silver mine. The play's notable scene occurs when, caught in a compromising situation, Rhy defends her honor and repudiates the assumption that she needs a male protector: "My honor! Do you think it's in your hands? It's in my own and I'll take care of it, and everyone who *belongs* to me. I don't need you—either of you."[13]

Crothers's other notable plays of this period include *He and She* (1911), about a New Woman who capitulates to domestic pressures at the cost of a promising artistic career; *Ourselves* (1913), which examines prostitution; and *Young Wisdom* (1914), a satire of the New Woman and the notion of trial marriages. In later plays Crothers shifted direction from dramatizing the problems of New Women to comic depictions of flappers in such plays as *Nice People* (1921) and *Mary the Third* (1923). As the economic hardships of the Great Depression began to be felt, she began exploring the concerns of women disillusioned about the new freedoms in such plays as *Let Us Be Gay* (1929), *As Husbands Go* (1931), *When Ladies Meet* (1932), and *Susan and God* (1937). After a long and distinguished career that included heading the Stage Relief Fund during the Depression and the American Theater Wing for War Relief (known for its Stage Door Canteen) during World War II, Crothers died on July 5, 1958.

A Man's World, first performed in Washington, D.C., on October 18, 1909, is the first detailed exploration on the American stage of the choices society presents for women: to be a "True Woman" and face limited possibilities for personal growth and remain a passive object defined in relation to men; or to be a "New Woman" and face censure by men and women alike and be caught in a bind concerning the possibilities for fulfillment in love. The story concerns Frank Ware, a successful novelist and social reformer, who has taken the name of a man so that her work will be more readily accepted by a society reluctant to tolerate an inde-

pendent woman. Frank lives in a Greenwich Village boardinghouse ten-
anted by various artists, many of whom assume that she owes her success
to a man. As one male European resident condescendingly remarks, "She
is a very brilliant woman, but she cannot do what is impossible. She cannot write like a man unless a man help her—and no man could make her
write like zat unless she love him."

The rather spare plot focuses on the problems created for women by
a double standard of morality, embodied symbolically in questions that
arise over the paternity of Kiddie, whom Frank adopted after his unwed
mother died during childbirth. Kiddie has become the chief motivation
for Frank's social reform writing and settlement work, and she personifies
in his birth mother's seducer all that is wrong with gender relations. Most
of the roominghouse tenants mistakenly assume that Frank is really Kiddie's natural mother, and this fallacious assumption gives Crothers the
opportunity to underscore the destructive effects of the double standard.
The opera singer Lione Brune is especially harsh in her condemnation,
echoing the conventional perception of women as the chief enforcers of
social morality: "I don't propose to help a woman of that sort keep up appearances by pretending that I don't see what's right under my nose."

The play's dramatic interest is the ongoing verbal battle between
Frank and her fiancé Malcolm Gaskell, who serves as a particularly annoying mouthpiece for chauvinist attitudes. Despite the universal approval of
Frank's book, an exposé of tenement conditions, Gaskell tells Frank it is
"only a story. You haven't got at the social evil in the real sense. You
couldn't tackle that. It's too big for you. . . . You keep banging away
about woman—woman and what she could do for herself if she would.
Why—this is a man's world. Women'll never change anything." He
mouths the conventional view of women as moral exemplar, to be judged
by a separate standard: "Man sets the standard for woman. He knows
she's better than he is and he demands that she be—and if she isn't she's
got to suffer for it." Gaskell's comment appropriately echoes a remark by
Bronson Howard, one of the nineteenth century's leading playwrights,
and it suggests the continued currency of dramatic expectations. In an address before Harvard University in 1886, Howard offered several "laws"
concerning dramatic construction, one of which concerned the role of
the "erring woman": "The wife who has once taken the step from purity
to impurity can never reinstate herself in the world of art on this side of
the grave; and so the audience looks with complacent tears on the death
of an erring woman."[14]

With such attitudes concerning the separate spheres of men and
women, it is inevitable that Gaskell become revealed as Kiddie's father,
and the third and fourth acts contain some vigorous verbal sparring as

Frank weighs her principles against her love for Gaskell. To Gaskell's comment that "A man wants the mother of his children to be the purest in the world," Frank rejoins, "Yes, and a man expects the purest woman in the world to forgive him anything—everything. It's wrong. It's hideously wrong." Crothers complicates Frank's feminism by demonstrating the very real problems love poses for a New Woman, which meant a radically altered set of assumptions about the connection between social and personal roles and the emotion of love. For both men and women "love" means a certain set of behaviors in addition to a type of feeling. Gaskell, for instance, once he declares his love for Frank, expects her to quit work so that he may "take care" of her. And Frank is genuinely conflicted about her admission of love for Gaskell because she too has been raised with the expectation that love and marriage mean narrowly defined gender roles:

> You're the one man, Malcolm. That's why I've tried to resist it because it means so terribly much to me. My life has been filled with other things you know—with Kiddie—and my work. They absorbed me and satisfied me; and when you—when love began to crowd in—to overpower me—I was afraid. It seemed almost like being a traitor to myself. Oh, it means such a—such an overwhelming thing for a woman to give up to love after—she's—she's been . . . let me lean on you and worship you.

The play is thus as much a drama about the problem of the proper expression of "love" for the New Woman as it is a criticism of the double standard, and Crothers develops this theme through two other casualties of the conflict between the old and new conceptions of womanhood.

Clara Oakes is an unattractive, thirty-seven-year-old miniaturist with mediocre talent who has tried to live up to the role of a New Woman but who has become tired of trying to make it in a man's world. "I've tried just as hard as I can for ten years," she tells Frank, "and scrimped and scraped and taken snubs and pretended I was ambitious and didn't care for anything but my work. . . . I'm so sick and tired of it all I don't know what to do. I'd marry any man that asked me." Crothers is sensitive to the fact that not all women are capable of being independent in 1909, given their training in the cult of true womanhood, as Frank compassionately tells Clara: "I believe in women doing the thing they're most fitted for. You should have married, Clara, when you were a young girl—and been taken care of all your life." When asked why she hasn't married, Clara replies that she was too "superfluous and plain" to attract a husband—thus underscoring one of society's more trenchant means of acculturation. "There's nobody to take care of me and I'm simply not capable of taking care of myself," Clara explains to Frank. "If I were a man—the most insignificant little runt of a man—I could persuade some woman to marry me—and could have a home and children and hustle for my living—and life would mean something."

Lione Brune illustrates the other extreme: the woman who is so insecure in her life that she is willing to tolerate behavior by men she despises because she has given up hope of changing male attitudes. "Men are pigs of course," she tells Frank. "They take all they can get and don't give any more than they have to. It's a man's world—that's the size of it. What's the use of knocking your head against things you can't change?" Although Frank holds a loftier standard, believing male attitudes *can* be changed if women demand it, Lione's reply is particularly suggestive of the latent fear even independent women hold: "When it comes to morality a woman never holds anything against a man. What good would it do if she did? She'd be alone." Like Clara, Lione feels incomplete without a love in her life, and in a man's world love requires women to accept a double standard or risk losing that love. So Lione capitulates to that double standard and advises Frank to accept Gaskell: "He's the man you want—take him and thank your lucky stars you have him."

A Man's World was revolutionary in its time because the play did not provide a tidy ending that would reconcile the sparring lovers—such reconciliation would require, according to accustomed dramatic treatment, that Frank forgive Gaskell his transgression. As Gaskell confidently tells Frank at the close: "We don't live under the same laws. It was never meant to be. Nature, nature made men different. . . . You're going to forgive me." Frank wants to forgive Gaskell, but only if he admits his attitude is wrong. He refuses, and the curtain falls upon Frank's dismissal of Gaskell, and her love for him, with the words "It is the end."

The play opened at the Comedy Theater in New York on February 8, 1910, with Crothers directing the staging. Though not a commercial success (seventy-one performances), *A Man's World* did provoke discussion in the press. The *New York Times* praised Crothers for not preaching, for having the views "come naturally out of the mouths of the characters." The *Nation* called the play "one of the strongest, and most interesting, logical, and dramatic pieces on the now dominant topic of the relations of the sexes, that has been seen in this city for years." The reviewer went on to laud the logic of the ending, pointing out that "For once sense has not been sacrificed to sentiment, or the desire for a happy ending." But not all reviewers agreed about the appropriateness of the close. Adolph Klauber, in a second review for the *New York Times*, while agreeing that the play was "one of the very best produced in New York this season," expressed dissatisfaction with the ending, clearly preferring a more conventional close. Indeed, he rewrites the ending in his review:

"Doubt remains as to the permanency of the separation. One feels that inevitably the man will come again and again to sue for pardon, that ultimately he will be forgiven, that bygones will be bygones, and that these two, mending the broken china, to use Pinero's phrase, will finally live out their lives together."[15]

IV

THIS DESIRE TO REAFFIRM the status quo prompted Augustus Thomas to draft a conservative reply to this by now well-worn theme in *As a Man Thinks*, one of the biggest hits of the 1911 season. Even by 1911 Broadway standards, the play's plot was complicated, seeking to unite discussion of the social necessity for a double standard of morality, the effect of emotions on mental health, the need for forgiveness of sin, and anti-Semitism. As Clayton Hamilton remarked in a review for *The Bookman*, "What the new piece lacks is unity of theme. . . . *As a Man Thinks* discloses a mosaic of many ideas instead of a thematic development of one; it produces on the mind an impression that is plural instead of single." Nonetheless, Hamilton concluded, "it is curiously coherent in expression."[16]

During the early 1900s Augustus Thomas was known as the "Dean of American drama," presenting a string of Broadway hits after a rather diverse apprenticeship. Born on January 8, 1857, in St. Louis, Thomas quit attending school regularly at age ten to serve as a page in the Missouri House of Representatives. In December 1870 he left school altogether to become a congressional page in Washington, sending his entire salary home to help support his family. He returned to St. Louis in 1871 to work for three St. Louis railroads and became a member of the Knights of Labor. Interested in the theater since he was a child, he attended plays regularly in St. Louis and began to compose his own while acting in a variety of amateur troupes. In 1883 he organized the Dickson Sketch Club and presented a series of his one-act plays in Chicago before taking them on the road in two tours. When the Sketch Club disbanded in 1885, he worked as a reporter and feature writer for the *St. Louis Post-Dispatch* and the *Missouri Republican* for three years before quitting to go to New York to work as a stage manager and foreign play adapter and reviser.

Thomas's experience as an actor on the road with the Sketch Club (appearing in some of his own plays) enabled him to gauge what would please the ethnically diverse audiences of the Midwest. His background as a newspaper reporter honed his skills of observation, description, and selection of the dramatic moment, which provided plenty of material for his playwriting. Because New York managers did not produce plays they did not think would do well on the road, Thomas profited from his experience to create dramatic situations and characters pointed to satisfy his audience's tastes, and his efforts were rewarded in 1891 with the production of *Alabama*, his first major success, a drama concerning the reconstruction of the South. It was followed by a series of plays focusing on American regions, all of which are historically important as contributions to dramatic realism. *In Mizzoura* appeared in 1893; two plays on political themes debuted in 1894 (*New Blood*) and 1895 (*The Capitol*); *Arizona* followed in 1899; and *Colorado* in 1902.

Thomas's achievement in drama was rewarded in 1906 when he became president of the Society of American Dramatists, an office he held until 1912. In 1914 he received the Gold Medal award for his life's work in drama from the National Institute of Arts and Letters, and he was elected that year as its president for the next two years. In 1919 he was selected to mediate the Actors Equity strike, which had closed most New York theaters. Thomas died on August 12, 1934, after seeing some thirty-five original full-length plays produced on the professional stage.

As a Man Thinks followed the enormous success of *The Witching Hour* (1907), which combined Thomas's interest in telepathy and hypnotism with issues of social responsibility. In the latter play the central conflict concerns the gentleman gambler Jack Brookfield, who manipulates a jury through telepathic suggestion and hypnotizes an assailant into dropping a gun. Its sensational plot is a vehicle to demonstrate Thomas's theme that individuals bear responsibility for their actions and that the emotions are interconnected with both conscious and unconscious motivations.

This issue becomes the focus of *As a Man Thinks*. The principal plot concerns a debate over why a double standard of morality is necessary for the social good. Elinor Clayton has discovered that her husband, Frank, has had another affair. Frank tries to excuse his actions by offering a rather bald defense of the double standard: he is only indulging "a man's natural curiosity about her type. Hang it—there must be some freedom." When Elinor asks whether women also have the freedom to indulge that "natural curiosity," Frank asserts, "Curiosity of that kind in a woman is idle and immoral!" Feeling neglected and peeved with Frank, and seeking to repay him in kind, Elinor goes to the room of Benjamin De Lota, where she remains for half an hour. When her husband discovers her "transgression," he threatens to have her thrown out of the house, but he goes to his club instead and sues for divorce. Although Elinor has not committed adultery, Frank refuses to believe her. When he discovers that De Lota was once Elinor's suitor, he doubts his paternity of their child Dick and becomes psychosomatically ill.

This situation—despite "the staleness of its major theme," as the *New York Times* review remarked—gives Thomas much opportunity to discourse upon the relations between the sexes and woman's place in the social order.[17] He sidesteps the issue by making Elinor guilty only of the indiscretion of going to De Lota's room and not of adultery; but with an eye to the moral effect of drama upon his audience, he makes Elinor suffer nonetheless, as Bronson Howard claimed the erring woman should. And Elinor admits her error: "I'm to blame," she tells Mrs. Seelig, the sympathetic wife of the play's raisonneur, Dr. Seelig. "I deserve it all—I did go to his rooms." In an expression of solidarity, Mrs. Seelig consoles her: "That woman dramatist with her play was right. It is 'a man's world.'" Lest his audience miss the point about the necessity of upholding the status quo, Dr. Seelig explains clearly and eloquently albeit chauvinistically the social benefit of the double standard. "This is a *woman's world*," he tells Elinor:

> Men work for the children because they believe the children are—their own—*believe*. Every mother *knows* she is the mother of her son or daughter. Let her be however wicked, no power on earth can shake that knowledge. Every father believes he is a father only by his faith in the woman. . . . There is a double standard of morality because upon the golden basis of woman's virtue rests the welfare of the world.

This scene and the ensuing business of Elinor's suffering as she tries to win back her husband's faith in her pleased 1911 audiences immensely. "What he [Thomas] has to say on this point is thoroughly sound," remarked Clayton Hamilton in his review, "and, therefore, entirely commonplace." The conservative William Winter, nearing the end of a long and distinguished career, offered a lengthy review in *Harper's Weekly* and applauded the social utility of Dr. Seelig's speech while recognizing that it was simply old wine in a new bottle. Winter chided John Mason, who played Dr. Seelig, for remarking to a newspaper that "'Dr. Seelig makes *a point that has never been made before*,'" but Winter went on to affirm the sentiment nonetheless, quoting from one of his own speeches, "As long as woman is pure and man continues to worship her, society is safe and civilization will advance." And Arthur Hobson Quinn cemented the historical take on the scene by writing in his *A History of American Drama* that in this scene "Thomas gave the answer to the sentimental discussion of the double standard which is rampant in literature."[18]

Had Thomas stopped with this remark, the play would be of interest only as a now-dated conservative reaffirmation of gender roles. But Thomas's chief interest in this tawdry situation is not, as most recent commentators have suggested, with the double standard itself but with the scene's utility as a prompt for the mental ailments that afflict both Elinor and Frank.[19] As a devotee of psychic phenomena, among them the "science" of mental healing, Thomas believed in "the toxic and tonic properties of the emotions: selfish emotions, such as anger, resentment, and anxiety, generating poisons in the body, and altruistic emotions producing physical well being." Thomas had formerly been an advance man for the psychic Washington Irving Bishop, and his association with the telepathist engendered in him a lifelong fascination with psychic phenomena.[20] He owned a copy of James Allen's *As a Man Thinketh*, which supplied the title for the play and influenced the development of its themes. Allen advocated positive thinking as a remedy for physiological ills, arguing for a direct connection between the quality of thought and its effect on one's health:

> Sickly thoughts will express themselves through a sickly body. Thoughts of fear have been known to kill a man as speedily as a bullet, and they are continuously killing thousands of people just as surely though less rapidly. The people who live in fear of disease are the people who get it. Anxiety quickly demoralises the whole body, and lays it open to the entrance of disease, while impure thoughts, even if not physically indulged, will soon shatter the nervous system.
>
> Strong, pure, and happy thoughts build up the body in vigour and grace.[21]

The effect of Frank's adultery is to produce insomnia in Elinor and illness in Frank; their son Dick also becomes sick, for the "sickly thoughts" produced by his parents telepathically affect his health. Dr. Seelig ministers to the ailments of all three, first by diagnosing the causes of the emotional ill-health and then by treating the body through ministering to the mind. For Elinor's insomnia he prescribes a form of talk therapy, drawing an analogy to surgery: when a wound has healed too quickly the surgeon must "re-open it entirely. A mental trouble has its analogy." By making Elinor talk out what is troubling her, he discovers the cause for her insomnia: she has not forgiven Frank. By making her realize how much she owes to Frank, and his importance and her influence upon his success, Seelig effects a "cure": "I saw the care go out of those eyes—and the peace come into them," Seelig observes. And Elinor accepts Seelig's diagnosis: "You're a dear," she tells him, and *"gratefully and impulsively takes* SEELIG*'s hand."* Thomas thus scores a twin victory for mental healing and for male chauvinism.

Upon learning of Elinor and De Lota's previous acquaintance, Frank doubts his paternity of Dick, thus affirming part of Seelig's comment about the need for man's faith in woman. The effects of his doubt soon lead to psychosomatic illness: he becomes listless, fretful, impatient, tired. Frank is suffering principally from the "poisons" of doubt and hate. Hate kills the hater, Seelig tells Frank. "Now, you lie here with this grouch of yours and generate an internal poison." To effect a cure, Seelig first forces Frank to talk out his troubles, getting him to recognize his own errors, and then he prescribes a "cure": to take the "imperfect" Elinor—"overlook what she's done"—and "perfect" her by completing her moral education. Thus Seelig tidily cures Frank's illness and resolves a social issue. By extending the necessity of forgiveness to both Elinor and Frank, a marriage is saved, a woman is relegated to her "place," an adulterous husband escapes condemnation, and the status quo remains firmly entrenched.

As a contemporary observer noted, *As a Man Thinks* "represents a sex-ethics that is more or less typical." The play "is a fair enough picture of that American home in which the function of the wife is to be the ornamental symbol of her husband's prosperity."[22] This "typical" presentation of the double standard proved to be a moderately popular success when it opened at the Thirty-Ninth Street Theater on March 13, 1911, playing for 128 performances. Male reviewers, however, mostly raved. The *New York Times* called it "an exceptionally gratifying experience," "a work of which the American theatre may be proud, and it establishes Mr. Thomas in the very first place among our native playwrights." Clayton Hamilton regarded it as "the most notable" play of the season. And William Winter, who spent his career denouncing any drama that violated his sense of decorum, composed a lengthy article in which he applauded the didacticism of the drama, arguing that "the influence of the play is a potent, decisive, far-reaching benefit to society."[23]

V

BECAUSE THE PROFIT MOTIVE so dominated the commercial stage, Broadway producers were not very receptive to plays that were experimental in theme or form. In order to stage their plays, playwrights would need to find alternative venues for their efforts. The little theater, with its stripped-down budget, amateur spirit, and enthusiasm for innovation, provided such an alternative to the commercial theater, for upon its amateur stage writers and actors could experiment with controversial topics or new staging techniques without risking financial disaster. The transitional role played by the Washington Square Players and the Provincetown Players is well known in literary history. The former troupe (and its successor, the Theater Guild) introduced American audiences to innovative European dramas and staging methods; the latter produced two playwrights of stature: Eugene O'Neill and Susan Glaspell. But the Washington Square Players and the Provincetown Players were only the two signal successes of a much larger movement that was simultaneously educating audiences to appreciate innovative drama. Little theaters blossomed in every major American city during the first two decades of the twentieth century, and these theaters provided an alternative venue for many writers for whom the professional stage was not a viable option.

The little theater movement in America began in 1891 when Hamlin Garland and James A. Herne formed the Boston Independent Theater Association to stage Herne's Ibsenesque *Margaret Fleming*. Although the production was a critical success, audiences proved to be not much interested, preferring more conventional fare, and the Association folded in a few weeks. By 1906 reaction to the stranglehold imposed by the Syndicate and the Shubert Brothers had set in, and early independent theater groups such as Victor Mapes's Chicago New Theater (1906–1907), the Donald Robertson Players (1907–1909), and Winthrop Ames's New York New Theater (1909–1911) were experimenting with means of subsidizing plays considered too risky for the commercial stage. Although their methods of staging and acting differed little from those of the commercial theater, they were interested in "uplifting" the theater by providing a forum for controversial European and domestic dramas.[24]

By 1912 at least nine noncommercial theaters had been formed to foster the ideals of the "art" theater. Dissatisfied with the general vulgarity of commercial productions, such groups as the Chicago Little Theater (1912–1917), the Wisconsin Dramatic Society (1911–1915), and the Boston Toy Theater (1912–1915) consciously sought to embody the "new stagecraft" ideals of Gordon Craig and Adolphe Appia. Craig insisted upon the primacy of the artist-director whose vision unified play, acting, setting, and lighting into an impressionistic whole; Appia subordinated realistic setting through simplification and emphasized emotional effects through the manipulation of light and shadow. Both sought to replace the standardized productions of the commercial theater with a performance that expressed a unified, synthetic artistic vision. In practice the art theater ideal meant that realistic sets were gradually abandoned in favor of impressionistic and expressionistic staging methods which emphasized visual experimentation rather than fidelity to the text.[25]

The growth of the little theaters was truly astounding. In 1912 there were nine; by 1917, fifty; by 1922, three hundred to four hundred; by 1929, more than one thousand.[26] What was responsible for this explosion of noncommercial theater? Publicity played a significant role, for newspaper reviewers widely covered early productions and often accompanied their reviews with columns extolling the principles of experimental theater. In 1914 Samuel Hume, who had studied with Gordon Craig, presented his New Stagecraft Exhibition in Cambridge, Massachusetts. Widely reviewed and praised, the exhibition toured during the next year to New York, Chicago, and Detroit, at each stop attracting crowds of theater enthusiasts (fifteen thousand in Chicago alone). The exhibit consisted of a variety of stage designs, including "five hundred drawings and photographs, . . . twenty-one electrically lighted models, and . . . two working models of the sliding stage and the skydome."[27] To meet this interest in the new stagecraft, several books appeared, among them Sheldon Cheney's *The New Movement in the Theatre* (1914) and *The Art Theatre* (1917), Thomas Dickinson's *The Insurgent Theatre* (1917), and Constance D'Arcy Mackay's *The Little Theatre in the United States* (1917). In 1916 Sheldon Cheney founded *Theatre Arts Magazine*, which served as the principal organ for the movement. Universities began offering workshops in playwriting, among them the Harvard 47 Workshop (1913), the Dartmouth Laboratory Theatre (1913), and the Laboratory Theatre of the Carnegie Institute (1914). To meet the need for scripts, volumes of one-act plays soon began appearing from such publishers as Frank Shay, Mitchell Kennerley, and Brentano's Bookstore, as well as from the little theaters themselves.[28]

This flowering of little theaters heightened interest in the one-act play as an art form. Little theaters favored the one-act play partly because the compressed form did not overextend the capabilities of the actors, most of whom were amateurs, and the plays, usually presented in a bill of three or four for a period of less than a week, enabled the actors to try a variety of roles. The generally small royalties for one-act plays facilitated their production by troupes constantly fighting to make ends meet. The brief compass also invited experimentation in staging methods—especially in those theaters devoted to the new stagecraft—enabling the director to distill the dramatic intention into a unified whole. As the little theaters grew in numbers, they began to clamor for more plays by American authors, and many devoted themselves entirely to American authorship.

Because the chief desire was artistic integrity, dramatic experiment, or the cultivation of American playwrights, these little (or noncommercial) theaters did not need to pay attention to the proven moneymaking potential of conventional plots, staging techniques, or star players. Instead, since productions were never intended to wring as much money as possible from a play, but rather to develop actors, playwrights, and staging methods for runs, in most cases, of less than a week, these theaters could take risks with the sort of play they staged and its method of production.

Alice Gerstenberg was a founding member of the Chicago Little

Theater, one of the most influential troupes in the little theater movement. Born on August 2, 1885, in Chicago, Gerstenberg was the only daughter of a wealthy and socially prominent grain merchant who encouraged her interest in the arts. After graduating in 1907 from Bryn Mawr, where she wrote and acted in plays, she enrolled in Anna Morgan's acting studio in Chicago. Morgan encouraged her playwriting ambitions, and the four one-act plays she composed for student productions were published in 1908 as *A Little World*. Gerstenberg then studied theater in New York and wrote her first full-length play, *The Conscience of Sarah Platt*, which was accepted for production in 1910 by David Belasco (and later published in 1915 as a novel). The play went unproduced, however, when the actress Belasco wanted for the play, Nance O'Neill, married.

For Gerstenberg, 1912 proved to be an important year. Her comedy *Captain Joe* was produced in New York by students of the Academy of Dramatic Arts; she published a novel, *Unquenched Fire;* and she auditioned for Maurice Browne's Chicago Little Theater, acting in *The Trojan Women* and *Anatol*. In 1915 she developed her interest in psychology by adapting Lewis Carroll's *Alice in Wonderland*, which appeared in both Chicago and New York, and the play gave "Broadway its first really authentic glimpse into unconscious life."[29] Now professionally established, Gerstenberg published a series of novels and plays over the next forty years, the most important of which include *Ten One-Act Plays* (1921), *Four Plays for Women* (1924), and *Comedies All* (1930). She founded the Playwrights' Theater of Chicago (1922–1945) to encourage the production of works by local authors, and she staged a three-act version of *Overtones*. Her work in theater was honored in 1938 when she won the Chicago Foundation for Literature award. Gerstenberg died on July 28, 1972.

Overtones, written in 1913 and first produced in 1915, exemplifies the one-act play favored by the little theater. The plot is simple but innovative: Harriet and Margaret are fashionable women conducting polite but shallow conversation while their "primitive selves," Hetty and Maggie, reveal the jealous, backbiting one-upmanship that seethes beneath the surface, underscoring the hypocrisy of both the cultured self and fashionable speech. To stage this embodiment of the unconscious, Gerstenberg relies upon nuances of color and lighting in her stage directions, as well as the placement of the actors on stage, to clarify the relations between the cultured and primitive self:

> HARRIET*'s gown is a light, "jealous" green. Her counterpart,* HETTY, *wears a gown of the same design but in a darker shade.* MARGARET *wears a gown of lavender chiffon while her counterpart,* MAGGIE, *wears a gown of the*

same design in purple, a purple scarf veiling her face. Chiffon is used to give a sheer effect, suggesting a possibility of primitive and cultured selves merging into one woman.

The darker colors of Hetty and Maggie suggest their richer, more fundamental passions as opposed to the artificialities of their cultured selves. Gerstenberg also directs the placement of the actors on the stage to emphasize the dualism of the characters: Harriet and Margaret do not acknowledge their counterparts but rather look off into space while their counterparts speak, to give an impression of thinking aloud. Additionally, the voices of the cultured selves are "*affected and lingering*" while those of the primitive selves are "*impulsive and more or less staccato.*" Finally, the spare set, containing only a tea table and two chairs, is admirably suited to the equally spare economy of the little theater stage.

Overtones has been called "the first departure from realism for the purpose of dramatizing the unconscious," and its dramatization of the separation of the ego and the id is the first such embodiment on the American stage. The play likely influenced Eugene O'Neill's *Strange Interlude* (1928) and *Days Without End* (1934), which employ similar methods of dramatizing the unconscious.[30]

The play opened at the Bandbox Theater in New York on November 8, 1915, as part of the Washington Square Players' first season. Appearing with it were three other plays by continental authors: *Literature* by Arthur Schnitzler; *The Honorable Lover* by Robert Bracco; and *Whims* by Alfred de Musset. The *New York Times* devoted most of its review to the European offerings, noting of *Overtones* merely that "The idea was more clever than its execution."[31] *The New Republic*, however, called the play "the most interesting event" of the week—not because of the quality of the theme or of the acting but because "It points the way to other things. Miss Gerstenberg's success will incite other dramatists to try their hands at plays in which the suppressed self is also at moments the irrelevant, and we shall be the richer by droll scenes of contrast between what a man says and the superficially unrelated things he is thinking about."[32]

While earlier reviewers may have delighted in "droll scenes of contrast" and may have seen the play as a confirmation of women's shrewishness, subsequent critics have valued the play for its dramatization of women's split consciousness as a result of conforming to patriarchal pressures. Mary Maddock argues that Harriet and Margaret's "alter egos are the natural outcome of the socialized women's denial of their autonomous selves and represent their desperate efforts to save their outlaw identities." While Harriet and Margaret observe conventional proprieties, their "primitive," more fundamental selves—Hetty and Maggie—seethe at the restrictions demanded by the artifice of convention and rebel by voicing their true thoughts. The play ends with a clash of cymbals and a blackout to "interrupt, not resolve, the action, because there can be no real solution to Hetty and Maggie's conflict."[33]

Another innovator in staging and form is Susan Glaspell, who is, with Eugene O'Neill, the most famous of the playwrights who wrote for the little theaters. Born in Davenport, Iowa, on July 1, 1876, Glaspell graduated from Drake University in 1899 and worked for two years as a reporter for the *Des Moines Daily News*. She published several stories in the local color tradition in such magazines as *Youth's Companion* and *Harper's Bazaar* and in 1901 became a full-time writer, publishing in addition to short fiction the novels *The Glory of the Conquered* (1909), *The Visioning* (1911), and *Fidelity* (1915). In 1907 she met George Cram Cook, who shared with her his vision of a classical revival in America, founded upon Greek ideals. The couple were among the early admirers of the Chicago Little Theater, and when they married in 1913 and moved to Provincetown, Massachusetts, they formed the Provincetown Players in a makeshift theater on a wharf to put on plays written by their friends.[34]

Glaspell is perhaps best known for her much-anthologized one-act play *Trifles* (1915), which has become something of a textbook staple, appearing in nearly every American literature collection as well as most drama anthologies. In addition to this play, she collaborated with Cook on *Suppressed Desires*, a satire of Greenwich Village Freudianism and the fad of "psyching," which was first produced in August 1915 and quickly became a favorite of the little theaters. Unlike the Washington Square Players, whose goal was to produce plays of "artistic merit," of whatever national origin, under Cook's leadership the Provincetown Players formed to stage plays exclusively of American authorship. Glaspell was, with O'Neill, the Provincetown's most important playwright, and she saw some eleven of her plays produced by them, beginning in 1915 with *Trifles* and concluding in 1922 with *Chains of Dew*. Notable productions included *Inheritors* (1921), an indictment of America's tendency to sacrifice the visionary idealism of its founders for money; and *The Verge* (1921), an expressionistic portrayal of a woman botanist and her search for meaning divorced from conventional expectations of women's "proper" sphere. Dissatisfied with the Provincetown's increasing commercialism, Cook disbanded the players in 1922 and went to Greece, where he and Glaspell lived until Cook's death in 1924. Glaspell published a biography of her husband, *The Road to the Temple*, in 1927. Other important books include her 1920 collection, *Plays;* the Pulitzer Prize–winning *Alison's House* (1930), a drama based on the life of poet Emily Dickinson; and the novel *Judd Rankin's Daughter* (1945). Glaspell died on July 27, 1948.

The Outside, which opened at the Provincetown Playhouse on December 28, 1917, is an impressive meditation on the meaning of life, dramatized through an allegorical battle between the life and death forces. Two women have removed themselves from society and live together in an abandoned lifesaving station. Mrs. Patrick has been abandoned by her husband, and her bitterness has caused her to stifle anything that smacks of life, symbolically suggested through her attempt to bury beach grass with sand. Allie Mayo (played by Glaspell in the original production) has lost her husband to the sea, and the ice that claimed him extends to her heart: she has not spoken "an unnecessary word for twenty years." Two men enter the house, bringing with them a drowning victim. Their attempt to resuscitate him causes Mrs. Patrick to try to drive them out, but their example revives Allie Mayo's will to live. She speaks to Mrs. Patrick, telling her that her desire for seclusion is a mistake. What ensues is a debate over the desire to live versus the will to die, communicated through the language of metaphor.

The opening scene description suggests a visual symbol for the linguistic battle that will ensue. Through a large open door is seen the line where sand dunes and vegetation meet: "*a sand hill is menacing the woods. . . . The dunes are hills and strange forms of sand on which, in places, grows the stiff beach grass—struggle; dogged growing against odds.*" When Mrs. Patrick stoops to bury the struggling grass, symbolically enacting her attempt to bury her own will to live, Allie Mayo attempts to dissuade her. She tells Mrs. Patrick that her attempt to "bury the life in you" will be countered by the woods: "*They* fight too. The woods! They fight for life the way that Captain fought for life in there!" "I have walked on the tops of buried trees," Mrs. Patrick responds. Allie Mayo counters, "And vines will grow over the sand that covers the trees, and hold it. And other trees will grow over the buried trees."

Glaspell's achievement in *The Outside* is her fusion of expressionistic language to theme. As Linda Ben-Zvi remarks, Glaspell's characters "are inarticulates": they "generally cannot find words because they are still in the process of discovering what they want to say and are often unable or unsure of their own thoughts."[35] Glaspell therefore mirrors that process in the language of the female characters, who stammer, pause, and make false starts. Thus when Allie tells her that the time has come to return from the "Outside" and engage in life, Mrs. Patrick's hesitating response indicates her attempt to find language appropriate to her still-forming thoughts:

I didn't *go* to the Outside. I was left there. I'm only—trying to get along. Everything that can hurt me I want buried—buried deep. Spring is here. This morning I *knew* it. Spring—coming through the storm—to take me—take me to hurt me. That's why I couldn't bear—[*she looks at the closed door*]—things that made me know I feel.

Allie Mayo's and Mrs. Patrick's struggle to find the words to express their thoughts is a verbal manifestation of their attempt to discover meaning in a life in which men are absent. Both women have cast themselves to the "Outside" because of sorrow and bitterness at having lost their husbands. Allie's successful attempt to make Mrs. Patrick see the value of life is therefore an affirmation of "women's autonomy."[36]

VI

ON DECEMBER 25, 1917, *Why Marry?* opened at New York's Astor Theater and quickly became the hit of the season. In this witty, Shavian discussion play, Jesse Lynch Williams mercilessly satirized the institution of marriage, to the delight of audiences. A popular success (120 performances), the play was voted the best play of the year and became the first drama to win the Pulitzer Prize.

Williams was born on August 17, 1871, in Sterling, Illinois. While enrolled at Princeton, he helped found the Triangle Club, an organization devoted to staging amateur plays, and he edited the *Nassau Literary Magazine*. After graduating from Princeton in 1892 (taking a master's in 1894), he distinguished himself in journalism. He became a reporter for the *New York Sun* for two years before resigning to work for *Scribner's Magazine* (1897–1900). He founded the *Princeton Alumni Weekly* in 1900 and contributed stories to a variety of New York newspapers. He soon turned his Princeton and journalism experience into fiction, publishing a popular series of stories centered on Princeton undergraduate life, *Princeton Stories* (1895), *Adventures of a Freshman* (1899), and *The Girl and the Game, and Other Stories* (1908). His newspaper stories appeared as *The Stolen Story* (1899), which he later turned into a successful play in 1906; *Newspaper Stories* appeared in 1899; and he published seven novels, adapting some of them into plays. During his lifetime he won several honors, among them election to the National Institute of Arts and Letters and to the Author's League of America (serving as its president in 1921); he was a Pulitzer Prize juror (1923–1925); and he occupied the Chair of Creative Arts at the University of Michigan (1925–1926). Williams died on September 14, 1929.

Why Marry? is not, as Arthur Hobson Quinn observed, "an attack upon marriage; it is a scrutiny of the institution."[37] Williams presents five couples in various stages of marriage, examines their reasons for marrying, and finds those reasons to be hypocritical, cynical, and destructive. John is a wealthy businessman and a stereotypical chauvinist along the lines of Malcolm Gaskell of *A Man's World*, who believes in economic Darwinism (those with the most money are the fittest), and who treats his wife Lucy as a possession. Lucy wants a divorce but has no grounds for it and no means of supporting herself. John's youngest sister, Jean, pursues the promiscuous playboy Rex, though she doesn't love him because, as a True Woman, she has been raised only to become a wife. Although she is fully aware that she's entering what she refers to as "legalized prostitution," she is determined not "to be a dependent old maid." Her uncle, Judge Everett, is in the midst of a divorce but discovers that, although he no longer loves his wife, he has become habituated to marriage. Their cousin Theodore, a minister, has had to commit his wife to a sanitarium after a lifetime of economic impoverishment, and he voices the conventional religious reasons for marriage. Finally, John's other sister, Helen, a New Woman who is a self-supporting scientist in love with her boss, Ernest Hamilton, has resolved not to marry him because to do so would destroy their careers.

These relationships become the backdrop for an often hilarious exposé of the reasons people marry, the causes of divorce, and the methods by which society enforces its social codes, all centered upon Helen and Ernest's attempt to defy conventional expectations. As Brenda Murphy observes, *Why Marry?* reverses our normal expectations of the typical comedy plot. Rather than serving as blocking figures, preventing the lovers from getting married, Helen's family is trying to overcome her objections to marriage and to prevent her from living with Ernest as an unmarried couple.[38] Helen and Ernest reject marriage because they cannot afford to live on Ernest's pitiful salary, because Helen does not wish to give up her career, because she despises domestic duties, and because the example of their family suggests that marriage destroys love. Although Helen is depicted as a radical New Woman in her advocacy of "free love," the playwright evidently could not conceive of a marriage divorced from conventional gender-specific roles.

Like Rachel Crothers's Frank Ware, Helen is torn between her desire for a rewarding career and her desire to marry the man she loves. For both Ernest and Helen, marriage means sacrifice, not fulfillment: for Ernest, marriage means giving up poorly paid science for a less rewarding but better-paid job to support a home; for Helen, marriage means giving up challenging work for the drudgery of housework. "The right to work, the right to love—those rights are inalienable," Helen says. "No, we'll give up marriage but not each other." When Lucy points out that she'll be ostracized by society, Helen sketches love-without-marriage as an idyllic companionship: "Instead of making a tired husband work for me, I'll have my days free to work with him, like the old-fashioned women you admire! Instead of being an expense, I'll be a help to him; instead of being separated by marriage and divergent interests, we'll be united by love and common peril." Although Williams presents Helen's radical solution to the work-marriage dilemma with impeccable logic, he was not able to resist the conventional comic closure, so he contrives a solution that undercuts that logic. Uncle Everett manipulates the lovers into admitting their love for one another "in the eyes of God," and he quickly announces a civil marriage. And so they were married, despite their wishes. Williams dissects a social problem but offers no solution. As Uncle Everett, the play's raisonneur, declaims, "Respectability has triumphed this time, but let Society take warning and beware! beware! beware!"

Much of the appeal of *Why Marry?* stems from its witty pronouncements on marriage, many of which still resonate today. "What does the modern home amount to?" asks the Judge. "Merely a place to leave your wife." "It's curious," Ernest remarks, "but when working with women of ability one learns to respect them so much that one quite loses the habit of insulting them." Or this exchange:

> JOHN: True women enjoy sacrificing themselves.
> JUDGE: Yes, that's what we tell them. Well, we ought to know. We make 'em do it.

In addition, the actor playing Uncle Everett was Nat Goodwin, who had achieved considerable notoriety for his five marriages and five divorces, as well as for a 1914 book he entitled *Nat Goodwin's Book* (which one biographer referred to as *Why Beautiful Women Marry Nat Goodwin*), and his appearance in the play was a considerable draw. As the reviewer for the *New York Times* wryly remarked, "His strictures on the marital relation are a source of incessant laughter; and it was only in part due to the fact that they emanated from an actor whose authority on the subject is recognized."[39]

Why Marry? had a circuitous route to fame as a Pulitzer Prize winner. Williams began the play as a story but soon decided on a dramatic treatment, publishing it in 1914 under the title "*And So They Were Married.*" Williams was unable to interest Broadway managers because, as he explained in a letter to Arthur Hobson Quinn, "It was written ahead of its time—i.e., ahead of the public's time for such treatment of such ideas." Students at the American Academy of Dramatic Art asked for permission to stage the play at their annual graduation exercise, and when they did so (on January 3, 1917), demonstrating its comic appeal, three "well-known managers opened negotiations" for rights to the play, all three of whom had refused the play in manuscript.[40] The play received its professional debut under the title *Why Marry?* on November 1, 1917, in Columbus, Ohio, where it ran for 10 weeks before moving to New York. After its 120-performance run it went on the road, but the death of Nat Goodwin (who had become identified with the play) on February 1, 1919, caused managers to cancel bookings.

The play opened to good reviews, with the *New York Times* calling it "perhaps the most intelligent and searching satire on social institutions ever written by an American." The reviewer noted its tendency "to hammer away at current standards in conduct and to underline ideas," but believed that "Short of Shaw, no one has ventilated such a subject with such telling satire and explosive humor. And there are certain respects in which, as it seemed, the play surpasses even Shaw."[41]

Lawrence Gilman, however, writing for the *North American Review*, ridiculed Williams's sophomoric depiction of sentiment (by quoting speeches about love from Helen and Ernest), and pointed particularly to the closing line of the *New York Times* review: "If he had been as scrupulous and vigilant in his expression of feeling as he is shrewd and delightful in his manipulation of comedy," Gilman declared, "Mr. Williams might have given us, if not (as we have been told) 'the most intelligent and searching satire on social institutions ever written by an American,' at least a satire of uncommon point and distinction." Indeed there is some justice to Gilman's remark, for the love talk between Helen and Ernest is conventionally sentimental stuff. Yet as Gilman acknowledges, the play's "surgical wit" redeems it.[42]

Williams proved to be a contentious playwright. John Corbin, the *New York Times* drama editor, praised him for "the keen intelligence of his economic disquisitions and the brilliancy of his dialogue." But Corbin also ridiculed Williams for his sleight-of-hand in contriving the play's ending, called him a propagandist for "free love," and claimed that Ernest Hamilton's salary ($2,000) was too little to be plausible—thus undermining Williams's point about the economic disadvantage of marriage. The next week Williams published a lengthy defense of his play in which he argued, albeit unconvincingly, for his play's economic and social theses: "I thought I was writing comedy, not propaganda, and that my moral was not immoral at all. In fact, I should say that my message is a warning against, not an argument for, what is usually meant by 'Free Love.'" Williams noted that his intent was to show why society makes it difficult to stay married and insisted that marriage is "the most sacred and important relationship in life. . . . So it really looks as though society would have to reform the rules and regulations of marriage if it expects its young people to keep on playing the game for it." He concluded his letter by offering a vision of his heroine as a "true woman" who has become "radical in order to conserve woman's ancient share of the work of the world, ready to seem ridiculous, or even wrong, in order to serve and protect those whom she loves."[43]

Corbin's reply to *this* response must have infuriated Williams. He repeated his charges, castigating Williams for not respecting "the 'logical conclusion' of his own premises and preachments," and concluded that the play was "eloquent in declamation against modern marriage, but ending in matrimony" nonetheless. Williams evidently had enough of this journalistic quibble. In his next play he turned his satire to divorce, ridiculing divorce laws that prevented unsuited couples from separating and entitling the result simply *Why Not?* (1922).[44]

VII

WHAT HAPPENED to the New Woman? While all of these plays were popular successes in their day, playing to the audience's fascination with the war over gender roles, several events occurred in the 1920s that signaled the end of the New Woman. With the passage of the Nineteenth Amendment in 1920, giving women the right to vote, much of the women's movement lost focus. The cause of women's suffrage had always been the linchpin of turn-of-the-century feminism, and with the goal achieved, the feminist movement no longer had a *raison d'être*. The new sexual freedom also undermined feminism. As the New Woman came to be identified as a female libertine who abandoned traditional values of family and home, a backlash set in. New Women were depicted in the popular press as "mannish lesbians" and as unattractive spinsters unable to catch a man. As one writer warned in 1901, "It is now obvious to impartial observers that these 'rights' are in reality demanded by only a very small group of women—mostly mannish women, too, belonging to what has aptly been called 'the third sex'; and that to grant them the 'rights' demanded would in reality be to inflict a grievous *wrong* on the vast majority of women—the womanly women—as well as on children, on men, and on society in general." As a result, women's gains in education and employment from 1890 to 1920 began to reverse. The historian Carroll Smith-Rosenberg observes that "From the 1870s through the 1920s, between 40 and 60 percent of women college graduates did not marry, at a time when only 10 percent of all American women did not." As the backlash against women's social progress set in, specifically with accusations of lesbianism levied at women who chose to remain single, this proportion reversed, and 65 percent of women college graduates now married. After 1920 the rate of increase of working women began to decline as did the percentage of women who were college graduates. In fact, there were more women college students, professors, and professionals in 1920 than there were in 1960.[45]

The decline of the New Woman was also reflected on the stage. Rachel Crothers, who had achieved some eminence for her sympathetic portrayal of the New Woman in *A Man's World* and *He and She*, abandoned her earlier theme in favor of portraying independent women who were dissatisfied with their freedom and who longed for domestic stability. In *Mary the Third* (1923), for instance, the youngest Mary flirts with economic and sexual independence briefly but chooses a mate after pledging to divorce if their love ends. The play ends with traditional romantic endearments. In *Let Us Be Gay* (1929), Kitty Brown divorces her husband because of his infidelity and then engages in three years of casual sexual encounters. Discovering that imitating her husband's behavior is emotionally barren, she and her husband remarry, hoping to restore some stability to their meaningless lives. And in *When Ladies Meet* (1932), a woman writer tires of her independence and sexual freedom and longs for the stability of home and husband.

Despite the waning of the New Woman phenomenon, the plays reprinted in this anthology still have the ability to speak to audiences. *The Great Divide* was performed in 1988 by the Indiana Repertory Company to good reviews; *Overtones* and *The Outside* appear regularly on college campuses. Perhaps the time is right to revive *A Man's World, As a Man Thinks,* and *Why Marry?*

NOTES

1. Florence Kiper, "Some American Plays from the Feminist Viewpoint," Forum 51 (1914), 921.

2. Elizabeth Ammons, "The New Woman as Cultural Symbol and Social Reality: Six Women Writers' Perspectives," in Adele Heller and Lois Rudnick, eds., *1915, The Cultural Moment* (New Brunswick, N.J., 1991), 82.

3. Thomas H. Dickinson, *Playwrights of the New American Theater* (1925; reprint Freeport, 1967), 184–185.

4. Jack Poggi, *Theatre in America: The Impact of Economic Forces, 1870–1967* (Ithaca, N.Y., 1966), 13, 11–18.

5. David Perkins, *A History of Modern American Poetry: From the 1890s to the High Modernist Mode* (Cambridge, Mass., 1976), 106.

6. Lois Gottlieb, "The Double Standard Debate in Early 20th-Century American Drama," *Michigan Academician* 7 (1975), 449.

7. Ibid.

8. William Vaughn Moody, *Letters to Harriet*, ed. Percy MacKaye (Boston, 1935), 282–283.

9. For discussion of Moody's revisions, see MacKaye, Introduction to *Letters to Harriet*, 40–47; and Maurice F. Brown, *Estranging Dawn: The Life and Works of William Vaughn Moody* (Carbondale, Ill., 1973), 221.

10. "A Powerful Play Beautifully Acted," *New York Times* (October 5, 1906), 9.

11. Brown, *Estranging Dawn*, 220.

12. Charlotte Hughes, "Women Playmakers," *New York Times Magazine* (May 4, 1941), 27.

13. Lois Gottleib, *Rachel Crothers* (Boston, 1979), 27.

14. Arthur Hobson Quinn, *A History of American Drama From the Civil War to the Present Day*, I, rev. ed. (New York, 1936), 45.

15. "Splendid Play by Rachel Crothers," *New York Times* (February 9, 1910), 5; "Drama," *Nation* 90 (February 10, 1910), 146; Adolph Klauber, "Drama, Moral, and the Point of View," *New York Times* (February 13, 1910), sec. 6:7.

16. Clayton Hamilton, "The Plays of the Spring Season," *Bookman* 33 (1911), 354–355, 357.

17. "Augustus Thomas Excels in His Best Previous Effort [*sic*]," *New York Times* (March 19, 1911), sec. 7:1.

18. Hamilton, "Plays," 357; William Winter, "Shadows of the Stage: A Great Play Greatly Acted," *Harper's Weekly* 55 (April 15, 1911), 18; Quinn, *A History of American Drama*, 256.

19. Scholars who discuss *As a Man Thinks* as an attack upon the emerging New Woman include Brenda Murphy, *American Realism and American Drama, 1880–1940* (Cambridge, England, 1987); Deborah S. Kolb, "The Rise and Fall of the New Woman in American Drama," *Educational Theatre Journal* 27 (1975), 149–160; and Gottlieb, *Rachel Crothers*, 47–48.

20. Ronald J. Davis, *Augustus Thomas* (Boston, 1984), 97, 10.

21. Ibid., 103.

22. Kiper, "Some American Plays," 923–924.

23. "Augustus Thomas," 1; Hamilton, "Plays," 357; Winter, "Shadows of the Stage," 18.

24. For further discussion of early independent theaters, see James L. Highlander, "America's First Art Theatre: The New Theatre of Chicago," *Educational Theatre Journal* 11 (1959), 285–290; and Thomas H. Dickinson, *The Insurgent Theatre* (New York, 1917).

25. Craig's *The Art of the Theatre* (1905) was widely read and was adopted as the movement's bible. Appia's *La musique et la mise en scène* (1899), translated into German as *Die Musik und der Inscenierung* (1899), was not translated into English until 1962. But many of those involved in the little theater knew of his theories secondhand, often through the influence of German productions. Some directors read Appia in German, and Sheldon Cheney was an enthusiastic proponent of both Craig and Appia, disseminating their theories through his *Theatre Arts Magazine* (founded in 1916) and through his two books on the new stagecraft, *The New Movement in the Theatre* (1914) and *The Art Theatre* (1917).

26. Dickinson, *Insurgent Theatre*, 227–233; Poggi, *Theatre in America*, 107.

27. John Seelye Bolin, "Samuel Hume: Artist and Exponent of American Art Theatre" (unpublished Ph.D. dissertation, University of Michigan, 1970), 76, 66.

28. Among others, the Washington Square Players, the Provincetown Players, the Chicago Little Theater, the Portmanteau Players, the Wisconsin Players, the Morningside Players, the Harvard Dramatic Club, and the 47 Workshop published plays performed on their stages. Plays also regularly appeared in such periodicals as *Smart Set, Forum, Drama, Seven Arts,* and *Poet Lore.*

29. W. David Sievers, *Freud on Broadway: A History of Psychoanalysis and the American Drama* (New York, 1970), 49.

30. Sievers, *Freud on Broadway,* 51; for Gerstenberg's probable influence upon O'Neill, see Mary Maddock, "Alice Gerstenberg's *Overtones:* The Demon in the Doll," *Modern Drama* 37 (1994), 474; and Beverly M. Matherne, "Alice Gerstenberg," in Lina Mainiero, ed., *American Women Writers,* II (New York, 1980), 119.

31. "Comedy Playlets at the Bandbox," *New York Times* (November 10, 1915), 13.

32. Q. K., "After the Play," *New Republic* 5 (November 20, 1915), 74.

33. Maddock, "Alice Gerstenberg's *Overtones,*" 476, 480.

34. For Glaspell's role in the founding of the Provincetown Players, see Robert K. Sarlós, *Jig Cook and the Provincetown Players: Theatre in Ferment* (Boston, 1982); and Helen Deutsch and Stella Hanau, *The Provincetown: A Story of the Theatre* (New York, 1972).

35. Linda Ben-Zvi, "Susan Glaspell and Eugene O'Neill," *The Eugene O'Neill Newsletter* 6 (Summer/Fall 1982), 25.

36. Christine Dymkowski, "On the Edge: The Plays of Susan Glaspell," *Modern Drama* 31 (1988), 96.

37. Quinn, *A History of American Drama,* II, 69.

38. Murphy, *American Realism,* 163.

39. "'Why Marry?' A Hit at the Astor Theatre," *New York Times* (December 26, 1917), 7.

40. Williams's letter to Quinn appears as part of Quinn's preface to the revised version of the play published in Quinn, ed., *Contemporary American Plays* (New York, 1923), 2–3.

41. "'Why Marry?,'" 7.

42. Lawrence Gilman, "Drama and Music," *North American Review* 207 (1918), 281.

43. John Corbin, "The Katydid Comedy," *New York Times* (February 3, 1918), sec. 8:8; Jesse Lynch Williams, "Is 'Why Marry?' a Katy-Did Comedy?" *New York Times* (February 10, 1918), sec. 5:8.

44. Williams, "Is 'Why Marry?'" 8.

45. Henry T. Finck, "Are Womanly Women Doomed?" *Independent* (January 31, 1901), 268. For the decline of women in education and employment, see Carroll Smith-Rosenberg, "The New Woman as Androgyne: Social Disorder and Gender Crisis, 1870–1936," in *Disorderly Conduct: Visions of Gender in Victorian America* (New York, 1985), 253, 281; Kolb, "The Rise and Fall of the New Woman in American Drama," 158; and Lois Rudnick, "The New Woman," in Heller and Rudnick, 70.

Bibliography

Ammons, Elizabeth. "The New Woman as Cultural Symbol and Social Reality: Six Women Writers' Perspectives." *1915: The Cultural Moment.* Adele Heller and Lois Rudnick, eds. New Brunswick, N.J., 1991, 82–97.

Atlas, Marilyn J. "Innovation in Chicago: Alice Gerstenberg's Psychological Drama." *Midwestern Miscellany* 10 (1982), 59–68.

"Augustus Thomas Excels in His Best Previous Effort [*sic*]" [*As a Man Thinks*]. *New York Times.* March 19, 1911, sec. 7:1.

Bach, Gerhard. "Susan Glaspell, Provincetown Playwright." *Great Lakes Review* 4.2 (1978), 31–43.

Ben-Zvi, Linda. "Susan Glaspell and Eugene O'Neill." *The Eugene O'Neill Newsletter* 6 (Summer/Fall 1982), 21–29.

Bolin, John Seelye. "Samuel Hume: Artist and Exponent of American Art Theatre." Dissertation, University of Michigan, 1970.

Brown, Maurice F. *Estranging Dawn: The Life and Works of William Vaughn Moody.* Carbondale, Ill., 1973.

"Comedy Playlets at the Bandbox" [*Overtones*]. *New York Times.* November 10, 1915, 13.

Corbin, John. "The Dawn of American Drama." *Atlantic Monthly* 94 (May 1907), 632–644.

———. "The Katydid Comedy" [*Why Marry?*]. *New York Times.* February 3, 1918, sec. 8:8.

Davis, Ronald J. *Augustus Thomas.* Boston, 1984.

Deutsch, Helen, and Stella Hanau. *The Provincetown: A Story of the Theatre.* 1931. Reprint, New York, 1972.

Dickinson, Thomas H. *The Insurgent Theatre.* New York, 1917.

———. *Playwrights of the New American Theater.* 1925. Reprint, Freeport, 1967.

"Drama" [*A Man's World*]. *Nation* 90. February 10, 1910.

Dymkowski, Christine. "On the Edge: The Plays of Susan Glaspell." *Modern Drama* 31 (1988), 91–105.

Finck, Henry T. "Are Womanly Women Doomed?" *Independent* (January 31, 1901), 267–71.

Gilman, Lawrence. "Drama and Music" [*Why Marry?*]. *North American Review* 207 (1918), 278–283.

Gottlieb, Lois. "The Double Standard Debate in Early 20th-Century American Drama." *Michigan Academician* 7 (1975), 441–452.

———. *Rachel Crothers*. Boston, 1979.

Hamilton, Clayton. "The Plays of the Spring Season." *Bookman* 33 (1911), 352–360.

Hecht, Stuart J. "The Plays of Alice Gerstenberg: Cultural Hegemony in the American Little Theatre." *Journal of Popular Culture* 26.1 (1992), 1–16.

Heller, Adele, and Lois Rudnick, eds. *1915, The Cultural Moment*. New Brunswick, N.J., 1991.

Highlander, James L. "America's First Art Theatre: The New Theatre of Chicago." *Educational Theatre Journal* 11 (1959), 285–290.

Hughes, Charlotte. "Women Playmakers." *New York Times Magazine*. May 4, 1941, 10–11, 27.

K., Q. "After the Play" [*Overtones*]. *New Republic* 5 (November 20, 1915), 74.

Kiper, Florence. "Some American Plays from the Feminist Viewpoint." *Forum* 51 (1914), 921–931.

Klauber, Adolph. "Drama, Moral, and the Point of View" [*A Man's World*]. *New York Times*. February 13, 1910, sec. 6:7.

Kolb, Deborah S. "The Rise and Fall of the New Woman in American Drama." *Educational Theatre Journal* 27 (1975), 149–160.

Maddock, Mary. "Alice Gerstenberg's *Overtones*: The Demon in the Doll." *Modern Drama* 37 (1994), 474–483.

Matherne, Beverly M. "Alice Gerstenberg." *American Women Writers*, II. Lina Mainiero, ed. New York, 1980, 118–120.

Moody, William Vaughn. *Letters to Harriet*. Percy MacKaye, ed. Boston, 1935.

Murphy, Brenda. *American Realism and American Drama, 1880–1940*. Cambridge, England, 1987.

Perkins, David. *A History of Modern American Poetry: From the 1890s to the High Modernist Mode*. Cambridge, Mass., 1976.

Pickering, Jerry V. "William Vaughn Moody: The Dramatist as Social Philosopher." *Modern Drama* 14 (1971), 93–103.

Poggi, Jack. *Theatre in America: The Impact of Economic Forces, 1870–1967*. Ithaca, N.Y., 1966.

"A Powerful Play Beautifully Acted" [*The Great Divide*]. *New York Times*. October 5, 1906, 9.

Quinn, Arthur Hobson. *A History of American Drama From the Civil War to the Present Day*, rev. ed. New York, 1936.

Richardson, Gary. *American Drama From the Colonial Period Through World War I: A Critical History.* New York, 1993.

Sarlós, Robert K. *Jig Cook and the Provincetown Players: Theatre in Ferment.* Boston, 1982.

Sievers, W. David. *Freud on Broadway: A History of Psychoanalysis and the American Drama.* 1955. Reprint, New York, 1970.

Smith-Rosenberg, Carroll. "The New Woman as Androgyne: Social Disorder and Gender Crises, 1870–1936." *Disorderly Conduct: Visions of Gender in Victorian America.* New York, 1985, 245–96.

"Splendid Play by Rachel Crothers" [*A Man's World*]. *New York Times.* February 9, 1910, 5.

Stephens, Judith L. "*Why Marry?*: The 'New Woman' of 1918." *Theatre Journal* 34 (1982), 183–196.

Sutherland, Cynthia. "American Women Playwrights as Mediators of the 'Woman Problem.'" *Modern Drama* 21 (1978), 319–336.

Tibbetts, John. "The 'New Woman' on Stage: Women's Issues in American Drama, 1890–1915." *Helicon Nine* 7 (1982), 6–19.

"'Why Marry?' A Hit at the Astor Theatre." *New York Times.* December 26, 1917, 7.

Williams, Jesse Lynch. "Is 'Why Marry?' a Katy-Did Comedy?" *New York Times.* February 10, 1918, sec. 5:8.

Winter, William. "Shadows of the Stage: A Great Play Greatly Acted" [*As a Man Thinks*]. *Harper's Weekly* 55 (April 15, 1911), 18.

A Note on the Texts

THIS COLLECTION reproduces the texts of the first editions of each play: *The Great Divide* (New York: Macmillan Co., 1909); *A Man's World* (Boston: Richard G. Badger, 1915); *As a Man Thinks* (New York: Duffield & Co., 1911); *Overtones*, from *Washington Square Plays* (Garden City: Doubleday, Page & Co., 1916); and *The Outside*, from *Plays*, by Susan Glaspell (Boston: Small, Maynard & Co., 1920).

Jesse Lynch Williams's *Why Marry?* was first published by Scribner in 1914 under the title *"And So They Were Married."* After the play appeared on Broadway, Scribner reissued the play in 1918 under the title *Why Marry?* This edition simply took the plates of the 1914 edition and added a new title page, an introduction by the author, and four photographs from the Broadway production. Williams later revised and abridged the play for inclusion in Arthur Hobson Quinn's anthology *Contemporary American Plays* (Scribner, 1923) to reflect changes made during performance. The text reproduced here is that of the 1914 edition. I have emended the amount of Ernest Hamilton's salary to reflect changes Williams made during the initial performance. In the 1914 printing Ernest's salary is three thousand per year, but in the 1918 printing Williams decreased it to two thousand to emphasize Ernest's relative poverty—a figure mentioned in reviews of the first run. I have therefore emended all salary citations to accord with the lower figure.

The texts of all plays save *A Man's World* have been faithfully reproduced, except for the silent correction of a very few errors in punctuation, typography, and the occasional grammatical slip. Old-fashioned spellings and hyphenations have been retained (*gayety, to-day*). For *A Man's World*, however, I have spelled out scene direction abbreviations (*left* for *L.*, *center* for *C.*) and spelling reform contractions which did not gain currency (*thought* for *tho't*, *through* for *thro'*). Finally, typographical inconsistencies among the texts in matters of signaling scene changes and dialogue cues have been regularized.

THE GREAT DIVIDE

A Play in Three Acts

by

William Vaughn Moody

First performed at the Princess Theater, New York City, on October 4, 1906.

CHARACTERS

PHILIP JORDAN
POLLY JORDAN, *Philip's wife*
MRS. JORDAN, *his mother*
RUTH JORDAN, *his sister*
WINTHROP NEWBURY
DR. NEWBURY, *Winthrop's father*
STEPHEN GHENT
LON ANDERSON
BURT WILLIAMS
DUTCH
A MEXICAN
A CONTRACTOR
AN ARCHITECT
A BOY

ACT I

Interior of PHILIP JORDAN*'s cabin in southern Arizona, on a late afternoon in spring. A large room rudely built, adorned with blankets, pottery, weapons, and sacred images of the local Indian tribes, and hung with tro-*

*phies of the chase, together with hunting-knives, saddles, bridles, nose-bags for
horses, lariats, and other paraphernalia of frontier life. Through a long low
window at the back the desert is seen, intensely colored, and covered with the
uncouth shapes of giant cacti, dotted with bunches of gorgeous bloom. The entrance door is on the left (from the spectator's standpoint), in a projecting
elbow of the room; farther to the left is a door leading to the sleeping-
quarters. On the right is a cook-stove, a cupboard for dishes and household
utensils, and a chimney-piece, over which hangs a bleached cow's-skull supporting a rifle.*

At a rude table in the centre sits PHILIP JORDAN, *a man of thirty-four,
mending a bridle.* POLLY, *his wife, kneels before an open trunk, assisted in
her packing by* WINTHROP NEWBURY, *a recent graduate of an Eastern medical college.* RUTH JORDAN, PHILIP'*s sister, a girl of nineteen, stands at the
window looking out.*

WINTHROP: [*As he hands the last articles to* POLLY.] What on earth pos-
sessed you to bring such a load of duds to Arizona?

POLLY: They promised me a good time, meaning one small shindig—
one—in the three months I've spent in this unholy place.

[PHILIP *makes an impatient movement with the bridle, speaks gruffly.*]

PHILIP: You'd better hurry. It's getting late.

RUTH: [*From the window.*] It's getting cooler, which is more to the point.
We can make the railroad easily by sunrise, with this delicious breeze
blowing.

POLLY: [*Gives the finishing touches to the trunk and locks the lid.*] There, at
last! Heaven help the contents.

PHILIP: [*Gruffly, as he rises.*] Give me a lift with the trunk, Win.

[*They carry the trunk outside.* POLLY, *with the aid of a cracked mirror,
puts on her travelling hat and cloak.*]

RUTH: My, Pollikins! You'll be the talk of all the jack-rabbits and sage hens
between here and the railroad.

POLLY: Phil is furious at me for going, and it is rather mean to sneak off
for a visit in a grand house in San Francisco, when you poor dears
have to slave on here. But really, I can't endure this life a day longer.

RUTH: It isn't in nature that you should. Fancy *that*—[*she indicates* POLLY
with a grandiose gesture]—nourishing itself on salt-pork, chickory
beans, and air-tight!

POLLY: Do you really mean to say that apart from your pride in helping
your brother, making the project go, and saving the family fortunes,
you really *enjoy* yourself here?

RUTH: Since Phil and I came out, one day has been more radiantly excit-

ing than the other. I don't know what's the matter with me. I think I
shall be punished for being so happy.

POLLY: Punished for being happy! There's your simon-pure New Englan-
der.

RUTH: True! I was discovered at the age of seven in the garret, perusing
"The Twelve Pillars and Four Cornerstones of a Godly Life."

POLLY: [*Pointing at* RUTH*'s heart, speaks with mock solemnity.*] If Massachusetts and Arizona ever get in a mixup in there, woe be!—Are you
ever going to have that coffee done?

RUTH: I hope soon, before you get me analyzed out of existence.

POLLY: [*As* RUTH *busies herself at the stove.*] The main point is this, my
dear, and you'd better listen to what the old lady is a-tellin' of ye.
Happiness is its own justification, and it's the sacreder the more un-
reasonable it is. It comes or it doesn't, that's all you can say about it.
And when it comes, one has the sense to grasp it or one hasn't.
There you have the Law and the Prophets.

[WINTHROP *and* PHILIP *enter from outside.* RUTH, *who has set out the
coffee and sandwiches on the table, bows elaborately, with napkin over
arm.*]

RUTH: *Messieurs et Mesdames!*

WINTHROP: Coffee! Well, rather, with an all-night ride in the desert ahead
of us. [*They drink their coffee,* PHILIP *standing sullenly apart.*] Where
do we get our next feed?

RUTH: With luck, at Cottonwood Wash.

WINTHROP: And how far may Cottonwood Wash be?

RUTH: Thirty miles.

WINTHROP: [*Sarcastically.*] Local measurement?

POLLY: [*Poking* PHILIP.] Phil, for Heaven's sake say something. You dif-
fuse the gloom of the Pit.

PHILIP: I've had my say out, and it makes absolutely no impression on
you.

POLLY: It's the impression on the public I'm anxious about.

PHILIP: The public will have to excuse me.

POLLY: I *am* horribly sorry for you two poor dears, left alone in this
dreadful place. When Dr. Newbury goes, I don't see how you'll support life. I should like to know how long this sojourn in the wilder-
ness is going to last, anyhow.

[*During the following,* RUTH *takes a candle from the shelf, lights it, and
brings it to the table. The sunset glow has begun to fade.*]

RUTH: Till Cactus Fibre makes our eternal fortune.

WINTHROP: And how long will that be?

RUTH: [*Counts on her fingers.*] Two years to pay back the money we raised on mother's estate, two years of invested profits, two years of hard luck and marking time, two years of booming prosperity. Say eight years!

POLLY: Shades of the tomb! How long do you expect to live?

RUTH: Forever! [*The sound of a galloping horse is heard, muffled by the sand.*]

WINTHROP: Listen. What's that?

[*A boy of fifteen, panting from his rapid ride, appears at the open door.*]

PHILIP: [*Rising and going toward the door.*] What's the matter?

BOY: I've come for the doctor.

PHILIP: Who wants a doctor?

BOY: Your man Sawyer, over to Lone Tree.—He's broke his leg.

RUTH: Broken his leg! Sawyer? Our foreman?

PHILIP: There's a nice piece of luck!—How did it happen?

BOY: They was doin' some Navajo stunts on horseback, pullin' chickens out of the sand at a gallop and takin' a hurdle on the upswing. Sawyer's horse renigged, and lunged off agin a 'dobe wall. Smashed his leg all to thunder.

[WINTHROP *looks vaguely about for his kit and travelling necessaries, while* POLLY *gives the boy food, which he accepts shyly as he goes outside with* PHILIP. RUTH *has snatched saddle and bridle from their peg.*]

RUTH: I'll have Buckskin saddled for you in a jiffy. How long will it take you to set the leg?

WINTHROP: Perhaps an hour, perhaps three.

RUTH: It's a big détour, but you can catch us at Cottonwood Wash by sunrise, allowing three hours for Sawyer. Buckskin has done it before. [*She goes out.*]

POLLY: [*Pouting.*] This will spoil all our fun! Why can't the creature wait till you get back?

WINTHROP: Did you ever have a broken leg?

POLLY: Well, no, not exactly a leg. But I've had a broken heart! In fact, I've got one now, if you're not going with us.

WINTHROP: To tell you the truth, mine is broken too. [*Pause.*] Did you ever dream of climbing a long hill, and having to turn back before you saw what was on the other side? [POLLY *nods enthusiastically.*] I feel as if I'd had my chance to-night to see what was over there, and lost it.

POLLY: You'll excuse me if it sounds personal, Dr. Newbury, but did you expect to discern a—sort of central figure in the outrolled landscape?

WINTHROP: [*Embarrassed, repenting of his sentimental outburst.*] No. That is—

POLLY: [*With a sweep of her arm.*] O, I see. Just scenery!
  [*She laughs and goes into the inner room, left.* RUTH *reënters. The sky has partly faded and a great full moon begins to rise.*]
RUTH: Buckskin is ready, and so is the moon. The boy knows the trails like an Indian. He will bring you through to Cottonwood by daylight.
WINTHROP: [*Taking heart.*] We shall have the ride back together, at any rate.
RUTH: Yes.—I would go with you, and try to do something to make poor Sawyer comfortable, but we haven't another horse that can do the distance. [*She holds out her hand.*] Good-bye.
WINTHROP: [*Detaining her hand.*] Won't you make it up to me? [*He draws her toward him.*]
RUTH: [*Gently but firmly.*] No, Win. Please not.
WINTHROP: Never?
RUTH: Life is so good just as it is! Let us not change it.
  [*He drops her hand, and goes out, without looking back.* POLLY *reënters. The women wave* WINTHROP *goodbye.*]
POLLY: [*Takes* RUTH *by the shoulders and looks at her severely.*] Conscience clear?
RUTH: [*Humoring her.*] Crystal!
POLLY: [*Counts on her fingers.*] Promising young physician, charming girl, lonely ranch, horseback excursions, spring of the year!
RUTH: Not guilty.
POLLY: Gracious! Then it's not play, it's earnest.
RUTH: Neither the one nor the other. It's just your little blonde romantic noddle. [*She takes* POLLY*'s head between her hands and shakes it as if to show its emptiness.*] Do you think if I wanted to flirt, I would select a youth I've played hookey with, and seen his mother spank? [*Suddenly sobered.*] Poor dear Win! He's so good, so gentle and chivalrous. But—[*with a movement of lifted arms, as if for air*] ah me, he's—finished! I want one that isn't finished!
POLLY: Are you out of your head, you poor thing?
RUTH: You know what I mean well enough. Winthrop is all rounded off, a completed product. But the man I sometimes see in my dreams is— [*pausing for a simile*]—well, like this country out here, don't you know—? [*She breaks off, searching for words, and makes a vague outline in the air, to indicate bigness and incompletion.*]
POLLY: [*Drily*]. Yes, thank you. I do know! Heaven send you joy of him!
RUTH: Heaven won't, because, alas, he doesn't exist! I am talking of a sublime abstraction—of the glorious unfulfilled—of the West—the Desert.
POLLY: [*Lifts* RUTH*'s chin, severely.*] We haven't by chance, some spring

morning, riding over to the trading-station or elsewhere—just by the merest chance *beheld* a sublime abstraction—say in blue overalls and jumper? [RUTH *shakes her head.*] Honest?

[*More emphatic head-shaking.* POLLY *drops* RUTH*'s chin with a shrug of the shoulders.* PHILIP *enters.*]

RUTH: [*Putting on her riding-hat.*] Is Pinto saddled?

PHILIP: Pinto is gone.

RUTH: [*Astonished.*] Gone where?

PHILIP: To that Mexican blow-out over at Lone Tree. Every man-jack on the ranch has disappeared, without leave asked or notice given, except this paper which I just found nailed to the factory door. [RUTH *takes the note and reads it anxiously. Then she slowly removes her hat and lays it away.*] What are you up to now? We've no time to lose!

RUTH: [*With quiet determination.*] I am not going.

POLLY: [*As* PHILIP *turns in surprise.*] Not going?

RUTH: I must stay and look after the ranch.

PHILIP: O, come, that's out of the question!

RUTH: We have put all mother's money into this venture. We can't take any risks.

PHILIP: The men will be back to-morrow. It's not to be thought of—your staying here all alone.

POLLY: [*Seats herself with decision.*] One thing is certain: either Ruth goes or I stay.

PHILIP: [*Takes off his hat and sets down the provision basket.*] That suits me perfectly!

POLLY: [*Hysterical.*] But I can't stay! I won't stay! I shall go mad if I spend another night in this place.

RUTH: No, you mustn't stay. You would never get us worked up to the point of letting you go, another time. [*She lifts* POLLY, *and with arm around her waist leads her to the door.*]

PHILIP: I refuse to leave you here alone, just to satisfy a whim of POLLY's. That's flat!

RUTH: But, Phil, you forget the stores you're to fetch back. They will be dumped out there on the naked sand, and by to-morrow night—[*She blows across her palm, as if scattering thistledown.*]

PHILIP: Well, what of it? A few hundred dollars' worth of stuff.

RUTH: A few hundred dollars means sink or swim with us just now.—Besides, there's poor Sawyer. He'll be brought back here to-morrow, and nobody to nurse him. Then inflammation, fever, and good bye Sawyer.

[PHILIP, *with a gesture of accepting the inevitable, picks up the grain-sacks and basket.*]

POLLY: [*At the door, embracing* RUTH.] Good bye, dear. Aren't you really afraid to stay?

RUTH: I'm awfully sorry to miss the fun, but as for danger, the great Arizona Desert is safer than Beacon Hill.

POLLY: You're sure?

RUTH: If marauders prowl, I'll just fire the blunderbuss out the window, and they won't stop running this side of the Great Divide.

POLLY: [*Kissing her.*] Good-bye, dear.

RUTH: Good-bye.

[POLLY *goes out.*]

PHILIP: [*Pausing beside* RUTH, *at the door.*] Mind you put out the light early. It can be seen from the Goodwater trail. There's no telling what riffraff will be straggling back that way after the dance.

RUTH: Riff-raff! They're my sworn knights and brothers.

PHILIP: In that case, what makes you uneasy about the property?

RUTH: O, property! That's different.

PHILIP: Well, you mind what I say and put out the light.

RUTH: Yours for prudence! [*She puts her arm around his waist and draws him to her, kissing him tenderly.*] Good-bye, Phil. [*He kisses her and starts to go. She still detains him. When she speaks again, her voice is softened and awed.*] What a lovely night! Who would ever think to call this a desert, this moonlit ocean of flowers? What millions of cactus blooms have opened since yesterday!

PHILIP: [*Looking at her dubiously.*] What's the matter with you to-night?

RUTH: Nothing. Everything. Life!—I don't know what's got into me of late. I'm just drunk with happiness the whole time.

PHILIP: Well, you're a queer one.—Good-bye. I shall get back as soon as horseflesh will do it. [*He goes out.*]

RUTH: [*As the rumble of the wagon is heard.*] Good-bye! Good-bye, Pollikins! Good-bye!

[*She takes the candle from the table and stands in the door for a time, then raises the light in one hand and waves her handkerchief with the other. She sets the candle again on the table, goes to the mantel-shelf, and takes down a photograph.*]

Dear Win! I forgot how disappointed *you* were going to be.

[*Pause, during which she still gazes at the picture.*]

Clear, kind heart!

[*After a moment she replaces it brusquely on the mantel-shelf, and raises her arms above her head with a deep breath. She stands thus, with arms crossed behind her head, looking at the photograph. Her gaze becomes amused and mischievous; she points her finger at the picture and whispers mockingly.*]

Finished! Finished!

[*She begins to prepare for bed, taking down her hair, and re-coiling it loosely during the following. She hums a tune vaguely and in snatches, then with a stronger rhythm; at last she sings.*]

> Heart, wild heart,
> Brooding apart,
> Why dost thou doubt, and why art thou sullen?
> Flower and bird
> Wait but thy word—

[*She breaks off, picks up a photograph from the table, and looks at it for a moment in silence.*]

Poor little mother! You look out at me with such patient, anxious eyes. There are better days coming for you, and it's troublesome me that's bringing them. Only you trust me!

[*A man's face appears at the edge of the window, gazing stealthily in. As* RUTH *turns, he disappears. She lays down the picture and sings again.*]

> This is the hour,
> And thine is the power.
> Heart, high heart, be brave to begin it.
> Dare you refuse?
> Think what we lose!
> Think what we gain—

[*The words grow indistinct as she takes up the candle and passes into the other room, from which her voice sounds from time to time in interrupted song. The man again appears, shading his face with a peaked Mexican hat so as to see into the darkened room. He turns and waves his hand as if signalling distant persons to approach, then enters through the open door. He looks cautiously about the room, tiptoes to the inner door and listens, then steals softly out, and is seen again at the window, beckoning.* RUTH *reënters carrying the candle. She is shod in moccasins, and clad in a loose, dark sleeping-dress, belted at the waist, with wide, hanging sleeves and open throat. As she crosses to the table she sings.*]

> Heart which the cold
> Long did enfold—
> Hark, from the dark eaves the night thaw drummeth!
> Now as a god,
> Speak to the sod,
> Cry to the sky that the miracle cometh!

[*She passes her hand over a great bunch of wild flowers on the table.*]

Be still, you beauties! You'll drive me to distraction with your color and your odor. I'll take a hostage for your good behavior.

[*She selects a red flower, puts it in the dark mass of her hair, and looks out at the open door.*]

What a scandal the moon is making, out there in that great crazy world! Who but me could think of sleeping on such a night?

[*She sits down, folds the flowers in her arms, and buries her face in them. After a moment she starts up, listens, goes hurriedly to the door, and peers out. She then shuts and bolts the door, draws the curtains before the window, comes swiftly to the table, and blows out the light. The room is left in total darkness. There are muttering voices outside, the latch is tried, then a heavy lunge breaks the bolt. A man pushes in, but is hurled back by a taller man, with a snarling oath. A third figure advances to the table, and strikes a match. As soon as the match is lighted* RUTH *levels the gun, which she has taken from its rack above the mantel. There is heard the click of the hammer, as the gun misses fire. It is instantly struck from her hand by the first man* (DUTCH), *who attempts to seize her. She evades him, and tries to wrest a pistol from a holster on the wall. She is met by the second man* (SHORTY), *who frustrates the attempt, pocketing the weapon. While this has been going on the third man* (GHENT) *has been fumbling with the lamp, which he has at last succeeded in lighting. All three are dressed in rude frontier fashion; the one called* SHORTY *is a Mexican half-breed, the others are Americans.* GHENT *is younger than* DUTCH, *and taller, but less powerfully built. All are intoxicated, but not sufficiently so to incapacitate them from rapid action. The* MEXICAN *has seized* RUTH *and attempts to drag her toward the inner room. She breaks loose, and flies back again to the chimney-piece, where she stands at bay.* GHENT *remains motionless and silent by the table, gazing at her.*]

DUTCH: [*Uncorking a whiskey flask.*] Plucky little catamount. I drink its health. [*Drinks.*]

RUTH: What do you want here?

DUTCH: [*Laughs, with sinister relish.*] Did you hear that, Steve? [*He drinks again, and reaches out the flask to* RUTH.] Take one, and pull in its purty little claws, eh? Jolly time. No more fuss and fury. [RUTH *reaches for a knife, hidden behind the elbow of the chimney.* DUTCH *wrests the knife from her and seizes her in his arms.*] Peppery little devil! [*With desperate strength she breaks from his clutch and reels from him in sickness of horror.* GHENT *remains gazing at her in a fascinated semi-stupor. Meanwhile, after closing the door, the* MEXICAN *has taken dice from his pocket, and, throwing them into a small vase on the table, shakes them and holds out the vase to* DUTCH. *He takes it and turns to* GHENT; *the latter has moved a step or two toward* RUTH, *who in her retreat has reached the chimney-piece and stands at bay.*]

DUTCH: Come, get into the game, curse you, Steve! This is going to be a free-for-all, by God!

[*As he rattles the dice,* RUTH *makes a supplicating gesture to* GHENT.]

RUTH: Save me! save me! [*Her gesture is frozen by his advancing towards her. She looks wildly about, shrinking from him, then with sudden desperate resolution speaks.*] Save me, and I will make it up to you! [GHENT *again advances; she goes on pantingly, as she stands at bay.*] Don't touch me! Listen! Save me from these others, and from yourself, and I will pay you—with my life.

GHENT: [*With dull wonder.*] With—your life?

RUTH: With all that I am or can be.

GHENT: What do you mean?—[*Pause.*] You mean you'll go along with me out of this? Stick to me—on the square?

RUTH: [*In a tragic whisper.*] Yes.

GHENT: On the dead square?

RUTH: Yes.

GHENT: You won't peach, and spoil it?

RUTH: No.

[*Pause, during which he looks at her fixedly.*]

GHENT: Give me your hand on it!

[*She gives him her hand. The other men, at the table, have drawn their weapons, and hold them carelessly, but alert to the slightest suspicious movement on the part of* GHENT.]

DUTCH: [*As* GHENT *turns to them.*] Shorty and me's sittin' in this game, and interested, eh, Shorty? [*The* MEXICAN *nods.* GHENT *comes slowly to the table, eyeing the two.* DUTCH *holds out the vase containing the dice.*] Shake for her!

GHENT: Shake how?

DUTCH: Any damn way! Sole and exclusive rights. License to love and cherish on the premises!

[GHENT *takes the vase, shakes the dice meditatively, is about to throw, then sets the vase down. He searches through his pockets and produces a few bills and a handful of silver, which he lays on the table.*]

GHENT: There's all I've got in my clothes. Take it, and give me a free field, will you?

DUTCH: [*Leaning over the table to* GHENT, *in plaintive remonstrance.*] You don't mean me, Steve!

GHENT: [*To the* MEXICAN.] Well, you, then!

[*The* MEXICAN *spreads the money carelessly with his left hand to ascertain its amount, then thrusts it away with a disgusted grunt of refusal.*]

DUTCH: Don't blame you, Shorty! A ornery buck of a dirt-eatin' Mojave'd pay more'n that for his squaw.

[RUTH *covers her face shudderingly.* GHENT *stands pondering, watching the two men under his brows, and slowly gathering up the money. As if on a sudden thought, he opens his shirt, and unwinds from his neck a string of gold nuggets in the rough, strung on a leather thread.*]

GHENT: Well, it ain't much, that's sure. But there's a string of gold nuggets I guess is worth some money. [*He throws it on the table, speaking to both men.*] Take that, and clear out.

DUTCH: [*Draws up angrily.*] I've give you fair warning!

GHENT: We'll keep everything friendly between me and you. A square stand-up shoot, and the best man takes her.

DUTCH: [*Mollified.*] Now you're comin' to!

GHENT: [*To the* MEXICAN.] Then it's up to you, and you'd better answer quick!

THE MEXICAN: [*Eyeing* GHENT *and* RUTH, *points to the gun lying on the floor.*] I take him, too.

GHENT: No, you don't. You leave everything here the way you found it.

THE MEXICAN: Alla right. [*He pockets the chain and starts for the door.*]

GHENT: Hold on a minute. You've got to promise to tie the man who falls, on his horse, and take him to Mesa Grande. Bargain? [*The* MEXICAN *nods.*] And mouth shut, mind you, or—[*He makes a sign across his throat.*]

THE MEXICAN: [*Nods.*] Alla right. [*He goes out.*]

GHENT: [*Motioning toward the door.*] Outside.

DUTCH: [*Surprised.*] What for?

GHENT: [*Sternly.*] Outside! [*They move toward the door.* DUTCH *stops and waves his hand to* RUTH.]

DUTCH: Don't worry, my girl. Back soon.

GHENT: [*Threateningly.*] Cut that out!

DUTCH: What's eatin' you? She ain't yours yet, and I guess she won't be, not till hell freezes over.

[*He taps his pistol and goes out.* GHENT *picks up the rifle which has previously missed fire; he unloads it, throws it on the window seat, and follows* DUTCH. RUTH *stands beside the table, listening. Four shots are heard. After a short time* GHENT *appears and watches from the door the vanishing horses. He comes to the table opposite* RUTH.]

RUTH: [*In a low voice.*] Is he dead?

GHENT: No; but he'll stay in the coop for a while.

[*She sinks down in a chair.* GHENT *seats himself at the other side of the table, draws a whiskey flask from his pocket, and uncorks it awkwardly, using only his right hand.*]

RUTH: [*As he is about to drink.*] Don't!

GHENT: [*Lowers the bottle and looks at her in a dazed way.*] Is this on the square?

RUTH: I gave you my promise.

[*Gazing at her, he lets the bottle sink slowly by his side; the liquor runs out, while he sits as if in a stupor.* RUTH *glances toward the door, and half starts from her seat, sinking back as he looks up.*]

GHENT: Give me a drink of water.

[*She brings the water from a bucket in the corner. He sets the empty bottle on the table, drinks deeply of the water, takes a handkerchief from his neck, wets it, and mops his face.*]

GHENT: Where are your folks?

RUTH: My brother has gone out to the railroad.

GHENT: Him and you ranching it here by yourselves?

RUTH: Yes.

GHENT: Write him a note. [*He shoves paper, pen, and ink before her.*] Fix it up anyway you like.

RUTH: Tell me first what you mean to do with me.

GHENT: [*Ponders awhile in silence.*] Have you got a horse to ride?

RUTH: Yes.

GHENT: We can reach San Jacinto before sun-up. Then we're off for the Cordilleras. I've got a claim tucked away in them hills that'll buy you the city of Frisco some day, if you have a mind to it! [*She shrinks and shudders.*] What you shivering at? [RUTH *does not answer, but begins to write.* GHENT, *still using only one hand, takes a pistol from his pocket, examines it, and lays it carelessly on the table, within* RUTH's *reach. He rises and goes to the fireplace, takes a cigarette from his pocket and lights it, and examines the objects on the mantel-shelf.* RUTH *stops writing, takes up the pistol, then lays it down, as he speaks without turning round.*] Read what you've written. [RUTH, *about to read, snatches up the pistol again, rises, and stands trembling and irresolute.*] Why don't you shoot? [*He turns round deliberately.*] You promised on the square, but there's nothing square about this deal. You ought to shoot me like a rattlesnake!

RUTH: I know that.

GHENT: Then why don't you?

RUTH: [*Slowly.*] I don't know.

GHENT: I guess you've got nerve enough, for that or anything.—Answer me; why not?

RUTH: I don't—know—You laid it there for me.—And—you have no right to die.

GHENT: How's that?

RUTH: You must live—to pay for having spoiled your life.

GHENT: Do you think it is spoiled?

RUTH: Yes.

GHENT: And how about your life?

RUTH: I tried to do it.

GHENT: To do what?

RUTH: To take my life. I ought to die. I have a right to die. But I cannot,
I cannot! I love my life, I must live. In torment, in darkness—it
doesn't matter. I want my life. I will have it! [*She drops the weapon on
the table, pushes it toward him, and covers her eyes.*] Take it away!
Don't let me see it. If you want me on these terms, take me, and may
God forgive you for it; but if there is a soul in you to be judged,
don't let me do myself violence. [*She sinks down by the table, hiding
her face in her hands.*] O, God have pity on me!
[GHENT *puts the pistol back into his belt, goes slowly to the outer door,
opens it, and stands for some moments gazing out. He then closes the
door, and takes a step or two toward the table. As he speaks,* RUTH'*s sobs
cease, she raises her head and looks strangely at him.*]

GHENT: I've lived hard and careless, and lately I've been going down hill
pretty fast. But I haven't got so low yet but what I can tell one
woman from another. If that was all of it, I'd be miles away from
here by now, riding like hell for liquor to wash the taste of shame out
of my mouth. But that ain't all. I've seen what I've been looking the
world over for, and never knew it.—Say your promise holds, and I'll
go away now.

RUTH: O, yes, go, go! You will be merciful. You will not hold me to my
cruel oath.

GHENT: And when I come back? [RUTH *does not answer. He takes a step
nearer.*] And when I come back?

RUTH: You never—could—come back.

GHENT: No, I guess I never could.

RUTH: [*Eager, pleading.*] You *will* go?

GHENT: For good?

RUTH: Yes.

GHENT: Do you mean that?

RUTH: [*Wildly.*] Yes, yes, ten thousand times!

GHENT: Is that your last word?

RUTH: Yes. [*Pause. She watches him with strained anxiety.*] O, why did you
come here to-night?

GHENT: I come because I was blind-drunk and sun-crazy and looking for
damnation the nearest way. That's why I come. But that's not why
I'm staying. I'm talking to you in my right mind now. I want you to
try and see this thing the way it is.

RUTH: O, that is what I want you to do! You did yourself and me a
hideous wrong by coming here. Don't do us both a more hideous
wrong still! I was in panic fear. I snatched at the first thing I could.
Think what our life would be, beginning as we have begun! O, for
God's pity go away now, and never come back! Don't you see there
can never be anything between us but hatred, and misery, and horror?

GHENT: [*Hardening.*] We'll see about that!—Are you ready to start?
[RUTH, *conscious for the first time of her undress condition, shrinks, and
folds her gown closer about her neck.*] Go, and be quick about it. [*She
starts toward her room; he detains her.*] Where's your saddle?
[*She points at it and goes out.* GHENT *picks up the note she has written,
reads it, and stands for a moment in reflection before laying it down.
He gets more water from the bucket, drinks deeply, mops his face, and
rolls up the sleeve of his left arm, which is soaked with blood. He tries
awkwardly to stanch a wound in his forearm, gives it up in disgust, and
rolls down his sleeve again. He reads the note once more, then takes
RUTH's saddle and bridle from the wall and goes out.* RUTH *comes in;
her face is white and haggard, but her manner determined and collected. She comes to the table, and sees the bloody handkerchief and basin
of water. As* GHENT *enters, she turns to him anxiously.*]

RUTH: You are hurt.

GHENT: It's no matter.

RUTH: Where? [*He indicates his left arm. She throws off her hooded riding-
cloak, and impulsively gathers together water, towels, liniment, and
bandages; she approaches him, quite lost in her task, flushed and eager.*]
Sit down.—Roll up your sleeve. [*He obeys mechanically. She rapidly
and deftly washes and binds the wound, speaking half to herself, between
long pauses.*] Can you lift your arm?—The bone is not touched.—It
will be all right in a few days.—This balsam is a wonderful thing to
heal.

GHENT: [*Watching her dreamily, as she works.*] What's your name?

RUTH: Ruth—Ruth—Jordan. [*Long pause.*] There, gently.—It must be
very painful.
[*He shakes his head slowly, with half-humorous protest.*]

GHENT: It's not fair!

RUTH: What isn't fair?

GHENT: To treat me like this. It's not in the rules of the game.

RUTH: [*As the sense of the situation again sweeps over her.*] Binding your
wound? I would do the same service for a dog.

GHENT: Yes, I dare say. But the point is, I ain't a dog; I'm a human—the worst way! [*She rises and puts away the liniment and bandages. He starts up with an impulsive gesture.*] Make this bad business over into something good for both of us! You'll never regret it! I'm a strong man! [*He holds out his right arm, rigid.*] I used to feel sometimes, before I went to the bad, that I could take the world like that and tilt her over. And I can do it, too, if you say the word! I'll put you where you can look down on the proudest. I'll give you the kingdoms of the world and all the glory of 'em. [*She covers her face with her hands. He comes nearer.*] Give me a chance, and I'll make good. By God, girl, I'll make good!—I'll make a queen of you. I'll put the world under your feet! [RUTH *makes a passionate gesture, as if to stop her ears.*] What makes you put your hands over your ears like that? Don't you like what I'm saying to you?

RUTH: [*Taking the words with difficulty.*] Do you remember what that man said just now?

GHENT: What about?

RUTH: About the Indian—and—his squaw.

GHENT: Yes. There was something in it, too. I was a fool to offer him that mean little wad.

RUTH: For—me!

GHENT: Well, yes, for you, if you want to put it that way.

RUTH: But—a chain of nuggets—that comes nearer being a fair price?

GHENT: O, to buy off a greaser!

RUTH: But to buy the soul of a woman—one must go higher. A mining-claim! The kingdoms of the world and all the glory of them! [*Breaking down in sudden sobs.*] O, be careful how you treat me! Be careful! I say it as much for your sake as mine. Be careful!

GHENT: [*Turns from her, his bewilderment and discomfiture translating itself into gruffness.*] Well, I guess we'll blunder through.—Come along! We've no time to lose.—Where are your things? [*At her gesture, he picks up the saddle-pack which she has brought out of the bedroom with her, and starts toward the door.*]

RUTH: [*Taking a hammer from the window-ledge and handing it to* GHENT.] Fix the bolt. My brother must not know.

[*He drives in the staple of the bolt, while she throws the blood-stained water and handkerchief into the fire. He aids her in replacing the weapons on the walls, then takes the saddle-pack and stands at the door, waiting. She picks up her mother's picture, and thrusts it in her bosom. After standing a moment in hesitation, she takes the picture out, kisses it, lays it on the mantel, face down. She extinguishes the lamp, and goes out hastily. He follows, closing the door.*]

ACT II

STEPHEN GHENT's *home, in the Cordilleras. At the right, crowning a rude terrace, is an adobe cabin, stained a pale buff, mellowed to ivory by sun and dust. Over it clamber vines loaded with purple bloom. The front of the cabin is turned at an angle toward the spectator, the farther side running parallel with the brink of a cañon, of which the distant wall and upper reaches are crimsoned by the afternoon light. In the level space before the rocky terrace is a stone table and seats, made of natural rocks roughly worked with the chisel. The rude materials have manifestly been touched by a refined and artistic hand, bent on making the most of the glorious natural background. Against the rocks on the left stands a large hand-loom of the Navajo type, with weaving-stool, and a blanket half woven. On the table lies a half-finished Indian basket, and strips of colored weaving-materials lie in a heap on the ground. Cactus plants in blossom fill the niches of the rocks and lift their fantastic forms above the stones which wall the cañon brink. At one point this wall is broken, where a path descends into the cañon.*

LON ANDERSON, *a venerable looking miner, with gray hair and beard, sits smoking before the cabin.* BURT WILLIAMS, *a younger man, peeps up over the edge of the cañon, from the path.*

BURT: Hello, Lon. Is the Missus inside? [LON *smokes on, without looking at the questioner.*] Look here, I put a nickel in you, you blame rusty old slot machine. Push out something!

LON: [*Removes his pipe deliberately.*] What you wantin' off 'n her now? A music lesson or a headache powder?

BURT: Boss's waitin' down at the mine, with a couple o' human wonders he's brought back with him from wherever he's been this time. Something doin' on the quiet.

LON: You can tell him his wife ain't nowheres about.

[BURT *produces an enormous bandana from his pocket, mounts the wall, and waves it. He sits on the wall and smokes for a moment in silence, looking down into the cañon, as if watching the approaching party. He points with his pipe at the cabin.*]

BURT: Funny hitch-up—this here one—I think.

LON: [*After a pause.*] How much you gittin' a day now?

BURT: Same little smilin' helpless three and six-bits.

LON: Anything extry for thinkin'?

BURT: Nope! Throwed in. [*They smoke again.* BURT *glances down to reassure himself, then points at the loom and basket.*] Queer business—this rug-weavin' and basket-makin', ain't it?—What d' ye s'pose she wants to sit, day in and day out, like a half-starved Navajo, slavin' over them fool things fur?—Boss ain't near, is he? Don't keep her short of ice-cream sodas and trolley-rides, does 'e? [LON *rises and approaches* BURT, *regarding him grimly.*] Saw 'er totin' a lot o' that stuff burro-back over to the hotel week 'fore last.—An' Dod Ranger—you know what a disgustin' liar Dod is—he tells how he was makin' tests over in the cross-cañon, an' all of a sudden plump he comes on her talkin' to a sawed-off Mexican hobo, and when she sees Dod, she turns white's a sheet.

LON: [*With suppressed ferocity.*] You tell Dod Ranger to keep his mouth shet, and you keep yourn shet too—or by Jee-hosophat, I'll make the two of ye eat yer Adams's-apples and swaller the core!

BURT: O, git down off'n yer hind legs, Lon! Nobody's intendin' any disrespect.

LON: You boys keep yer blatherin' tongues off'n her! Or you'll get mixed up with Alonzo P. Anderson—[*he taps his breast*]—so's it'll take a coroner to untangle ye!

BURT: [*Deprecatingly.*] I guess I'd stick up fur 'er 's quick as you would, come to that.

LON: Well, we don't need no stickin' up fur 'er. What we need is less tongue. [*He leans down and speaks lower.*] Especially when the boss is round. You tell the boys so.

[BURT *looks at him in surprise and is about to speak;* LON *makes a warning signal, indicating the approach of the party below.* BURT *descends, saluting* GHENT *respectfully.*]

GHENT: [*Peeping up over the edge of the cañon.*] Coast clear, eh, Lon?

LON: Yes, sir.

GHENT: Where is she?

LON: [*Points along the brink of the cañon.*] Kind o' think she went out to Look-off Ledge.—Guess she didn't expect you back to-day.

GHENT: [*Speaking below.*] Come up, gentlemen. [GHENT *emerges from the cañon, followed by an* ARCHITECT, *a dapper young Easterner, and a* CONTRACTOR, *a bluff Western type.* GHENT *is neatly dressed in khaki, with riding-boots and broad felt hat. He has a prosperous and busy air, and is manifestly absorbed in the national game of making money.*] Take a seat.

CONTRACTOR: [*Seats himself by the table.*] Don't care if I do. That new stage of yours just jumped stiff-legged from the go-off. And the trail up here from the mine is a good deal of a proposition for the seedentary.

ARCHITECT: [*As he takes in the stupendous view.*] What a wonderful place! Even better than you described it.

GHENT: Yes. My wife picked it out.—Let's see your plans. [*He removes bas-*

ket from the table, where the ARCHITECT *unrolls several sheets of blue paper.*]

ARCHITECT: I have followed your instructions to the letter. I understand that nothing is to be touched except the house.

GHENT: Not a stone, sir; not a head of cactus. Even the vines you've got to keep, exactly as they are.

ARCHITECT: [*Smiling.*] That will be a little difficult.

GHENT: You can put 'em on a temporary trellis.—A little pains will do it.

CONTRACTOR: Maybe, with a man to shoo the masons off with a shot-gun.

GHENT: [*Over the plans.*] Provide a dozen men, if necessary, with machine guns.

CONTRACTOR: As you please, Mr. Ghent. The owner of the Verde mine has a right to his whims, I reckon.

ARCHITECT: I have designed the whole house in the Spanish style, very broad and simple. This open space where we stand—[*points to the plans*]—I have treated as a semi-enclosed *patio,* with arcaded porches.

GHENT: [*Dubiously.*] Good.

ARCHITECT: This large room fronting the main arcade is the living-room.

GHENT: I guess we'll have 'em all living-rooms. This place is to be lived in, from the word go.

ARCHITECT: [*Humoring him.*] To be sure, everything cheerful and open.—Here on the left of the inner court is the library and music-room.

GHENT: I'm afraid we won't have much use for that. My wife don't go in much for frills. I used to play the concertina once, but it was a long while ago.

ARCHITECT: It can be used for other purposes. For instance, as a nursery, though I had put that on the other side.

GHENT: [*Embarrassed and delighted.*] Um, yes, nursery.—Stamping-ground for the—? [*The* ARCHITECT *nods; the* CONTRACTOR *follows suit, with emphasis.* LON *nods solemnly over his pipe.*] Good. [*The* ARCHITECT *bends over to make a note with his pencil.* GHENT *restrains him and says somewhat sheepishly in his ear.*] You can leave it music-room on the map.

ARCHITECT: [*Continuing his explanation.*] This wing—

[GHENT, *interrupting him, holds the plan at arm's length, with head on one side and eyes squinted, as he looks from the drawings to the cabin and surroundings.*]

GHENT: Looks a little—*sprawly* on paper. I had sort of imagined some-thing more—more up in the air, like them swell tepees on the Hill in

Frisco. [*He makes a grandiose outline of high roofs and turrets in the air.*]

ARCHITECT: I think this is more harmonious with the surroundings.

CONTRACTOR: [*In answer to* GHENT*'s inquiring look.*] Won't look so showy from the new hotel across yonder. [*He points to the left, down the curve of the cañon wall.*]

GHENT: What's your estimate on this plan, now you've seen the location?

CONTRACTOR: It's a long way to haul the stuff.—Say somewheres between twenty and twenty-five thousand. Twenty-five will be safe.

GHENT: [*Slightly staggered.*] That's a big lot of money, my friend!

CONTRACTOR: [*With cold scorn.*] I thought we was talkin' about a *house*! I can build you a good sheep-corral for a right smart less.

GHENT: Well, I guess we don't want any sheep-corrals.

CONTRACTOR: I should think not, with the Verde pumping money at you the way they tell she does.

GHENT: [*Holds up the plans again and looks at them in perplexed silence.*] I'll tell you, gentlemen, I'll have to consult my wife about this before I decide. The fact is, I've been working the thing out on the sly, up to now.

CONTRACTOR: Expect to build it of an afternoon, while the lady was takin' her see-ester?

GHENT: I thought I'd smuggle her off somewhere for a while. [*He is silent a moment, pondering.*] No! It's her house, and she must O.K. the plans before ground is broke. [*He looks along the cañon rim.*] Would you mind waiting a few minutes till I see if I can find her? [*He starts irresolutely, then turns back.*] Or better still, leave the plans, and I'll see you at the hotel to-morrow morning. I haven't been over there since it was opened. I'd like to know what they're making of it.

CONTRACTOR: [*Astonished.*] Hain't been over to the Buny Visty yet?

GHENT: Too busy.

CONTRACTOR: Well, you'll find it an up-to-date joint, and chock full of tourist swells and lungers.

GHENT: Good-afternoon, gentlemen. You'll excuse me. You can find your way back all right? Take the left-hand path. It's better going.
[*The* ARCHITECT *bows ceremoniously, the* CONTRACTOR *nods.* GHENT *disappears along the cañon brink behind the cabin.*]

ARCHITECT: [*Has been examining the work on the loom, and has then picked up the unfinished basket, admiringly.*] What a beautiful pattern! I say, this is like those we saw at the hotel. [*To* LON.] May I ask who is making this? [LON *smokes in silence. The* ARCHITECT *raises his voice, slightly sharp.*] May I ask who is making this?

LON: [*Benignly.*] You kin, my friend, you kin!

ARCHITECT: Well, then, the question is put.

LON: And very clear-put, too. You'd ought to be in the law business, young man. [*He gets up deliberately.*] Or some other business that'd take up all yer time.

ARCHITECT: [*Between wrath and amusement.*] Well, I'll be hanged! [*He follows his companion down the cañon path, stopping a moment at the brink to look round with a professional air at the house and surroundings, then at LON.*] Tart old party! [*He descends.*]

[LON *crosses to the table, looks over the plans, makes outlines in the air in imitation of* GHENT, *then shakes his head dubiously, as he rolls up the plans.* RUTH *appears, emerging from the cañon path. She wears the same dress as at the close of Act I, with a dark scarf-like handkerchief thrown over her head. She is pale and exhausted. She sinks on the rocks at the edge of the cañon.*]

LON: [*Approaching her, anxiously.*] It's too much fer you, ma'am. You'd oughter let me go. [*He brings her a glass of water from an Indian water-jar before the cabin.*]

RUTH: [*Tasting the water.*] O, I thought I should never get back! [*She leans against a rock, with closed eyes, then rouses herself again.*] Lon, take the glass, and see if you can make out any one down yonder, on the nearer trail. I—I thought some one was following me.

LON: [*Speaks low.*] Excuse me askin', Mis' Ghent, but is that dod-blamed Mexican a botherin' you again?

RUTH: No. He has gone away, for good. It's some one I saw at the hotel—some one I used to know.—Look if you can make out a man's figure, coming up.

LON: [*Takes the glass from the niche in the rocks, and scans the cañon path.*] Can't see nothin' but a stray burro, an' he ain't got no figger to speak of.—Might be t'other side o' Table Rock, down in the pinyon scrub. [RUTH *gets up with an effort, takes the glass and looks through it, then lays it on the ledge.*] Excuse me, ma'am, but—Mister Ghent come home this afternoon.

RUTH: [*Startled.*] Where is he?

LON: Huntin' for you down Look-off Ledge way. I 'lowed you was there, not knowin' what else to say.

RUTH: Thank you, Lon.—You can go now. [*He goes down the cañon path. RUTH looks once more through the glass, then crosses to the table, where she sits down and begins to finger the roll of plans. GHENT reënters. He approaches with soft tread and bends over RUTH. She starts up with a little cry, avoiding his embrace.*] You frightened me.—When did you come back?

GHENT: An hour ago.

RUTH: Was your journey successful?

GHENT: Yes. But my home-coming—that looks rather like a failure. [*Pause.*] I expected to find you out on the bluff.

RUTH: Lon was mistaken. I had gone the other way. [*As she stands at the table, she begins to unroll the plans.*] What are these papers?

GHENT: Haven't you one word of welcome for me, after five days? [RUTH *remains silent, with averted head, absently unrolling the packet.*] Not a look even? [*He waits a moment, then sighs and seats himself moodily by the table.*] I never can remember! After I've been away from you for twelve hours, I forget completely.

RUTH: Forget what?

GHENT: How it stands between us. It's childish, but for the life of me I can't help it.—After I've been away a few hours, this place gets all lit up with bright colors in my mind, like—[*searching for a simile*]— well, like a Christmas tree! I dare say a Christmas tree don't amount to much in real life, but I saw one once, in a play,—I was a little mining-camp roust-about, so high,—and ever since it has sort of stood to me for the gates o' glory.

RUTH: [*With a hysterical laugh.*] A Christmas tree! [*She bows her head in her hands, and repeats the words, as if to herself, in a tone in which bitterness has given place to tragic melancholy.*] A Christmas tree!
[GHENT, *watching her moodily, crumples up the plans and throws them upon the ground. He goes toward the cabin, hesitates, turns, and comes back to the table, where* RUTH *still sits with buried head. He draws from his pocket a jewel-case, which he opens and lays before her.*]

GHENT: There is a little present I brought home for you. And here are some more trinkets. [*He takes out several pieces of jewelry and tumbles them together on the table.*] I know you don't care much for these things, but I had to buy something, the way I was feeling. And these papers—[*picks them up and spreads them out on the table*]— these mean that you're not to live much longer in a mud shanty, with pine boxes for furniture. These are the drawings for a new house that I want to talk over with you. [*He points at the map and speaks glibly, trying to master his discomfiture at her lack of interest.*] Spanish style, everything broad and simple! Large living-room opening on inner court. Library and music-room, bless your heart. Bedrooms; kitchen and thereunto pertaining. Wing where the proprietor retires to express his inmost feelings. General effect sprawly, but harmonious with the surroundings. Twenty thousand estimated, twenty-five limit. Is she ours?

RUTH: [*In a dead, flat tone.*] How much did you say the house is to cost?

GHENT: Twenty-five thousand dollars at the outside.

RUTH: And these—trinkets?

GHENT: O, I don't know.—A few hundred.

RUTH: [*Draws the plans toward her and pours the jewels in a heap upon them from her lifted hands.*] Twenty-five thousand dollars and the odd hundreds! [*She laughs suddenly and jarringly.*] My price has risen! My price has risen! [*She laughs again, as she rises from the table and looks down the cañon path.*] Keep those displayed to show to our visitors! My honor is at stake. [*She points down the path.*] There is one coming now!

GHENT: Visitors? What visitors?

RUTH: Only an old school-friend of mine; a Mr. Winthrop Newbury.

GHENT: What are you talking about? Are you crazy? [*He joins her, where she stands looking down into the cañon.*] This fellow, is he really what you say? [RUTH *nods, with unnaturally bright eyes and mocking smile.*] What does this mean?

RUTH: It means that he caught sight of me, an hour ago, in the hotel.

GHENT: In the hotel? What were you doing there?

RUTH: [*With biting calm.*] Nothing wicked—as yet. They don't pay twenty-five thousand dollars over there—at least not yet! [GHENT *turns sharply, as if stung by a physical blow. She raises her hands to him, in a swift revulsion of feeling.*] O, don't judge me! Don't listen to me! I am not in my right mind.

GHENT: [*Sweeps the jewels together, and throws them over the cliff.*] Do you want me to be here, while you see him? [*She does not answer.*] Won't you answer me?

RUTH: [*Again cold.*] Act as you think best.

GHENT: It's a question of what will be easiest for you.

RUTH: O, it's all easy for me!

[GHENT *stands irresolute, then raises his hand in a gesture of perplexity and despair, and goes into the house, closing the door.* WINTHROP NEWBURY *appears at the top of the cañon path, looks curiously about, catches sight of* RUTH's *averted figure, and rushes toward her.*]

WINTHROP: Ruth! Is it really you?

[RUTH *starts involuntarily toward him, stretching out her arms. As he advances, she masters herself, and speaks in a natural voice, with an attempt at gayety, as she takes his hand.*]

RUTH: Well, of all things! Winthrop Newbury! How did you find your way to this eagle's nest?

WINTHROP: I—we saw you—we caught a glimpse of you at the hotel, but we weren't sure. We followed you, but lost you in the cañon.

RUTH: We? Who is we?

WINTHROP: Your brother and his wife.

RUTH: [*Turning the shock, which she has been unable to conceal, into conventional surprise.*] Philip and Polly here!

WINTHROP: They took the other turn, down there where the path forks. We didn't know which way you had gone.

RUTH: Yes, but why on earth are they here at all?

WINTHROP: They are on their way East. They stopped over to see me.

RUTH: To see you? Are you—living here?

WINTHROP: I have been here only a week. [*He starts impulsively, trying to break through the conventional wall which she has raised between them.*] Ruth—for God's sake—!

RUTH: [*Interrupting him, with exaggerated animation.*] But tell me! I am all curiosity. How do you happen to be here—of all places?

WINTHROP: What does it matter? I am here. We have found you, after all these miserable months of anxiety and searching. O Ruth—why—

RUTH: I have acted badly, I know. But I wish not to talk of that. Not now. I will explain everything later. Tell me about yourself—about Philip and Polly—and mother. I am thirsty for news. What have you been doing all these months, since—our queer parting?

WINTHROP: [*Solemnly.*] Looking for you. [*Pause.*] O, Ruth—how could you do it? How could you do it?

RUTH: [*Touches him on the arm and looks at him with dumb entreaty, speaking low.*] Winthrop!

WINTHROP: [*In answer to her unspoken words.*] As you will.

RUTH: [*Resumes her hard, bright tone.*] You haven't told me about mother. How is she?

WINTHROP: Well. Or she will be, now. Ruth, you ought at least to have written to her. She has suffered cruelly.

RUTH: [*Quickly, with a nervous uplift of her arms.*] Yes, yes, I know that!— And you are—settled here? You mean to remain?

WINTHROP: I am physician at the End-of-the-Rainbow mines, three miles below. At least I—I am making a trial of it. [*Pause.*] How pale and worn you are.—Don't turn away. Look at me. [*She flinches, then summons her courage and looks him steadily in the face.*] You are—you are ill—I fear you are desperately ill!

RUTH: [*Moving away nervously.*] Nonsense. I was never better in my life. [*She goes toward the cañon brink.*] *You* haven't praised our view. We are very proud of it.

WINTHROP: [*Following her.*] Yes, very fine. Magnificent.

RUTH: But you're not looking at it at all! Do you see that bit of smoke far down yonder? That is the stamp mill of the Rio Verde mine.

WINTHROP: [*Compelling himself to follow her lead.*] Yes—the Rio Verde.

One of the big strikes of the region. Dispute about the ownership, I believe.

RUTH: None that I ever heard of, and I ought to know. For—[*she makes a sweeping bow*]—*we* are the Rio Verde, at your service.

WINTHROP: You—your—husband is the owner of the Verde mine?

RUTH: No less!

WINTHROP: [*Embarrassed.*] We found the record of your marriage at San Jacinto. The name was Ghent—Stephen Ghent.

RUTH: Yes. He will be so glad to see some of my people. [WINTHROP*'s eyes have fallen on the basket at the foot of the table. He picks it up, examines it curiously, and looks meaningly at* RUTH, *who snatches it from his hand and throws it over the cliff.*] A toy I play with! You know I always have to keep my hands busy pattering at some rubbishy craft or other.

WINTHROP: [*Is about to speak, but checks himself. He points at the loom.*] And the blanket, too?

RUTH: Yes, another fad of mine. It is really fascinating work. The Indian women who taught me think I am a wonder of cleverness.

WINTHROP: So do—the women—over there. [*He points across the cañon.*]

RUTH: [*Flushing.*] Ah, yes, you saw some of my stuff at the hotel. You know how vain I am. I had to show it.

WINTHROP: Perhaps. But why should the wife of the man who owns the Verde mine *sell* her handiwork, and under such—such vulgar conditions?

RUTH: [*Brilliantly explanatory.*] To see if it will sell, of course! That is the test of its merit!

[*He looks at her in mute protest, then with a shake of the head, rises and puts on his hat.*]

WINTHROP: Do you want to see the others?

RUTH: Why, yes, to be sure I do. How should I not?

WINTHROP: You haven't seemed very anxious—these last eight months.

RUTH: True. I have been at fault. I so dread explanations. And Phil's tempests of rage! Poor boy, he must feel sadly ill-used.

WINTHROP: He does. [*Hesitates.*] If there is any reason why you would rather he didn't see you, just now,—

RUTH: There is no reason. At least, none valid.

WINTHROP: Then I will bring them up.

RUTH: By all means. [*She holds out her hand, smiling.*] Auf wiedersehen! [WINTHROP *releases her hand and goes toward the cañon path. He waves, and turns to* RUTH.]

WINTHROP: They are just below. [*As* RUTH *advances he takes her hand and looks searchingly into her eyes.*] For old friendship's sake, won't you give me one human word before they come? At least answer me honestly one human question?

RUTH: [*Keeping her hard, bright gayety.*] In the great lottery of a woman's answers there is always one such prize!

WINTHROP: [*Dejectedly, as he drops her hand.*] It's no use, if that is your mood.

RUTH: My mood! Your old bugbear! I am as sober-serious as my stars ever let me be.

WINTHROP: Did you, that night you bade me good-bye, know that—this was going to happen?

RUTH: [*Cordially explanatory.*] No. It was half accident, half wild impulse. Phil left me at the ranch alone. My lover came, impatient, importunate, and I—went with him.

WINTHROP: And your—this man—to whom you are married—pardon me, you don't need to answer unless you wish—for how long had you known him?

RUTH: [*Solemnly, as she looks him straight in the eyes.*] All my life! And for aeons before.

[*He looks at her for a moment, then goes toward the cañon path. POLLY's voice is heard calling.*]

POLLY: [*Not yet visible.*] Win! Win!·

WINTHROP: [*Calls down the cañon.*] Come up! Come up!

[*RUTH goes past him down the cañon path. In a moment she reappears, with POLLY. They are laughing and talking as they come.*]

POLLY: Ruth!

RUTH: Dear old Polly!

POLLY: You *naughty* girl!

RUTH: If our sins must find us out, you are the kind of Nemesis I choose.

POLLY: My! But you're a shady character. And sly!

[*PHILIP appears. RUTH hurries to embrace him, while POLLY, fanning herself with her handkerchief, examines the house and surroundings with curiosity.*]

RUTH: O Phil!—Dear old man! [*She covers his face lightly with her hands.*] No scolding, no frowns. This is the finding of the prodigal, and she expects a robe and a ring.

POLLY: [*Seating herself on a rock.*] Heavens, what a climb!—I'm a rag.

RUTH: [*Motions to the men to be seated.*] The cabin wouldn't hold us all, but there's one good thing about this place; there's plenty of outdoors.

WINTHROP: [*Looking about.*] I should say there was!

POLLY: To think of our practical Ruth doing the one really theatrical thing

known in the annals of Milford Corners, Mass.!—And what a setting! My dear, your stage arrangements are perfect.

RUTH: In this case Providence deserves the credit. We may have come
here to have our pictures taken, but we stayed to make a living.

[PHILIP *has drawn apart, gloomy and threatening.* POLLY *keeps up her
heroic efforts to give the situation a casual and humorous air.*]

POLLY: [*With jaunty challenge.*] Well, where is he?

RUTH: Who?

POLLY: He! [RUTH *points at the cabin, smiling.*] Well, produce him!

RUTH: [*Following, with gratitude in her eyes, the key of lightness and raillery
which* POLLY *has struck.*] You insist?

POLLY: Absolutely.

RUTH: O, very well!

[*She goes up the rocky incline, and enters the cabin, calling: "Steve!
Steve!"* POLLY *goes to* PHILIP, *and shakes him.*]

POLLY: Now you behave! [*Indicates* WINTHROP.] He's behaving.

[RUTH *reappears in the doorway, followed by* GHENT.]

RUTH: [*With elaborate gayety, as they descend the rocks.*] Well, Stephen,
since they've run us to earth, I suppose we must put a good face on
it, and acknowledge them.—This is Polly, of whom I've talked so
much. Polly the irresistible. Beware of her! [POLLY *shakes his hand
cordially.*] And this is—my brother Philip. [GHENT *extends his hand,
which* PHILIP *pointedly ignores.* RUTH *goes on hastily, to cover the insult.*] And this is my old school-friend, Winthrop Newbury. [*They
shake hands.*]

WINTHROP: [*To* PHILIP, *formally explanatory.*] Mr. Ghent is the owner of
the famous Verde mine.

GHENT: Part owner, sir. I hadn't the capital to develop with, so I had to
dispose of a half-interest.

WINTHROP: Isn't there some litigation under way?

RUTH: [*Looking at* GHENT, *surprised.*] Litigation?

GHENT: Yes—a whole rigmarole.

POLLY: [*Catching at a straw to make talk.*] Heaven help you if you have
got entangled in the law! I can conceive of nothing more horrible or
ghostly than a court of law; unless [*she glances at* PHILIP] it is that
other court of high justice, which people hold in private to judge
their fellows, from hearsay and half-knowledge!

RUTH: [*Keeping up the play desperately, as she blesses* POLLY *with a look.*] But
there must be law, just the same, and penalties and rewards and all
that. Else what's the use of being good?

POLLY: Like you—for instance!

RUTH: Well, yes, like me!

POLLY: You are not good, you are merely magnificent. I want to be magnificent! I want to live on the roof of the world and own a gold mine! [*To* GHENT.] Show me where the sweet thing is.

GHENT: We can get a better view of the plant from the ledge below. Will you go down?

[GHENT, POLLY, *and* WINTHROP *go down the cañon path.* RUTH *takes* PHILIP *by the arm, to lead him after.*]

PHILIP: No. We must have a word together, before the gabble begins again. Winthrop has given me your explanation, which explains nothing.

RUTH: [*Trying to keep up the light tone.*] Hasn't that usually been the verdict on explanations of my conduct?

PHILIP: Don't try to put me off! Tell me in two words how you came to run away with this fellow.

RUTH: [*Hardening.*] Remember to whom you are speaking, and about whom.

PHILIP: I got your note, with its curt announcement of your resolve. Later, by mere accident, we found the record of your marriage at San Jacinto—if you call it a marriage, made hugger-mugger at midnight by a tipsy justice of the peace. I don't want to question its validity. I only pray that no one will. But I want to know how it came to be made, in such hurry and secrecy—how it came to be made at all, for that matter. How did you ever come to disgrace yourself and your family by clandestine meetings and a hedge-row marriage with a person of this class? And why, after the crazy leap was taken, did you see fit to hide yourself away without a word to me or your distracted mother? Though that perhaps is easier to understand!

RUTH: The manner of your questions absolves me from the obligation to answer them.

PHILIP: I refuse to be put off with any such patent subterfuge.

RUTH: Subterfuge or not, it will have to suffice, until you remember that my right to choose my course in life is unimpeachable, and that the man whose destiny I elect to share cannot be insulted in my presence.

PHILIP: Very well, I can wait. The truth will come out some day. Meanwhile, you can take comfort from the fact that your desertion at the critical moment of our enterprise has spelled ruin for me.

RUTH: [*Overwhelmed.*] Philip, you don't mean—!

PHILIP: Absolute and irretrievable ruin.

RUTH: Then you are going back East—for good?

PHILIP: Yes.

RUTH: But—mother's money! What will she do? [PHILIP *shrugs his shoulders.*] Is everything gone—everything?

PHILIP: I shall get something from the sale. Perhaps enough to make a fresh start, somewhere, in some small way.

RUTH: [*Comes to him, and lays her arms on his shoulders.*] Phil, I am sorry, sorry!

[*He caresses her; she bursts into suppressed convulsive weeping and clings to him, hiding her face in his breast.*]

PHILIP: Ruth, you are not happy! You have made a hideous mistake. Come home with me. [RUTH *shakes her head.*] At least for a time. You are not well. You look really ill. Come home with us, if only for a month.

RUTH: No, no, dear Phil, dear brother! [*She draws down his face and kisses him; then lifts her head, with an attempt at lightness.*] There! I have had my cry, and feel better. The excitement of seeing you all again is a little too much for me.

PHILIP: If there is anything that you want to tell me about all this, tell me now.

RUTH: O, there will be plenty of time for explanations and all that! Let us just be happy now in our reunion.

PHILIP: There will not be plenty of time. We leave to-morrow morning.

RUTH: Then you will take me on trust—like a dear good brother. Perhaps I shall never explain! I like my air of mystery.

PHILIP: Remember that if you ever have anything to complain of—in your life—it is my right to know it. The offender shall answer to me, and dearly, too.

RUTH: [*Takes his head between her hands, and shakes it, as with recovered gayety.*] Of course they will, you old fire-eater!

PHILIP: [*Pointing to the blanket on the loom.*] Ruth, at least tell me why—.
[RUTH *does not see his gesture, as she is looking at the others, who come up from below. The men linger in the background,* GHENT *pointing out objects in the landscape.*]

RUTH: [*To* POLLY, *who advances.*] Well, what do you think of us, in a bird's-eye view?

POLLY: In a bird's-eye view you are superb! [*She draws* RUTH *to her, and speaks in a lower tone.*] And looked at near, you are an enthralling puzzle.

RUTH: [*Half to herself.*] If you only knew how much!

POLLY: [*Taking* RUTH *by the chin as in Act I.*] So you *had*—just by chance riding over to the trading-station or so—met the glorious unfulfilled—in blue overalls and a jumper! I thought so! [RUTH *bows her head in a spasm of pain.* POLLY, *who does not see her face, goes on teasingly.*] I see now what you meant about wanting one that wasn't finished. This one certainly isn't finished. But when he is, he'll be grand! [RUTH *moves away with averted head.* POLLY *follows her, peeping round to view her face.*] Don't sulk! I meant nothing disrespectful. On the contrary, I'm crazy about him. [*In a louder tone.*] And now that I've seen the outside of you, I must peep into that fascinating little house!

RUTH: [*To* GHENT, *who has drawn nearer.*] Polly wants to go inside the cabin. I can't let her until we have shown her what it's going to be. [*With* GHENT*'s aid she spreads out the plan, which* POLLY *examines with curiosity.*] These are the plans for our new house. You call us magnificent. We will show you that we are not. We are overwhelming!

WINTHROP: [*Looking at his watch.*] I am afraid we must be getting back. It grows dark very suddenly in the cañon.

RUTH: [*To* POLLY.] Well, then you may come in, if you will promise to view the simple present in the light of the ornate future.

[POLLY *goes in.* RUTH, *lingering at the door for an instant, looks back anxiously at the men.*]

PHILIP: [*Curtly, to* GHENT.] If you will permit me, I should like a word with you.

GHENT: Certainly.

[WINTHROP *effaces himself, making and lighting a cigarette, as he looks out over the cañon.*]

PHILIP: In deference to my sister's wishes, I refrain from asking you for the explanation which is due me. [GHENT *bows in silence.*] But there is one thing which I think I am at liberty to question.

GHENT: Do so.

PHILIP: I hear of your interest in a valuable mine. I hear of plans for an elaborate house. Why, then, is my sister compelled to peddle her own handiwork in a public caravansary?

GHENT: What do you mean? I don't understand you.

PHILIP: [*Points at the loom.*] Her rugs and baskets are on sale in the corridor of the hotel, fingered and discussed by the tourist mob.

GHENT: [*Astonished.*] This can't be true!

PHILIP: It is, however.

GHENT: I know nothing of it. I've had to be away a great deal. I knew she worked too hard over these things, but I took it for a mere pastime. Perhaps—No, I can't understand it at all!

PHILIP: I advise you to make inquiries. She has taken pains to conceal her identity, but it is known nevertheless, and the subject of public curiosity.

[POLLY *and* RUTH *come out from the cabin.*]

POLLY: [*To* PHILIP.] Take me away quickly, or I shall never enjoy uphol-
stery again. [*To* RUTH.] Please change your mind, dear, and come
with us for the night.

RUTH: No. I will see you in the morning.

WINTHROP: We leave by the early stage.

RUTH: [*Looking at him quickly.*] You too?

WINTHROP: Yes, I have decided so.

RUTH: I will be there in good time, trust me. [*She kisses* POLLY *and*
PHILIP.] Good-bye, till morning. [*Gives her hand to* WINTHROP.]
Good-bye.

[PHILIP *ignores* GHENT *pointedly in the leave-takings.* POLLY *bids him
farewell with corresponding cordiality.*]

POLLY: Good-bye, Mr. Ghent. [*As they descend the cañon path, she is heard
chatting enthusiastically.*] O Phil, you ought to have seen the inside
of that delightful little house! [*Her voice is heard for some time, indis-
tinctly.* RUTH, *at the top of the path, waves to them as they descend.*]

GHENT: [*Looks long at her, with deep gratitude.*] God bless you! [*She sits
down on the rocks of the cabin terrace. He walks up and down in anxious thought. Once or twice he makes as if to speak. At length he stops before her.*] You must go in and lie down. You are worn out.

RUTH: [*Rousing herself.*] No, there is something I must tell you first.

GHENT: [*Points at the rug.*] It's about this—work you have been doing?

RUTH: [*Slightly startled.*] *You* know of that?

GHENT: Your brother told me. I should have found it out to-morrow anyhow. [*Pause.*] Have you wanted money?

RUTH: Yes.

GHENT: I thought I—I thought you had enough. I have often begged you
to take more.

RUTH: I haven't spent what you gave me. It is in there. [*She points toward
the house.*]

GHENT: [*Astonished.*] You haven't spent—any of it?

RUTH: A little. Nothing for myself.

GHENT: But there has been no need to save, not after the first month or
two. You surely knew that!

RUTH: Yes, I knew it. It was not economy.

GHENT: [*Slowly.*] You haven't been willing to take money from me?

RUTH: No. I know it was small of me, but I couldn't help it. I have paid
for everything.—I have kept account of it—O, to the last dreadful
penny! These clothes are the ones I wore from my brother's house
that night. This shelter—you know I helped to raise that with my
own hands. And—and some things I paid for secretly, from the little

hoard I brought away with me. You were careless; you did not notice.

GHENT: [*Sits down, dizzy from the shock of her words.*] I must try to grasp this! [*There is a silence, during which he sits perfectly motionless. At last he turns to her.*] Why—why did you stand up so plucky, so splendid, just now? Put a good face on everything about our life? Call me by my first name and all that—before your own people?

RUTH: We are man and wife. Beside that, my own people are as strangers.

GHENT: [*Eagerly.*] You say that? You can still say that?

RUTH: [*Looks up, startled.*] Can't you? [*She awaits his answer tensely.*]

GHENT: [*Desperately.*] O, I don't know. I can't say or think anything, after what you have just told me!

RUTH: [*Wails.*] You can't say it! And it isn't true! It is. we who are strangers.—Worse, a thousand times worse!

GHENT: [*Rises and stands over her.*] Don't let us dash ourselves to hell in one crazy minute! [*He pauses and hesitates. When he speaks again it is with wistful tenderness.*] Ruth, do you remember our journey here? [*She lifts her head, looking at him with white, thirsty face.*] I thought—it seemed to me you had—begun to care for me.

RUTH: That night, when we rode away from the justice's office at San Jacinto, and the sky began to brighten over the desert—the ice that had gathered here—[*she touches her heart*]—began to melt in spite of me. And when the next night and the next day passed, and the next, and still you spared me and treated me with beautiful rough chivalry, I said to myself, "He has heard my prayer to him. He knows what a girl's heart is." As you rode before me down the arroyos, and up over the mesas, through the dazzling sunlight and the majestic silence, it seemed as if you were leading me out of a world of little codes and customs into a great new world.—So it was for those first days.—And then—and then I woke, and saw you standing in my tent-door in the starlight! I knew before you spoke that we were lost. You hadn't had the strength to save us!

GHENT: [*Huskily.*] Surely it hasn't all been—hateful to you? There have been times, since that.—The afternoon we climbed up here. The day we made the table; the day we planted the vines.

RUTH: [*In a half whisper.*] Yes!—Beautiful days! [*She puts her hands suddenly before her face and sobs.*] O, it was not my fault! I have struggled against it. You don't know how I have struggled!

GHENT: Against what? Struggled against what?

RUTH: Against the hateful image you had raised up beside your own image.

GHENT: What do you mean?

RUTH: I mean that sometimes—often—when you stand there before my eyes, you fade away, and in your place I see—the Other One!

GHENT: Speak plainly, for God's sake! I don't understand this talk.

RUTH: [*Looking steadfastly, as at an invisible shape, speaks in a horrified whisper.*] There he stands behind you now!—The human beast, that goes to its horrible pleasure as not even a wild animal will go—*in pack, in pack!* [GHENT, *stung beyond endurance, rises and paces up and down.* RUTH *continues in a broken tone, spent by the violence of her own words.*] I have tried—O, you don't know how I have tried to save myself from these thoughts.—While we were poor and struggling I thought I could do it.—Then—[*she points toward the cañon*]—then that hole down there began belching its stream of gold. You began to load me with gifts—to force easy ways upon me—

GHENT: Well, what else did I care to make money for?

[RUTH *does not answer for a moment, then speaks slowly, taking the words with loathing upon her tongue.*]

RUTH: Every time you give me anything, or talk about the mine and what it is going to do, there rings in my ears that dreadful sneer: "A dirt-eating Mojave would pay more than that for his squaw!" [*She rises, lifting her arms.*] I held myself so dear! And you bought me for a handful of gold, like a woman of the street! You drove me before you like an animal from the market! [GHENT *has seated himself again, elbows on knees and face in his hands.* RUTH *takes slowly from her bosom the nugget chain and holds it crumpled up in her palm. Her tone is quiet, almost matter-of-fact.*] I have got back the chain again.

GHENT: [*Looks up.*] Chain?—What chain?

RUTH: [*In the same tone, as she holds it up, letting it unwind.*] The one you bought me with.

GHENT: [*Dumfounded.*] Where the devil—? Has that fellow been around here?

RUTH: It would have had no meaning for me except from his hand.

GHENT: So that's what you've been doing with this rug-weaving and basket-making tomfoolery? [RUTH *does not answer, but continues looking at the chain, running it through her fingers and weighing it in her hand.*] How long has this been going on?

RUTH: How long?—How long can one live without breathing? Two minutes? A few lifetimes? How long!

GHENT: It was about a month after we came here that you began to potter with this work.

RUTH: [*Draws her hand about her neck as if loosening something there; convulsively.*] Since then this has been round my neck, around my limbs, a chain of eating fire. Link by link I have unwound it. You will never know what it has cost me, but I have paid it all. Take it and let me go free. [*She tries to force it upon him, with wailing entreaty.*] Take it, take it, I beseech you!

GHENT: [*Holding himself under stern control.*] You are killing yourself. You mustn't go on this way. Go and rest. We will talk of this to-morrow.

RUTH: Rest! To-morrow! O, how little you have understood of all I have said! I know it is only a symbol—a make-believe. I know I am childish to ask it. Still, take it and tell me I am free.

[GHENT *takes the chain reluctantly, stands for a moment looking at it, then speaks with iron firmness.*]

GHENT: As you say, your price has risen. This is not enough. [*He throws the chain about her neck and draws her to him by it.*] You are mine, mine, do you hear? Now and forever! [*He starts toward the house. She holds out her hand blindly to detain him.*]

RUTH: [*In a stifled voice.*] Wait! There is—something else. [*He returns to her, anxiously, and stands waiting. She goes on, touching the chain.*] It isn't only for my sake I ask you to take this off me, nor only for your sake. There is—another life—to think of.

GHENT: [*Leaning to look into her averted face.*] Ruth!—Is it true?—Thank God!

RUTH: Now will you take this off me?

GHENT: [*Starts to do so, then draws back.*] No. Now less than ever. For now, more than ever, you are mine.

RUTH: But—*how* yours? O, remember, have pity! *How* yours?

[PHILIP *appears at the head of the cañon path. Hearing their voices, he waits, half-concealed.*]

GHENT: No matter how! Bought if you like, but mine! Mine by blind chance and the hell in a man's veins, if you like! Mine by almighty Nature whether you like it or not!

RUTH: Nature! Almighty Nature! [*She takes the chain slowly from her neck.*] Not yours! By everything my people have held sacred! [*She drops the chain.*] Not yours! Not yours! [*She turns slowly.* PHILIP *has come forward, and supports her as she sinks half fainting upon his neck.*]

PHILIP: [*To* GHENT.] I came back to get my sister for the night.—I don't know by what ugly spell you have held her, but I know, from her own lips, that it is broken. [*To* RUTH.] Come! I have horses below.

GHENT: No!

PHILIP: [*Measuring him.*] Yes. [*Pause.*]

GHENT: Let her say!

RUTH: [*Looks long at* GHENT, *then at the house and surroundings. At last she turns to her brother.*] Take me—with you. Take me—home!

[PHILIP, *supporting her, leads her down the cañon path.* GHENT *stands gazing after them as they disappear below the rim. He picks up the chain and goes back, looking down after the descending figures. The sunset light has faded, and darkness has begun to settle over the mountain world.*

ACT III

Sitting-room of MRS. JORDAN'*s house at Milford Corners, Massachusetts. An old-fashioned New England interior, faded but showing signs of former distinction. The walls are hung with family portraits, several in clerical attire of the eighteenth century, one in the uniform of the Revolutionary War. Doors open right and left. At the back is a fireplace, flanked by windows, the curtains of which are drawn. On the left is a small table, with a lamp, books, and magazines; on the right, near the fireplace, a sewing-table, with lamp and sewing-basket. A bookcase and a writing-desk occupy opposite corners of the room, forward.*

WINTHROP *and* PHILIP *stand near the desk, chatting.* POLLY *is reading a newspaper at the table, left.* RUTH *sits before the grate, sewing; her face is turned away toward the fire.*

PHILIP: [*Offers* WINTHROP *his cigar-case.*] Have another cigar.

WINTHROP: Well, as a celebration. [*Takes one and lights it.*]

PHILIP: Rather small business for the Jordan family, to be celebrating a bare escape from the poor-house.

WINTHROP: Where did you scare up the benevolent uncle? I never heard of him before.

PHILIP: Nor I, scarcely. He's always lived abroad.

[WINTHROP, *strolling about, peeps over* POLLY'*s shoulder.*]

WINTHROP: [*To* PHILIP, *with a scandalized gesture.*] Stock reports!

PHILIP: Her latest craze.

WINTHROP: Last week it was Japanese Samurai.

POLLY: [*Crushingly.*] And next week it will be—Smart Alecks.

[*The door on the left opens, and* MRS. JORDAN *enters, with* DR. NEWBURY. *During the preceding conversation* RUTH *has sat sewing, paying no heed to the chatter.* MRS. JORDAN *and the* DOCTOR *look at her as they come in, but she does not look up.*]

MRS. JORDAN: Sit down, Doctor, at least for a moment.

DR. NEWBURY: [*Seats himself,* MRS. JORDAN *near him.*] I can never resist such an invitation, in this house.

MRS. JORDAN: Dear Doctor, you've been a wonderful friend to me and mine all these years, since poor Josiah was taken.

DR. NEWBURY: But just when you needed help most—

MRS. JORDAN: I know how gladly you would have offered it, if you could.

DR. NEWBURY: Your brother-in-law in England was able to redeem the property?

MRS. JORDAN: [*Hastily.*] Yes, yes.—But what we are to do for the future, with my little capital gone—[*She speaks lower.*] O, that dreadful West! If my children had only stayed where they were born and bred. [*She glances at* RUTH, *who has let her sewing fall in her lap and sits staring into the fire.*]

DR. NEWBURY: [*Sotto voce.*] Poor child!

[POLLY *looks up from the newspaper excitedly, holding her finger at a place on the sheet.*]

POLLY: I say, Phil! Win! Look here.

[PHILIP *and* WINTHROP, *who have been chatting and smoking apart, come to the table.*]

PHILIP: What is it now?

POLLY: [*Tapping on the paper.*] Something about your Arizona scheme.

PHILIP: [*Bending over her, reads:*] Allegheny pig-iron, 93¾, National Brick—

POLLY: [*Pointing.*] No, there!

PHILIP: Arizona Cactus Fibre, 84. [*He picks up the paper, astounded.*] Cactus Fibre listed! Selling at 84! [*He tosses the paper to* WINTHROP.] This is the last straw!

MRS. JORDAN: [*Who has been listening anxiously.*] What does it mean, Phil?

PHILIP: Only that the people who bought our plant and patents for a song, have made a fortune out of them.

[RUTH *has resumed her needlework.* WINTHROP *offers her the paper, with his finger at the line. She takes it, looks at it vaguely, and lays it on the table.*]

POLLY: [*Leaning across.*] Doesn't that interest you?

RUTH: [*Tonelessly.*] O, yes. [*She rises, lays her work aside, and goes toward the door, left.*]

DR. NEWBURY: [*As she passes him.*] Won't you bid me good-night, my child?

RUTH: [*Giving him her hand.*] Good-night, Doctor.

DR. NEWBURY: [*Shaking his finger.*] Remember, no more moping! And from to-morrow, outdoors with you.

[RUTH *looks at him vacantly, attempting to smile. She moves toward the door, which* WINTHROP *opens for her.*]

WINTHROP: [*Holding out his hand.*] You must bid me good-night, too, and good-bye.

RUTH: [*With a faint kindling of interest.*] Are you going away?

WINTHROP: Only back to Boston. Some time, when you are stronger, you will come down and see our new sailors' hospital.

RUTH: Yes.—Good-bye. [*She goes out,* WINTHROP *closing the door.*]

WINTHROP: [*To* DR. NEWBURY.] I must be going along, father. Good-night, everybody! [*Patting* PHILIP*'s shoulder.*] Hard luck, old man! [*He goes out by the hall door on the right,* PHILIP *accompanying him.*]

DR. NEWBURY: [*Looking after his son.*] Brave boy! Brave boy! He keeps up a good show.

MRS. JORDAN: You think he still grieves over her?

DR. NEWBURY: Ah, poor chap! He's made of the right stuff, if he is mine.

MRS. JORDAN: Let us not talk of it, It is too sad, too dreadful.
[PHILIP *reënters.*]

DR. NEWBURY: About part of it we must talk. [*He speaks so as to include* PHILIP *and* POLLY *in the conversation.*] Mrs. Jordan, I don't want to alarm you, but your daughter—I may as well put it bluntly—is in a dangerous state.

MRS. JORDAN: [*Frightened.*] Doctor! I thought she seemed so much stronger.

DR. NEWBURY: She is, so far as her body is concerned.
[MRS. JORDAN *sits in an attitude of nervous attention, gazing at the doctor as if trying to formulate one of many questions pressing upon her.* PHILIP *comes forward and sits by the table, near them.*]

PHILIP: Don't you think that the routine of life which she has taken up will soon restore her to a normal state of mind?

DR. NEWBURY: Perhaps.—I hope so.—I would have good hope of it, if it were not for her attitude toward her child.

MRS. JORDAN: [*Overwhelmed.*] You have noticed that, too! I haven't spoken to you of it, because—I haven't been willing to see it myself.

PHILIP: I can't see that there is anything particularly strange in her attitude. She takes care of the brat scrupulously enough.

POLLY: Brat!

MRS. JORDAN: Brat! [*To* DR. NEWBURY, *after a reproachful gaze at* PHILIP.] With the most watchful, the minutest care, but—[*she speaks in a constrained voice, with a nervous glance at the door*]—exactly as if it were a piece of machinery!—Phil, do please lay down that paper-knife before you break it! Your father brought that to me from India. [*He obeys, but picks it up again absent-mindedly, after a few seconds.*] Pardon me, Doctor. She goes about her daily business, and answers when she is spoken to, but as for her really being here—[*She breaks out.*] Doctor, what *shall* we do?

DR. NEWBURY: She must be roused from this state, but how to do it, I don't know.

POLLY: [*Rising, with heightened color and nervous emphasis.*] Well, I do!

MRS. JORDAN: [*Looking at her with frightened interrogation.*] Polly—?

POLLY: What she needs is her husband, and I have sent for him!

PHILIP: [*Inarticulate with surprise and anger.*] You—!

POLLY: Yes. He's been here a week. And he's an angel, isn't he, mother? [PHILIP *snaps the paper-knife in two, flings the pieces to the floor, and rises, pale with rage.*]

MRS. JORDAN: [*Gathering up the pieces with a wail.*] O, Phil! How could you! One of my most precious relics!

PHILIP: [*To* MRS. JORDAN.] Is this true, or is it another of her tedious jokes?

POLLY: [*Protesting.*] O, my dear, tedious!

MRS. JORDAN: [*Wipes her eyes, after ruefully fitting the broken pieces of the knife together and laying them tenderly on the table.*] You don't deserve to have me answer you, but it is true.

PHILIP: Was this action taken with your knowledge?

MRS. JORDAN: I do not expect to be spoken to in that tone. Polly telegraphed merely the facts. He came at his own instance.

PHILIP: But you have consented to enter into relations with him?

MRS. JORDAN: I have seen him several times.

POLLY: [*Triumphantly.*] And yesterday we showed him the baby! Such fun, wasn't it, mother?

MRS. JORDAN: [*Wiping her eyes, sheepishly.*] Yes, it was rather—enjoyable.

PHILIP: He can't be in this town. I should have heard of it.

POLLY: We've hid him safe.

PHILIP: Where?

POLLY: Never mind. He's on tap, and the sooner we turn on the spigot, the better, is what I think. Doctor, what do you think?

DR. NEWBURY: Let me ask you again to state your view of Ruth's case. I don't think I quite grasp your view.

POLLY: [*Pluming herself, doctrinaire.*] Well! Here on the one hand is the primitive, the barbaric woman, falling in love with a romantic stranger, who, like some old Viking on a harry, cuts her with his two-handed sword from the circle of her kinsmen, and bears her away on his dragon ship toward the midnight sun. Here on the other hand is the derived, the civilized woman, with a civilized nervous system, observing that the creature eats bacon with his bowie knife, knows not the manicure, has the conversation of a preoccupied walrus, the instincts of a jealous caribou, and the endearments of a dancing crab in the mating season.

MRS. JORDAN: Polly! What ideas! What language!

DR. NEWBURY: Don't be alarmed, Mrs. Jordan. The vocabulary has changed since our day, and—the point of view has shifted a little. [*To* POLLY.] Well?

POLLY: Well, Ruth is one of those people who can't live in a state of divided feeling. She sits staring at this cleavage in her life, like—like that man in Dante, don't you know, who is pierced by the serpent, and who stands there in hell staring at his wound, yawning like a sleepy man.

MRS. JORDAN: O, Polly, do please try not to get our heads muddled up with literature!

POLLY: All I mean is that when she married her man she married him for keeps. And he did the same by her.

[PHILIP *rises, with uncontrollable impatience, and goes back to the mantelpiece, against which he leans, nervously tearing a bit of paper to pieces.*]

DR. NEWBURY: Don't you think that a mere difference of cultivation, polish—or—or something of that sort—is rather small to have led to a rupture, and so painful a one too?

POLLY: [*A little nonplussed.*] Well, yes, perhaps it does *look* small. But we don't know the particulars; and men *are* such *colossal* brutes, you know, dear Doctor!

DR. NEWBURY: [*Judicially.*] Yes, so they are, so they are!

POLLY: And then her pride! You know when it comes to pride, Ruth would make Lucifer look like a charity-boy asking for more soup.

DR. NEWBURY: I think perhaps the plan should be tried. [*After a pause.*] Yes, I think so decidedly.

PHILIP: I call this a plot against her dignity and peace of mind!

DR. NEWBURY: [*Rising.*] Well, this conspirator must be going. [*He shakes hands with* POLLY *and* MRS. JORDAN, *takes his hat and stick.* PHILIP *remains plunged in angry reflection.* DR. NEWBURY *taps* PHILIP *jestingly on the shoulder with the tip of his cane.*] When you have lived as long as I have, my boy, you'll—you'll be just as old as I am!

[*He goes out,* POLLY *accompanying him to the door.* PHILIP, *disregarding his mother's conciliatory look and gesture as he passes her, goes out left.* POLLY *stretches her arms and draws a deep breath as the door closes after him.*]

MRS. JORDAN: [*Looking at her severely.*] Pray what does that mean?

POLLY: O, Phil is such a walking thunder-cloud, these days. It's a relief to get rid of him.

MRS. JORDAN: Have you done what you could to make his life brighter?

POLLY: I never had a chance. He has always been too much wrapped up in Ruth to think of me.

MRS. JORDAN: How can you say such a thing? What do you suppose he married you for?

POLLY: Heaven knows! What do they ever do it for? It is a most curious and savage propensity. But immensely interesting to watch.

MRS. JORDAN: [*With a despairing gesture.*] If you hold such heathenish views, why are you so bent on bringing those two together?

POLLY: [*Soberly.*] Because they represent—what Philip and I have missed.

MRS. JORDAN: And pray what have "Philip and I" missed?

POLLY: O, we're all right. But we're not like those two.

MRS. JORDAN: I should hope not!

POLLY: Even I believe that now and then a marriage is made in Heaven. This one was. They are predestined lovers!

MRS. JORDAN: [*Mournfully, hypnotized by the evangelical note.*] I pray it may be so. [*She looks suspiciously at* POLLY.] You wretched girl! Predestined lovers and marriage made in Heaven, after all you've just been saying about how impossible he is.

POLLY: He is quite impossible, but he's the kind we can't resist, any of us. He'd only have to crook his little finger at me.

MRS. JORDAN: [*Lifting her hands in despair.*] What are you young women coming to! [*Pause.*] He seems to me a good man.

POLLY: [*Delighted.*] O, he's *good!* So is a volcano between eruptions. And commonplace, too, until you happen to get a glimpse down one of the old volcanic rifts in his surface, and see far below—underneath the cold lava-beds—fire, fire, the molten heart of a continent!

MRS. JORDAN: I only hope you have some vague general notion of what you are talking about.

POLLY: Amen.—And now let's consider when, where, and how we are to hale this dubious pair together.

MRS. JORDAN: One thing is sure, it mustn't be here.

POLLY: Why not?

MRS. JORDAN: On Philip's account.

POLLY: O, bother Philip!—Wasn't that the doorbell?

MRS. JORDAN: Yes. You had better go.

[POLLY *goes out. After a moment she reënters, excitedly.*]

POLLY: It's Mr. Ghent!

MRS. JORDAN: [*Amazed.*] Mr. Ghent? [POLLY *nods enthusiastically.* GHENT *enters. He is conventionally dressed, a black string tie and the broad-brimmed hat which he carries being the only suggestions of Western cos-*

tume remaining. MRS. JORDAN *receives him in a flutter of excitement and alarm.*] Mr. Ghent—! Surely at this hour—!

GHENT: I beg your pardon. There was no other way. I am going West to-night.—Can I see you alone?

MRS. JORDAN: [*Looks at* POLLY, *who goes out, pouting.*] Going West to-night?

GHENT: Yes. Trouble at the mine.

MRS. JORDAN: Isn't your business partner competent to attend to it?

GHENT: He's competent to steal the whole outfit. In fact, is doing it, or has done it already.

MRS. JORDAN: [*Vaguely alarmed.*] And—my property here? Is that involved in the danger?

GHENT: Certainly not.

MRS. JORDAN: [*Relieved.*] I have gone through such months of misery at the thought of losing the dear old place!—If Ruth only knew that we owe the very roof over our heads to you—

GHENT: Well, she isn't to know, that's understood, isn't it? Besides, it's nothing to speak of. Glad if you think it a service. She wouldn't.

MRS. JORDAN: You mean—?

GHENT: I mean that if she knew about it, she wouldn't stay here overnight.

MRS. JORDAN: Sit down. [*She motions him to a seat at the table; she sits near him, speaking with nervous impulsiveness.*] Tell me what is the trouble between you! It has all been a dreadful mystery from the beginning!

GHENT: Is it a mystery that a woman like your daughter—? [*He stops and sinks into gloomy thought.*]

MRS. JORDAN: Should have chosen you?—Pardon me, I don't mean anything unkind—[*He makes a gesture of brusque exoneration.*] But having chosen—and broken faith with her brother to do it—

GHENT: [*Nervously.*] Let's drop that! [*Pause.*] Mrs. Jordan, you come of the old stock. Do you believe in the devil?

MRS. JORDAN: Perhaps not in the sense you mean.

GHENT: [*Tapping his breast.*] I mean the devil inside of a man—the devil in the heart!

MRS. JORDAN: O, yes. We are all forced by our lives to believe in that.

GHENT: Our lives! [*He looks slowly round the room.*] How long have you lived here?

MRS. JORDAN: For thirty years, in this house. Before I was married, I lived in the old house down the road yonder, opposite the church.

GHENT: [*To himself.*] Think of it!

MRS. JORDAN: What did you say?

GHENT: [*Gathers himself together.*] Mrs. Jordan, I want you to promise

that what I put in your hands from time to time comes to your
daughter as if from another source.

MRS. JORDAN: You are going away for good?

GHENT: Yes.

MRS. JORDAN: You give her up?

GHENT: A man can't give up what isn't his.

MRS. JORDAN: What isn't his? She is your wife.

GHENT: No. Never has been.

MRS. JORDAN: [*Terrified.*] O, pitiful heavens!

GHENT: I beg your pardon.—I was only trying to say—I used to think
that when a couple was married, there they were, man and wife, and
that was the end of it. I used to think that when they had a child,
well, sure enough it was their child, and all said.—And there's something in that, too. [*He stares before him, smiting the table and speaking with low intensity.*] Damn me if there ain't something eternal in
it! [*He sits for a moment more in gloomy thought.*] Do you think she'll
make up to the young one, after a bit?

MRS. JORDAN: O, surely! To think otherwise would be too dreadful!

GHENT: I'd give a good deal to know.—It's kind of lonesome for the little
rooster, sitting out there all by himself on the world's doorstep!—I
must see her for a minute before I go.—Do your best for me.

MRS. JORDAN: I will do what I can.

GHENT: You can put it as a matter of business. There is a matter of business I want to talk over with her, if I can get up the gumption.

MRS. JORDAN: Hadn't you better tell me what it is?

GHENT: Well, it's about your son Philip. That little scheme he started out
in my country—the Cactus Fibre industry.

MRS. JORDAN: Yes?

GHENT: I believe he thinks his sister's going away when she did queered
his game.

MRS. JORDAN: It was a severe blow to him in every way. She was the life
and soul of his enterprise.

GHENT: I want her to give him back the Cactus Fibre outfit, worth something more than when he dropped it.

MRS. JORDAN: Give it back to him? She?

GHENT: [*Takes papers from his pocket.*] Yes. I happened to hear it was
knocking around for nothing in the market, and I bought it—for the
house, really. Hated to see that go to the dogs. Then I looked over
the plant, and got a hustler to boom it. I thought as a matter of
transfer, to cancel her debt, or what she thinks her debt—[*Pause.*]

MRS. JORDAN: [*Fingering the paper with hesitation.*] Mr. Ghent, we really
can't accept such a thing. Your offer is quixotic.

GHENT: Quix—what?

MRS. JORDAN: Quixotic, it really is.

GHENT: [*Doubtfully.*] I guess you're right. It depends on the way you look at it. One way it looks like a pure business proposition—so much lost, so much made good. The other way it looks, as you say, quix— um—. Anyway, there are the papers! Do what you think best with them. [*He lays the papers on the table, and picks up his hat.*]

MRS. JORDAN: Wait in the parlor. [*He opens the hall door.*] The second door on the left.

[*With an awkward bow to* MRS. JORDAN, *he partly closes the door after him, when the inner door opens and* RUTH *appears. She goes to the sewing-table and picks up her sewing. Her mother, with a frightened glance at the half-open hall door, draws her back and kisses her.* GHENT, *unseen by* RUTH, *remains standing, with his hand on the door-knob.*]

MRS. JORDAN: Ruth, you are a brave girl, and I will treat you like one.— Your husband is here.

RUTH: Here?—Where?

[GHENT *pushes the door open, and closes it behind him.* RUTH, *sinking back against the opposite wall, stares at him blankly.*]

MRS. JORDAN: He is leaving for the West again to-night. He has asked to see you before he goes. [RUTH *covers her face with her hands, then fumbles blindly for the latch of the door. Her mother restrains her.*] It is your duty to hear what he has to say. You owe that to the love you once bore him.

RUTH: He killed my love before it was born!

MRS. JORDAN: It is your duty to hear him, and part with him in a Christian spirit, for our sakes, if not for your own.

RUTH: For whose sake?

MRS. JORDAN: For mine, and your brother's.—We owe it to him, as a family.

GHENT: [*Raises his hand restrainingly.*] Mrs. Jordan—!

RUTH: Owe?

MRS. JORDAN: We owe it to him, for what he has done and wishes to do.

RUTH: What he has done?—Wishes to do?

MRS. JORDAN: Yes, don't echo me like a parrot! He has done a great deal for us, and is anxious to do more, if you will only let him.

RUTH: What is this? Explain it to me quickly.

MRS. JORDAN: [*With growing impatience.*] Don't think to judge your mother!

RUTH: I demand to hear what all this is! Tell me.

MRS. JORDAN: [*Losing control of herself.*] He has kept us from being turned into the street! [GHENT, *who has tried dumbly to restrain her, turns away in stoic resignation to his fate.*] He has given us the very roof over our heads!

RUTH: You said that uncle—

MRS. JORDAN: Well, it was not your uncle! I said so to shield you in your stubborn and cold-hearted pride.

RUTH: Is there more of this?

MRS. JORDAN: Yes, there *is* more. You wronged your brother to follow your own path of willful love, and now you wrong him again by following your own path of willful aversion. Here comes your husband, offering to make restitution—

RUTH: What restitution?

MRS. JORDAN: He has bought Philip's property out there, and wants you to give it back to him.

[RUTH *stands motionless for a moment, then looks vacantly about, speaking in a dull voice, as at first.*]

RUTH: I must go away from this house.

MRS. JORDAN: You don't understand. He claims nothing. He is going away himself immediately. Whatever this dreadful trouble is between you, you are his wife, and he has a right to help you and yours.

RUTH: I am not his wife.

MRS. JORDAN: Ruth, don't frighten me. He said those same words—

RUTH: He said—what?

MRS. JORDAN: That you were not his wife.

RUTH: He said—that?

MRS. JORDAN: Yes, but afterward he explained—

RUTH: [*Flaming into white wrath.*] Explained! Did he explain that when I was left alone that night at the ranch he came—with two others— and when gun and knife had failed me, and nothing stood between me and their drunken fury, I sold myself to the strongest of them, hiding my head behind the name of marriage? Did he explain that between him and the others money clinked—[*she raps on the table*]— my price in hard money on the table? And now that I have run away to the only refuge I have on earth, he comes to buy the very house where I have hidden, and every miserable being within it! [*Long pause. She looks about blankly and sinks down by the table.*]

MRS. JORDAN: [*Cold and rigid.*] And you—married him—after that? [*She turns away in horror-stricken judgment.*] You ought to have—died— first! [PHILIP *opens the door and enters, staring at* GHENT *with dislike and menace.*] O, Philip, she has told me!—You can't imagine what horrors! [RUTH *rises, with fright in her face, and approaches her brother to restrain him.*]

PHILIP: Horrors? What horrors?

MRS. JORDAN: It was your fault! You ought never to have left her alone in that dreadful place! She—she married him—to save herself—from—O horrible!

[PHILIP *waits an instant, the truth penetrating his mind slowly. Then, with mortal rage in his face, he starts toward* GHENT.]

PHILIP: You—dog! [RUTH *throws herself in* PHILIP'S *path.*]

RUTH: No, no, no!

PHILIP: Get out of my way. This is my business now.

RUTH: No, it is mine. I tell you it is mine.

PHILIP: We'll see whose it is. I said that if the truth ever came out, this man should answer to me, and now, by God, he shall answer! [*With another access of rage he tries to thrust* RUTH *from his path.* MRS. JORDAN, *terrified at the storm she has raised, clings desperately to her son's arm.*]

RUTH: I told him long ago it should be between us. Now it shall be between us.

MRS. JORDAN: Philip! For my sake, for your father's sake! Don't, don't! You will only make it worse. In pity's name, leave them alone together. Leave them alone—together!

[*They force* PHILIP *back to the door, where he stands glaring at* GHENT.]

PHILIP: [*To* GHENT.] My time will come. Meanwhile, hide behind the skirts of the woman whose life you have ruined and whose heart you have broken. Hide behind her. It is the coward's privilege. Take it.

[PHILIP, *with* MRS. JORDAN *still clinging to his arm, goes out,* RUTH *closing the door after them. She and* GHENT *confront each other in silence for a moment, across the width of the room.*]

RUTH: God forgive me! You never can.

GHENT: It was a pity—but—you were in a corner. I drove you to it, by coming here.

RUTH: It was base of me—base!

GHENT: The way your mother took it showed me one thing.—I've never understood you, because I don't understand your people.

RUTH: You mean—her saying I ought to have died rather than accept life as I did?

GHENT: Yes.

RUTH: She spoke the truth. I have always seen it.

GHENT: Ruth, it's a queer thing for me to be saying, but—it seems to me, you've never seen the truth between us.

RUTH: What is the truth—between us?

GHENT: The truth is—[*He pauses, then continues with a disconsolate gesture.*] Well, there's no use going into that. [*He fumbles in his pocket, and takes from it the nugget chain, which he looks at in silence for a time, then speaks in quiet resignation.*] I've got here the chain, that's

another, to have a meaning for us. For you it's a
, all the same, I want you to keep it. Show it some
l tell him—about me. [*He lays it on the desk and
r.*]

h—between us?

only of myself I was thinking.

ut yourself?

se.*] I drifted into one of your meeting-houses last
wing where else to go, and I heard a young fellow
t what he called "The Second Birth." A year and a
ld have thought it was all hocus-pocus, but you can
not, the way he went on he might have been behind
night in that little justice den at San Jacinto, saying to
Angel: "Do you see that rascal? Take notice! There
e of bone or a drop of blood in him but what's new

it has been all my fault—the failure we've made of our

n no failure. However it is, it's been our life, and in my
k it's been—all—right!

! O, how can you say that? [*She repeats the words with a
we and wonder.*] All right!

of it has been wrong, but as a whole it has been right—
now that doesn't happen often, but it has happened to us,
—[*he stops, unable to find words for his idea*]—because—be-
e first time our eyes met, they burned away all that was bad
neeting, and left only the fact that we *had* met—pure good—
y—a fortune of it—for both of us. Yes, for both of us! You'll
ourself some day.

ou had only heard my cry to you, to wait, to cleanse yourself
ne—by suffering and sacrifice—before we dared begin to live!
ou wouldn't see the need!—O, if you could have felt for your-
what I felt for you! If you could have said, "The wages of sin is
h!" and suffered the anguish of death, and risen again purified!
instead of that, what you had done fell off from you like any
ly trifle.

GH   eps impulsively nearer her, sweeping his hand to indicate the por-
tr atts on the walls.*] Ruth, it's these fellows are fooling you! It's they
who keep your head set on the wages of sin, and all that rubbish.
What have we got to do with suffering and sacrifice? That may be the
law for some, and I've tried hard to see it as our law, and thought I
had succeeded. But I haven't! Our law is joy, and selfishness; the
curve of your shoulder and the light on your hair as you sit there says

that as plain as preaching.—Does it gall you the way we came together? You asked me that night what brought me, and I told you
whiskey, and sun, and the devil. Well, I tell you now I'm thankful on
my knees for all three! Does it rankle in your mind that I took you
when I could get you, by main strength and fraud? I guess most
good women are taken that way, if they only knew it. Don't you
want to be paid for? I guess every wife is paid for in some good coin
or other. And as for you, I've paid for you not only with a trumpery
chain, but with the heart in my breast, do you hear? That's one thing
you can't throw back at me—the man you've made of me, the life
and the meaning of life you've showed me the way to! [RUTH's face is
hidden in her hands, her elbows on the table. He stands over her, flushed
and waiting. Gradually the light fades from his face. When he speaks
again, the ring of exultation which has been in his voice is replaced by a
sober intensity.] If you can't see it my way, give me another chance to
live it out in yours. [He waits, but she does not speak or look up. He
takes a package of letters and papers from his pocket, and runs them
over, in deep reflection.] During the six months I've been East—

RUTH: [Looking up.] Six months? Mother said a week!

GHENT: Your sister-in-law's telegram was forwarded to me here. I let her
think it brought me, but as a matter of fact, I came East in the next
train after yours. It was rather a low-lived thing to do, I suppose,
hanging about and bribing your servant for news—[RUTH lets her
head sink in her hands. He pauses and continues ruefully.] I might
have known how that would strike you! Well, it would have come
out sooner or later.—That's not what I started to talk about.—You
ask me to suffer for my wrong. Since you left me I have suffered—
God knows! You ask me to make some sacrifice. Well—how would
the mine do? Since I've been away they've as good as stolen it from
me. I could get it back easy enough by fighting; but supposing I
don't fight. Then we'll start all over again, just as we stand in our
shoes, and make another fortune—for our boy. [RUTH utters a faint
moan as her head sinks in her arms on the table. With trembling hands,
GHENT caresses her hair lightly, and speaks between a laugh and a sob.]
Little mother! Little mother! What does the past matter, when we've
got the future—and him? [RUTH does not move. He remains bending
over her for some moments, then straightens up, with a gesture of stoic
despair.] I know what you're saying there to yourself, and I guess
you're right. Wrong is wrong, from the moment it happens till the
crack of doom, and all the angels in Heaven, working overtime, can't
make it less or different by a hair. That seems to be the law. I've
learned it hard, but I guess I've learned it. I've seen it written in

mountain letters across the continent of this life.—Done is done, and lost is lost, and smashed to hell is smashed to hell. We fuss and potter and patch up. You might as well try to batter down the Rocky Mountains with a rabbit's heart-beat! [*He goes to the door, where he turns.*] You've fought hard for me, God bless you for it.—But it's been a losing game with you from the first!—You belong here, and I belong out yonder—beyond the Rockies, beyond—the Great Divide! [*He opens the door and is about to pass out.* RUTH *looks up with streaming eyes.*]

RUTH: Wait! [*He closes the door and stands waiting for her to speak.* RUTH *masters herself and goes on, her eyes shining, her face exalted.*] Tell me you know that if I could have followed you, and been your wife, without struggle and without bitterness, I would have done it.

GHENT: [*Solemnly.*] I believe you would.

RUTH: Tell me you know that when I tore down with bleeding fingers the life you were trying to build for us, I did it only—because—I loved you!

GHENT: [*Comes slowly to the table, looking at her with bewilderment.*] How was that?

RUTH: O, I don't wonder you ask! Another woman would have gone straight to her goal. You might have found such a one. But instead you found me, a woman in whose ears rang night and day the cry of an angry Heaven to us both—"Cleanse yourselves!" And I went about doing it in the only way I knew—[*she points at the portraits on the wall*]—the only way my fathers knew—by wretchedness, by self-torture, by trying blindly to pierce your careless heart with pain. And all the while you—O, as I lay there and listened to you, I realized it for the first time—you had risen, in one hour, to a wholly new existence, which flooded the present and the future with brightness, yes, and reached back into our past, and made of it—made of all of it—something to cherish! [*She takes the chain, and comes closer.*] You have taken the good of our life and grown strong. I have taken the evil and grown weak, weak unto death. Teach me to live as you do! [*She puts the chain about her neck.*]

GHENT: [*Puzzled, not yet realizing the full force of her words.*] Teach you—to live—as I do?

RUTH: And teach—*him!*

GHENT: [*Unable to realize his fortune.*] You'll let me help make a kind of a happy life for—the little rooster?

RUTH: [*Holds out her arms, her face flooded with happiness.*] And for us! For us!

A MAN'S WORLD

A Play in Four Acts

by

Rachel Crothers

First performed at the Shubert Theater, New York City, on February 8, 1910.

CHARACTERS

FRANK WARE
LIONE BRUNE
CLARA OAKES
KIDDIE
MALCOLM GASKELL
FRITZ BAHN
WELLS TREVOR
EMILE GRIMEAUX

ACT I

TIME: *The present—Eight o'clock a winter evening.*
SCENE: FRANK WARE's *living room in an old house in lower New York. There is a door at center back leading into hall. One at left leading into sleeping room. A wide window cuts off the upper right corner diagonally. Another window is down right. At left a large old-fashioned fire-place of white marble. Low open book shelves fill the wall spaces. In the upper corner left is a large round table on which are magazines, a lamp, a box of ciga-rettes and a bowl of red apples. At left center a very large upholstered daven-port facing the fire at a slanting angle. Below the fire a large arm-chair.*
    At back a baby grand piano stands right of the door center—the key-board facing the window—a single chair before it. Below piano a small

round table holding books and a work basket—a chair at left of this table. Well out from the window right is a large table desk with a chair on either side. The desk holds a student's lamp—magazines, newspapers, brass desk furnishings—and a great quantity of mss., letters, etc.

On the book shelves are vases, several busts in bronze and white—old bowls, a large Victory in white, and a great quantity of pictures on the walls—water colors, oils, sketches—all good.

The walls and ceilings are done in faded, old frescoes—and there is a center gas chandelier of an old-fashioned design. The furniture is all old, but solid and the general air is that of past elegance grown shabby and invaded by up-to-date comfort and cheerfulness.

AT CURTAIN: KIDDIE WARE, *a sturdy boy of seven, is lying full length on sofa looking into fire. After a slight pause he rises—punches pillow and sulkily crosses to piano. With one finger he plays "Can you come out to-night boys" three times, with one note always wrong. He then crosses to window and looks eagerly out into the street. There is a soft rap at the door center. Pause—and the rap is repeated.*

KIDDIE: [*Lifelessly.*] Come.
FRITZ: [*Opening the hall door.*] Wie gehts. Hello.
KIDDIE: [*Without turning.*] Hello!
    [FRITZ BAHN *is a young German. He is in evening clothes and carries a shabby top-coat, a cap and a violin case.*]
FRITZ: Where is de Frankie mutter?
KIDDIE: [*Still not turning.*] She hasn't come yet.
FRITZ: Ach! She is late. Don't you worry. She come soon. It is not eight o'clock all ready. [*Goes to child at window.*]
KIDDIE: I want Frankie.
FRITZ: Ach Gott, so do I—but we don't get everything we want.
KIDDIE: [*Still not turning from window.*] Why don't she come?
FRITZ: I tink she has had a very busy day with dot old publisher down town to-day. She will be so tired. Un? Yah, I tink it. Don't look all de time on de outside. She not come so. Look a liddle on de inside an she come. So.
KIDDIE: Light all the gas. She likes it.
FRITZ: [*Lighting the gas.*] So. Dere iss one—dere iss two—dere iss dree. So. Better? Un? Who lighted the first one for you all ready?
KIDDIE: Old Grumper, when she brought my supper. She was awful cross to-night.
FRITZ: No, iss dot so?
KIDDIE: Light the lamp.

FRITZ: [*Lighting student lamp on desk.*] Oh, yah. De light at de shrine. So. We are ready for her. Un? Wat did you do to-day?

KIDDIE: Nothing.

FRITZ: Nothing? Didn't you go to school?

KIDDIE: Yes.

FRITZ: And didn't that nice girl wat takes care of you, take you to de park dis afternoon?

KIDDIE: Yes.

FRITZ: And did she go home already?

KIDDIE: Yes.

FRITZ: And you was alone dis evening waiting for de Frankie mudder. Ain't you going to smile yet? Wat will make you smile now? Shall I tell you—oh—such a funny story aboud Chris Kringle, wat's coming down your chimney next month already? [KIDDIE *shakes his head.*] No? shall I—

KIDDIE: [*Solemnly.*] Be a monkey.

FRITZ: [*Hopping on a chair and imitating a monkey.*] Ach Gott! Dot iss too easy.

KIDDIE: I like that.

FRITZ: Well I am glad you like something.

KIDDIE: [*Going to kick the end of a couch.*] I want Frankie to come.

FRITZ: Du Leiber! Can't you forget a liddle? She come soon, now. I tink she iss eating her dinner all ready down in de restaurant.

KIDDIE: She's going to take me to dinner to eat with her down in that restaurant, she said so.

FRITZ: No! How fine! I will haf to get invited on that time. You tink I can?

KIDDIE: Sing a song.

FRITZ: All my tricks, un? [*Going to piano he begins a German song—extravagantly—after first few bars—loud voices are heard in hall singing same tune.* WELLS *and* EMILE *bang on the door and enter arm in arm singing.*]

WELLS: For Heaven's sake, can't you hear anything but your own voice.

EMILE: Que faites—vous? Oh, la, la, Tenez! Où est la Divinité? Où est la Divinité? [WELLS TREVOR *is a happy go lucky young American, good looking and good natured. He wears a shabby lounging coat.* EMILE GRIMEAUX *is a small Frenchman of the unmistakable artist type. He wears a blue working blouse.*]

WELLS: Where's Frankie? Kiddie?

KIDDIE: She hasn't come home yet.

FRITZ: [*Rising from piano and going to* WELLS *thumping him in the ribs.*] It's too early all ready. Don't you know anything?

EMILE: Um—he knows nossing.

WELLS: I know a good sport when I see one. [*Going to* KIDDIE.] Kiddie, old man, doesn't care when Frank gets home, do you? He can take care of himself, can't you? [WELLS *doubles his fist and makes a pass at* KIDDIE, *to which* Kiddie *quickly responds. They move to center going on with mock fight.*]

FRITZ: Gif it to him, Kiddie. Goot! See! Ach du leiber Himmel! Keep at him! You have him going! [WELLS *doubles back to left towards the couch.* KIDDIE *is excited with his victory.*]

EMILE: Voila! See ze liddle champion! En garde! Bien! Voila!

FRITZ: Reach for de chin.

EMILE: Non, no,—Kick him wiz ze feet! [WELLS *falls full length backwards on couch among pillows.* KIDDIE *wildly excited.*]

FRITZ: [*Snatching a newspaper from the desk and giving it to* KIDDIE.] Here—here—fan him! You must be goot to a man when he iss down.

WELLS: [*Gasping.*] Where am I?

FRITZ: You are wid friends. [KIDDIE *takes paper and holding it at arm's length, in both hands, fanning* WELLS *laboriously.*] Haf you got your wind all ready?

EMILE: [*Laughing.*] I wonder where iss a cigarette. Oh—le voila!

WELLS: Let me have that paper, Kiddie. Did you see a criticism of Frank's book this morning?

EMILE: Non—I had not ze time. I haf painted all day like mad. I have had ze most wonderful—

WELLS: Here you are. [*Finding the article.*] "The Beaten Path" is the strongest thing that Frank Ware has ever done. Her first work attracted wide attention when we thought Frank Ware was a man, but now that we know she is a woman we are more than ever impressed by the strength and scope of her work. She has laid her scenes this time on the East side in the wretched poverty of the tenement houses, and the marvel is that any woman could see and know so much and depict crime and degradation so boldly. Her great cry is for women—to make them better by making them freer. It is decidedly the most striking book of the year. [KIDDIE *with a heavy sigh goes back to the window.*] Bully good criticism.

FRITZ: It's a bully good book.

WELLS: You bet it is. Where does she get her stuff, anyway? After all, that's the point! How does she get it?

EMILE: Sere iss only one way. [*Rising and stretching himself complacently, standing with back to fire.*] A woman only gets what a man gives her. [FRITZ *draws* KIDDIE *away from the window and sitting right of desk, takes him on his knee.*]

WELLS: [*Still lying on couch.*] Lione says the man is Gaskell.

EMILE: Zut! Gaskell has not ze romanse—ze mystery—ze charm for a secret love.

FRITZ: [*Attracting* KIDDIE'*s attention from the others by showing him a trick with his fingers.*] Can you do dot? It iss not so easy. Un?

WELLS: I'm hanged if I can tell whether it *is Gaskell* or not—but if it is—why the devil won't she marry him? I tell you Malcolm Gaskell's going to be a big man some day. He's got the grip on this newspaper all right, all right, and he's not going to let go till he's got a darned good thing.

EMILE: Zat would be nossing to her. She wants ze love of ze poet—ze artist. It is not—

FRITZ: Wat are you talking about? It is not dis—it is not dat. It is not nobody.

EMILE: Oh, la, la! She is a very brilliant woman, but she cannot do what is impossible. She cannot write like a man unless a man help her—and no man could make her write like zat unless she love him.

FRITZ: [*Frowning fiercely and shaking his head at* EMILE, *takes up picture to show* KIDDIE.] Mine gracious! Look at dis beautiful ladies.

KIDDIE: I don't like 'em.

FRITZ: Ach Gott! Der is Fraulein Keppel who used to sing wid dot beautiful voice when I played in the orchestra in Berlin.

KIDDIE: There ain't anything funny in that old paper. Why don't they have Buster Brown every day?

FRITZ: Ach no. They have to keep Buster so we can tell ven it iss Sunday.

WELLS: [*In a lower voice to* EMILE.] You can't see beyond the love idea. Frank isn't a Frenchwoman. What if there *is* a man helping her—it might be only a business deal.

EMILE: Oh—mon enfant!

FRITZ: [*Rising quickly as he puts* KIDDIE *to the floor.*] You are two big fools. [*To* KIDDIE.] Kiddie, why don't you go down to the lower hall and wait dere for Frankie mutter?

KIDDIE: [*Going up to hall door.*] I'll stay by the door and when she comes in, I'll jump out at her. [*He goes out.*]

FRITZ: [*Going out into hall after him.*] Oh my! Dot will be so funny! She will jump so high.

EMILE: [*At fire-place.*] Au revoir, mon mignon.

WELLS: So long, old man.

KIDDIE: [*Calling from the hall.*] I'm going to slide down the banisters.

FRITZ: [*In the door way.*] Don't break your neck, all ready. I vill watch! Ach Got! Be careful! Der you go. [*He closes door and goes down center.*] So you—her friends—are talking too.

EMILE: Oh—la—la!

FRITZ: You have listened to de gossip, de—

WELLS: [*Throwing down paper and sitting up.*] Oh, come off Fritz. Don't get excited. I say I don't know whether it's a love affair or not. *If* it is Gaskell—

FRITZ: If—if—if! Why do you always use dot mean little "if?" Are you cowards? Are you afraid to say it is a lie?

EMILE: She does not deny it.

FRITZ: She would not stoop to deny it.

WELLS: I think Frank has had some grand smash up of a love affair sometime. I don't know whether Kiddie's her child or not—don't care—none of my business—but after she's had the courage to adopt the boy, and refuses to explain who he is—after she's made people respect her and accept the situation—I can't see for the life of me, why she lets *another* thing come up for people to talk about.

FRITZ: There *is* no other thing! That iss a lie.

EMILE: How do you know?

FRITZ: *You* know—*you* know it iss a lie! Why don't you kill it?

EMILE: How can you kill a lie about a woman?

FRITZ: Wid de truth.

EMILE: Mais! What *is* ze truth?

FRITZ: De truth iss—that she is a good woman and you are too small too liddle—too—too—too bad in your mind to know wat dot means.

EMILE: [*Following him to center.*] Prenez-garde! I am a Frenchman!

FRITZ: Yah, dot iss yust it. You don't know a good woman when you see one.

EMILE: "Good!" I said nossing about good or bad. It iss you—you who make her bad. You say she must live like zis or like zat—or like one little way *you* think—or she iss bad! Bah! What is bad? She iss good because she has a great heart—a great nature. She is brave enough to keep ziz child wiz her—and snap ze fingers at ze world. She is kind as an angel—she is free—she is not afraid—but she must love because she is too great to live without love. Does zat make her bad? Allons donc! Because she does not tell who ze lover is does zat make her bad? Bah! It is you who are too small—too little too bête—too German to understand.

FRITZ: Oh, yah! yah, yah. You can talk wid your French talk. You mix up de good and de bad like you mix your black and white paint till you get a dirty something and say it iss beautiful. You say "Oh, yah, she iss a good woman," and you damn her wid dat nasty liddle shrug of dat nasty liddle shoulder.

EMILE: Wat do you—

FRITZ: You cannot do dat wid me. You are her friend or you are not her friend. You know dat she is what I know she is, and if you don't stop winking and wiggling and smiling—I vill—

EMILE: You will? What will you? It is not to you to tell me what I sink of her. You are only jealous. You say zer is no ozzer man because you are crazy wiz ze jealous. Hein! If you was ze man you would not care what I zink—[FRITZ *rushes at* EMILE.]

WELLS: [*Springing up from couch and going between them*]. Drop it, you fools!

KIDDIE: [*Bursting into the room and getting behind the hall door.*] Don't tell 'er where I am.

FRANK: [*Coming in with a rush.*] Oh, I'm so frightened! Something jumped out at me and ran up the stairs. Where's my Kiddie man to save me? Where is he I say.

EMILE: Il n'est pas ici. I do not see him.

WELLS: Didn't you see him? He went down to meet you. [KIDDIE *and* FRANK *both cautiously peer near edge of the door which is between them until they see each other and* KIDDIE *springs into* FRANK's *arms.*]

FRANK: [*Catching* KIDDIE *to her and covering his face with kisses.*] My Kiddie man! Was I long? I tried so hard not to be late tonight. I must have a bigger hug than that.

KIDDIE. [*With a bear-like hug.*] You was awful scared—wasn't you?

FRANK: 'Deed I was—all to pieces!

KIDDIE: She jumped awful high, Fritz!

FRITZ: Yah, I told you.

FRANK: Well, how are you? You're lucky dogs to be so poor that you don't have to work. [*She smiles at them all with the frank abandon of being one of them—strong, free, unafraid, with the glowing charm of a woman at the height of her development. Her clothes are simple and not new—but have a certain artistic individuality and style.*]

EMILE: Zen why do you kill yourself to get rich?

FRANK: I have to get rich for my Kiddie, don't I? See what you think of that, boy. [*Giving him a small package.*]

FRITZ: [*Helping* FRANK *off with her coat.*] Have you had some dinner?

FRANK: Yes, I had a bite down town, but I'm hungry.

FRITZ: [*Putting her cloak on piano.*] I will get you some-ding.

WELLS: No, I'll chase out and get it.

EMILE: I will make you a salad, toute de suite.

FRANK: [*Sitting on the couch.*] No—no—no. Stay where you are—all of you. I know what I want. It's an apple. Give it to me, Wells. Oh—This is good! Be it ever so high up, there's no place like home. Take off my gloves, will you, Emile? Somebody might poke up the fire a bit. [*To* KIDDIE *who is struggling with the toy.*] Can't you make it go, old man? Wind it up for him, Fritz. [EMILE *having taken the gloves off goes back of couch and takes off her hat.* FRITZ *takes the toy and sits on the floor tailor fashion.* KIDDIE *sits in front of him with his back to audience. There is a long pause.* WELLS, *peeling and slicing the apple, sits on the left arm of couch, holding the slices out to* FRANK *on the end of the knife.*] What's the matter with you all? Anybody had bad luck? You're a cheerful set. Why don't you talk? Amuse me. What are you good for? You look as cross as sticks, Fritz. Have you had a fight?

EMILE: Oui. We have had a grand fight.

FRANK: What about?

EMILE: About you.

FRANK: That's good. Who was on my side?

EMILE: We were all on your side, only in ze different way.

FRANK: What's your way? [KIDDIE *runs to* FRANK, *sitting on her lap.*]

EMILE: I say I have ze advantage of zem all—because I can put you in my pictures as I see you—as I understand you. You are in zem all—many women—in many moods. Mon Dieu! I have had a wonderful day! I have painted every minute till ze light is gone.

FRANK: You look it.

EMILE: I haf got it to-day—what I want—and it iss you zat I see in ziz picture.

FRITZ: [*Working with the toy on the floor.*] Nobody else vill see it.

EMILE: Ah, not ze nose—ze ears—ze chin, maybe—I am not painting the photograph. I am painting the soul—ze soul of a woman.

FRITZ: How can you paint what you know nudding about?

FRANK: [*Laughing.*] How's the play, Wells?

WELLS: I rewrote the great third act to-day. May I read it to you in the morning?

FRANK: Yes. [*As* KIDDIE *hugs her.*] Aw—Kiddie—between you and the apple I am choking to death. What have you been doing to-day, Fritz?

FRITZ: [*Reaching for the toy which has run away from him.*] I have been gifing a five dollar violin lesson for a dollar fifty.

WELLS: Cash?

FRITZ: Yah.

WELLS: Then you haven't got any kick coming.

FRANK: Go and see that thing, Kiddie. Don't you like it? [KIDDIE *goes to sit on the floor again.*]

FRITZ: [*Winding the toy.*] One of his legs is a liddle longer than he really ought to be.

KIDDIE: Make him go.

FRANK: What are you doing in your glad rags, Fritz? You ought not to be sitting on the floor so dressed up.

FRITZ: I am going to play Lione's accompaniments. She says it is a very fashionable function.

FRANK: Oh, yes, I remember. Get up and brush yourself off. What is she going to sing?

FRITZ: [*Rising and going to piano.*] She is going to sing dis for an encore.

WELLS: [*Putting apple and tray back on table up left.*] Lione's encores are her long suite.

FRANK: That's because she always sings Fritzie's songs for them. [FRITZ *plays a tender little German song, singing a strain here and there.* WELLS *whistles.* FRANK *closes her eyes listening.*] Um—sweet. I could tell that was Fritzie's in the moon. Come and listen, Kiddie. [KIDDIE *runs to kneel on couch by* FRANK *with his head on her shoulder.* LIONE's *voice is heard singing the song from the hall. She throws open the hall door on a high note.* WELLS *and* EMILE *applaud her with good natured guying.* LIONE BRUNE *is a tall woman with rather striking beauty of a bold type, emphasized by her black gown which is very low and long.*]

WELLS: Bravo! Bravo! Make your entrance again, my dear,—and I'll throw the lights on the door.

LIONE: I'm on now. You're too late for the cue.

FRANK: No one will dispute your Italian blood to-night, Lione.

LIONE: [*Sweeping down to fire.*] Why should they dispute it?

WELLS: [*Imitating her.*]—Why should they—but they do.

EMILE: A man say to me ze ozzer day—"Wat iss Miss Brune?" and I say— "Can you not see by ze look—ze voice—ze temperament?" And he says to me—"You mean Irish?"

LIONE: Beast! [*Sitting in arm chair down left.*]

WELLS: Italian extraction. Lione from Lena—Brune—from Brown.

LIONE: That's brilliant dialogue, Wells. Put it in a play. Give me a cigarette, Emile. [EMILE *lights a cigarette for her.* FRITZ *plays again—they all whistle or sing for a moment with comfortable abandon.* CLARA OAKES *opens the door. She is a medium-sized woman of about 37—with a generally drab and nondescript appearance, looking thrown into her clothes which are somewhat passé. One refractory lock of hair falls over her face and her hat is on one side of her head—both of these she constantly tries to adjust. She speaks in a nervous gasping way and is just now very much out of breath.*]

CLARA: Hello, everybody.

ALL: "Hello Clara."

LIONE: [*Condescendingly.*] Ah, cara mia, where have you been all day?

CLARA: Did you miss me, dearest?

LIONE: Of course I did. I wanted you to hook my gown.

CLARA: I am so sorry.

FRANK: Sit down, child.

CLARA: [*Sitting on the edge of the couch by* FRANK.] I went into Cousin
Mabel's and she asked me to stay to dinner. So I did of course.

WELLS: Of course. Don't miss any of Cousin Mabel's dinners, Clara.

CLARA: [*Still out of breath.*] She sent me home in the motor.

FRANK: Too bad she didn't send you all the way up stairs in it.

CLARA: Yes. I ran up three flights I was in such a hurry to see you I have
an idea.

LIONE: Well, sit back and either take your hat off or pin it on straight.

CLARA: Oh, is it crooked?

EMILE: It make ze whole room crooked—out of drawing. I cannot see
anything else.

CLARA: [*Struggling with her hat and hair.*] Well—I'm going to give an exhibition.

FRITZ: [*From the piano where he is still playing very softly.*] Ach gott!

WELLS: What?

LIONE: Now, Clara, don't be a fool.

EMILE: And what are you going to exhibit?

FRANK: Be quiet. [*To* CLARA.] Go on. Why shouldn't you give an exhibition? I wish to goodness you'd finish that miniature of Kiddie you
began about six months ago.

CLARA: I will. I'll get to work at it right away. I'll make it *the* important
picture of the exhibition.

FRANK: Kiddie can be there and walk up and down in front of it to show
how good it is.

WELLS: I wouldn't run any unnecessary risks, Clara.

CLARA: You mean thing!

FRANK: Shut up, Wells. [*Throwing a pillow at him.*]

CLARA: You just wait—you just wait, you people. You don't believe in me.
You don't think I am in earnest. I'll show you. I am going to get to
work right away.

EMILE: Oh, you have some orders, zen?

CLARA: No—I didn't mean that. But Cousin Mabel says she'll let me do
her miniature.

LIONE: *Let* you? For nothing?

CLARA: Well, yes. I don't mind that.

WELLS: Good Lord! [*An uproar from the others.*]

CLARA: Now, listen!

FRANK: Listen! Listen! Go on, Clara.

CLARA: Then if she likes it, she'll interest other people. That's what I've always wanted her to do, you know. Because if Cousin Mabel really wanted to she could do anything with her social position.

LIONE: Your Cousin Mabel and her social position make me sick. Why doesn't she give you an income?

CLARA: Oh, I couldn't accept that.

WELLS: You couldn't—if you didn't get it.

CLARA: You don't understand how conservative my people are.

LIONE: How stingy—you mean.

EMILE: Why don't you tell them all to go to ze devil?

CLARA: Oh, I couldn't do that. I can't afford to cut loose entirely from my family—though of course they object horribly to my working.

LIONE: They're a pack of snobs. Why don't they boost you along in society then, if they object to this?

CLARA: Well, I really think if I succeeded, they wouldn't mind so much.

LIONE: No—you bet. They'd all be running after you then.

EMILE: Zat is ze trouble. You are still hanging to ze petticoats of your fashionable world—and what do it do for you? Look at me—I am alone in a strange country. I have no influence—no rich friends. I am working for ze art—not for ze money.

FRITZ: [Rising, getting pipe from overcoat and going to window.] Dat is a good thing den.

EMILE: Bah! What is money?

WELLS: Don't ask me.

EMILE: Why don't you live for your art—and starve for it if it must be.

FRITZ: Yah! And when you are hungry—eat one of your beautiful miniatures.

EMILE: Art has nossing to do wiz money.

WELLS: No, but money has something to do with art.

EMILE: In America, yes. Oui—zat is ze truth—ze sad truth. You have no art in America—and what you have is French. [A laugh of tolerance from the others.]

LIONE: I suppose you'll be swelling it, Frank, now that you don't have to make any sacrifices for the sake of your work.

FRANK: I never have made any for it.

LIONE: I'd be ashamed to confess it.

FRANK: Neither have you—none of you have. We're all working for money. We'd be fools if we didn't.

LIONE: Well—really—I thought you had a few ideals.

FRANK: Never mind ideals. I've got a little talent and I'm trying to sell it. So are we all—because we haven't got anything else to sell. It's only genius that forgets money. Only the glory of creating that compensates for being hungry. No—no—talent wants three meals a day—genius can live in spite of none.

WELLS: Well, by God—I guess you're right, Frank. I want to sell—and I'm going to hang on. I think I've got a chance, not because my plays are any good—but because other people's are so damned bad. [*All laugh and there is a general movement.*]

FRANK: [*Rising.*] Come, Kiddie, say good night.

KIDDIE: Aw—

FRANK: Not another minute. Past time now.

FRITZ: Gute nacht—mine kint.

KIDDIE: Gute nacht.

EMILE: Bonne nuit, mon petit. Dormez bien.

KIDDIE: Good night.

EMILE: Comment? Que dis tu? Ah! Mon Dieu! I will never make you a Frenchman if you do not speak ze language.

FRITZ: Don't speak den, Kiddie.

WELLS: Good night old man—I'll have to practice an uppercut for you.

KIDDIE: I'll do you up again.

CLARA: [*Catching* KIDDIE *as he passes her.*] Good night, angel sweetheart. [*Kissing him on both cheeks.*]

KIDDIE: [*Rubbing his cheek.*] Night.

FRANK: Excuse me two minutes, good people. [*She follows* KIDDIE *out closing the door.*]

CLARA: [*After pause.*] Dear Frank is so devoted to Kiddie.

LIONE: Yes, isn't she—as devoted—as a mother.

CLARA: Oh, I didn't mean *that.* That is—I—I—you know what I mean. [*She looks from one to the other much embarrassed. A conscious pause.*] Oh, dear, I'm always saying the wrong thing. You know I just love Frank. I wouldn't criticize her for the world. Of course I do think you have to be very broad minded when you come into this atmosphere. Cousin Mabel says I am getting entirely too liberal—but then she—

WELLS: You're very liberal with your hair pins—they're all over the place. [*Giving her two from the floor.*]

CLARA: Oh, thank you, Wells. She also said my hair was too loose and that I was getting just like a bohemian. [*Laughing foolishly.*] She doesn't like it—but then she doesn't understand—you know.

WELLS: That's it. She doesn't understand. Cousin Mabel doesn't understand. You tell her it takes more than loose hair to make a bohemian—and you're getting to be an out and outer.

CLARA: [*Rising, laughing again—nervous—but immensely flattered.*] Oh, no, I'm not.

EMILE: Oui—Oui—I can see it. It is there—that something—mysterious and illusive—the true mark of ze bohemian.

CLARA: Oh, don't say that. I—I think I'm just as I always was.

WELLS: No, Clara, you're not. The change is so subtle that you don't know it yourself. But we feel it, you know.

LIONE: You want to be careful, Clara.

CLARA: Why what do you mean? Oh, dear!

FRITZ: You better make your hair tight again already.

CLARA: Well—I'm sure I don't know what you mean. I don't believe it any way. I'm going. [*Running out the hall door.*]

LIONE: [*Calling to her.*] I'm coming. Clara, get my coat out, will you?

WELLS: Poor Clara, she'd like to tip-toe through bohemia, but she's afraid of her petticoats.

EMILE: She will never be an artist.

FRITZ: But she makes very nice little pictures already.

LIONE: [*Sneeringly.*] Nobody said she didn't. You have charity to burn.

FRITZ: I would like to give some of it away.

LIONE: Oh, you mean I am uncharitable. Just because I'm not a fool and can see what's what as plain as the nose on your face.

WELLS: [*Dreading* LIONE*'s temper.*] Well, I must skip. I've got to rewrite a whole play to-night. Come on, Emile. [*Pulling* EMILE *to the door.*]

EMILE: No, I vill not—

WELLS: Come on. Come on. Good night. Hope you make a hit to-night, Lione. [*He pulls* EMILE *out, closing the door.*]

LIONE: Pray, what did you mean by that speech?

FRITZ: You seem to tink you know.

LIONE: I wish you wouldn't imply before other people that you think I'm uncharitable to Frank. I have the greatest charity. I don't care what she has done, or is doing, or how many lovers she has. All I ask is that she doesn't *pose.* It's absurd the attitude she takes of being strong minded and independent and it makes me sick—simply *sick* to see her fool you and lead you around by the nose.

FRITZ: Sh! Be careful!

LIONE: Anybody—*anybody* can see that it's Gaskell. She's flirting with you and fooling you and using you as a blind—

FRITZ: What if she do lof Gaskell? What of it?

LIONE: What of it?

FRITZ: Dot—don't mean der is anything wrong or dot dere iss any reason for everybody in de house to talk and whisper and hint.

LIONE: I don't know whether you are so simple that you don't see—or so crazy about her that you lie for her.

FRITZ: Lie for her? Ah, Lione, why do you do dis? Are you out of your head? You are making it all up.

LIONE: Don't you say that to me. I not only believe what I say—but something else.

FRITZ: What?

LIONE: Have you ever thought—Does Kiddie make you think of anyone?

FRITZ: What do you mean?

LIONE: I'll tell you some day—when I'm sure.

FRITZ: I don't understand you. [*He turns sharply and goes to lower window. She follows him.*]

LIONE: You're a fool! a fool—a fool! I'm only trying to save you. Now you've made me angry, Fritz, and I won't sing well.

FRITZ: Oh, yes, you will. You are very beautiful to-night.

LIONE: You only say that to—[*Lifting her face to him.*] Do you really think I am, Fritzie?

FRITZ: I tink it, yah. Und I tink it iss time to go already.

LIONE: Come on then—I'll get my coat.

FRITZ: You get your coat und I come.

LIONE: You want to see *her*. Stay with her then. I don't want you to go with me.

FRITZ: I will come as soon as I—

LIONE: Stay with her. I won't be made a fool of.

FRITZ: I vill come in ten minutes.

LIONE: I don't want you. [*Rushing out and closing the door with a bang.*]

FRITZ: [*Calling.*] I will come. [FRITZ *sighs and going to piano, plays again as* FRANK *enters. She goes quietly to her desk—drawing pen and paper towards her.* FRITZ *goes to stand at left of desk. She smiles up at him with comfortable affection.*]

FRITZ: You are tired to-night, Yah? Un?

FRANK: A little Fritz.

FRITZ: Und you must work yet?

FRANK: I'm going out later.

FRITZ: Oh, no. Don't do dot!

FRANK: Oh, I must. If I get what I'm after to-night I'll have a fine study. I'm going to have supper with a girl from the East side.

FRITZ: I vill be back. I vill go with you.

FRANK: Indeed you won't.

FRITZ: But, I don't want you to go—alone—at night.

FRANK: Now—now—Fritzie—if you get fidgety—

FRITZ: Oh—but de talk—de talk—I can't stand it for you. When you go out like dis people don't believe it is for your work. They say you have a lover—they say he writes your books.

FRANK: That's very flattering. It means that they think they are too good for a woman to do.

FRITZ: But you see you make dem talk when you do foolish things.

FRANK: Foolish? You mean going out alone? Good Heavens! You don't suppose I'm going to give up all my chances of seeing and knowing and understanding just because a few silly people are talking about me?

FRITZ: But you are a woman. You must not expect people to trust you— too much.

FRANK: I'm not going to spend my life explaining.

FRITZ: [*Sitting at left of desk.*] No—but you—

FRANK: Oh, Fritz, don't. You've been so nice and so comfortable. And now you're beginning to worry. You see how much better it would have been for both of us if I'd never told you anything about myself and about Kiddie.

FRITZ: Don't say that. You have to talk to somebody—sometimes. Don't say you are sorry you told me, dot was de most natural ting I haf ever seen you do.

FRANK: Natural? Surely, I am nothing but natural. I'm a natural woman— because I've been a free one. Living alone with my father all those years made me so. He took me with him every possible place.

FRITZ: Ah—but he was with you to protect you.

FRANK: I didn't need much protection. Dad wanted me to see—to know—to touch all kinds of life—and I surely did. He developed all his stories by telling them aloud to me. He used to walk up and down the little library and talk out his characters. So I began to balance men and women very early—and the more I knew—the more I thought the women had the worst of it.

FRITZ: Something has made you bitter to men.

FRANK: Kiddie has made me bitter. Poor little nameless fellow! I shall never forget the night his mother came to us. I didn't know her very well—she was only one of the hundreds of American girls studying in Paris—but she came to me because she wanted to get away from her own set. We kept her and she died when Kiddie was born—and then we kept him—because we didn't know what else in God's world to do with him—and then we loved him—and after father died—some how that poor, little, helpless baby was the greatest comfort in the world to me. I couldn't bear Paris without dad, so I came back to America. Kiddie was two then, and we set up house in this old place three years ago—and here we are—and it's nobody's business who he is. I don't *know* who his father was—I don't *care* who he was— but my name is better for the boy than his—for mine is honest.

FRITZ: I tink it iss a too bad ting to be a woman wid a big mind, a big soul. Yah, I tink it. But I am glad you are one already.

FRANK: Dear old Fritz!

FRITZ: I only wonder wat vill be de end.

FRANK: Kiddie will be the end of everything for me.

FRITZ: No—he vill not. Someday you vill lof a strong man—and he vill change it all.

FRANK: You don't believe me of course. But it's Kiddie—Kiddie I am living for. Everything I believe about men and women has been so intensified by him that he has become a sort of symbol to me of what women suffer through men—and he's given me a purpose—something to do.

FRITZ: I tink Malcolm Gaskell has cut me out wid—Kiddie.

FRANK: Nonsense! Nobody could do that.

FRITZ: I am not so sure. I think Gaskell can get most anything he want—if he try.

FRANK: Why don't you like him, Fritz?

FRITZ: He isn't de kind of a man dot every body knows all about and can trust de first time you see him.

FRANK: Yes, he is. That's just what Gaskell is. Whatever his faults may be at least they're honest, right out from the shoulder!

FRITZ: I am not—so sure. [*A pause.*] Don't be sorry to-morrow that you haf talked a liddle to-night. It's gute for you—und don't tink I don't understand. Gute nacht. [*Giving her his hand.*]

FRANK: Good night Fritz. [FRITZ *goes up to table by piano and picks up his violin case and overcoat. There is a knock at hall door.*]

FRANK: Open the door. [FRITZ *opens door and* MALCOLM GASKELL *stands in the doorway. He is a tall, powerful looking man, about 40. The face is strong and reckless.*]

FRITZ: Speaking of the devil—here iss the old boy himself.

GASKELL: Hello, Bahn, you here? Good evening, Miss Ware.

FRANK: Good evening, Mr. Gaskell.

FRITZ: Yah—I am here—but I am going. She is very tired and very busy.

GASKELL: You must have stayed too long. [*To* FRANK.] Why didn't you send him away?

FRITZ: She did.

GASKELL: That's good. I came to borrow a book.

FRANK: Help yourself.

GASKELL: [*Going to table up left and selecting book he sits carelessly on couch.*] Thanks. [FRITZ *still stands by door watching* GASKELL.] You don't seem to be going?

FRITZ: No, I'm holding the door open for you.

GASKELL: I'd rather you'd shut it for me.

FRITZ: Vell—I haf done my best—you see he is going to stay. [FRANK *watches both men, much amused.* FRITZ *starts to go as* LIONE *appears in doorway. She wears a long coat and is drawing on her gloves petulantly.*]

LIONE: Well—really, I thought you were coming for me.

FRITZ: Yah—I am just coming.

LIONE: I am not in the habit of going after my escorts.

FRITZ: Ach—Lione.

LIONE: It's frightfully late. Of course some people are such *sirens.* [*With a withering glance at* FRANK.] Oh—Mr. Gaskell—too. You're so popular, Frank.

FRANK: I am with some people. You don't appreciate me, Lione.

LIONE: At least I understand you. I'm ready, Fritz. [*She sweeps out*—FRITZ *following meekly, nodding to* FRANK *as he closes door.*]

GASKELL: You ought to took out for the stiletto under that Italian cloak. I am sure she's got it ready for you.

FRANK: Don't laugh.

GASKELL: [*Rising and going center.*] Why not?

FRANK: It isn't a joke—poor girl.

GASKELL: It is decidedly a joke to see that big tempestuous Lione bow down to the little pink and white Fritz.

FRANK: You're decidedly off when you call Fritz pink and white.

GASKELL: He couldn't be that and love you, I suppose?

FRANK: [*Sitting sidewise in the chair at left of desk.*] What did you come for?

GASKELL: Your book. I want to read it again. You haven't given me a copy.

FRANK: Why don't you buy one and help the sale?

GASKELL: I did buy one—but I threw it away—it irritated me.

FRANK: Then you don't need another one.

GASKELL: No—I don't need it—I admit, but I want it. I want to read it again. I want to see why people are talking about it.

FRANK: You don't see then?

GASKELL: I don't see why they say it's so strong. It's clever as the deuce and it's got a lot of you in it—but it isn't big. Our paper gave you a darned good criticism. Did you see it? [*Handing her a paper from his pocket.*]

FRANK: [*Taking paper and getting scissors from desk she goes to couch.*] Yes, I saw it. Much obliged to your paper.

GASKELL: [*Following her.*] Your story's all right—a man couldn't have done it any better—your people are clean cut as a man's.

FRANK: Oh, thank you.

GASKELL: [*Standing with his back to fire looking down at her.*] But—it's only a story. You haven't got at the social evil in the real sense. You couldn't tackle that. It's too big for you. You've taken the poverty and the wrongs of the woman on the East Side as an effective background for your story, and you've let your dare-devil profligate girl rail against men and the world. She says some darn good things—more or less true—but—you don't get *at* the thing. You keep banging away about woman—woman and what she could do for herself if she would. Why—this is a man's world. Women'll never change anything.

FRANK: Oh! [*Smiling.*]

GASKELL: Man sets the standard for woman. He knows she's better than he is and he demands that she be—and if she isn't she's got to suffer for it. That's the whole business in a nut shell—and you know it.

FRANK: Oh, don't begin that again. I know your arguments backwards.

GASKELL: How did you happen to come here anyway? This isn't a good place for you to live.

FRANK: Why did you?

GASKELL: Oh, this is all right for a man.

FRANK: Rather good for me too. The house is filled with independent women who are making their own living.

GASKELL: And you also have a little court of admirers here—all more or less in love with you—all curious—most of them doubting and all of them gossiping about you to beat the band. Don't you know that?

FRANK: Let's talk about something else for a change.

GASKELL: Hang it! Somebody's got to tell you. You can't live the way you do and do the things you do—without running your head into a noose—just as any other woman would.

FRANK: I don't know why you take the trouble to say all this.

GASKELL: I don't know why I do myself, for Lord knows, I wouldn't stop you in anything you're trying to do. I like your pluck. I say go on. I understand you—but you needn't think for a moment anybody else does. I don't question you. I take you just as you are. I suppose you think this Dutchman understands you?

FRANK: He isn't impertinent to say the least.

GASKELL: No, I suppose not. He wouldn't dare to disagree with you.

FRANK: Oh, yes he would. Fritz has a mind of his own and a very strong character. He is a genius beside. If he only had a chance to be heard. I wish you'd do something for him, you know so many people. You've got a lot of influence in that direction. Don't you want to?

GASKELL: Do you really want me to?

FRANK: Oh, awfully. He has the real thing—you know he has. Don't you know it?

GASKELL: Oh, I suppose so,—the real thing is fiddling—but that's not much for a man.

FRANK: He's here without friends—without money. He ought to be heard.

GASKELL: What do you want me to do?

FRANK: Talk him up to somebody. He can't do that sort of thing for himself. He's too sensitive and too fine.

GASKELL: Sensitive and fine—be hanged. That won't get him any where.

FRANK: [*Rising to go back to desk with the clipping.*] I hate you when you say things like that.

GASKELL: [*Catching her hand as she passes him.*] Do you hate me! Do you?

FRANK: Then don't be so—

GASKELL: So what—? Don't you think I'm—What do you think of me? Tell me.

FRANK: I think you don't mean half you say.

GASKELL: Oh, yes, I do. And a good deal more. You don't mean half *you* say—they're only ideals.

FRANK: Oh!

GASKELL: You'll acknowledge it some day—when you care for a man. You won't give a hang for anything you ever believed then.

FRANK: Oh, yes, I will—and I'll care what he believes.

GASKELL: [*Bending close to her.*] You'll believe that you've got to live while you are young and you'll believe that love is the only thing that counts much for a woman.

FRANK: No—no—no!

GASKELL: It is. Women are only meant to be loved—and men have got to take care of them. That's the whole business. You'll acknowledge it some day—when you do—love somebody.

FRANK: It would only make me feel more—more than ever the responsibility of love of life. [*She moves back from him—looking at him while she speaks.*]

GASKELL: [*After a pause.*] Come out after while and have a bite of supper with me. Will you?

FRANK: Oh, couldn't—possibly. [*Sitting at her desk and drawing a ms. towards her.*]

GASKELL: Please.

FRANK: No—really I can't. I have to work.

GASKELL: Well—get to work and I'll come back for you—any time you say.

FRANK: Can't. I'm going out at twelve anyway.

GASKELL: Oh, that's different—if you're going out to supper anyway.

FRANK: I'm going to have supper with a girl from the East side.

GASKELL: Why in the name of heaven are you going at 12 o'clock?

FRANK: She is going to bring her sweetheart for me to see and he can't get off any other time.

GASKELL: I'll go with you.

FRANK: No, you—

GASKELL: Yes, I will.

FRANK: Indeed you won't. I want them to be natural and talk. She's had a tragic story and this fellow knows all about it and is going to marry her. She is helping me a lot in my club for girls over there—she can get at them because she's been through it all and has come out a fine, decent woman.

GASKELL: I can't see for the life of me why you go banging around over there—wasting your time—getting into all sorts of disagreeable things. What's the use?

FRANK: What's the use? I call it some use to get hold of about a dozen girls a year and make them want to lead decent lives.

GASKELL: [*After a pause.*] Are you going to let your Fritz go with you?

FRANK: Of course not.

GASKELL: Thought perhaps you would. He makes a pretty good watch dog trotting around after you. Doesn't he?

FRANK: He makes a pretty good friend. [*Rising.*] You must skip now. I've got to get to work!

GASKELL: I don't want to go.

FRANK: Come on. [*They walk together to door.*]

GASKELL: [*Standing in the open door.*] You're awfully hard on me.

FRANK: Poor you!

GASKELL: That's right. You don't know how nice I could be if you didn't fight with me.

FRANK: You always begin it.

GASKELL: Will you come to dinner to-morrow night and see a show? Will you—will you? [*After a pause she nods smilingly.*] Good. [*Taking her hand.*] And we won't fight? [*She shakes her head.*] Not a bit?

FRANK: [*Drawing her hand away.*] Not a bit.

GASKELL: If you were only as kind to me as you are to everybody else—I'd be—

FRANK: You wouldn't like me at all.

GASKELL: Try it.

FRANK: I couldn't. Nobody could get on with you without fighting.

GASKELL: Oh, don't say that.

FRANK: It's the truth. You're a head-strong, domineering—

GASKELL: Just because I don't crawl at your feet the way the other fellows do. Do you hate me?

FRANK: You said that before. Skip now. Good-night.

GASKELL: [*Taking book out of pocket.*] Are you going to give me this?

FRANK: I said no.

GASKELL: But I've got it.

FRANK: [*Putting her hand on the book.*] But I haven't given it to you.

GASKELL: You'll never give me anything. I'll have to fight for it. [*He snatches her hand and kisses her wrist and arm and goes out closing the door. Hesitating, she puts her hand over the arm where he kissed it and puts her arm on the door hiding her face in it.*]

ACT II

SCENE: *A room in the same house, occupied by* CLARA *and* LIONE. *Long double windows at back. A single door at left leading into hall. A single door at right opening into a closet. An old-fashioned fire-place below closet at right.*

Down right below the fire-place a large hassock. Before upper end of fire-place a large arm chair. To the right of windows at back a couch bed—covered with a dark cover, and holding two pillows. Before the windows are two screens for holding pictures. They have only a single panel and stand on spreading feet, and are made of a plain wood and brown canvas. To the left of windows is a wash stand, with bowl, pitcher, etc., of flowered china. Above the door at left is a bureau crowded with toilet articles, a small china bowl, a few books, cigarettes, matches, etc.

Half hiding the bureau and wash stand is a large screen of four leaves. Below the screen an upright piano, and at left center a good sized round table with a chair between it and the piano. A chair to right of table, and one below it to the left.

At left below the door is another couch bed, covered with a dark cover, and holding several pillows. On the table center are a brass tea service and a dozen teacups and saucers of various kinds—and a white lace cover.

On the piano are piles of music and a small clock. The mantel holds a brass candle stick, a few ornaments, and a great many photographs.

The furniture is old-fashioned, heavy black walnut. The walls are covered with a dull faded paper—which is badly torn above the couch at right. There are a few effective pictures—water-colors, prints, etc., on the walls.

TIME: *Four weeks later, 2 o'clock in the afternoon.*

AT CURTAIN: LIONE, *with the front of her skirt turned up and a towel pinned over it as an apron, is sitting on the couch down left, polishing a brass candle stick with a flannel rag.* CLARA *wears a skirt and shirt-waist, which do not meet in the back, and a much be-smeared painting apron. The same lock of hair of act one is constantly falling over her face and she mechanically pushes it back.*

CLARA: [*Going to take a work-basket from the table to put it on bureau at left.*] Oh, dear! I hope it pays for all the trouble. Cousin Mabel may have one of her headaches at the last minute and not come at all. She's really awfully pleased with her miniature. It flatters her horribly. I do want to be honest and true in my work, but what are you going to do? No woman will accept a miniature unless it does flatter her.

LIONE: I hope to goodness somebody gives you an order after this affair. I'm ruining my hands cleaning these things.

CLARA: Don't do them well. We'll never be ready by four o'clock. It's two now. [*Taking hat from arm chair and dropping on her knees before the couch up right. She draws a hat box from under the bed and puts the hat in it.*]

LIONE: If your cousin doesn't come, I'd never speak to her again in all my life, if I were you.

CLARA: [*Getting flat on the floor to reach a dress box under the bed.*] Oh, pooh! She wouldn't care whether I did or not.

LIONE: Your cousin Mabel's a damned snob—that's what she is.

CLARA: [*Taking a shabby afternoon gown from the box.*] Oh, she doesn't mean to be. She's just like everyone else in her world. [*Examining the gown.*]

LIONE: I hate 'em. Ignorant, idle, society women. That's all they are.

CLARA: You'd give your ears to be one, though.

LIONE: [*Rising and leaving candles on the couch, as she goes to look at herself at bureau.*] I wouldn't. I wouldn't give up my career for anything on earth.

CLARA: Yes, that's what I used to think—but somehow, I'm not so keen about my—Goodness, this is mussed and shabby! Absolutely the only rag I've got to wear. [*Hanging the gown on the chandelier below the fire-place she pushes the box back—and arranges the cover on couch.*] Oh, I must get the rest of the miniatures up. Here's Kiddie's picture. Where's the best place to put this?

LIONE: I think Frank's got an awful nerve to let you display it at all.

CLARA: Why?

LIONE: Why? Because people will ask who he is.

CLARA: Oh, well, I'll just say he's a little boy that Frank Ware adopted.

LIONE: [*Going to put a candle stick on mantel.*] Yes, that sounds well.

CLARA: Well, it's plausible. [*Putting the miniature on the screen and standing back to see how it looks.*]

LIONE: Not to me. The men say she isn't in love with Gaskell. Why, she is, head over heels—and sometimes I think—

CLARA: What?

LIONE: Sometimes—I think—[*going to* CLARA]—*he* is Kiddie's father.

CLARA: What? Oh, horrible, Lione. She never saw Gaskell till she came here.

LIONE: Yes, so *they* say. Let me see Kiddie's picture. Frank used to live in Paris, and so did Gaskell.

CLARA: Oh, Goodness! I never dreamed of such a thing.

LIONE: [*Going to sit at right of table and looking closely at miniature.*] Several times I've thought—

CLARA: You'd better keep on working. The tea table isn't ready at all. I hope to goodness nobody looks behind this screen.

LIONE: [*Starting as she looks at picture.*] It isn't imagination. I do see it— as true as I live.

CLARA: What's the matter?   .

LIONE: Look! Come here.

FRITZ: [*Calling as he knocks.*] Can I come in?

CLARA: Yes, come. [FRITZ *enters carrying a screen like the others. He is in his shirt-sleeves.*] Oh, you angel! Put it over there. The screens are perfectly splendid. I'm so grateful. Really I am. You've so clever to have made them. I never could have afforded to have them if you hadn't—

FRITZ: [*Putting screen near the others.*] I like to do it.

CLARA: You're a genius, Fritz.

FRITZ: Yah—but I am too many kinds of a one. Dat iss my trouble.

CLARA: [*As they adjust the screens.*] You ought to stick to your violin. That's where your genius is.

FRITZ: Yah. But de great American public doesn't seem to know it.

CLARA: Yes—I know—I know. Isn't it awful? I hope to goodness somebody gives me at least one order from this exhibition.

FRITZ: Oh, yah, you get some.

CLARA: I wish I were as cheerful as you are. Did you ask Emile if I could have his tapestry for this afternoon?

FRITZ: Ach du lieber! You ask him. He vill not gif it to me. Dot tapestry is de apple core of his eye.

CLARA: I'm going to ask him now. It won't hurt it a bit and I want it awfully to put above that couch over there—to hide the hole in the paper. [*She goes out.*]

FRITZ: [*Going to look over* LIONE*'s shoulder.*] What are you looking at?

LIONE: [*Hiding the miniature.*] Nothing.

FRITZ: Let me see.

LIONE: I've just decided something. Something I've half way believed for a long time.

FRITZ: What is dot?

LIONE: I don't know that I'll tell you.

FRITZ: Please.

LIONE: I've found out something and you'll pretend not to see it.

FRITZ: How do you know that unless you tell me what it iss?

LIONE: Because I know *you*.

FRITZ: Tell me, please—please. You have very pretty eyes.

LIONE: Had you forgotten that?

FRITZ: No.

LIONE: It's the last woman who comes along with you, Fritz.

FRITZ: Every woman keeps her own place in a man's heart.

LIONE: What I don't understand about you is—how can you let a woman flirt with you when you know she is crazy about another man.

FRITZ: You mean Frank? She does not flirt with me. She iss a friend.

LIONE: Will you admit that she's in love with Gaskell?

FRITZ: She don't want to love any man.

LIONE: Oh, is that what she tells you?

FRITZ: No—she tells me nodding. Dat iss what I tink.

LIONE: You do? Well, you're about as wise as a kitten. I know she's in love with Gaskell and I think she always has been—that is—long before she came here.

FRITZ: Ach! Why? Why you tink dot? She never know him.

LIONE: [*Lifting the miniature.*] Whom does Kiddie look like?

FRITZ: What do you mean?

LIONE: Look.

FRITZ: No, no—I will not look.

LIONE: [*Catching his arm.*] Why won't you look? Are you afraid to?

FRITZ: No—no—I am not afraid. Why should I be?

LIONE: Why you are so excited?

FRITZ: I am not excited.

LIONE: You are. Oh! You see the resemblance too, do you?

FRITZ: What resemblance? I don't know what you are talking about.

LIONE: Don't you? Who is he like through the eyes?

FRITZ: Who? He iss like himself.

LIONE: [*Holding the picture before him.*] It's Malcolm Gaskell!

FRITZ: [*Closing his eyes.*] Ach Gott! What do you mean?

LIONE: You know what it means. Frank came here alone with this child.

There is a mystery about her—then Gaskell comes—they're in love with each other and pretend not to be. I'll bet anything you like, Gaskell is this boy's father.

FRITZ: You have made it all up.

LIONE: You either know it's the truth or you're *afraid* it is. I'll tell her that I know.

FRITZ: No.

LIONE: I will—I will—I will. There's no reason why I shouldn't and there's every reason why I should.

FRITZ: Listen to me. If you will promise to keep still—if you will promise to say nodding to anybody about it, I will tell you what I tink.

LIONE: [*Looking at him keenly.*] What's that?

FRITZ: Frank has told us he is de child of a woman who died.

LIONE: Yes—but who is the father?

FRITZ: *She* don't know who de fadder was. But when Gaskell first came here *I* see dis resemblance and *I* believe he is de boy's fadder. Maybe he don't know it—maybe he do—but Frank don't know it. I am as sure of dat as I am standing here.

LIONE: Fritz, you must think I'm an awful fool. Of all the cock and bull stories I ever heard—that's the worst.

FRITZ: It might—it might be. Dis iss a strange und funny old world.

LIONE: But it isn't as funny as that. Oh, Fritz, I want to save you from this woman, from her influence.

FRITZ: She iss de best influence dot efer came into my life.

LIONE: What's going to come of it?

FRITZ: Nodding.

LIONE: You love her?

FRITZ: You are two women, Lione. You and I used to haf such good times togedder. I lof your voice, Lione, you haf someding great in it. I like to play for you when you sing. You are so jolly and so sweet when you—when you are nice. Why can't it always be so? Why can't we always be friends?

LIONE: She's changed everything. She's spoiled everything. She's ruining your life—and I'm trying to save you.

FRITZ: No—Lione—you don't—

LIONE: I've wasted my friendship on you—wasted it—wasted it—!

CLARA: [*Opening the door.*] Yes—yes—if I get an order from this exhibition I'll blow you all to a supper. [EMILE *follows. He is in his blouse and carries a large tapestry over his shoulder.* WELLS *comes next carrying a quantity of curious daggers, foils, Indian weapons, etc.*]

EMILE: Where will you have it?

CLARA: There—over there. [*Pointing above couch up right.*] Put that stuff on the arm chair, Wells—till we put it up. I'm so much obliged.

WELLS: [*Striding across the room with the tapestry dragging, he stops center and recites elaborately.*] Clara, I've composed an ode to the occasion. Ahem!

> Clara, Clara's giving a show,
> She makes miniatures, you know;
> She gives you cake, she gives you tea,
> She's polite as she can be.
> But don't just eat her cake and tea,
> She would like some cash you see.
> Don't say just—"How charming dear.
> Oh, how quaint and sweet and queer!"
> But let her paint your pretty faces
> With a rose bud and the laces.
> Then the checks that you have sent
> Will pay our Clara's board and rent.

[*The others laugh and applaud.*]

WELLS: [*Suddenly seeing* CLARA's *gown hanging below fire-place, and springing back.*] Great Heavens! Is that your astral body?

CLARA: No, it's my last year's body.

EMILE: Where did you say to put zis?

CLARA: [*Going to couch right.*] Right over this. It will cover the hole.

EMILE: Mais! Mon Dieu! Ze tapestry will not show. It belong to Napoleon.

WELLS: [*Holding out Indian hatchet.*] This belonged to George Washington.

CLARA: Get up there, Emile. You take the other end, Wells, and I'll get you some tacks.

WELLS: [*As he and* EMILE *get on couch.*] Where are you going to put the weapons of warfare?

CLARA: [*Going to bureau and taking tacks out of china bowl.*] Right over the tapestry.

EMILE: Sacré! You are not going to put ze relics of your savages with ze tapestry of Napoleon!

CLARA: [*With tacks in her mouth.*] Why not? It will be effective and nobody will notice whether they really go together or not.

EMILE: Zat is ze American. You mix your Art until nobody knows what you mean.

CLARA: I don't want it to *mean* anything. I want it to cover the hole. Here—[*Holding up shabby slipper and tacks.*]

EMILE: [*Taking slipper.*] What is zis for?

CLARA: To pound with, of course.

WELLS: You wouldn't expect that artistic temperament to have a hammer, would you? Go on. Hold up your end and fire away, Napoleon. Don't stop for details. [EMILE *and* WELLS *begin to hang the tapestry.* LIONE *has sat on the floor by the couch down left and taking a box from under it gets out teaspoons which she rubs with a towel.*]

CLARA: That isn't straight. Lift your end—

FRANK: [*Coming in carrying a large bunch of roses in a paper. She is wearing a very charming afternoon gown and hat.*] Hello, everybody.

ALL: [*Except* LIONE.] Hello! Hello, Frank!

FRANK: How're you getting on? Oh, how nice you're going to look.

CLARA: And how nice *you* look.

FRANK: I bought these for your tea table.

CLARA: You darling! Just what I wanted. But, how awfully extravagant!

FRANK: Not extravagant at all. Marked down on the corner. Not warranted to last over night—but I think they'll get through the afternoon. Have you got anything to put them in?

CLARA: Nothing high enough.

FRANK: Get the tall vase out of my room—will you, Fritz? And isn't there anything else you want?

LIONE: We have everything we want thank you.

FRANK: You're lucky. Here's the key, Fritz, will you get the vase?

FRITZ: Yah, I get it. [*Going out with the key.*]

CLARA: [*Moving the large screen so the bureau and wash stand are hidden.*] You'll sit here, Frank, when you serve the tea.

FRANK: [*Squeezing into the chair between the table and piano.*] Give me room enough to get in.

CLARA: Oh, well, you can get in before the people come. Now, Emile, listen. You said you'd help Frank with the tea. When you take the cups away don't move the screen what ever you do. Just hand them around like this. See—

EMILE: Bien.

CLARA: And Mrs. Grumper will be behind the screen washing.

WELLS: What?

CLARA: Washing cups, you goose!

WELLS: Oh!

CLARA: And all you have to do, Emile—

WELLS: All you have to do is to whisper—"One wash."

FRANK: [*Laughing.*] What are you going to have—just tea?

CLARA: Heavens yes. Don't you think it's enough?

FRANK: Oh, of course. I only wanted to know.

WELLS: Nothing else—on the side?

CLARA: Oh, I wouldn't dare. Cousin Mabel would say there was drinking and carousing going on.

WELLS: Give Cousin Mabel a drink or two and she might pay for her picture.

FRANK: Kiddie's quite excited about his picture being displayed. [LIONE *looks up at* FRANK *quickly and watches her a moment.*] He said this morning—"Don't you think I ought to be there and see if they could guess who it is?"

CLARA: Bless his heart!

WELLS: Yes, you might make it a guessing party, Clara.

LIONE: To guess who Kiddie is, you mean? [*There is a slight pause as they all look from* LIONE *to* FRANK.]

WELLS: I meant to guess which is Kiddie's picture.

FRANK: We might all guess now—what Lione means. [*A pause*—LIONE *rises, puts spoons on table—looks at* FRANK *and goes up to window.*]

FRITZ: [*Enters with medium sized glass vase.*] Here you are.

FRANK: No, you aren't. That isn't it at all. I meant the tall one.

FRITZ: Ach du lieber! Dis iss all I see.

FRANK: [*Rising.*] I'll get it.

FRITZ: No—I'll go back. I am sorry.

FRANK: I'd rather go—thank you. I want to get something else. Oh, Clara,—don't you want some more pillows and rugs and things?

CLARA: I'd just love them.

FRANK: And are you going to wear that? [*Pointing to the gown hanging on the chandelier.*]

CLARA: Yes—It's all I've got.

FRANK: Don't you think it would be rather pretty with that little lace jacket of mine over it?

CLARA: Oh, heavenly! May I?

FRANK: Of course. [CLARA *pushes her lock of hair back.*] And I wish you'd let me do your hair. I'd love to try it a different way.

CLARA: You're an angel. I wish you would. I don't seem to be able to make it stay up. It drives Cousin Mabel crazy. Wells says it's temperament, you know. [*Giggling.*]

FRANK: Well, let's see if we can't hold your temperament in a little.

CLARA: You're awfully good, Frank. Really you are.

FRANK: Nonsense! Fritz, will you come and help me bring some things? Fritz!

FRITZ: Yah?

FRANK: Will you come and help me bring some things?

FRITZ: Oh, yah, I come. [*He goes out with* FRANK *closing the door.*]

CLARA: Frank's a dear. She's got the biggest heart.

EMILE: I do not sink Fritz tinks her heart is quite big enough. He would like to get in.

WELLS: [*Kicking* EMILE *and looking at* LIONE.] You don't know anything about her heart.

CLARA: I wish I did. I think it would be awfully interesting to know whether she really cares for Gaskell or not.

WELLS: Give us more bric-a-brac, Clara, if you want it all up.

CLARA: Oh, yes, use it all. [*Giving* WELLS *another weapon from chair.*]

EMILE: I tell you she love somebody. Zat iss her charm—her mystery. She could not be what she iss wiz out love.

WELLS: She's a mystery to me all right, all right.

CLARA: She certainly is to me.

LIONE: She certainly is not to me. Look here—all of you. [*Holding out the picture.*] Whom does Kiddie look like?

CLARA: Oh, gracious! What do you mean?

LIONE: Simply what I say. Whom does he look like?

EMILE: You mean like Frank?

LIONE: No, no. Not like Frank. Look now—through the eyes.

CLARA: I don't see it—and I ought to if anybody does—I painted it. What do you mean, Lione, anybody we know?

WELLS: You couldn't very well see a resemblance to anybody you didn't know.

CLARA: Well, dear me. I don't see—through the eyes—Oh, Heaven's— yes—I do.

LIONE: You see it! Wait!—Don't say anything.

WELLS: Oh, you can imagine anything.

LIONE: You can't imagine anything as strong as that.

CLARA: Yes—I actually—

EMILE: Ah! Mon Dieu! I see what you mean. It is Gaskell.

WELLS: What—

EMILE: Ah! C'est extraordinaire!

LIONE: [*Looking triumphantly at* WELLS.] We *all* see it.

WELLS: Rot—rot! Nothing of the sort. I don't see the slightest—

LIONE: We see it. All of us.

CLARA: I think I do—I did. It sort of comes and goes.

WELLS: Especially goes. I don't see it.

LIONE: You're blind. Look—it's Gaskell. That child looks like Malcolm Gaskell—and *any* body can see it. Unless they don't want to.

EMILE: Mais oui! I see it. It is here, the eyes. For *you*—Clara, it iz wonder- ful—you haf caught ze trick wiz ze eyes.

LIONE: Of course it's there.

CLARA: Oh my! I think it's awful. What do you mean, Lione? I don't know what you mean.

WELLS: Nothing. It doesn't mean anything.

LIONE: Oh, no. Nobody means anything—nobody knows anything—nobody says anything—but you all *think* what I do—and you haven't got the courage to say so. I have you know. I believe in saying what you think—and not pretending to be fooled.

WELLS: Well, now, what of it? What if what you imply is true. What of it? What's the good of digging it up?

CLARA: Oh, dear! I don't believe it at all.

EMILE: I tell you all—all ze time—you are foolish as babies not to understand.

WELLS: Oh, yes, you understand a lot, you do. I say, what's the use of talking about it? Let it alone.

LIONE: Oh, very well, if that's the sort of thing you accept and believe in—that's your affair—but I don't propose to help a woman of that sort keep up appearances by pretending that I don't see what's right under my nose.

CLARA: Oh, dear! I never was in anything like this before. I think you have to have strict ideas even if you are broadminded. I do think—Oh, dear! I don't know what to think.

EMILE: You amuse me—all. You pretend to live in ze world of art and freedom and yet you make ze grand fight about—about what? What are you talking about? What do you expect—you funny Americans. She is a great woman—she must live and love and—

LIONE: You needn't say that to me. I don't—[FRANK *knocks and opens the door.* LIONE *puts the miniature back in her blouse.* FRANK *has taken off her hat and coat. She carries a sofa pillow under each arm, and the lace coat. She has also the vase and the two framed pictures in silver frames in her hands.* FRITZ *follows with four pillows and a rug.*]

FRANK: [*Laughing.*] We met old Grumper in the hall and she thought the house was on fire. [*An uncomfortable pause.*] You don't seem to think that is funny. [*Putting vase on table and throwing the two pillows onto the couch left she hangs the coat over screen.*] This is the vase I meant. [FRITZ *goes behind piano and filling vase from pitcher puts it on table and remains up center.*]

WELLS: Come on, girls, your lunch is ready. Sorry we didn't know you'd be home, Frank. We've only got enough for four.

FRANK: That's all right. I've had my luncheon.

LIONE: Come on, Clara.

CLARA: You don't mind my going, do you, Frank?

FRANK: Of course not. I'll do the flowers for you.

WELLS: We've only got salad and cheese. Thought the girls wouldn't have time to go out to-day—so we're setting them up.

FRANK: How nice of you!

EMILE: [*To* FRANK.] You are an angel. Je vous adore.

CLARA: I hate to go and leave you—but—

LIONE: Come on Clara, don't keep everybody waiting—[LIONE *goes out.*]

WELLS: [*Catching* CLARA *by left hand and pulling her to door.*] On, Clara, on, to the feast. On, Clara, let us be mad and gay while life is fleeting. [*Exit* WELLS, EMILE, *and* CLARA *laughing.*]

FRANK: Weren't you invited to the party?

FRITZ: Nein. No, I was not invited.

FRANK: Put the pillows on the other couch. I do hope this affair does Clara some good. The screens are splendid. Where's Kiddie's picture? Do you know?

FRITZ: A—no, I don't know.

FRANK: [*Going to look on the screens.*] I don't see it.

FRITZ: Oh, I think she has not yet hung them all.

FRANK: It looks as if she had. I don't see it. Funny! Is it on that one?

FRITZ: No.

FRANK: Here's a vacant space. Maybe she's taken it down. I wonder where it is. Oh!

FRITZ: What it is?

FRANK: I just thought of something.

FRITZ: What is dot you tink of?

FRANK: I thought maybe Lione took it down. I have a sort of feeling about the miniature from something she said just now. Fritz, tell me honestly. Do they talk about it much? Do they? Oh, they do.

FRITZ: Frankie, I want you to do something. You must tell them—more about Kiddie.

FRANK: No! Fritz, do you doubt what I've told you about him?

FRITZ: If I do not believe you, I believe nodding in de world. But—

FRANK: But what?

FRITZ: But you see you haf gifen me your confidence. You haf only tell a little to dem—just enough to make dem doubt—and it hurts you.

FRANK: All I want to do is to keep still and help Kiddie make his life clean and honest, and then let the world judge him by himself. I don't see anything foolish in that.

FRITZ: That's all very well for him—but you must think of yourself too—your reputation.

FRANK: Now, see here, Fritz, I care just as much about my reputation as any woman in the world, but this talk is only idle gossip and curiosity and I'm not going to let that force me to do a thing that I know isn't right.

FRITZ: Den I ask you something else—Tell Lione—

FRANK: No!

FRITZ: You tink I'm crazy—but I tell you if you make Lione your friend— if you make her understand you—she will kill all de talk—she will be a help. You need a woman on your side, and if once you get Lione, she fight for you—and she wipe up de floor mit everybody else.

FRANK: I don't want to buy her friendship.

FRITZ: No—no, it would not be dot. She—I tell you she need you, too. She need a good woman friend. Lione has a big heart, if it is—if it just get hold de right ting. She fight you now—but it is only like a big child dat don't know how to control its badness. If you just get her once—you could make her lof you, if you try—but first she has got to belief you.

FRANK: You're a funny, dear old boy, Fritz. I'm just as much to blame as Lione when we scrap.

FRITZ: Will you do it? Will you tell her? Will you?

FRANK: Yes, I will.

FRITZ: Ah—I am so glad. [*There is a knock at the hall door.*]

FRANK: Yes, come in.

GASKELL: [*Opening door wearing his hat and coat.*] Hello! [*Looking jealously from one to the other.*]

FRANK: [*Moving toward* GASKELL.] Oh, hello, what are you doing here this time of day? Did you come to the exhibition? You're rather early. It doesn't begin till four o'clock.

GASKELL: Oh, is this the day for the show? No—I came to—I went to your room, Bahn, and I went to yours—[*To* FRANK.] There's a concert on for this afternoon—and the young violinist who was booked to play is laid up—fell and broke his arm this morning. The manager—Holbrooke, is a friend of mine, and called me up because I had spoken to him about you. [*Nodding to* FRITZ.]

FRANK: Oh—

GASKELL: Will you go on? Will you play? Chance of your life. Cracker-jack audience.

FRANK: Oh, your chance has come at last Fritz! It's too splendid—I could cry—it's too splendid. You'll play the concerto and then you must play your own slumber song. It's too splendid—I can't believe it. [*Turning to* GASKELL.] Think what it means to him—Oh, Fritz! I'm so glad. I'm so—What will you play, Fritz?

FRITZ: I cannot play.

FRANK: What?

FRITZ: I cannot play.

FRANK: What do you mean?

FRITZ: Dot is what I mean. I cannot play.

FRANK: Have you gone mad? It's the chance of your life, as Mr. Gaskell says. Are you fooling? Here's the opportunity—in your hand—are you going to take it?

FRITZ: We cannot always take what comes. [*Looks at* GASKELL.] I cannot take dis. [*He goes out closing the door.* FRANK *and* GASKELL *stare at the door for an instant.*]

FRANK: I don't understand.

GASKELL: Impudent pig-headed—irresponsible set—every one of them. How do they expect to get along if they don't take a chance when you hand it out to them? Bohemians! Geniuses! Damn fools, I say.

FRANK: Oh, Fritz isn't like that. There's something else—some reason. What was the matter with him? Something came over him—I don't—

GASKELL: Why, it's me—that's what's the matter with him. He won't take it from me, because he's so jealous of you he's crazy. If I'd known he was such a fool, I'd have had them send to him direct, so he wouldn't have known I had anything to do with it. That would have pleased you? But I thought the safest and quickest way to get him was to come and find him myself. Sorry I've balled it up. Your friend's so fine and sensitive I don't know how to handle him.

FRANK: Don't be unjust to Fritz just because you've lost your temper. I must say I don't blame you for that—he did seem awfully rude and ungrateful, but I know he didn't mean it. He—

GASKELL: Mean it? Good Lord, what did he mean then?

FRANK: That's just what I don't know.

GASKELL: You're trying to find another reason for what's just plain ordinary jealousy. Do you want me to keep out of his way?

FRANK: Don't be ridiculous.

GASKELL: [*Taking both her hands.*] Do you want me to clear out and let you alone?

FRANK: [*Trying to draw her hands away.*] This has nothing to do with the case.

GASKELL: Yes, it has. Everything to do with it. He doesn't make any more difference to me than a mosquito—but if you—good God, I love you—and you know it. [*He catches her to him and kisses her, then slowly lets her go. She puts her hands over her face and turns away.*]

GASKELL: I—you've kept me outside. I know he knows—the whole business—what ever it is. You've shut me out. But I know you're making a mistake by making a mystery of your life.

FRANK: You mean I ought to tell about Kiddie—explain and prove every bit of my life?

GASKELL: I don't put it that way. I mean everything ought to be—open—understood.

FRANK: I thought you said you accepted me just as you see me here—just as you accept a man.

GASKELL: In the beginning I thought I did. But, when a man loves a woman—the whole world changes to him. He wants to protect her—he wants to understand her. He wants to look into her eyes and see the truth.

FRANK: You're afraid of what you might see in mine?

GASKELL: Tell me—what ever it is.

FRANK: Why should I?

GASKELL: Frank, don't fool with me. I love you. That's why I ask. That's why I care. I want to understand you. Why won't you tell me? Have you told this other man?

FRANK: He never asked me.

GASKELL: Do you love him? Are you going to marry him? Are you? You've got to tell me that. Are you going to marry him?

FRANK: No.

GASKELL: Then I'm going to make you love me. I love you. I love you—I tell you. This child is the most important thing in your life. I ask you to tell me what he is to you.

FRANK: How dare you say that to me?

GASKELL: Because I love you. That gives me the right.

FRANK: What if I said to you: "I love you, but I don't believe you. You must prove to me that everything in your life has been just what *I* think it ought to be."

GASKELL: I'm a man. You're a woman. I love you. I have the right to know your life.

FRANK: You mean if Kiddie were my own child, you couldn't ask me to marry you?

GASKELL: Is he?

FRANK: And if he were? Can't a woman live through that and be the better for it? How dare a man question her! How dare he!

GASKELL: Do you mean—[LIONE *throws open the door and stops in supercilious surprise.*]

LIONE: Oh—I beg your pardon! I didn't know Mr. Gaskell was here. I should have knocked.

GASKELL: It's always a pretty good idea to knock, don't you think?

LIONE: Oh, I don't know. I'm such an open, frank sort of a person that somehow it never occurs to me that I ought to knock at the door of my own room. [EMILE, WELLS *and* CLARA *follow her in.*]

FRANK: There are some people who think all doors ought to be open—always—even to the innermost rooms of one's soul—so that all the curious world may walk in and look about and see if he approves of what he finds there.

LIONE: Do you mean I am one of those?

FRANK: You know whether you are or not.

LIONE: If you mean I am curious about you, you're mistaken. I'm not curious—and I am not deceived.

FRANK: Deceived?

LIONE: No. The real situation is too apparent for me to pretend not to see it.

FRANK: You'll have to speak plainer than that.

LIONE: Do you really want to discuss it here?

FRANK: I do.

LIONE: Well, really, if you insist. A certain resemblance in Kiddie's miniature attracted my attention. We all see it.

WELLS: I object, Lione—

EMILE: If you please—

CLARA: How can you, Lione?

FRANK: Where is Kiddie's miniature? I couldn't find it.

CLARA: It must be there.

FRANK: No, it isn't.

CLARA: Why, I—

LIONE: [*Holding it out to* FRANK.] Here it is.

FRANK: A certain resemblance—you say? [FRITZ *comes into the open door.*]

LIONE: [*Looking at* FRITZ.] We all see it.

FRITZ: [*Stepping forward.*] You have broken your promise.

LIONE: No! I promised if you told the truth—but you told me an absurd thing. Fritz saw it too, but he has a different explanation, of course.

FRITZ: [*Looking at* FRANK *in agony of appeal.*] No! Don't—

GASKELL: What do you all mean? What resemblance are you talking about? Confound your impertinence! What do you mean?

LIONE: I'll tell you—

FRITZ: No, you will not.

LIONE: I will. Why shouldn't I? I will.

FRITZ: No, I say you will not.

GASKELL: Tell it—tell it! Say it. What do you mean?

LIONE: I mean—

FRANK: You needn't. They mean that Kiddie looks like me.

[*A pause. They stare at* FRANK *as she walks out quietly.*]

ACT III

TIME: *Six hours later. Eight o'clock the same evening.*

PLACE: *Same as Act I. Chandelier and both lamps are lighted—shades
are drawn in windows.*

AT CURTAIN: FRANK *wearing a house gown of striking simplicity, is
seated by table sewing.* KIDDIE *on the couch, is reading aloud.*

KIDDIE: [*Reading.*] And—Fido—runs and—gets—the ball—f-r-o-m—
from—the water—and takes—it—to his m-a-s-t-e-r.

FRANK: Master.

KIDDIE: Master—and Willie—takes—it—to his f-a-t-h-e-r?

FRANK: You know that.

KIDDIE: No, I don't.

FRANK: Look at it again.

KIDDIE: F-a-t fatter.

FRANK: No—no.

KIDDIE: F-a-t-h—father.

FRANK: Of course.

KIDDIE: What's my father?

FRANK: Why do you ask that?

KIDDIE: 'Cause today at school two boys were talking about their fathers
and one said his was a lawyer and one of 'em said his was a barber.

FRANK: A barber?

KIDDIE: Or a banker—I don't remember.

FRANK: Oh!

KIDDIE: And they asked me what mine was. What is he?

FRANK: [*Going to sit beside* KIDDIE.] He went away a long time ago—you
don't want him. Aren't I a good father? Don't I give you all you
need?

KIDDIE: Maybe I don't need one—but I'd like—

FRANK: Like what?

KIDDIE: Oh, I'd just like to see him sittin' round.

FRANK: I love you as much as if I were your father and mother and sisters
and brothers and uncles and aunts. You have to be all those to me,
too, you know, because I haven't any. We must tell each other everything and keep close and think all the time of how we can make each
other happy. Mustn't we?

KIDDIE: If you want to make me happy, why didn't you take me to see my
picture this afternoon? That made me very *un*happy.

FRANK: It made me unhappy too, but I really couldn't take you, dearie.
Something happened. I really couldn't take you. I'm so sorry.

KIDDIE: But it's just down stairs. I could have gone by myself. [*Looking at her closely.*] Have you been crying?

FRANK: No—no. Are my eyes red?

KIDDIE: Your nose is.

FRANK: Do you love me?

KIDDIE: You bet.

FRANK: How much?

KIDDIE: As much as—[*Stretching his arms out full length. There is a knock at door.*]

FRANK: Oh—

FRANK: You open the door, Kiddie. [KIDDIE *marches to the door and opens it wide.* GASKELL *stands in the doorway.*]

KIDDIE: Goodie! It's Mr. Gaskell.

GASKELL: May I come in?

FRANK: I—don't—

GASKELL: I'm coming. I want to talk to you.

KIDDIE: Don't you want me to hear it?

GASKELL: Well—to be very honest, I would like to talk to just Miss Ware—if you don't mind.

KIDDIE: I've got to pick up my paints I left all over the floor then I'll be back. [*He goes out left closing the door.*]

GASKELL: I've been thinking—since that—since this afternoon. I was a cad. At least that's what I seemed to you. I don't know what those other duffers were driving at—Oh, I do know in a way—but—All I mean is that I love you and ask for your—confidence.

FRANK: I'm not angry now, but I was then—so horribly angry and hurt. I could tell you who his mother was and prove it in a hundred ways but don't ask me to do that. Oh, Malcolm—You must believe me— just *me*. Look at me. I give you the one love of my life.

GASKELL: [*Catching her in his arms.*] Frank!

FRANK: I love you. I love you.

GASKELL: My darling! It was hell to doubt you, but I couldn't help it, dear. It was only because I love you so. Because I want you to be the most perfect woman in the world. Do you understand?

FRANK: And don't you see why I wanted you—of all people in the world to trust me—in every way? Don't you understand?

GASKELL: No, not quite. [*Sitting beside her.*] When will you marry me?

FRANK: Oh, I don't know.

GASKELL: I want to take care of you. You need it as much as any woman does. Do you love me?

FRANK: I've tried—not to.

GASKELL: Don't say that. Why?

FRANK: I haven't wanted to love anybody—and when I knew I was beginning to care—I didn't want to.

GASKELL: When did you know you—cared?

FRANK: Oh—When I began to fight with you. You made me so awfully angry—and then I was always wretched until we made up. I began to know your step in the hall, and when you opened the door and stood there I knew something strong and sweet, something stronger than myself was coming in.

GASKELL: I'm a beast in lots of ways and stubborn as a mule—but I can take care of you and I'll be good to you.

FRANK: When did you first know *you* cared?

GASKELL: From the first minute I saw you.

FRANK: Oh, every man says that. You know that isn't true. I wouldn't want it to be. I'll tell you when I first knew you cared.

GASKELL: When?

FRANK: Do you remember that day—it was—it was Sunday evening about three months ago. You were here and Fritz came in with some roses for me and you didn't look at me for the rest of the evening. You talked to Clara every minute.

GASKELL: Oh, come, I wasn't quite such an ass as that.

FRANK: You were. You were just as silly as you could be, and perfectly adorable. When you'd gone I—

GASKELL: You what—

FRANK: I won't tell you.

GASKELL: Oh, please tell me.

FRANK: No.

GASKELL: Oh, please. What did you do when I'd gone?

FRANK: I won't tell.

GASKELL: I don't believe you love me at all. Do you?

FRANK: Um—you haven't the faintest idea how much.

GASKELL: Well—tell me—tell me how much.

FRANK: I never can. You don't know what it means for a woman to love only one man in all her life.

GASKELL: Oh, now Frank—

FRANK: It's true. You're the one man, Malcolm. That's why I've tried to resist it because it means so terribly much to me. My life has been filled with other things you know—with Kiddie—and my work. They absorbed me and satisfied me; and when you—when love began to crowd in—to overpower me—I was afraid. It seemed almost like being a traitor to myself. Oh, it means such a—such an overwhelming thing for a woman to give up to love after—she's—she's been—

GASKELL: After she's been as strong and independent as you've been. I'm the luckiest dog on earth. I don't see how I got you.

FRANK: Just because you are you. Oh, don't ever disappoint me. Be big and fine and honest always—let me lean on you and worship you.

GASKELL: Kiss me. [*She puts her head back and he bends over her kissing her.* KIDDIE *opens the door and comes in, standing amazed.*]

KIDDIE: Is that what you were talking about—kissing her?

GASKELL: No, a man never talks much about that.

KIDDIE: [*Going to* FRANK *and throwing his arms about her and kissing her fiercely.*] She says I am the only man that can kiss her.

GASKELL: Well, let me see if I can do it like that.

FRANK: No—no!

KIDDIE: What made you let him do it, Frankie?

GASKELL: I'll tell you.

FRANK: No—no! Please. I'll tell you after awhile, Kiddie—when I put you to bed.

GASKELL: Will you kiss me too?

KIDDIE: I'll kick you. [GASKELL *laughs.*]

FRANK: Oh, Kiddie, you don't mean that.

KIDDIE: Yes, I do. You said I always had to take care of you.

FRANK: Yes—but—[*There is a loud knocking at door center.*] Oh, heavens! Go over there. [*Motioning* GASKELL *away.*]

KIDDIE: I'll tell on you.

FRANK: Kiddie, you won't do that, will you? You never tell tales, you know. Will you? [*He hesitates a second, then shakes his head.*]

GASKELL: [*In a very loud voice, going to door.*] If you'll come down to my room with me, Kiddie, I'll give you—[*He opens the door—*CLARA *is there waiting, with the pillows, coat, etc., which were borrowed.*] Oh, I beg your pardon, did you knock?

CLARA: Yes, I did.

GASKELL: I'm afraid I was talking so loud nobody heard you. I say, Kiddie, if you'll come down I'll give you—well, you can tell me what you want most when we get there. [*After slight hesitation* KIDDIE *goes to* GASKELL.]

KIDDIE: I haven't forgiven him, but I'd like to see what he's got. [KIDDIE *goes out center—followed by* GASKELL.]

CLARA: Here's your coat. I am so much obliged. I wore it—but I must say I was rather ashamed to after what happened.

FRANK: I don't care now what happened.

CLARA: Why?

FRANK: Because something else has happened that makes that affair this afternoon seem very insignificant.

CLARA: Does it? I thought you'd be so furious with everyone of us that you'd never speak to us again. I was really afraid to come up—but I did.

FRANK: I am glad you did.

CLARA: But I want to tell you I wasn't in it. I didn't—

FRANK: Let's not talk about it. Sit down. How was the exhibition?

CLARA: A fizzle. A perfect fizzle.

FRANK: Oh, no. I am so sorry.

CLARA: Cousin Mabel didn't come at all. Some people she'd asked were there, and of all the snippy snobs I ever saw! They only stayed a minute and were so out of breath and asked me how I could possibly climb two flights. Only two mind.

FRANK: Good thing they didn't have to come to see me.

CLARA: One woman asked me why I didn't have one of those lovely studios on 57th Street. Oh, dear, what's the use. [*Bursting into tears.*] I'm so discouraged. I don't know what to do.

FRANK: Oh, no, you're not. You're tired and nervous.

CLARA: Yes, I am too discouraged. I've tried just as hard as I can for ten years—and scrimped and scraped and taken snubs and pretended I was ambitious and didn't care for anything but my work, and look at me—don't even know how I am going to pay my next month's rent. I'm so sick and tired of it all I don't know what to do. I'd marry any man that asked me.

FRANK: Now, you're not going to lose your nerve like this.

CLARA: I would. I'd marry anything that could pay the bills. Oh, I am so tired—so tired of it all.

FRANK: Poor little girl. It is a hard fight, isn't it?

CLARA: It doesn't pay. I've been too terribly respectable and conventional all my life to succeed. If I were like you—you're so strong and independent—you believe in women taking care of themselves.

FRANK: I believe in women doing the thing they're most fitted for. You should have married, Clara, when you were a young girl—and been taken care of all your life. Why didn't you? Don't you believe in that?

CLARA: No man has ever asked me to marry him. I've never had a beau—a real beau—in my life. I—I've always been superfluous and plain. Absolutely superfluous. I'm not necessary to one single human being. I'm just one of those everlasting women that the world is full of. There's nobody to take care of me and I'm simply not capable of taking care of myself. I've tried—God knows I've tried—and what is the use? What under Heaven do I get out of it? If I were a man—the most insignificant little runt of a man—I could persuade some woman to marry me—and could have a home and children and hustle for my living—and life would mean something. Oh, I can't bear it, Frank. I can't bear it! I often wish I were pretty and bad and could have my fling and die. [*Sobbing she falls on the couch—huddled and helpless.*]

FRANK: Life has been dull and common place and colorless for you—but there are worse things than that. You've learned that life is easier for men than for women—you know what it is to struggle for existence—come and help me in some of the things I'm trying to do for girls. I'd like to have you teach drawing and modeling in this new club we're opening.

CLARA: Oh—would you?

FRANK: Would you be willing to live there? To be one of the women in charge and help the girls in a personal way?

CLARA: Oh—do you think I could help anybody?

FRANK: Come over and try it, Clara, and see. You'll never wish again that you were pretty and bad, after you've seen a girl come off the streets and get to be a decent woman.

CLARA: I don't think I could actually do anything, but—Oh, Heaven's, Frank, I would like to get hold of something.

FRANK: You—[*A ra-ta-tat-tat at the door.*] That's Fritz.

CLARA: [*Wiping her eyes and blowing her nose.*] Oh dear, I don't want to see anyone. I am going out through your bedroom. I—I am so awfully grateful, Frank, but—I—can't—[*She chokes with tears and hurries out. Another rap—*FRANK *opens the door.*]

FRITZ: I would like to see you.

FRANK: Come in. [*She goes to sit in arm chair below the fire and* FRITZ *closing the door goes to couch.*]

FRITZ: You tink—I haf broken my promise? You tink—I haf been—dot I haf talked about you to Lione. Dot iss true—but not in de way that you tink. I was very foolish and I argue wid her and I say a very foolish ting—but it was not a bad ting—I mean it was not about you at all. It was about you—but it wasn't. I don't tink anything but what I always haf and dot iss dot you are de best and most honest woman in de world. Do you believe dot?

FRANK: I want to believe it—but, oh, Fritz, how could you discuss me at all? I thought you were so different from the others. I've told you everything. How could you talk about it?

FRITZ: I know. I know I was one big fool, but I lose my head—and I said a ting I wish back.

FRANK: And something else that disappointed me awfully this afternoon. Why on earth didn't you take the chance Mr. Gaskell gave you to play?

FRITZ: I couldn't.

FRANK: It can't be because of Malcolm Gaskell himself, can it?

FRITZ: You must not ask me.

FRANK: For goodness sake speak out. I'm sick of suspicion and curiosity. How dare they take Kiddie's picture down and try to squeeze something out of it? How dare they? Of course they decided that he looks like me. Isn't it a joke? Let's not have any more made up scandals. If you have anything against Gaskell go and tell him so—like a man.

FRITZ: You would like to believe in him above any man in the world?

FRANK: I do.

FRITZ: Den I will ask him some ding—somebody has got to do it for you—but—if anything bad should come of dis—

FRANK: Oh—I'm not afraid—and he wouldn't lie to you!

FRITZ: You are very sure of him.—Don't—don't let it—don't let it—mean too much to you if—if he is not de man you tink. It *would* mean everything to you, won't it? Frankie, don't—don't break your heart about a man. I—I couldn't bear it—if anybody hurt—you. [*He raises her hand to his lips and she slowly puts her other hand on his head.*]

FRANK: You—you've been so good to me, Fritz.

FRITZ: Don't tink I don't want to find him worthy of you—I want you to be happy. You know dot, don't you?

FRANK: I do.

FRITZ: He iss a strong man—he iss a success. He can take care of a woman—he has not failed.

FRANK: Neither have you, Fritz.

FRITZ: I haf nodding to offer a woman.

FRANK: You have to offer her what money can't buy for her.

FRITZ: No—the devotion of a life time don't count unless a man can say: "I can protect you from hunger and cold and keep you safe for always."—But—but I would like to know dot some man will do dot and dot he is worthy of you.

FRANK: You dear old Fritz! Your friendship is the most beautiful thing in my life. Oh, Fritz, life is so hard! Love is such a sad, mad, awful thing. It is the greatest danger in the world isn't it—the love of men and women. If we could only get along without it. We—you and I must be friends—always, Fritz. [*Her voice breaks. He tries to speak, but turns and goes quickly out.*]

FRITZ: [*Heard in the hall.*] No, no, don't go in.

LIONE: I will. Yes, I will. I guess I can see her if you can. [LIONE *rushes in.*] I don't know what Fritz has been telling you and I don't care. You said you wanted me to speak plainly—so I suppose you'd like to hear what I mean and why I mean it. I've come up as soon as I could get here.

FRANK: Well?

LIONE: Oh, we can't be blind, you know, even to please you.

FRANK: You mean Kiddie looks like me—and you draw the self evident conclusion.

LIONE: Oh, no, not at all. We mean he looks like Malcolm Gaskell.

FRANK: What?

LIONE: Why you ever let him come here—why you ever undertook such a pose and expected to carry it out is more—[*She stops as* FRANK *goes slowly toward her.*]

FRANK: What do you mean?

LIONE: I mean he's your child and Malcolm Gaskell is his father.

FRANK: Lione, don't say that. Don't lie about a thing like that—it's too awful. Why do you? Kiddie isn't my child. I can prove it by people who knew his mother.

LIONE: [*Impressed by the blaze of truth in* FRANK'*s eyes.*] Then—who—*who was his father?*

FRANK: I don't know who his father was.

LIONE: For God's sake, do you mean that? Haven't you ever had a— Haven't you ever seen the resemblance to Gaskell?

FRANK: No! No! No! No! Of course not! Not the slightest bit in the world. [*Hurrying to desk and taking miniature out of drawer.*] It isn't there at all. He doesn't look the least bit like him. See—look! [*They bend over the picture.*] What do you see? Where? What? I don't see it. Not a thing. Do you?

LIONE: Well—I—you—I—I thought I did.

FRANK: Did they all say they saw it? All of them?

LIONE: Yes—no, not all of them. You can imagine anything in a picture.

FRANK: What did Fritz say?

LIONE: He believes you—and always has. From the first.

FRANK: But *he* saw the resemblance to Gaskell—*thought* he saw it? [*Starting.*] That's what he meant. That's what he's going to ask Gaskell. Oh, it can't be. It can't be! Look again. What did you think was like him? I don't see a thing. I'm telling the truth, as I live. I'd see it if it were—there. What is it you think is like him? Tell me. What? What?

LIONE: Through the eyes.

FRANK: The eyes? No—I can't see it. I can't see it. It's imagination. You can imagine anything in a picture. You don't see it now do you? Oh, Lione, any man—any man in the world but Gaskell. [*Sinking into chair at right of desk.*]

LIONE: I'm sorry I stirred this up. I ought to have kept my mouth shut. It *was* imagination. Let it alone I say. It's the wildest—most improbable thing in the world.

FRANK: But I've got to know. I've got to know.

LIONE: Let it alone. Good Lord, you can't stir up any man's life. You're lucky if it looks right on top. If you love him—take him—that's the point. Let it alone.

FRANK: Um—you don't understand. Who ever Kiddie's father is I've hated him all these years. Every time I look at Kiddie and think that somewhere in the world is a man who branded him with the shame of—Every time I see a girl who's made a mess of her life because she's loved a man, I think of Kiddie's poor little mother, with the whole burden and disgrace of it—and the man scott free. I tell you it's horrible—the whole thing—the relation between men and women. Women give too much. It's made me afraid to love any man. I've prided myself that I never would—because of Kiddie. Because I saw and went through that—I feel almost as deeply—as bitterly—as if I really were his mother. Don't you see? Don't you see?

LIONE: I suppose it does make a difference when a thing is brought home to you. I've never thought much about the whole business myself. Men are pigs of course. They take all they can get and don't give any more than they have to. It's a man's world—that's the size of it. What's the use of knocking your head against things you can't change? I never believed before that you really meant all this helping women business. What's the use? You can't change anything to save your neck. Men are men.

FRANK: If women decided that men should be equally disgraced for the same sin, they *would* be.

LIONE: Oh, yes—if—if. That's easy enough to preach. When it comes to morality a woman never holds anything against a man. What good would it do if she did? She'd be alone. Why, see here—what if—just suppose—that Malcolm Gaskell *were* Kiddie's father. You love him, and love is no joke with you. You've let yourself go at last. You've found the one man. What are you going to do about it? Throw him over—because you happen to find a little incident in his life that doesn't jibe with your theory? Where will you be? What becomes of you? Um? Not much fun for you for the rest of your life. He's the man you want—take him and thank your lucky stars you have him. That's all I see in it.

FRANK: It's all you say. He's the one man—but if it—were true—

LIONE: Well?

FRANK: If it were true—[*She shakes her head.*]

LIONE: Oh, bosh! Then you can marry any man—they're all alike. You know—we've worked ourselves up over nothing after all. I've been at the bottom of all that picture business. It was easy enough to sort of hypnotize the others into it. You can see anything in a picture—in Clara's pictures. I've always been looking for something to get hold of about you because I was jealous. I'm a fool about Fritz. [FRANK *quickly puts a hand over* LIONE's.] I can't sing any more. I can't sleep. I can't eat. I'm a fool and I know it, but I can't help it.

FRANK: Go away from him for awhile, Lione, get away and he'll go after you.

LIONE: Oh, I don't know. I don't know.

FRANK: There it is! Love! What fools it makes us. Oh, I'm afraid of it!

LIONE: I don't believe this thing's true. Brace up. I don't believe it—not for a minute.

FRANK: l don't either—now. But it frightened me when you—

KIDDIE: [*Opening door and pulling* GASKELL *in by the hand.*] Come on. He didn't have anything I wanted—but this. [*Showing a large pocket knife.* FRANK *goes quickly into her room.*] It's got four blades. Look at this one.

LIONE: That's a stunner—isn't it?

KIDDIE: I can cut anything with it.

LIONE: Mind you don't cut the legs off the piano.

KIDDIE: I could. I could cut off your legs too. [KIDDIE *goes to curl up in the left end of couch—busy opening the blades of the knife. There is a pause.*]

LIONE: I think Frank wants you, Kiddie.

KIDDIE: Oh, no, she don't.

LIONE: [*Looking at* GASKELL.] I've just been telling Frank—

GASKELL: What?

LIONE: That I'm sorry for the row I kicked up this afternoon. I think everything is cleared up now.

GASKELL: A row's a pretty good thing once in a while for clearing the atmosphere.

LIONE: Well, I tell you, you never know anybody through and through till you fight with them. Good night, Kiddie. [LIONE *and* GASKELL *nod to each other and she goes out closing the door.*]

GASKELL: [*Going to right end of couch.*] Don't you think you had better go to bed now—and ask—Miss Ware, if I can't wait to see her?

KIDDIE: What do you want to see her for?

GASKELL: Well, several things.

KIDDIE: I don't know if I'll let you.

GASKELL: Oh, please. [FRANK *opens her door and stands watching them.*]

KIDDIE: I like you.

GASKELL: I'm glad.

KIDDIE: I'm much obliged for the knife. [*Giving his hand.*]

GASKELL: [*Taking* KIDDIE*'s hand.*] Don't mention it.

KIDDIE: But that isn't why I like you.

GASKELL: Why, then?

KIDDIE: 'Cause I do. [FRANK *moves a step toward them.*]

GASKELL: [*Taking* KIDDIE*'s other hand.*] That's the best reason in the world, isn't it?

FRANK: You must say good night, now, Kiddie.

KIDDIE: [*To* GASKELL.] Do you mind if I go?

GASKELL: I'll have to stand it. [FRANK *moves above the fire-place still watching them intently.*]

KIDDIE: [*Standing upon arm of couch.*] I'm as tall as you are.

GASKELL: [*Turning his back.*] Come on.

KIDDIE: [*Climbing on* GASKELL*'s back.*] Get up! Look, Frankie! [KIDDIE *laughs as* GASKELL *carries him across to the door left and puts him down.*]

GASKELL: Good night old man.

KIDDIE: Good night—Frankie you come in ten minutes. [*He goes in closing the door.*]

GASKELL: He gets hold of you when you're alone with him, doesn't he? When he says he likes you—it sort of makes a fellow throw out his chest. What's the matter? Why do you look at me like that?

FRANK: Nothing. Was I staring?

GASKELL: Tired?

FRANK: Perhaps I am a little.

GASKELL: It's been rather an exciting day. Your hands are as cold as ice. Have you got nerves?

FRANK: No—no—I haven't.

GASKELL: You know—the more I think about what you've done for Kiddie,—the more I like you for it.

FRANK: Do you?

GASKELL: [*Holding her by the arms.*] Yes, I do. It begins to sink into me what the boy means to you—and that you actually believe all your ideas. I begin to see how through your love for the boy—and his mother's tragedy—you've sort of taken up a fight for all women.

FRANK: Yes, yes,—that's it.

GASKELL: I never thought before that you actually believed that things ought to be—the same—for men and women.

FRANK: No,—I know you didn't.

GASKELL: But I see that you believe it so deeply that you think it's a thing to go by—live by.

FRANK: Of course.

GASKELL: You couldn't get far by it.

FRANK: Not far. No. You wouldn't have asked me to marry you—if Kiddie had been my own child.

GASKELL: Oh, I don't—I—I love you. I want you. But when I knew he was not—the greatest change came that can come to a man. A radiance went over you. I wanted to kneel at your feet and worship you. That's the way all men feel towards good women and you can't change it. No woman with that in her life could be the same to any man—no matter how he loved her—or what he said or swore. It's different. It's different. A man wants the mother of his children to be the purest in the world.

FRANK: Yes, and a man expects the purest woman in the world to forgive him anything—everything. It's wrong. It's hideously wrong.

GASKELL: It's life. Listen to me,—sweetheart. I want to help you do the sensible thing—about Kiddie.

FRANK: What do you mean?

GASKELL: Don't you see that you must let it be known positively who his mother was?

FRANK: That's just what I will not do.

GASKELL: Wait. You've hurt yourself by keeping still about him. What good can you do him by that? You can't take away the curse that will follow him. He'll have to fight that himself. Don't you see it would be much better to tell the whole business while he's little—too little to know anything about it—and then send him away—put him in some good school?

FRANK: Give him up, you mean?

GASKELL: No, not at all. I don't ask you to do that. Watch over him of course and be a sort of guardian—but—clear this thing about yourself. What's the matter?

FRANK: No, turn your head that way—side ways.

GASKELL: What are you looking at? What do you see? Gray hairs? The whole point, dear girl, is—that you can't, to save your life—make things right for the boy.

FRANK: You mean I can't take away the shame that his father put upon him?

GASKELL: Ye-s.

FRANK: What would you think—of Kiddie's father—if you ever saw him?

GASKELL: Oh,—let's not go into that again. Nobody knows the circumstances. You can't judge. Think about what I've said. We won't say anything more about it now. [*He goes to her and turns her toward him.*] Do you love me?

FRANK: I shall never—never give Kiddie up.

GASKELL: I wish you'd tell me what you are looking at. You look as though you saw—Frank!—what's the matter with you?

FRANK: Nothing. Stand over there.

GASKELL: This is very funny.

FRANK: Oh, don't. [*Quickly putting her hand over her eyes.*]

GASKELL: [*Going to her.*] Frank—are you ill? For Heaven's sake tell me what—

FRANK: I've got a blinding headache—I can't see anything.

GASKELL: Do you want me to go? [*She nods her head slowly—staring at him.*] I'm awfully sorry. Why didn't you tell me before and I wouldn't have—Frank—there's something the matter. You've got to tell me. What do you think you see? [*Taking hold of her.*]

FRANK: Please go.

GASKELL: Are you angry? Look at me. Tell me what it is.

FRANK: Please—Just go—I want to think. Go now—please—pl-ease. I can't see. [*Hurt and a little angry he moves backwards toward door.*] Oh—it can't be—it isn't—it can't be! It can't be! It isn't! It isn't!

GASKELL: What?

FRANK: Did you ever know a girl named—Alice Ellery?

GASKELL: [*After a pause.*] Who told you that?

FRANK: Oh, you *did*.

GASKELL: Who told you? Who told you?

FRANK: No one.

GASKELL: Was it anybody here—in this house?

FRANK: How did you—know her? I mean—oh—tell me!

GASKELL: Do you know the whole business?

FRANK: I don't know anything.

GASKELL: You do—you do.

FRANK: No. I don't. I—I'm not prying into your life. It isn't that. But you must tell me something. I've got to know. I've got to know. [*She drags herself to the couch, GASKELL goes to the fire and after a long pause speaks in a low hard tone.*]

GASKELL: It happened about six years ago. I never said anything about marrying her. She knew what she was doing.

FRANK: But, did you—did you desert her?

GASKELL: I didn't! She went away.

FRANK: And you never heard from her?

GASKELL: Never.

FRANK: Never knew what happened to her?

GASKELL: No. She left a note saying she knew then she'd been a fool—

and that she couldn't face the rest. I'm not proud of it, you know. I'd give a good deal to wipe it out—but—it happened. Are you going to hold it up against me? Is that one of your theories? Who told you?

FRANK: No one. I knew her. I was in Paris then. She came to me.

GASKELL: And she told you who—?

FRANK: Oh, not that it was you—no—no.

GASKELL: How did you know then?

FRANK: Her child was born in my house.

GASKELL: What?

FRANK: It was Kiddie!

GASKELL: No!

FRANK: They've seen the likeness—I've just seen it. I had to ask you. I had to know.

GASKELL: Kiddie!

FRANK: Kiddie—Kiddie.

GASKELL: Don't take it like that. I love you better than my life. [*Trying to take hold of her.*]

FRANK: Oh, don't.

GASKELL: Look here, Frank, we love each other, and we've got to face it.

FRANK: Yes, we've got to face it.

GASKELL: Nothing—nothing can separate us.

FRANK: We are separated.

GASKELL: Only by your ideas.

FRANK: My ideas! They're horrible realities now because it's you.

GASKELL: Frank—

FRANK: Every time I've looked at Kiddie I've cursed the man who ruined his mother and branded him with disgrace.

GASKELL: Frank, stop!

FRANK: I've loathed and despised that man, I tell you—and it's you. Before it was someone else—any one—some one unknown, but now it's you—you—*you.* [*She stops. They both turn with horror, as* KIDDIE, *in his night clothes, stands watching them, a little wondering figure.*]

ACT IV

TIME: *Immediately following Act III.*

PLACE: *Same as Act III.*

AT CURTAIN: FRANK *and* GASKELL *are standing as at end of Act III.*

KIDDIE: Why don't you come, Frankie?

FRANK: [*Moving slowly.*] Come, Kiddie. [KIDDIE *hangs his head, then looks up at* GASKELL *slowly.*] Kiddie. [KIDDIE *pushes past her and goes to* GASKELL—FRANK *goes in to her room.*]

KIDDIE: Don't you like me any more? [GASKELL *doesn't answer.*] Do you want me to give the knife back? [*Moving closer to* GASKELL.] It's the best knife I ever had. I found another blade—look. [*Taking knife out of pocket and leaning against* GASKELL *to show it.*] You open it. Don't you want to? [KIDDIE *looks steadily at* GASKELL *and then puts his hands on* GASKELL's *chest.*] Are you mad at me? Don't you like me any more? [KIDDIE *throws his arms about* GASKELL's *neck.* GASKELL *holds him tensely a moment.*]

FRANK: [*Calling from her room.*] Come, Kiddie.

KIDDIE: I've got to go now, but I'll see you tomorrow. [*He goes in. There is a knock at hall door. After a moment* GASKELL *opens it.* FRITZ *stands in door way.*]

FRITZ: I came to find you. I went to your room. Are you going back now?

GASKELL: No, I'm going out.

FRITZ: I have something to say to you.

GASKELL: Well, say it.

FRITZ: Not here.

GASKELL: Go on. Miss Ware is putting Kiddie to bed.

FRITZ: I would rather you—

GASKELL: Say what you've got to say now. I'm in a hurry.

FRITZ: I—der has been—you know—der has been some—some talk about—about Kiddie.

GASKELL: Confounded impertinent set here.

FRITZ: Miss Ware is in a wrong position and some one has got to make it right for her.

GASKELL: Look here. You're meddling with something that doesn't concern you.

FRITZ: No, I'm not meddling. Some one has got to do dis for her.

GASKELL: You needn't trouble yourself. You can tell the rest of your curious friends that I know who this boy is.

FRITZ: You know?

GASKELL: And I've asked Miss Ware to marry me. That clears the whole business.

FRITZ: No, it doesn't.

GASKELL: What are you trying to do? I know all about him, I tell you, and if there's any more of this damnable talk they'll answer to me.

FRITZ: You know who the mother was?

GASKELL: I not only knew who she was—I knew *her*. That's enough.

FRITZ: You knew the fadder also?

GASKELL: That has nothing to do with Miss Ware.

FRITZ: Yes, it has. Der has been a horrible thing said here in dis house. Dey say he is her child—and yours.

GASKELL: It's a lie!

FRITZ: Part of it is a lie—but he is *yours*.

GASKELL: Why damn you—what—

FRITZ: Listen to me. I haf seen dis strange and strong resemblance. I haf watch him—I haf watch you—till I haf come to tink you are his fadder. [*A pause*—GASKELL *looks at* FRITZ *then moves away.*] For de love of God if it is true don't marry dis woman without telling her—it will kill her if she ever find it out.

GASKELL: Now see here, Bahn. Miss Ware does know who Kiddie's father is.

FRITZ: No she does not know.

GASKELL: Yes she does and she is going to marry me. That clears the whole thing.

FRITZ: No, it does not clear her name, it will only make dem sure of what dey tink now—that he is her child and yours.

GASKELL: It's a hellish, infernal lie—and I'll—

LIONE: [*Rapping loudly and opening the hall door quickly.*] What are you doing? You're shouting so the whole house can hear you. [WELLS *appears in door behind her.*]

GASKELL: Come in here. Shut the door. [LIONE *enters.* WELLS *follows, closing the door.*] So this is what you've been saying about her? You've been lying about a good woman.

LIONE: What have you told him, Fritz?

GASKELL: The whole business and I'll tell you who the boy is. I knew—the—mother. Maybe you'll believe that when I tell you—the boy is mine. [*There is a pause. They all watch* GASKELL *as he goes to stand before fire—his back to them.*] I only found this out a little while ago,—from something Miss Ware told me about—his mother who died in her house. I hope this knocks the truth into you.

LIONE: For my part I'm pretty much ashamed of what I've had to do in this.

GASKELL: It's happened. That's the end of it.

WELLS: I consider what has just been said a sacred confidence. I take my oath it will be so with me. [LIONE *and* FRITZ *and* WELLS *look at each other and slightly bow their heads in acknowledgment of a pledge.*]

GASKELL: Whether Miss Ware will marry me now, I don't know. That's all

I have to say. [WELLS *opens the door for* LIONE *and follows her out.*
FRITZ *hesitates, takes a short step toward* GASKELL, *turns and goes out—*
closing the door. GASKELL *remains looking into the fire as* FRANK *comes*
back.] Frank, this thing isn't going to make any difference in our
lives, is it?

FRANK: [*Closing the door after her quietly.*] Whatever I do, Malcolm, you'll
know I do without bitterness—without any spirit of revenge.

GASKELL: You mean if you throw me over?

FRANK: I mean if the future doesn't seem possible for us together.

GASKELL: Why shouldn't it be possible?

FRANK: You know.

GASKELL: No, I don't. This thing has been a shock to you—of course. It's
shaken you terribly, but you haven't given me any real reason—any
facts why there shouldn't be a future for us. I love you and I am
going to have you.

FRANK: [*Moving away from him.*] Oh, don't, please. I must—I must—

GASKELL: [*Following her.*] There's little enough in the world worth having,
heaven knows. Why should we miss each other?

FRANK: Kiddie—Kiddie.

GASKELL: Well—well—we love each other. That's the first thing to reckon
with.

FRANK: Oh, you don't know yet what I mean.

GASKELL: Talk won't get us anywhere. We've got to look this thing square
in the face, as it is. Either you throw me over, or you let me give you
the rest of my life and make you happy.

FRANK: Oh, that isn't—

GASKELL: I love you, Frank. I'd lay down my life for you. You're the whole
world to me.

FRANK: Love isn't the only thing in the world.

GASKELL: It's the biggest thing. We've found each other. Look at me. You
know it's the one perfect thing on earth—a perfect love and we've
found it.

FRANK: It never could be perfect while you believe what you do.

GASKELL: What's that got to do with the facts?

FRANK: Do you believe it wasn't wrong—just because you are a man?

GASKELL: Oh—

FRANK: Do you believe that?

GASKELL: [*After a pause.*] Yes.

FRANK: Oh!

GASKELL: Good heavens, Frank, I thought you were so much bigger than
the average woman. All women kick against this and what good does

it do? Why since the beginning of time one thing has been accepted for a man and another for a woman. Why on earth do you beat your head against a stone wall? Why do you try to put your ideals up against the facts?

FRANK: I'm not talking about my ideals now, nor the accepted thing. I'm talking about *you*, that *girl*, this *child*. You think I must excuse what you did—that it really wasn't wrong at all, just because you are a man.

GASKELL: It's too late to say these things to me now. You know—must have known when you first knew me that I'd—well that I'd lived a man's life. When you first loved me why didn't you think of all this?

FRANK: Ah, that's just it—I loved you. I took you as all women take men—without question. Oh, don't you see I'm not looking for something bad in men. If it hadn't been for him—if he hadn't been put into my arms a little helpless, nameless thing—if I hadn't seen that girl suffer the tortures of hell through her disgrace, I probably wouldn't have thought any more about this than most women do.

GASKELL: Isn't our love more to you than that?

FRANK: No!

GASKELL: Good God, Frank! You're a woman. You talk like a woman—you think like a woman. I'm a man. What do you expect? We don't live under the same laws. It was never meant to be. Nature, nature made men different.

FRANK: Don't make nature the excuse for ruining the life of a good girl. Oh, Malcolm—[*Putting her hand on his arm.*] Do you think it wasn't wrong?

GASKELL: [*Drawing her to him.*] I only know I love you. You said you loved me. I won't give you up.

FRANK: Oh!

GASKELL: You're angry now. When you've had time to think you'll see. Frank, I love you. I love you.

FRANK: [*Getting away from him.*] Oh, no, no.

GASKELL: Frank, you're not as cold and hard as that. You're going to forgive me.

FRANK: Oh, I want to forgive you. If you could only see. If your soul could only see. Oh, dear God! Malcolm, tell me, tell me you know it was wrong—that you'd give your life to make it right. Say that you know this thing was a crime.

GASKELL: No! Don't try to hold me to account by a standard that doesn't exist. Don't measure me by your theories. If you love me you'll stand on that and forget everything else.

FRANK: I can't. I can't.

GASKELL: I'm not a man to beg, Frank. Do you want me to go? Is that it? Is this the end?

FRANK: There's nothing else.

GASKELL: Do you mean that?

FRANK: There's nothing else. It is the end. [*He goes out closing the door.*]

AS A MAN THINKS

A Play in Four Acts

by

Augustus Thomas

First performed at the 39th Street Theater, New York City, on March 13, 1911.

CHARACTERS

VEDAH
DR. SEELIG
HOLLAND, *Seelig's footman*
BUTLER
MRS. CLAYTON
JULIAN BURRILL
BENJAMIN DE LOTA
FRANK CLAYTON
MRS. SEELIG
SUTTON, *Clayton's footman*
MISS DOANE
JUDGE HOOVER
DICK

ACT I

SCENE: *Drawing room of the residence of* DOCTOR SEELIG. *Two small sofas set at right angles to the fireplace form a kind of inglenook. At the outer ends of the sofas are two marble pedestals, each surmounted by an antique vase.*

TIME: *An afternoon in late September.* VEDAH SEELIG, *a young girl, is at*

the piano and playing. After a few bars there is a sound of a door closing.
VEDAH *listens, then speaks.*

VEDAH: Papa?
SEELIG: Yes.
VEDAH: Alone?
SEELIG: Alone. [*He enters from the hall.* VEDAH *meets and kisses him.*]
    Mother home?
VEDAH: She is lying down.
SEELIG: Is mother ill?
VEDAH: Only resting.
SEELIG: Ah—where is the tea?
VEDAH: It isn't time.
SEELIG: [*Regarding his watch.*] Quarter of five.
VEDAH: [*Laughing.*] But no company.
SEELIG: Company? My dear Vedah. Tea with me is not a function—it's a
    stimulant. [*He calls to a footman passing.*] Holland.
HOLLAND: [*Pausing at doorway.*] Yes, sir.
SEELIG: Tell the butler—some tea. [HOLLAND *goes.*]
VEDAH: Now, Papa.
SEELIG: [*Affectionately imitating her.*] "Now, Papa." *You* want to drive me
    into dissipation.
VEDAH: But the others will think they're late.
SEELIG: I shan't grudge them that accuracy—they are late. I don't wonder
    at some of them, but I'm astonished at De Lota.
VEDAH: [*Pause.*] De Lota?
SEELIG: Yes.
VEDAH: Is Mr. De Lota coming?
SEELIG: I asked him to come.
VEDAH: Why?
SEELIG: Meet your artist—
VEDAH: But, Papa—
SEELIG: [*Playfully.*] Well, scold me.
VEDAH: But—Papa.
SEELIG: First to famish for a little tea—and then to be reprimanded for
    inviting a prospective son-in-law.
VEDAH: I don't want Mr. Burrill and Mr. De Lota to meet.
SEELIG: Not meet—?
VEDAH: Just yet.
SEELIG: Why not?
VEDAH: I haven't told anybody of my engagement to Mr. De Lota.

SEELIG: Well?

VEDAH: Well—he carries himself so—so—

SEELIG: Proudly?

VEDAH: So much like a proprietor that it's hard to explain to others—strangers especially.

SEELIG: By "strangers especially" you mean Mr. Burrill?

VEDAH: Yes.

SEELIG: Is Mr. Burrill's opinion important?

VEDAH: His refinement is important.

SEELIG: Refinement?

VEDAH: Yes—the quality that you admire in men—the quality that Mr. De Lota sometimes lacks.

SEELIG: When—for example?

VEDAH: I've just told you.

SEELIG: Well tell me again.

VEDAH: When he gives the impression of—of—owning me.

SEELIG: [*Pause.*] But after all, isn't there a compliment in that?

VEDAH: There's considerable annoyance in it.

SEELIG: Oh—[*A* BUTLER *enters, gets tea table, which he places center and goes out.*] If you and De Lota announced your engagement his manner might—seem more natural—to strangers especially.

VEDAH: I don't wish it announced.

SEELIG: It was to have been announced in September, wasn't it?

VEDAH: I know—but I'm waiting.

HOLLAND: [*Appearing in doorway and announcing.*] Mrs. Clayton. [MRS. ELINOR CLAYTON, *a blonde and blue-eyed woman of delicate charm and distinction enters.*]

VEDAH: Elinor! [*Kisses her.*] How good of you to come so early.

ELINOR: Doctor.

SEELIG: [*Shaking hands with* MRS. CLAYTON.] Elinor.

ELINOR: [*Seeing the empty tea table.*] Am I the first?

VEDAH: The very first.

SEELIG: If I'm not—counted.

ELINOR: *You're* first in every situation, Doctor. [*To* VEDAH.] I hope to have a moment with your father before the others call.

VEDAH: Professionally?

ELINOR: Don't I look the invalid? How's your mother?

VEDAH: Fine, thank you.

ELINOR: And to see her on a matter about as unimportant as my medical errand.

VEDAH: I'll leave you together while I tell Mama. [*She goes out.*]

ELINOR: [*Sitting.*] When I came to see you last time—?

SEELIG: Yes?

ELINOR: You told me the truth about myself?

SEELIG: My dear Mrs. Clayton.

ELINOR: Of course you did as far as you told me anything, but I thought you might be withholding something.

SEELIG: I don't know a woman in better physical condition. [*He takes a chair beside her.*]

ELINOR: Well, I want you to give me something to make me sleep.

SEELIG: Sleep!

ELINOR: I wake about four in the morning and—stay awake.

SEELIG: How often has this happened?

ELINOR: Ever since I came to see you—and a week before that.

SEELIG: 'M—[*Pause.*] Anything troubling you?

ELINOR: No.

SEELIG: Do you stay wide awake or—only partly so?

ELINOR: Awake.

SEELIG: Thinking?

ELINOR: Yes.

SEELIG: Of what?

ELINOR: Oh—everything.

SEELIG: But principally—?

ELINOR: Principally—[*Pause.*] That old trouble at Atlantic City.

SEELIG: Anything in Frank's conduct to revive that?

ELINOR: No—but—

SEELIG: What?

ELINOR: I think—sometimes that I felt that trouble more than any of us— even *I* thought I felt it.

SEELIG: You forgave Frank, didn't you?

ELINOR: Yes—but it was a good deal for a wife to overlook.

SEELIG: You mean you *didn't* forgive him?

ELINOR: I mean the hurt was deeper than I knew—deeper than I could know except as time taught me its depth.

SEELIG: Your thoughts on that are what wake you in the early morning?

ELINOR: And keep me awake.

SEELIG: Well, let's talk about it.

ELINOR: I don't wish to talk about it, Doctor. [*She moves to a seat near the window.*]

SEELIG: In surgery we sometimes find a condition where a wound has healed too quickly and on the surface only. The treatment is to re-open it entirely. A mental trouble has its analogy. Better talk of it. [*He goes to a seat beside her.*] Frank was foolish. Under the law you might have abandoned him to his folly. In that case, with his temperament—[*Pause.*] Two years? He'd have been—well—"a failure" is too gentle a description. As it is, consider his advancement in the two years—his development—power. All due to your wisdom, my dear Elinor—to your wisdom and forbearance—to your love for him—[*Pause.*] That sums it up—you do love him.

ELINOR: [*Earnestly.*] Yes.

SEELIG: Frank is important—he influences public opinion with his magazines and papers. He addresses an audience of two millions, let us say. In the great scheme of the world Frank is a factor—a big factor—isn't he?

ELINOR: Yes—I suppose he is.

SEELIG: [*Cheeringly.*] Well, there you are. Your abiding love for him made all the difference between success and failure. All the forces radiating from Frank really do so because of your loyalty at a supreme moment. That's a large commission, isn't it? The fates made you their chosen instrument—their deputy. If Frank hadn't needed help you couldn't have given it, could you?

ELINOR: Of course not.

SEELIG: [*Rising energetically.*] Well, don't regret having been useful—be proud of it.

ELINOR: But a man who has once committed such a fault—may do so again.

SEELIG: [*Pleasantly.*] You're assuming that we learn nothing from our mistakes—we men.

ELINOR: Well do you?

SEELIG: [*Smiling.*] As a physician—I'd hate to tell you how much.

ELINOR: I couldn't go through it again.

SEELIG: You won't have to.

ELINOR: [*Going to* SEELIG.] And you won't give me anything for my insomnia?

SEELIG: Isn't a point of view something?

ELINOR: Yes, if I can take it.

SEELIG: You did take it. I saw the care go out of those eyes—and the peace come into them.

ELINOR: [*Pause.*] You're a dear. [*She gratefully and impulsively takes* SEELIG's *hand.*]

VEDAH: May I come in?

SEELIG: Yes. [VEDAH *enters.*]

VEDAH: Mama wants you to come up, Elinor.

ELINOR: Yes—[*As* VEDAH *starts with her.*] Oh, I'll go alone.

VEDAH: But don't desert me entirely. [ELINOR *goes out.*]

SEELIG: Mama not coming down?

VEDAH: No.

[*The* BUTLER *enters with tea service—lighted lamp, etc., which he puts on the table and goes out.*]

SEELIG: When did you first meet Mr. Burrill?

VEDAH: With you—at his exhibition.

SEELIG: *That* was in September.

VEDAH: Yes.

SEELIG: [*Pause.*] Vedah, I want to help Mr. Burrill—

VEDAH: He has a lot of talent.

SEELIG: I'm going to take down my beautiful vases De Lota gave us. [*He caresses a vase on one of the pedestals.*]

VEDAH: They're deadly—

SEELIG: And put up Mr. Burrill's statuettes—

VEDAH: That's helping ourselves.

SEELIG: I'm going to enlist Clayton in Mr. Burrill's fight with the architects.

VEDAH: That's "copy" for Clayton's.

SEELIG: But Mr. Burrill is [*pause*] not a Jew.

VEDAH: [*Pouring tea.*] There's no race nor religion to art, is there?

SEELIG: There frequently is to the artist. [*Tenderly.*] Careful my pet. Remember—your happiness will be—with your own race. [VEDAH *gives* SEELIG *his tea.*]

HOLLAND: [*Appears and announces.*] Mr. Burrill.

VEDAH: Show Mr. Burrill in. [HOLLAND *goes.*]

SEELIG: Second call this week, isn't it?

VEDAH: Yes.

SEELIG: You know, he has *some rights*.

VEDAH: You mean—?

SEELIG: *His* heart—[*Enter* BURRILL, *a young man of twenty-eight years.*]

VEDAH: Good afternoon.

BURRILL: How do you do? [*They shake hands.*]

SEELIG: How are you?

BURRILL: Fine, thank you.

SEELIG: Any more news of the court house decoration?

BURRILL: Nothing different.

VEDAH: How will you take your tea, Mr. Burrill?

BURRILL: Submissively. I take it only because I admire its preparation.

SEELIG: We still struggle along with our vases. [*He indicates the vases on the pedestals.*]

BURRILL: I understand your reluctance to move them.

SEELIG: Only waiting for your statuettes.

BURRILL: They haven't come?

SEELIG: No.

VEDAH: I think they did, Papa. Something dreadfully heavy came this morning.

SEELIG: Well!

VEDAH: I was afraid to unpack them.

BURRILL: [*Laughing.*] They're bronze.

[VEDAH *gives* BURRILL *his tea. She then goes to the door and pushes the electric button.*]

SEELIG: Do you know Clayton—the publisher—Clayton's magazine?

BURRILL: Reputation.

SEELIG: He's a live wire—Clayton.

BURRILL: Yes. [*The* BUTLER *enters.*]

VEDAH: The expressman brought a package this morning?

BUTLER: Yes, M'm—two statues.

VEDAH: How do you know?

BUTLER: I opened it.

VEDAH: You opened it!

BUTLER: [*Looking to* SEELIG.] Mrs. Seelig told me to open it.

VEDAH: Mama told him to open it. Would you have thought it?

SEELIG: [*To* BURRILL.] How was the box addressed?

BURRILL: To you.

SEELIG: [*Dryly.*] I *would* have thought it—yes—

VEDAH: Bring the statuettes here.

BUTLER: They are in Mrs. Seelig's room.

VEDAH: I'll go with you and get them—Excuse me—[VEDAH *and the* BUT-LER *go out.*]

SEELIG: I've asked Clayton to drop in on his way uptown.

BURRILL: I shall be glad to meet him.

SEELIG: *Mrs.* Clayton is here. Have you met *her?*

BURRILL: No.

SEELIG: She was a Miss Hoover. Judge Hoover's daughter.

BURRILL: [*Nodding.*] The newspapers keep one pretty well informed.

SEELIG: Unfortunate, that notoriety.

BURRILL: Can't be agreeable.

SEELIG: Prosperity tries a man more than poverty does—

BURRILL: So I've read—

SEELIG: Clayton makes two millions a year from his publications—

BURRILL: Think of it!

SEELIG: His temptations were proportionate to his sudden success and— well, she is a most sensible woman.

BURRILL: Forgave everything I believe.

SEELIG: Not too meekly—I assure you—but—they have a little boy and—

as I say—she is a most sensible woman. As for Clayton—well I guess Clayton is sufficiently contrite.

[VEDAH *and the* BUTLER *re-enter, the* BUTLER *carries two bronze figurines.*]

VEDAH: [*Indicating a pedestal.*] I think the *girl* on that pillar—And the man on that one—

SEELIG: I'd put the girl here—

VEDAH: Why?

SEELIG: See it first. [*He takes the female figure from the* BUTLER *who places the male figure on the floor and goes out.*]

VEDAH: She's too darling for anything.

SEELIG: [*Placing the statuette on the tea table.*] Your figures are even handsomer here, than at the exhibition.

BURRILL: The room helps them.

SEELIG: [*With the statuette which he displays.*] Look, Vedah! Isn't she graceful in every view?

VEDAH: She is.

SEELIG: Do you know your nymph reminds me of those stunning little things by Theodore Riviere?

BURRILL: That's very interesting. The girl that posed for this was a model for Riviere.

SEELIG: [*Playfully.*] Well, there you are—I shall set up as a connoisseur.

VEDAH: You promised to bring her photograph.

BURRILL: I have brought it.

SEELIG: [*Half anxiously.*] But—posing?

BURRILL: Oh, no—street costume.

SEELIG: Oh—

BURRILL: There—[*He takes a photograph from his pocket and hands it to* VEDAH.]

SEELIG: [*Sitting comfortably.*] I don't know why sculpture is much more modest than photography—but—it is.

BURRILL: The artist is a mediator.

SEELIG: Does that explain it?

BURRILL: Doesn't it?

SEELIG: I don't know—I've never been an artist.

VEDAH: Nor a photographer.

SEELIG: Nor, for that matter, a beautiful female model.

VEDAH: [*Carrying the photograph to* SEELIG.] See, Papa—isn't that face angelic?

SEELIG: It is—It is—[*To* BURRILL.] And I dare say the lady herself was—[*Indicates abandon.*]

BURRILL: No—she wasn't a bad sort. She has a right to the face.

VEDAH: [*With girlish enthusiasm.*] Those eyes, Papa! And that beautiful nose and mouth. Why, anybody could *love* her.

BURRILL: Well—a good many did.

VEDAH: Of whom does she make you—think?

SEELIG: Some player.

VEDAH: Duse. [SEELIG *nods.*]

BURRILL: The resemblance is often remarked.

VEDAH: She should have been an actress.

BURRILL: [*Shaking his head.*] She tried acting and failed.

VEDAH: Did you see her?

BURRILL: Before my time. Antoine gave her a very good chance in his theatre, but—she was only a model.

SEELIG: Yes, if Antoine couldn't make her act. [VEDAH *returns the photograph to* BURRILL.]

BURRILL: But—a fine girl for all that—warm hearted—most grateful to the man who had got her the chance.

VEDAH: Well, if anybody got me a place in Antoine's theatre I'd be grateful. [*She returns to the statuette examining it closely.*] I'm sorry we can't see her mouth.

SEELIG: You can't? [*Also examines the statuette.*]

BURRILL: No—our early Greeks played with those pipes tied to the face.

VEDAH: I'm going to put her on her pedestal.

BURRILL: Let me. [*He takes the statuette from the table.*]

VEDAH: Take your old vases, Papa.

BURRILL: Old vases!

SEELIG: [*Taking the vases from the pedestals.*] The finest specimens in America, Mr. Burrill.

BURRILL: Exquisite—where did you find them.

SEELIG: Benjamin De Lota brought them from Genoa. De Lota does art and music for Clayton.

BURRILL: Charming.

SEELIG: I shall promote them to my library. [*He goes toward the door.*] I—I regard them somewhat as a bribe.

BURRILL: A bribe?

VEDAH: [*Expostulating.*] Papa!

SEELIG: De Lota gave them to me—and in the same interview asked me to—to become his father-in-law—an intimate and antique relation— a time-honored method. [*Regards vases.*] Ah, well. [SEELIG *goes out through the library door.*]

BURRILL: [*Dashed with the news.*] His father-in-law.

VEDAH: You hadn't heard? [BURRILL *shakes head, avoiding her gaze.*] Why, yes. [*Pause.*] May I pour you some more tea?

BURRILL: No, thank you. [*He walks away.*]

VEDAH: Do you know Mr. De Lota?

BURRILL: No.

VEDAH: He wrote that beautiful notice in Clayton's about your work.

BURRILL: [*Moodily at window.*] I know his articles, of course.

VEDAH: Shan't we put up the dancing man too?

BURRILL: [*Rousing himself.*] Let me. [*He puts the male figurine on the second pedestal.*]

VEDAH: They go well there, don't they?

BURRILL: Very well.

VEDAH: Attendant spirits of my fireside.

BURRILL: They are honored.

VEDAH: Do you know why I like them?

BURRILL: Why?

VEDAH: [*Impressively.*] They are just a girl and a man—nothing more—with their pan pipes—their freedom—the joy of existence—

BURRILL: [*Forcing a gayety.*] That sounds like paganism.

VEDAH: I am a pagan.

BURRILL: And the gentleman?

VEDAH: Mr. De Lota?

BURRILL: Yes.

VEDAH: Mr. De Lota—is a Jew.

BURRILL: [*Pause.*] Well, I'm a pagan myself—a Walter Pater pagan.

VEDAH: Oh, yes. I, too, must have the sunshine, the poetry festivals.

BURRILL: And you saw somewhat of that in my little figures?

VEDAH: Yes—

BURRILL: You hinted as much that day at the exhibition—thousands had walked by and looked at their catalogues you—only you—interpreted them. I can't tell you how much that meant to me.

VEDAH: I wonder if you know—that we—[*Pause.*]

BURRILL: We what?

VEDAH: Were never introduced to each other.

BURRILL: I hug that to my memory.

VEDAH: A friend offered—but I fibbed. I said I *knew* you already. An introduction would have been—well—[*Rises impatiently.*]

BURRILL: What?

VEDAH: A straight-jacket on your dancer. [*She pauses and comes near him.*] But it has been wrong to make you call here, hasn't it?

BURRILL: Has it?

VEDAH: Tell *me.*

BURRILL: [*With renewed fervor.*] Not if they are really to be the attendant spirits.

VEDAH: [*Evading his manner and going to the first statuette.*] Why did you get her a place in Antoine's theatre?

BURRILL: I didn't.

VEDAH: Then how do you know she was grateful?

BURRILL: The man who got her the place—afterwards committed—committed a crime and was on trial in Paris. Mimi had then become a model and was posing for Riviere and me and other artists. She dragged us—Antoine—Riviere—me—everybody—to the court house in a frenzied effort to free him.

VEDAH: Maybe she loved him.

BURRILL: I think not—simply gratitude for his interest. But that's a rare virtue. [MRS. ELINOR CLAYTON *returns to the room.*]

VEDAH: Mrs. Clayton, may I present Mr. Julian Burrill, the sculptor.

ELINOR: Mr. Burrill. [*She gives* BURRILL *her hand.*]

VEDAH: Mrs. Clayton is *the* Mrs. Clayton.

ELINOR: You must look as though you knew.

BURRILL: My struggle is to conceal, my knowledge—

ELINOR: [*To* VEDAH.] All that you've told me of him seems to be true.

BURRILL: So quickly?

VEDAH: One or two lumps? And look at my Greek playmates.

ELINOR: [*Seeing the statuettes.*] Charming. [*To* VEDAH.] Two please. [*She turns to the dancing nymph.*] Think of wanting to vote when one may do that.

BURRILL: Exactly.

VEDAH: And cream?

ELINOR: Lemon please. [*To* BURRILL.] You're a dangerous man.

BURRILL: I?

ELINOR: With that degree of flattery.

BURRILL: *That's* a servile portrait.

ELINOR: Really?

VEDAH: Show Mrs. Clayton the photograph.

BURRILL: [*Passing the photo to* ELINOR.] Model.

ELINOR: I know this woman.

VEDAH: Resembles Duse.

ELINOR: In Paris.

BURRILL: Yes.

ELINOR: She writes for the papers.

BURRILL: I hardly think writes for the papers.

ELINOR: French papers—yes. And she represents Mr. Clayton's publications.

BURRILL: I shouldn't have thought it.

VEDAH: You've met her?

ELINOR: A moment—yes—in this same hat and gown. [*She hands the photograph to* VEDAH.] Mr. Clayton said she spoke no English though she understood it fairly. Frank introduced her as a writer—she smiled assent—

BURRILL: [*Reclaiming the photograph.*] Possible.

HOLLAND: [*Entering and announcing.*] Mr. De Lota. [BENJAMIN DE LOTA *enters. He is a tall, aggressive and intellectual Spanish Jew of thirty-five years or so.* HOLLAND *goes out.*]

VEDAH: Good afternoon.

DE LOTA: [*Taking her hand with much manner.*] Vedah.

VEDAH: Mrs. Clayton you know?

DE LOTA: Yes—how are you. [ELINOR *nods to him.*]

VEDAH: And let me introduce Mr. Burrill.

DE LOTA: Mr. Burrill. [*The men shake hands.*]

BURRILL: [*Seriously.*] I've an impression of having met you in Paris.

DE LOTA: I'm often there.

VEDAH: Some tea?

DE LOTA: Not any, thank you. [*To* ELINOR.] I thought Frank was to be here?

ELINOR: He is.

DE LOTA: Good. [*To* BURRILL.] Doctor Seelig has told Frank—Mrs. Clayton's husband—about your row with the architects.

BURRILL: I hardly call it a row.

DE LOTA: Better call it a row and make it a row or you'll never get a chance at the big sculpture. Once let a ring do all the work and you young fellows can starve or be journeymen. Thank God, Clayton's a Westerner, believes in the open shop.

BURRILL: We want his influence, but not to involve him.

DE LOTA: Magazines must print something. [*He goes to* ELINOR.] Frank will clasp him and his row to our bosom with hooks of steel, won't he?

ELINOR: How do you spell steel?

DE LOTA: I follow the market. [*To* VEDAH.] Where's Papa?

VEDAH: Finding the post of honor in his library for your vases.

DE LOTA: [*Noting the pedestals.*] Oh—yours?

BURRILL: Yes.

DE LOTA: [*Regarding the dancing girl.*] Charming.

ELINOR: Does she impress you as a co-worker?

DE LOTA: Co-worker—no—co-respondent—yes.

ELINOR: I mean as a fellow member of the profession?

DE LOTA: Which profession?

ELINOR: Journalism.

DE LOTA: By nothing except the willingness to increase her circulation.

VEDAH: Mrs. Clayton says the lady represents your magazine in Paris.

DE LOTA: I dare say I'm dull—but—?

BURRILL: Not the statuette—the model—Mimi Chardenet.

DE LOTA: Mimi Chardenet—Europa?

BURRILL: Yes.

DE LOTA: Was Mimi your model? [BURRILL *nods*.] I might have known it. [*He turns admiringly to the bronze.*]

ELINOR: Why do you say "Europa?"

DE LOTA: Mimi *was* "Europa" at the Quat'z Arts ball this year.

ELINOR: Europa—mythological, isn't it?

DE LOTA: Yes.

VEDAH: [*As* ELINOR *looks to her.*] I remember something of Europa in our literature class—must be all right.

DE LOTA: Disappointingly proper.

ELINOR: But the lady at the ball?

DE LOTA: Costume—well, somewhat less than this.

ELINOR: Less?

DE LOTA: [*Nodding.*] Without the pipes—mounted on a sleek black bull which the students led about the ball room.

ELINOR: Show Mr. De Lota the photograph.

DE LOTA: [*Taking photo from* BURRILL.] That's Mimi.

ELINOR: Let me have it again. [DE LOTA *gives* ELINOR *the photograph.*]

BURRILL: Can she possibly have also written?

DE LOTA: Mimi a blue stocking? I leave it to you.

ELINOR: Frank knows this woman.

DE LOTA: Your husband?

ELINOR: Yes.

DE LOTA: Of course. I introduced him.

ELINOR: I was sure of it. [DE LOTA *is startled by* ELINOR*'s seriousness.*]

SEELIG: [*Calling from the library.*] Vedah.

VEDAH: Yes, Papa.

SEELIG: You and Mr. Burrill come here a moment.

VEDAH: [*To* BURRILL.] He wants us—[*To others.*] He doesn't know you are here.

DE LOTA: Don't disturb him on my account.

VEDAH: Your vases anyway—I expect—

BURRILL: [*Excusing his going.*] Pardon. [ELINOR *nods.* VEDAH *and* BURRILL *go to the library.*]

DE LOTA: [*Alone with* ELINOR.] Well?

ELINOR: Well?

DE LOTA: We do meet, don't we?

ELINOR: Vedah didn't tell me you were to be here.

DE LOTA: The Doctor invited me.

ELINOR: Meetings of this kind—I can't help.

DE LOTA: But you won't ask me to your home.

ELINOR: Frank asks you.

DE LOTA: I'll come when *you* ask me.

ELINOR: I shan't ask you.

DE LOTA: Why?

ELINOR: [*Pause.*] You know why.

DE LOTA: I don't.

ELINOR: [*Going to the statuette.*] This model—you say you introduced Frank to her?

DE LOTA: Yes.

ELINOR: When?

DE LOTA: This year.

ELINOR: Where?

DE LOTA: Paris—Quat'z Arts ball. It was her pose as Europa that caught—Frank's—caught his eye.

ELINOR: I remember the newspaper comment the day after. On that particular night—Frank went to a meeting of the American Chamber of Commerce.

DE LOTA: So did I. At those student dances the interesting things don't begin until midnight.

ELINOR: I see.

DE LOTA: [*Insistently.*] But you're changing the subject. Frank and I see a good deal of each other at the office. He begins to think it strange I don't accept his invitations to the house.

ELINOR: Why haven't you?

DE LOTA: He said he wanted me to call, to know you better—[*Smiles.*] I saw you'd told him nothing—so—I await *your* invitation.

ELINOR: You were away when Frank and I first met. [DE LOTA *nods.*] Away when we married—[DE LOTA *nods.*] I suppose all husbands ask their wives if they've ever cared for anyone else—[*She leaves the fireplace and goes to the window.*]

DE LOTA: [*Pause.*] And you said—?

ELINOR: I said no. Smile if you wish but—I hadn't loved anyone as I loved him.

DE LOTA: [*Following.*] Naturally.

ELINOR: So what I said was true.

DE LOTA: By the feminine standard—yes.

ELINOR: That's one of the things I always disliked in you, Ben.

DE LOTA: What?

ELINOR: Your talk of feminine standards and masculine standards. In morals there is just one standard.

DE LOTA: [*Laughing.*] Were there *many* other things you disliked in me?

ELINOR: This is one other.

DE LOTA: What?

ELINOR: Your mood of cat-like cruelty.

DE LOTA: Cruelty—cat-like?

ELINOR: Yes—cruelty—and it goes with your smile. That is like a cat's—your manner is like a cat's. When you play the piano it is a cat walking on the keys.

DE LOTA: There were times, however, when you asked me to play.

ELINOR: There are times when I like cats.

DE LOTA: Elinor—[*He starts impulsively toward her.*]

ELINOR: [*Avoiding him.*] No—

DE LOTA: [*Regarding her with admiration.*] Damn it—we'd have been happy together—you and I.

ELINOR: No.

DE LOTA: The history of my people supports me.

ELINOR: Spanish history?

DE LOTA: Jewish history. Our girls have often been unhappy when they've married outside. But our men—have absorbed the women of other races.

ELINOR: You mustn't talk to me in that strain. [*She walks angrily away.*]

DE LOTA: A man in sentimental bankruptcy may at least enumerate his assets. We *would* have been happy.

ELINOR: No.

DE LOTA: One of us would have been happy, of that—I'm sure. I loved you, Elinor, because you were a queen—me you sacrificed because—[*Pause.*] I was a Jew.

ELINOR: And because you are a Jew you still speak of it.

DE LOTA: Exactly.

ELINOR: But you must cease to speak of it.

DE LOTA: Not while you listen.

ELINOR: [*Starting toward the door.*] I will never be alone with you again.

DE LOTA: [*Interposing.*] Then I must tell you now.

ELINOR: [*Commandingly.*] Play something or I shall leave.

DE LOTA: Thank you—I prefer this way myself. [*He laughs and goes to the piano which he plays brilliantly and with passion.* SEELIG, VEDAH *and* BURRILL *re-enter in turn and join* ELINOR. *Enter* HOLLAND *who whispers to* SEELIG. SEELIG *goes out with* HOLLAND *and returns with* CLAYTON *as piano ceases.*]

VEDAH: [*Meeting* CLAYTON *and shaking his hand.*] We feared you were for-
getting us.

CLAYTON: Never—[*he nods to his wife*] my dear.

VEDAH: Mr. Clayton, may I present Mr. Julian Burrill.

CLAYTON: [*To* BURRILL.] I thought you an older man.

VEDAH: He is. [BURRILL *laughs.*]

CLAYTON: In the Salon six years ago, weren't you?

BURRILL: Yes.

CLAYTON: *Medal*, if I remember? [BURRILL *nods.* CLAYTON *turns to* SEELIG
with a shrug.]

SEELIG: No justice at all in the discrimination of these architects.

ELINOR: [*Calmly.*] That is Mr. Burrill's latest work. [*She indicates the
dancing figurine.*]

CLAYTON: Charming.

ELINOR: Do you recognize the lady?

CLAYTON: [*Playfully.*] I'd like to.

ELINOR: Mimi Chardenet.

CLAYTON: Chardenet?

ELINOR: You must remember—rode the black bull at the Quat'z Arts ball.
[*A swift glance passes between* DE LOTA *and* CLAYTON.]

CLAYTON: Ah, indeed. [*To* BURRILL.] From that celebrated model. [BUR-
RILL *nods.*]

ELINOR: [*To* BURRILL.] Let Mr. Clayton see the photograph.

BURRILL: I can't think it would interest him. [CLAYTON *tries to engage*
SEELIG *in conversation.*]

ELINOR: Oh, yes. [*To* CLAYTON.] Frank! [CLAYTON *turns to her.*] Look at
this photograph—please. [*To* BURRILL.]

BURRILL: [*Reluctantly yielding the photograph.*] Miss Seelig had some curiosity about it.

CLAYTON: Oh, yes.

ELINOR: Mr. Burrill was inclined to doubt that the lady represented your
magazines.

CLAYTON: [*Evasively.*] Oh, that arrangement was never completed—discussed but—[*He returns the photograph to* BURRILL.]

DE LOTA: [*Trying to help the strained situation.*] Mimi had more than one
side to her.

ELINOR: [*Regarding the bronze.*] So it appears.

DE LOTA: I mean she could think. Antoine told me that she caught the
meaning of a line—as quickly as any woman that ever came into his
theatre.

VEDAH: [*Starting at the name.*] Antoine?

DE LOTA: Yes, Antoine the manager. I got her a place in his company.

VEDAH: When was that?

DE LOTA: Oh, nine or ten years ago before she posed professionally. [VEDAH *looks to* BURRILL *who avoids her inquiry.*]

CLAYTON: She said she could write of the theatre.

ELINOR: Well—I must go.

VEDAH: Really? Am I to be the only woman in this council of war?

ELINOR: Leave it *all* to the men, my dear.

CLAYTON: The car's at the door—take it if you wish.

ELINOR: [*Frigidly.*] I'll walk, thank you. [*Pause.*] Mr. Burrill, I'm very glad to have seen you.

BURRILL: Thank you.

ELINOR: And your model—well—a delightful reminder of Paris, Mr. De Lota. [DE LOTA *turns to her.*] As you also know the lady, Mr. De Lota—*you* shall tell me more of her. I hope you'll call on us. [*She gives* DE LOTA *her hand.*]

DE LOTA: I've been promising Mr. Clayton to do so.

ELINOR: You must—[*Going with* VEDAH *to the hall.*] You'll bring Mr. Burrill to see me too?

VEDAH: Delighted, Mrs. Clayton. [VEDAH *and* ELINOR *go out.*]

DE LOTA: I put my foot in it—but—hang it, I was completely off guard. Mrs. Clayton said "Why Frank knows this woman" and I blurted "of course—I introduced him." [*Turns to* BURRILL *for confirmation.*]

CLAYTON: Forget it.

SEELIG: Trouble?

CLAYTON: *En promenade* with the girl—Elinor met us. I said business.

SEELIG: [*Seriously.*] 'Mmm. Too bad after—the—the other trouble so soon.

CLAYTON: Damn it—a man can't go to Paris and live on bread and milk. I've got to know the world I live in. I publish three magazines and a metropolitan newspaper.

SEELIG: The wife met you walking with the woman?

CLAYTON: That's all—[*To* DE LOTA *with some anxiety.*] You told her nothing more?

DE LOTA: [*Expostulating.*] My dear Frank—

CLAYTON: [*Relieved.*] Oh, I can fix it. [VEDAH *enters.*]

SEELIG: Well—shall we discuss this business of the architects?

CLAYTON: Yes.

SEELIG: Suppose we go into the library—I've your papers there, Mr. Burrill.

CLAYTON: Yes. [*The men start to the library.*]

VEDAH: Mr. Burrill! I'll send Mr. Burrill immediately.

BURRILL: [*To* SEELIG.] You permit me? [SEELIG *pauses, regards* VEDAH *intently*—DE LOTA, CLAYTON *and* SEELIG *go out.*]

VEDAH: [*In sudden alarm.*] He is the man—I saw your face when he said he had introduced this girl to Antoine.

BURRILL: Antoine's name startled me—that was all—and—

VEDAH: You thought you'd seen *him* in Paris.

BURRILL: Probably did—many times.

VEDAH: You think you saw him in that court room—on trial for a crime.

BURRILL: [*Evasively.*] No—no.

VEDAH: The man on trial had spoken to Antoine for the girl.

BURRILL: A dozen men may have done that. Engagements in the theatre require many introductions.

VEDAH: I read the doubt in your heart. You're not the conventional coward that most men are—tell me. I am promised to *marry* Benjamin De Lota—doesn't that mean anything to *you*?

BURRILL: Mean anything!—[*He starts impulsively toward* VEDAH, *stops and after a moment's effort at self-control says calmly and tenderly.*] I love you! [VEDAH *inhales quickly, her glance falls before* BURRILL'*s look, she turns irresolutely toward the room into which* DE LOTA *has gone—a pause.*]

ACT II

SCENE: *Lounging room of* MR. FRANK CLAYTON'*s house. The walls are covered with green canvas on which is a profusion of illustrations furnished to Clayton's magazines by various artists. The room, square and shallow and low, is furnished in mahogany and leather. Two five foot "arches" on either side of centre open to rooms back. That at right shows hallway in red, with staircase leading to second story. That at left shows music room in yellow with Chippendale furniture and pictures in gilt frames. A sofa above fireplace which is at right, stands at right angle to fireplace. A low table for tobacco is at end of this sofa. On this table is a big reading lamp. A large writing table is at back. A smaller table near the window at left side has a desk telephone.*

At Rise of Curtain *the stage is empty.* MRS. SEELIG *and* VEDAH *and* ELINOR *enter from the dining room by a door above the fireplace. They are in evening gowns.*

MRS. SEELIG: Vedah.

VEDAH: Mama?

MRS. SEELIG: [*To* ELINOR.] Mr. Clayton's found my gloves, but my handkerchief is gone.

ELINOR: [*Starting back to dining room.*] I'll get it.

MRS. SEELIG: Let Vedah.

ELINOR: No trouble. [*She goes out.*]

VEDAH: See this picture, Mama.

MRS. SEELIG: Which?

VEDAH: This.

MRS. SEELIG: What is it?

VEDAH: At Jerusalem. "The Wailing Wall."

MRS. SEELIG: Poor fellows. It's dreadful to take religion so seriously. [ELINOR *enters.*]

ELINOR: Mr. De Lota is bringing your handkerchief—wouldn't let me have it.

MRS. SEELIG: An excuse to join us. [DE LOTA *enters from the dining room waving a lace handkerchief playfully.*]

DE LOTA: Found! Lady's handkerchief—no marks.

MRS. SEELIG: [*Extending her hand.*] Thank you.

DE LOTA: [*Withholding the handkerchief.*] On one consideration. [*To* ELINOR.] Mrs. Seelig says the talking machine has spoiled—Celeste Aida—for her ears—[*To* MRS. SEELIG.] If you think you are mistaken when you hear Caruso tonight—you must stand up and wave this to me as a signal of surrender.

MRS. SEELIG: I agree—[*takes handkerchief*] because we shall be too late to hear that solo.

DE LOTA: Sharp practice, madam.

ELINOR: Are we so late!

VEDAH: Oh—let's not hurry.

DE LOTA: This room attracts me more than the opera. [*He regards the drawings on the wall.*]

MRS. SEELIG: Originals, aren't they?

ELINOR: Yes. They were in the offices of the magazine when Mr. Clayton bought it.

DE LOTA: Here's one by Frost. I used to watch for his sketches when I was a boy. [SUTTON, *the Clayton butler, enters with coffee.*]

MRS. SEELIG: [*At another drawing.*] And Remington—[*To the* BUTLER.] Thank you—[*Takes coffee.*]

[CLAYTON *and* BURRILL *come from the dining room.*]

CLAYTON: You found the cigars?

DE LOTA: I'll take a cigarette. [*He does so.*]

ELINOR: [*To* BURRILL.] Here's a libretto of Aida. Find that passage of which you spoke.

BURRILL: There were several.

MRS. SEELIG: Our coffee won't interfere with your cigars.

DE LOTA: Do you mind?

ELINOR: This room is dedicated to nicotine. [*To* MRS. SEELIG.] Besides, we're going to take Mr. De Lota to the piano.

DE LOTA: Are you?

ELINOR: [*To* VEDAH.] Aren't we?

VEDAH: We are.

BURRILL: Here's one place—[*His pencil breaks*]. Ah!

CLAYTON: [*Offering a pencil attached to his watch chain.*] Here.

BURRILL: [*Giving libretto to* CLAYTON.] Just mark that passage—"my native land," etc. [*To* ELINOR.] Now follow that when Aida sings Italian and note how the English stumbles.

ELINOR: Thank you. [*To* CLAYTON *as she takes book.*] Will you order the car?

CLAYTON: I have done so.

ELINOR: [*To* DE LOTA.] Come. [ELINOR, MRS. SEELIG, VEDAH *and* DE LOTA *go to the music room by the arch left.*]

BURRILL: [*To* CLAYTON *with whom he is alone.*] See here—I've an idea you'd go to the opera if it weren't for me.

CLAYTON: My boy, a box at the opera is the blackmail—a man pays for a quiet evening at home.

BURRILL: [*Laughing.*] Many men do go.

CLAYTON: And sleep on the rear chairs. No! I *planned* to stay home— you're part of the excuse. [SUTTON *enters with a note.*] Excuse me. [*Pause. Reads superscription on the note.*] Vedah—[BURRILL *gets a cigarette.* CLAYTON *goes to the door of the music room and calls.*] Vedah! [VEDAH *comes to him.*] They pursue you even here. [*He laughingly gives* VEDAH *the note which she opens and quickly scans.* SUTTON *goes.*]

VEDAH: [*Speaking to the ladies and* DE LOTA *who are not in view.*] Papa will be late. Mrs. Clayton mustn't wait for us.

CLAYTON: Our car carries seven. [ELINOR *and* MRS. SEELIG *appear in the doorway*—DE LOTA *follows, they enter.*]

ELINOR: I'm sure we can make room.

CLAYTON: *Make* room! You're only four!

ELINOR: Mr. De Lota and I are to stop for the Underwoods.

MRS. SEELIG: And we have our cousins Friedman.

DE LOTA: *I* can take a taxi.

VEDAH: That won't help—Papa is *coming* here—but later.

MRS. SEELIG: You go ahead, Mrs. Clayton.

VEDAH: Yes.

ELINOR: [*To* DE LOTA.] What do you think?

DE LOTA: Any time for me—but—the Underwoods—!
[SUTTON *enters.*]

SUTTON: The automobile. [ELINOR *nods;* SUTTON *goes.*]

MRS. SEELIG: It's all settled—you go. So much formality. [*She and* CLAYTON *go to music room.*]

ELINOR: Take this for me. [*Hands libretto to* DE LOTA.]

VEDAH: [*Going out with* ELINOR.] Papa will probably be here before you get away. [ELINOR *goes upstairs talking with* VEDAH. *They disappear.*]

BURRILL: [*As* DE LOTA *starts to music room.*] Mr. De Lota—were you in Paris eight years ago?

DE LOTA: [*Returning.*] Yes—and twenty-eight years ago—I'm there every year.

BURRILL: Did you ever—visit the Cour d'Assizes?

DE LOTA: Occasionally—if some interesting case were on—

BURRILL: I remember one very interesting case—A husband punished his wife and also her lover—by imprisonment.

DE LOTA: The French law *has* that absurd possibility.

BURRILL: The lover was sentenced to a year's imprisonment.

DE LOTA: He was fortunate—the court in its discretion might have given him two years.

BURRILL: You are more minutely informed on the subject than the average American.

DE LOTA: I am more minutely informed on *most* subjects than the average American. I know somewhat of character—of men's temperaments and motives, Mr. Burrill. And your interest in my life at Paris is very serviceable just now.

BURRILL: Indeed!

DE LOTA: Indeed yes. I've been at a loss to understand the change in Miss Seelig's deportment toward myself. I was charging it to your superior attraction. I see it was due to your power of insinuation.

BURRILL: I have insinuated nothing about you.

DE LOTA: You have been direct?

BURRILL: I've avoided discussing your life in Paris.

DE LOTA: That is wise, Mr. Burrill. In fact, you could do only one thing that would be more wise.

BURRILL: Yes?

DE LOTA: Avoid discussing *any* of my affairs.

BURRILL: My *instinct* is to do that.

DE LOTA: Thank you! [*He turns away.*]

BURRILL: [*Following.*] Except with one person.

DE LOTA: You mean—the lady?

BURRILL: I mean you. I expect to discuss them with *you* rather frankly.

DE LOTA: I shall be pleased. [*He throws the libretto on the table and confronts* BURRILL.]

ELINOR: [*Entering.*] Ready, Mr. De Lota?

DE LOTA: [*Smiling.*] You excuse me? [BURRILL *nods.* DE LOTA *disappears in the hallway.*]

ELINOR: I wish you were going with us.

BURRILL: I wish I were. [CLAYTON *re-enters from the music room.*]

ELINOR: You'll see Dick, won't you?

CLAYTON: Yes.

ELINOR: He's not started to undress yet. Miss Doane never knows how to manage him. [BURRILL *joins* VEDAH *and disappears with her in music room.*]

CLAYTON: [*Alone with* ELINOR.] Don't worry. Good night.

ELINOR: Good night. [CLAYTON *offers to kiss her.*] No.

CLAYTON: Still cross patch?

ELINOR: We can't laugh it off, Frank.

CLAYTON: Think we can *pout* it off?

ELINOR: I think you can't tread my sensibilities into the mire by your affairs with other women and expect me to smile at cue.

CLAYTON: Women!—One girl—and a man's natural curiosity about her type. Hang it—there must be some freedom.

ELINOR: Do you suggest more than you've had?

CLAYTON: I suggest domestic peace—or any other punishment than this deadly sulking.

ELINOR: You've admitted you went to the woman's room.

CLAYTON: Admitted nothing. I candidly told you I had gone there—*told* you in order that you might know all.

ELINOR: All that you were willing to tell.

CLAYTON: I can't keep pace with your imagination.

ELINOR: Your wish to have me "know all" is six months after the fact and when her photograph accidentally exposed you!

CLAYTON: If you're kicking on the tardiness of your news service, I'm with you.

ELINOR: I'm resenting your breach of faith.

CLAYTON: Don't assume any covenant, my dear, that doesn't exist.

ELINOR: Do you deny your promises after the affair of two years ago?

CLAYTON: I didn't promise to stagnate. I'm a publisher with a newsman's curiosity about the world he lives in.

ELINOR: And what of a woman's curiosity?

CLAYTON: Colossal! But not privileged. Curiosity of that kind in a woman is idle and immoral!

ELINOR: And in a man?

CLAYTON: A man's on the firing line—a woman's in the commissariat.

ELINOR: Which is a fine way of saying you have a license for transgression that your wife has not.

CLAYTON: If you will—yes.

ELINOR: [*After a defiant pause.*] You're mistaken. [DE LOTA *enters in wrap and carrying his hat.*]

DE LOTA: Ready?

ELINOR: Yes. [*To* CLAYTON.] You'll go up to Dick occasionally?

CLAYTON: Certainly.

ELINOR: [*Calls.*] Good night, Mr. Burrill—good night. [*To* MRS. SEELIG *and* VEDAH.] I feel awfully selfish. [MRS. SEELIG, VEDAH *and* BURRILL *come from music room.*]

MRS. SEELIG: Good night.

VEDAH: Lovely time at dinner. [ELINOR *and* DE LOTA *start out.*]

CLAYTON: [*Getting the libretto from table.*] Here—isn't this your libretto?

ELINOR: Thank you. [*Takes it and goes out with* DE LOTA. *Sound of front door closing.*]

[MRS. SEELIG, VEDAH, *and* BURRILL *are with* CLAYTON.]

MRS. SEELIG: Now, if Papa doesn't come for us—you have us both on your hands.

DICK: [*Coming down the stairs and calling.*] Mama—Mama.

CLAYTON: Mama's gone, Dick. Don't let him call that way, Miss Doane. [DICK *and* MISS DOANE, *the governess, appear in hallway.*]

DICK: I want Mama.

MRS. SEELIG: Here's Auntie Seelig, my dear—won't she do? [MISS DOANE *and* DICK *enter.*]

CLAYTON: It's much after his bed time.

MISS DOANE: I don't think he's well, Mr. Clayton.

DICK: My throat hurts.

CLAYTON: Throat *hurts*?

MISS DOANE: He complained at supper. I didn't tell Mrs. Clayton because she's so easily alarmed.

CLAYTON: [*Taking* DICK *to the lamp.*] Let me see your throat, Dick. Open your mouth. [*To* BURRILL.] You know anything about throats?

BURRILL: Not inside.

VEDAH: Mama does.

MRS. SEELIG: Papa Seelig's coming in a few minutes, Dick—he'll cure your throat. [*To* CLAYTON *as she takes the boy's face in her hands.*] Feverish.

CLAYTON: [*To* MISS DOANE.] Let him wait then and see the Doctor.

MRS. SEELIG: Doctor can see him better in the nursery. Come Dick—Auntie Seelig will tell you a pretty story while Miss Doane gets you to bed.

DICK: [*To* CLAYTON.] Carry me.

CLAYTON: [*Laughing.*] Carry you? You're taking advantage of all this sympathy. [*Picks him up.*] Excuse me—[*To* BURRILL *and* VEDAH.]

MRS. SEELIG: What is a father for—with his magazines and newspapers—if he can't carry a little boy upstairs, eh? [*Goes with* MISS DOANE *after* CLAYTON *who carries* DICK *upstairs.*]

VEDAH: Looks sick, doesn't he?

BURRILL: [*Nodding.*] Poor kid.

VEDAH: He wants his mother. If Papa says he's ill I can go to Mrs. Clayton's box and let her know.

BURRILL: Yes.

VEDAH: Have you noticed the disposition of our two parties?

BURRILL: Disposition?

VEDAH: Mr. De Lota escorts Mrs. Clayton.

BURRILL: *Mr.* Clayton doesn't care for the opera.

VEDAH: Some of my friends have been good enough to comment on the frequency of Mr. De Lota's calls.

BURRILL: [*Pause.*] Do you care?

VEDAH: A woman's natural—pride.

BURRILL: But—heartaches? [VEDAH *shakes head.*] Does Mrs. Clayton know of your engagement?

VEDAH: No. [*Pause.*] Have you done what I asked you?

BURRILL: What?

VEDAH: A letter to Paris.

BURRILL: There's none to whom I could write—on such a subject.

VEDAH: Your model friend—she is still there?

BURRILL: I suppose so.

VEDAH: Why not a line to her?

BURRILL: [*Evasively.*] She owes me nothing.

VEDAH: Well—?

BURRILL: She'd probably take alarm and forward the letter to the man himself.

VEDAH: Why "forward"—has he left the country?

BURRILL: [*Quickly recovering.*] Probably—or perhaps not—but—either way—nothing accomplished.

VEDAH: Either way nothing lost. Won't you try?

BURRILL: [*Disturbed.*] It isn't a manly thing to do—even against a *rival.*

VEDAH: [*Smiling.*] Thank you.

BURRILL: Why?

VEDAH: Rival.

BURRILL: Well?

VEDAH: So far you've said only that you loved me.

BURRILL: You don't resent—rival?

VEDAH: Does any woman?

BURRILL: [*With quick look about.*] You know, if there weren't so many doors here—[*Approaches her.*]

VEDAH: [*Retreating.*] No—[CLAYTON *re-appears on stairs.*]

BURRILL: [*Changing the subject.*] And all originals. [*Indicates framed sketches.*]

VEDAH: So wonderful to have them, isn't it? [*Enter* CLAYTON.]

CLAYTON: Boy's certainly not himself.

VEDAH: Poor child. [SUTTON *enters.*]

SUTTON: [*Announcing.*] Dr. Seelig. [*Enter* SEELIG. *He is in evening dress and wears a cloak.*]

SEELIG: Good evening Frank. [*Shakes hands with* CLAYTON.] Mr. Burrill.

BURRILL: Doctor.

SEELIG: [*To* VEDAH.] Sorry to be late. Where's Mama?

CLAYTON: With Dick—complains of his throat. Have you time to look at him?

VEDAH: Certainly.

SEELIG: What is more important? Go up?

CLAYTON: [*Nodding.*] The nursery. [SUTTON *takes* SEELIG*'s cloak and hat.*]

SEELIG: Get ready, my dear. [*Goes into hall and upstairs with* CLAYTON.]

VEDAH: [*Resuming the interrupted talk with* BURRILL.] But write to that girl.

BURRILL: [*Smiling.*] I did say I loved you.

VEDAH: A month ago.

BURRILL: Yes.

VEDAH: And now?

BURRILL: There isn't any stronger word or I'd use it.

VEDAH: [*Seriously.*] It isn't a thing a man says to a girl—betrothed to another man—is it?

BURRILL: Not generally.

VEDAH: That is another proof that you recognize Mr. De Lota as that man of the court room. You must—*do something.*

BURRILL: [*Easily.*] Does it really matter?

VEDAH: Matter? Why—we're engaged—aren't we—he and I?

BURRILL: I've said *I* love you.

VEDAH: Yes.

BURRILL: And you've listened to it—because—you love me.

VEDAH: [*Pause.*] Well?

BURRILL: [*Shaking head.*] Not *Mr. De Lota.* I shall marry you—so what difference does it make what he did in Paris?

VEDAH: I know my father. Mr. De Lota is of our faith, there would have to be good reason for breaking with him now. [CLAYTON *comes downstairs with* MRS. SEELIG.]

BURRILL: Breaking the engagement—would mean no distress to you?

VEDAH: [*In half coquetry.*] Why have I listened to you? [*Enter* MRS. SEELIG *and* CLAYTON.]

MRS. SEELIG: [*Getting her wrap.*] Not ready?

VEDAH: Where's Papa?

MRS. SEELIG: We are to send the car back to him. He wants to wait a while with Dick.

VEDAH: Excuse me. [*Goes to hall.*]

CLAYTON: [*To* MRS. SEELIG.] Can I help you?

MRS. SEELIG: It's very easy, this cloak. [CLAYTON *assists* VEDAH *with her wrap.*]

BURRILL: Allow me. [*Holds cloak for* MRS. SEELIG.]

MRS. SEELIG: [*To* CLAYTON *as she goes.*] I won't say anything to Elinor until Doctor comes.

VEDAH: Good night. [*Gives hand to* BURRILL *and goes out with* MRS. SEELIG. CLAYTON *and* BURRILL *come down to the fireplace.*]

CLAYTON: Wonderful man with children, this Seelig.

BURRILL: I thought principally surgical cases?

CLAYTON: He's at the head of the hospital for crippled children but great in diagnosis—medicine—anything.

BURRILL: Heidelberg, Miss Vedah tells me.

CLAYTON: [*Getting a cigar.*] Postgraduate yes—but New York family. *Father* left him ten millions.

BURRILL: Might have struggled through with that.

CLAYTON: His heart makes him a doctor. If ever I go to Heaven and that old Jew isn't there I'll ask for a rain check.

BURRILL: [*Lights cigarette.*] I understand they receive Jews.

CLAYTON: Heaven? [BURRILL *nods.*] Yes—very carelessly managed. Sit down. Judge Hoover will be here presently—he tells me you're acquainted. [*He sits as* BURRILL *takes a chair.*]

BURRILL: [*Nodding.*] We meet at the Club.

CLAYTON: Mrs. Clayton's father.

BURRILL: I know.

CLAYTON: I'd have had Judge to dinner but—[*Pause.*] How long you been in the Club?

BURRILL: Two years only.

CLAYTON: Perhaps you know?

BURRILL: What?

CLAYTON: The way Hoover's resisted the admission of Jews? He hates 'em.

BURRILL: No.

CLAYTON: Blackballed Seelig. What rot, eh?

BURRILL: Foolish antipathy.

CLAYTON: I *love* 'em—not the cheap ones. I hate cheap *Yankees* and cheap cattle of all kinds—but a classy Jew with education and culture—

BURRILL: I agree with you.

CLAYTON: While we think in vulgar integers—they think in compound fractions.

BURRILL: True.

CLAYTON: Damn it—[*Looks about in playful caution.*] *I'm* so wrong that I like their *noses.*

BURRILL: [*Laughing.*] Not all of them.

CLAYTON: Yes, all of them. Dismiss your prejudice for a while. See how insignificant our average Scandinavian and North Europe noses become. [BURRILL *nods.*] But—don't tell father-in-law Hoover you like 'em.

BURRILL: [*Laughs.*] I won't. [*Seeing* SEELIG *who re-appears on the stairs.*] The Doctor.

[CLAYTON *and* BURRILL *rise.* SEELIG *enters.*]

SEELIG: Don't disturb yourselves, gentlemen.

CLAYTON: How do you find him?

SEELIG: [*Pause.*] I'll look at him again when he's quiet. I hope some of the trouble may be only excitement.

CLAYTON: Cigar?

SEELIG: [*Shakes head.*] Thank you.

CLAYTON: [*Standing by the fire.*] His mother tells me a singular thing. She was holding Dick's hand as he napped on her bed this afternoon—*babies* him a good deal. She was reading—to herself—an old book of Stockton's—some treasure-trove—men carrying sacks of gold from cave to ship. Dick suddenly waked—sat up and said: "Where— where's all that money?" Elinor said, "What money?" Dick said "that gold those—those men had!" Reading to *herself!*

SEELIG: [*Easily.*] Yes. [*Pause.*] The connection between mother and child is more subtle, more enduring than our physiologies even suggest. [SEELIG *and* BURRILL *sit.*]

CLAYTON: Elinor invited the Underwoods to the opera—or I don't think she would have gone herself.

SEELIG: Courtlandt Underwoods?

CLAYTON: Yes.

SEELIG: Mrs. Underwood's suddenly ill. That's where I was delayed this evening.

CLAYTON: Too ill to go out?

SEELIG: Oh yes.

CLAYTON: [*Thoughtfully.*]—M'm.

SEELIG: [*To* BURRILL.] Doesn't the opera attract you?

BURRILL: Yes, but—more important business here.

CLAYTON: Those architects have sued us.

SEELIG: Sued you?

CLAYTON: [*Nodding.*] Libel. My editor insinuated graft in the sculpture awards and they jumped us.

SEELIG: [*Laughing.*] Well. [*Looks to* BURRILL.] You insurgent artists are getting prompt action.

BURRILL: Yes—I feel a little guilty at involving Mr. Clayton.

CLAYTON: [*Reassuringly.*] We'll take care of that. [*To* SEELIG.] The Judge is coming to confer with us—Judge Hoover. [SEELIG *nods.* HOOVER *appears in hall.*] Ah—here he is.

HOOVER: [*Removing his overcoat.*] Hello, Frank.

CLAYTON: Waiting for you. [*Meets* HOOVER *who comes into room.* SEELIG *rises.*] Dr. Seelig, you know.

HOOVER: Good evening.

SEELIG: Judge.

HOOVER: How are you, Burrill?

BURRILL: Good evening—[*Shake hands. Enter* SUTTON.]

SUTTON: Automobile for Dr. Seelig.

SEELIG: Tell him to wait, please. [SUTTON *goes.*]

CLAYTON: [*Answering* HOOVER*'s look.*] Doctor's been good enough to stay and see Dick.

HOOVER: [*Anxiously.*] Boy sick?

SEELIG: These sudden fevers; can't tell immediately.

HOOVER: [*To* BURRILL.] Poor little Dick—when he's ill it gets me right in the stomach. Man's an idiot to have grandchildren.

SEELIG: Still a pardonable weakness.

HOOVER: [*To* BURRILL.] I did a stupid thing. Left the copies of those letters you sent me—the photographs—all at my office.

BURRILL: Originals are at my studio—only two blocks. [*Starts out.*]

CLAYTON: [*To* HOOVER.] Do we need them?

HOOVER: Better have them.

BURRILL: Won't be five minutes. [*Goes out.*]

HOOVER: Doctor, may Dick see his grandfather?
    [MISS DOANE *appears down the stairs.*]

SEELIG: I'm waiting for him to get quiet, but—
    [MISS DOANE *enters.*]

HOOVER: You're the boss.

MISS DOANE: Doctor.

SEELIG: Ready? [MISS DOANE *nods.* SEELIG *goes with her and upstairs.*]

HOOVER: [*Alone with* CLAYTON.] Nearly scared me out of a year's growth.

CLAYTON: Dick?

HOOVER: Seelig. I feared you'd asked him to sit in this conference.

CLAYTON: [*Shaking head.*] I know your prejudice too well for that.

HOOVER: Not him expressly—but the whole breed—and it isn't prejudice. Observation and experience.

CLAYTON: I'll chance 'em.

HOOVER: Chance is the word. This libel suit's a proof of it. [*Gets a cigarette.*]

CLAYTON: An Irishman wrote the editorial.

HOOVER: [*Nods.*] On information furnished by a Jew. Wasn't it?

CLAYTON: De Lota! Yes—but De Lota's pretty cautious.

HOOVER: [*Shaking head in disapproval.*] Bad lot—I know him. He'll get in some nasty scandal before he finishes and it'll react on your business.

CLAYTON: Why do you say that?

HOOVER: A rounder—stamping ground the Great White Way.

CLAYTON: His contract's the Great White Way—he does art and music for us.

HOOVER: I passed his side street hotel on my way here. De Lota sneaking in with a girl.

CLAYTON: [*Easily.*] Guess you're mistaken.

HOOVER: I called him.

CLAYTON: His hotel? [HOOVER *nods.*] De Lota stops at the Ducal Apartments.

HOOVER: [*Nods.*] Ducal Apartments?

CLAYTON: That's a bachelor place—women not admitted.

HOOVER: Not *ad*mitted nor *per*mitted *after eleven o'clock.*

CLAYTON: I'd hate to know as much about this town as you do.

HOOVER: Wait 'till you're my age.

CLAYTON: [*After a disarming pause.*] What kind of a girl?

HOOVER: Didn't get her number—she scooted ahead.

CLAYTON: You spoke to him?

HOOVER: *Called* to him.

CLAYTON: Called?

HOOVER: Yes—I was forty feet away.

CLAYTON: Had your nerve with you.

HOOVER: The girl dropped something—I thought it was a fan.

CLAYTON: Well?

HOOVER:. 'Twasn't—but that's why I called De Lota.

CLAYTON: How do you know it wasn't?

HOOVER: I picked it up.

CLAYTON: What was it?

HOOVER: A libretto.

CLAYTON: What libretto?

HOOVER: Don't know—but grand opera—I remember that and libretto.

CLAYTON: You threw it away?

HOOVER: No—kept it.

CLAYTON: Where is it?

HOOVER: Overcoat pocket.

CLAYTON: [*Pause.*] I'd like to see it. Think I could have some fun with De Lota.

HOOVER: [*Going up to hallway.*] My idea too—fun—and word of caution. [*Gets coat and returns feeling in pocket for libretto.*]

CLAYTON: Caution—naturally.

HOOVER: Here it is. [*Reads.*] Aida.

CLAYTON: [*Taking libretto savagely.*] Aida—let me see it.

HOOVER: What's the matter? [*Puts coat on a chair.*]

CLAYTON: [*In sudden anger, throws book.*] The dog! Damn him—damn both of them!

HOOVER: What is it? See here—Who's with Dick?

CLAYTON: Not his mother—no! [*Points to libretto on floor.*] Marked. *I* did that myself, not an hour ago, and gave it to her.

HOOVER: To Elinor?

CLAYTON: [*Calling as he rushes to the hall.*] Sutton! Sutton!

HOOVER: Hold on, Frank—there's some mistake.

CLAYTON: [*Gets overcoat and hat.*] Get me a cab—never mind—I'll take Seelig's machine. [*Disappears.*] Here! Doctor Seelig says to take me to—[*He goes out. Door bangs.* SUTTON *enters from dining room.*]

SUTTON: Is master Dick in danger, sir?

HOOVER: [*Nervously.*] I don't know, Sutton. Where's his mother?

SUTTON: Opera, sir.

HOOVER: With whom?

SUTTON: Mr. De Lota. [*Enter* SEELIG *from upstairs.*]

HOOVER: That'll do. [SUTTON *goes.*]

HOOVER: Doctor Seelig.

SEELIG: Judge Hoover.

HOOVER: Mr. Clayton was summoned hurriedly—he took your automobile.

SEELIG: I'm glad it could be of service.

HOOVER: I'll get *you* a cab. [*Goes to telephone.*]

SEELIG: I'm not going, thank you—simply sending a prescription [*Starts toward push button.*]

HOOVER: Perhaps you'd—better go—Doctor Seelig.

SEELIG: [*Stopping.*] Why so, Judge? I've a very sick little patient upstairs.

HOOVER: Your pardon! But—[*Pause.*] Mr. Clayton's just had some disturbing news—. The—I think the family would rather be left to themselves this evening.

SEELIG: I shan't intrude past professional requirement—believe me. [*Rings.*]

HOOVER: I *do* believe you! Doctor. [*Nervously getting his coat from the chair.*] You and I are not especially intimate—but in your own sphere of usefulness I respect you.

SEELIG: Thank you.

HOOVER: A physician is not unlike a lawyer in his relations to to his client. [SEELIG *nods.*] I ask you to treat sacredly and with discretion—any matter that comes to your knowledge *here—tonight.*

SEELIG: My obligation to do that, Judge Hoover—has a firmer anchorage than even your request.

HOOVER: I know it—excuse me. Clayton's news—bears on me, too, a little. [*Enter* SUTTON *in response to* SEELIG'*s ring.*]

HOOVER: Sutton—Mr. Burrill will return. Say that important business has called me away.

SUTTON: Yes, sir.

HOOVER: And we'll make another appointment. [*Quickly goes out.*]

SEELIG: Sutton—

SUTTON: Yes, sir. [*Returns.*]

SEELIG: Is there someone who can take this prescription to the druggist and wait for it?

SUTTON: Yes, sir.

SEELIG: And go quickly?

SUTTON: Yes, sir.

SEELIG: Frazer's. [SUTTON *nods and leaves.*]

SEELIG: [*At 'phone.*] Bryant 6151. [*Pause, regards watch.*] Hello—Frazer's? [*Pause.*] Doctor Seelig. I'm sending a prescription by messenger— from Mr. Frank Clayton's. Will you please fill it as promptly as possible? [*Pause.*] Thank you. [*Hangs up 'phone.* BURRILL *and* SUTTON *appear in hall.* BURRILL *carries a package of papers.*]

SUTTON: Mr. Clayton and Judge Hoover have been called away. Judge Hoover said he'd make another appointment.
[SUTTON *and* BURRILL *enter.*]

BURRILL: Oh—[*Pause.*] Well—I'll leave this envelope for them—they may care to see it when they come in. [*Seeing* SEELIG.] How's the boy, Doctor?

SEELIG: Quite ill—poor baby.

BURRILL: Too bad—[*To* SUTTON.] I'll speak with the Doctor a moment. [SUTTON *bows—and goes out.*]

BURRILL: You have a minute or two?

SEELIG: [*Still seated at 'phone table.*] I've sent for some medicine—and am free until it comes.

BURRILL: [*Approaching.*] I want to thank you, Doctor, for your interest in my work.

SEELIG: It's been a pleasure, Mr. Burrill.

BURRILL: It's been a lesson to me.

SEELIG: Lesson?

BURRILL: [*Nodding.*] I'm reprehensibly ignorant on most subjects, especially religion and—well—your interest in sculpture—your toleration of it surprised me.

SEELIG: Why?

BURRILL: I always thought there was something in your tenets that forbade any graven image.

SEELIG: Only as objects of idolatry I think. The words are: "Nor bow down and worship them." As works of art I don't know any prohibition. My dear old father was a very orthodox believer—closed his office on Saturday and all that—but he was a liberal patron of the arts. In fact, I don't know a Jew among a fairly extensive circle—that feels as you—as you feared, Mr. Burrill.

BURRILL: You are not so orthodox as your father then?

SEELIG: Not orthodox at all.

BURRILL: I got a contrary impression.

SEELIG: From Judge Hoover?

BURRILL: From Miss Vedah.

SEELIG: Vedah?

BURRILL: Yes. It is of her I wish to speak.

SEELIG: Ah!

BURRILL: I wouldn't speak of her—if—if I didn't think a mistake was being made, Dr. Seelig.

SEELIG: A mistake!

BURRILL: Yes—I mean that my own feelings are not my sole guide. I think that Miss Vedah—likes me.

SEELIG: I'm glad you see it. I have cautioned her myself—and now perhaps you will aid me.

BURRILL: I speak to you about it as a matter of honor. You—you've been so ready to invite me to your house and all that—and—

SEELIG: And to tell you early of Vedah's engagement?

BURRILL: Yes—so my duty is to be a trifle old-fashioned, if you will, and to tell you that—I mean to increase her—regard for me—all I can.

SEELIG: Her regard? Only that?

BURRILL: I've no right to speak for her—so—

SEELIG: Has Vedah said more?

BURRILL: *I've* said more. She knows that I *love* her.

SEELIG: You told her so ?

BURRILL: Yes.

SEELIG: Then this caution to me is somewhat late, isn't it?

BURRILL: But unavoidably. If I didn't think she cared more for me than for—the man to whom she's engaged, I don't think I'd have spoken.

SEELIG: You mean to me?

BURRILL: To either of you.

SEELIG: Why not *first* to me?

BURRILL: Until I was sure there was no need to distress you, as I felt you would be, as I feel you are. [*Walks away as having said all that is possible.*]

SEELIG: [*Pause, slowly rises and approaches* BURRILL.] In asking your patient understanding, Mr. Burrill—I am fortunate that you are a sculptor.

BURRILL: How so, Doctor?

SEELIG: Most sculptors think in large symbols. The little span of human life takes its true proportion.

BURRILL: Life is all *I'm* sure of. I fear it's rather important to me.

SEELIG: It's all any of us is sure of. [*Pause.*] I'm not a religionist, Mr. Burrill—but—[*Pause.*] It has been wisely written, "Of all factors that make races and individuals what they are the most potent is religion." It would be a very sorry world without it.

BURRILL: There can be more than one religion, however, can't there?

SEELIG: There should be. Even to grind corn there must be two millstones. And for the world to grow in religion there must be more than one idea. [*Pause.*] The belief in one God is the trust given to the Jew—the precious idea of which every Jewish woman is custodian and which to transmit—the Jew suffers and persists. You see, Mr. Burrill, that there is something here to think of.

BURRILL: Yes.

SEELIG: The Christian faith itself needs our testimony. It is built upon our foundation—and whenever a daughter quits us the religious welfare of the whole world is the loser.

BURRILL: I don't see that.

SEELIG: Pardon the pride, which our proverb says "Goes often before a fall," and let me call your recollection to the nobility of this trust which a Jewish girl abandons if she marries elsewhere. [BURRILL *nods. A pause.*] When Egypt worshipped Isis and Osiris and Thoth, Israel proclaimed the one God. When India knelt to Vishnu and Siva and

Kali, Israel prayed only to Jehovah and down past Greece and Rome, with their numerous divinities from Jove to Saturn, Judah looked up to one God. What a legacy—what a birthright! How small our personal desires grow in comparison. As a sculptor, who writes in bronze that all time may read, what message can you leave if one so grand as this fails of your respect?

BURRILL: It has my respect sir.

SEELIG: I was sure of it. Is it too much to ask that a girl shall have time to think of this?

BURRILL: No, sir! I shall say nothing to her more than I have said, which is I love her and I know she loves me. [SEELIG *bows slowly.* BURRILL *respectfully acknowledges the bow.* ELINOR *enters excitedly, sees* BURRILL *and* SEELIG *and quickly passes to the music room.* HOOVER *comes in.*]

HOOVER: [*Nervously.*] Mr. Burrill—you will have to excuse Mr. and Mrs. Clayton tonight?

BURRILL: I know—good night. [*Goes quickly out.* HOOVER *turns helplessly toward* SEELIG, *who with a gesture of comprehension, goes upstairs. As* SEELIG *goes,* ELINOR *enters by the other arch.*]

ELINOR: Don't leave me, father. [*She walks excitedly.*]

HOOVER: I won't. But I'm not only your father—I'm an attorney—a counsellor. Let me have the truth, Elinor. The door was locked?

ELINOR: [*Sitting.*] De Lota locked it in sheer playfulness. I was begging him to open it when Frank came.

HOOVER: But why there at all? Why in De Lota's rooms?

ELINOR: Just plain madness. Twice at dinner the conversation got onto Mr. Burrill's sculpture. Frank has had an affair with Burrill's model. [*Rises and walks; throws her cloak onto the table.*]

HOOVER: When? Not since the trouble of Atlantic City?

ELINOR: This year in Paris—I've made him almost admit it. De Lota introduced them. Tonight when we found the Underwoods couldn't go—and we were alone for the evening, De Lota and I—he proposed seeing some Japanese carvings he has in his rooms.

HOOVER: But, Elinor—you're not an infant. A proposal of that kind is only a mask for lawlessness.

ELINOR: I *am* lawless. *He* claims the right to follow *his* fancy, and does follow it—my right is equal. He introduced me to this very woman on the Boulevard—but I didn't strike her, did I?

HOOVER: Did Frank strike De Lota?

ELINOR: Like a cheap bully. [*The front door is slammed violently.* CLAYTON *enters, pale with excitement.*]

CLAYTON: You came *here*, did you?

ELINOR: Why shouldn't I? You haven't made it such a sanctified temple that I'm unworthy to enter it.

CLAYTON: [*To* HOOVER.] She can't stay.

HOOVER: [*Going to* CLAYTON.] See here, Frank. You're in no state of mind to make any important decision.

CLAYTON: The facts make the decision—

HOOVER: You haven't got the facts?

CLAYTON: I've got all I can stand and we won't vulgarly discuss them. I decline to live with an adulteress.

ELINOR: I'm not that—but I am an indignant and cruelly neglected woman.

CLAYTON: She's your daughter. Now take her from my house or—I'll have the servants do it! [*Strides into the music room.*]

ELINOR: [*Impetuously.*] Coward! His house—

HOOVER: Elinor—that's not the way.

ELINOR: I haven't worked in his office—but every step in his success we consulted and agreed upon. *His house!* You know that every investment—

HOOVER: He doesn't mean it. He's excited beyond control—any husband would be.

ELINOR: In every tight place it was *your* legal advice that—

HOOVER: We can't go into that now, my dear. Humor him—avoid a scene before the servants. I'll take you to a hotel and—

ELINOR: Hotel! The cruelty of it—turned like a common woman onto the street. [*Sinks overwhelmed into a chair.*]

HOOVER: Only a day or two. If things were only as you say at De Lota's we can get Frank to believe us—

ELINOR: After what I've forgiven him! Oh, dad—

HOOVER: Don't—don't! Change your gown and we'll go. Tomorrow will put another color on everything. [*Helps her up and leads her protesting toward the hall.*]

ELINOR: [*Resentfully.*] The injustice of it—! The cruelty—! The—[SEELIG *comes downstairs and meets* HOOVER *and* ELINOR *in the doorway.*]

SEELIG: Pardon—

HOOVER: [*Trying to pass.*] Mrs. Clayton isn't well. [SEELIG *enters.*]

SEELIG: [*Taking* ELINOR'*s hand.*] I see—but come from the hall. Dick will hear you.

ELINOR: Dick?

SEELIG: Yes.

ELINOR: Dick's ill—? I'll go to him.

SEELIG: [*Restraining* ELINOR.] One moment—[*To* HOOVER.] *You* go to him.

HOOVER: The situation here, Doctor—

SEELIG: I think, Judge Hoover, I comprehend the situation here. Please go. [HOOVER *goes upstairs.*]

ELINOR: [*As* SEELIG *brings her further into the room.*] I can't *leave* without seeing my boy.

SEELIG: Leave! [*Slowly.*] No—no—but you must be calm when you go to him. There must be no excitement whatever.

ELINOR: [*Hysterically.*] I can't be calm and go away from him—if he's ill. You know the boy, Doctor. How much we are to each other—all his life—I've never neglected him.

SEELIG: I know.

ELINOR: It's too much to bear—[*Falls weeping into the chair at fireplace.* CLAYTON *enters.*]

CLAYTON: [*With suppression.*] If there's any man, Doctor, your people should have run straight with—I'm the man.

SEELIG: My people?

CLAYTON: [*Pointing to* ELINOR.] Locked in Ben De Lota's rooms.

SEELIG: My people! [*Pause.*] A Jew!

CLAYTON: [*Vehemently.*] A Jew.

SEELIG: [*Pause.*] There was another Jew—if one of *His* people may quote Him—[*Puts hand on* ELINOR'*s head.*] "Are *you* to cast the first stone?"

CLAYTON: I'm no hypocrite—I never subscribed to his code—and I'll begin the living hell—of life with a dishonored woman.

ELINOR: [*Rising defiantly.*] I'm not dishonored. I only *claim* the right you *exercise* for yourself to go where life interests me. If it's honorable and moral for *you*—it's equally honorable and equally moral for me.

CLAYTON: Every right you may possibly claim you have fully earned by your visit to Ben De Lota's room. I'm going to make your equality complete. From now on, you'll protect yourself and you'll earn the substance your vanity squanders.

ELINOR: Ah!—

SEELIG: [*Interrupting* ELINOR'*s outburst.*] One moment—don't speak, my child. [*Pause. Calms* ELINOR *to her chair.*] Your difference must wait. Just now Mrs. Clayton must be composed.

CLAYTON: [*Explosively.*] We're past the consideration of her nerves. Just now Mrs. Clayton must take what she needs for the night and leave—her trunks will follow her. [*Goes to the push button and rings.*]

SEELIG: [*In masterful calm.*] No Frank—she shall not leave.

CLAYTON: She'll not—

SEELIG: She shall not.

CLAYTON: [*Angrily.*] What have *you* got to do with it?

SEELIG: Every thing! There's a little *boy* upstairs—no one shall move him until I give permission, and his life for the next few days will depend on the mother that gave it him. [*Enter* SUTTON.]

CLAYTON: [*Pause.*] Sutton—[*pause*—SEELIG *looks sharply and steadily at* CLAYTON]—pack my valise—and send it to the Club.

SUTTON: Yes, sir. [*Goes out.*]

CLAYTON: [*Leaving the room.*] Good night, Doctor Seelig.

SEELIG: [*Quietly.*] Good night. [ELINOR *still seated turns weeping to* SEELIG *who embraces her paternally.*]

ACT III

SCENE: *Library in house of* DOCTOR SEELIG. *Door at back lets into drawing room which formed the first act. Another door to left lets into the hallway. Large diamond paned and leaded window with seat at right. Mantel and fireplace are at back. Over mantel is picture of Judith. Other pictures are heavily framed on wall. Book-cases height of mantel are at all walls. The ceiling is carved and heavily beamed. Near window is library table with lamp. In front of table and masking it is heavy sofa. Big easy chairs flank and half face the fire. A second table has a telephone. On mantel are* DE LOTA'*s two vases. Other ornaments complete shelf furniture. General tone of scene and carpet is red and gold.*

At Rise of Curtain BURRILL *is discovered waiting.*

[HOLLAND *enters.*]

HOLLAND: Miss Seelig will be down immediately.

BURRILL: Thank you. [*Exit* HOLLAND. BURRILL *scans the book shelves.* VEDAH *enters.*]

VEDAH: Julian! [*Extends both hands.*]

BURRILL: My sweetheart! [*Kisses her.*]

VEDAH: Together after all the talk and tears and family councils.

BURRILL: Have there been tears?

VEDAH: [*Nodding.*] Some.

BURRILL: You poor dear.

VEDAH: I've tried so hard not to care for you.

BURRILL: Have you? [*They sit together on the sofa.*]

VEDAH: Yes. Read the persecutions of my ancestry and blamed all on yours and then said, with Mercutio, "A plague on both your houses."

BURRILL: I hope you are as incurably smitten as Mercutio was when he said that.

VEDAH: I think I must be. Wasn't there something about a church door?

BURRILL: You angel!

VEDAH: Our critics write that the vice of our race is display.

BURRILL: Well?

VEDAH: And I fear it's true. I have a great *envie* to have the noted American sculptor in our box and all the opera glasses saying, "Vedah Seelig! She's caught him at last."

BURRILL: Have you manœuvred greatly?

VEDAH: Shamelessly—not even introduced to you.

BURRILL: I know it—but we've met, haven't we? [*Kisses her.*]

VEDAH: [*Resisting tardily.*] That isn't being done, you know, until the engagement is announced.

BURRILL: How does one tell?

VEDAH: I suppose—one doesn't *tell*?

BURRILL: What have you been doing since I saw you?

VEDAH: Home mostly. You know Mrs. Clayton is visiting us?

BURRILL: Mrs. Clayton?

VEDAH: And little Dick. He has the room that was my nursery. I've spent a lot of time with Dick.

BURRILL: And what operas—what parties?

VEDAH: Twice to the opera.

BURRILL: With—?

VEDAH: Mama. Then once to the theatre.

BURRILL: With—?

VEDAH: Mama and Papa.

BURRILL: No suitors? [VEDAH *shakes her head.*] Not even one?

VEDAH: You mean have I seen Mr. De Lota?

BURRILL: Well?

VEDAH: He is out of the city.

BURRILL: Oh. [MRS. SEELIG *enters.*]

MRS. SEELIG: Vedah! [BURRILL *and* VEDAH *rise.*]

VEDAH: Mama.

MRS. SEELIG: Mr. Burrill. [*Gives hand.*]

BURRILL: Mrs. Seelig.

MRS. SEELIG: You didn't tell me Mr. Burrill had called.

VEDAH: Did you wish to know?

MRS. SEELIG: Of course. [*She goes to the telephone.*] Give me 2500 Plaza, please. [*Pause.*] I want to speak to Doctor Seelig if he's there. [*Pause.*] Mrs. Seelig.

VEDAH: Why do you want him, Mama?

MRS. SEELIG: You'll see in good time.

VEDAH: [*To* BURRILL.] A girl never grows up in her mother's mind.

MRS. SEELIG: Yes. That you, Samuel? [*Pause.*] Will you be home soon? [*Pause.*] Well, nothing important—except—[*Pause.*] Mr. Burrill is here and—I thought I'd ask him to wait for you—[*Pause.*] No [*Pause.*] No—well—I think it much better for you to do it yourself— [BURRILL *and* VEDAH *quickly exchange glances and* BURRILL *comically interests himself in the books.*] Perhaps—but are you coming? [*Pause.*] Thank you. [*Hangs up 'phone.*]

VEDAH: What is it?

MRS. SEELIG: You know—[*To* BURRILL.] Sit down, Mr. Burrill—[MRS. SEELIG *and* VEDAH *sit together.*] Vedah's father and I have had a good many talks about—about you and Vedah.

BURRILL: Yes?

MRS. SEELIG: We haven't always agreed—

BURRILL: I'm sorry to be the cause of any difference.

MRS. SEELIG: It's Doctor's fault. I've always said to him, don't invite any men to your house in whom you wouldn't be willing to see your daughter interested.

VEDAH: But Mama, Papa didn't invite Mr. Burrill.

MRS. SEELIG: I know, but Papa was *with* you. That was the time for him to have been firm. And not go locking the stable after—

VEDAH: Oh, Mama, don't make me into a stolen horse.

BURRILL: No—see what I'd be—

MRS. SEELIG: [*To* VEDAH.] You'd better listen.

BURRILL: Pardon.

MRS. SEELIG: Vedah's our only child, Mr. Burrill, and my first wish is to see her happy—but—

VEDAH: Mama means that any unhappiness of mine wouldn't matter if she had another daughter.

MRS. SEELIG: Mr. Burrill understands me, I'm sure.

BURRILL: I do, Mrs. Seelig.

MRS. SEELIG: But Doctor and I agree that Vedah should *think* calmly.

VEDAH: That's expecting a good deal.

MRS. SEELIG: The Doctor is—going to—well, not let you see so much of each other, and I want to prepare you, Mr. Burrill, for his talk with you. [*Enter* HOLLAND.]

HOLLAND: Mr. De Lota and Judge Hoover.

MRS. SEELIG: Judge Hoover! Excuse me. [*Follows* HOLLAND *out.*]

BURRILL: Mr. De Lota?

VEDAH: Yes. And now with Papa going to talk—you haven't informed yourself about that Paris affair.

BURRILL: I wouldn't talk that no matter what I knew.

VEDAH: It's on my mind all the time. [*Enter* MRS. SEELIG.]

MRS. SEELIG: You go to the living room—[VEDAH *and* BURRILL *start out.*] I'll join you. [VEDAH *and* BURRILL *go to drawing room.*] Come in, gentlemen. [*Enter* HOOVER *and* DE LOTA *from the hall.*]

HOOVER: Some years since we met, Mrs. Seelig.

MRS. SEELIG: Yes—[*To* DE LOTA.] *You've* been away, Benjamin?

DE LOTA: [*Nods.*] How is Mrs. Clayton's son?

MRS. SEELIG: Doctor says he may go out in a day or two.

DE LOTA: [*To* HOOVER *in tone of congratulation.*] Ah!

HOOVER: It's been very good of you, Mrs. Seelig, to have him and his mother here.

MRS. SEELIG: A change of surroundings—and Dick's always called me Auntie. [ELINOR *enters by the door from hall.*]

ELINOR: Father!

HOOVER: My dear. [*Kisses her.*]

MRS. SEELIG: We shall see *you* later, Mr. De Lota?

DE LOTA: Oh—yes—yes. [MRS. SEELIG *goes into the drawing room closing the door after her.*]

ELINOR: You two come—here *together.*

HOOVER: I *brought* Mr. De Lota—yes.

ELINOR: Why?

HOOVER: Sit down, my dear. It's going to take more than a minute. [ELINOR *sits.*] And you—[DE LOTA *sits.*] When have you heard from Frank?

ELINOR: [*Anxiously rising.*] Don't they know where he is?

HOOVER: Good Heavens, Elinor—don't answer my question by asking another.

ELINOR: But don't they?

HOOVER: Don't *who* know where he is?

ELINOR: Anybody.

HOOVER: Hundreds I suppose—but have *you* heard from him?

ELINOR: No.

HOOVER: Doesn't he ask after little Dick?

ELINOR: He 'phones Doctor Seelig every day.

HOOVER: But you?

ELINOR: No. [*Pause.*]

HOOVER: Frank has instructed Colonel Emory to begin suit.

ELINOR: You mean?

HOOVER: Divorce.

ELINOR: Oh!

HOOVER: You expected it, didn't you?

ELINOR: Not after his conduct with this second woman—this sculptor model in Paris.

HOOVER: That wasn't condoned, eh?

ELINOR: Not after I discovered it.

HOOVER: What—what proof have you of that affair?

ELINOR: He *admitted* it.

HOOVER: [*Quickly.*] He did?

ELINOR: Almost.

HOOVER: I fear "almost" won't go in court.

ELINOR: And—Mr. De Lota *knows* it. He told me so.

DE LOTA: [*As* HOOVER *turns to him.*] My opinion.

HOOVER: You *told* Mrs. Clayton that, did you?

DE LOTA: My opinion—yes.

HOOVER: Have you and she met since—Clayton and I—came to your hotel?

DE LOTA: No.

HOOVER: Communicated? [DE LOTA *shakes head.*] Oh—then you told her—this opinion of yours with an idea of its influence upon *her?*

DE LOTA: I answered her questions.

HOOVER: And a damn fine mess you've made of it.

DE LOTA: Perhaps, Judge Hoover, we'd better get to the purpose of our call.

HOOVER: Perhaps. [*To* ELINOR.] I don't need to tell you, Elinor, that this thing's awkward for *me.*

ELINOR: I know.

HOOVER: The other side can subpoena me—and my testimony can't help you—[*Pause.*] If we go about it rightly, however, Colonel Emory thinks Frank can be persuaded to let you get the decree.

ELINOR: No.

HOOVER: No?

ELINOR: The reason for not getting a divorce two years ago is much greater now.

HOOVER: You mean—?

ELINOR: I mean Dick.

HOOVER: It's better for Dick to have the blame fixed on his father than upon you.

ELINOR: I'm not guilty.

HOOVER: My dear Elinor, I'm your father—and—and I believe you—but—[*Pause.*] I'm an attorney and I have been a Judge. The case is against you.

ELINOR: [*To* DE LOTA.] You know I'm not a guilty woman.

DE LOTA: I do—but your father is right. We must face the situation as it is. I love you, Elinor. [*Comes to her.*]

ELINOR: [*Recoiling.*] Don't say that to me.

HOOVER: My dear, I've brought Mr. De Lota here that, unpleasant as it is, he *might* say it—in my hearing.

ELINOR: You?

HOOVER: Yes. If we can't arrange it as Colonel Emory proposes—[*Pause.*] Mr. De Lota's willing to marry you.

ELINOR: Oh! [*Covers her face in revulsion.*]

HOOVER: [*Soothing her.*] Don't—don't do that. It isn't what any of us hoped for some years ago—but it's a devilish sight better, my dear, than it all looked last month.

ELINOR: There can't be such injustice in the world—that he may go un-scathed and little Dick and I—no—no—I can't live and have it come to that. I won't consent to any such arrangement of it all.

HOOVER: It's little Dick I'm asking you to think of.

ELINOR: He's all I am thinking of. He's like his father—it's his father's name he'll carry through his life and I'm not going even to *propose* to blacken it.

HOOVER: What are you going to do?

ELINOR: Defend myself—defend my boy's mother.

HOOVER: Against the boy's father?

ELINOR: Yes.

HOOVER: And if the court gives Clayton a decree of divorce?

ELINOR: Then I shall *live*—live so that he'll see some day he was mistaken.

HOOVER: There's one point we mustn't overlook. Dick's how old?

ELINOR: He's seven.

HOOVER: The court may award his custody to Clayton.

ELINOR: [*Greatly agitated.*] Oh no! Father! They won't—they can't do that.

HOOVER: I don't know.

ELINOR: You can think—arrange some way to avoid that.

HOOVER: I have thought of one way—you won't listen. If we can per-suade Clayton to be the defendant, that settles it. If we fight him as you propose, his anger may lead him to take the boy.

ELINOR: Divorce!

DE LOTA: And no certainty it can be kept quiet.

ELINOR: You mean the papers?

DE LOTA: Yes. If Mr. Clayton lets you get the decree—only the Chardenet girl will be named. [ELINOR *rings push button by fireplace.*]

HOOVER: What are you doing?

ELINOR: Tell Mrs. Seelig—

DE LOTA: No—no—

HOOVER: Why?

ELINOR: Because Doctor Seelig has told her nothing. [*Enter* HOLLAND.]

HOOVER: One minute.

HOLLAND: [*Going.*] Yes, sir.

ELINOR: Holland—ask Mrs. Seelig to come here. [HOLLAND *goes.*]

HOOVER: Wait 'till Frank decides.

ELINOR: *I've* decided.

HOOVER: But you may reconsider.

DE LOTA: Yes—why tell her now?

ELINOR: She has a right to know.

HOOVER: What right?

ELINOR: A wife's right—a mother's right. The right of a woman who has taken an outcast into her home.

HOOVER: You were not an outcast, Elinor—you could have come to me.

ELINOR: In your club?

HOOVER: I'd have gone to a hotel.

DE LOTA: I beg of you, Elinor—wait—or at least don't tell *everything*. My position in this house is—peculiar.

HOOVER: *Your* position?

DE LOTA: Yes—a tacit engagement—to Vedah.

ELINOR: Oh! How vile it all makes me.

DE LOTA: The more reason to be careful. [*Enter* MRS. SEELIG.]

MRS. SEELIG: My dear?

HOOVER: [*Cautioning.*] Elinor!

MRS. SEELIG: What is it? [*Starts to* ELINOR.]

ELINOR: Wait—[*pause*]—until I tell you—[*pause*]—Doctor told you only that it would be good for Dick to come here? Nothing more?

MRS. SEELIG: Nothing.

ELINOR: Not—my trouble—with Frank?

MRS. SEELIG: No—and don't you tell it, my dear, if it agitates you. Besides, Frank has lots to worry him. We mustn't judge too quickly.

ELINOR: He wants a divorce.

MRS. SEELIG: *He* does?

ELINOR: [*Nodding.*] He's already gone to a lawyer about it—father has just told me.

MRS. SEELIG: Because [*looks at* HOOVER *who nods toward* DE LOTA] Frank's jealous—of Benjamin? [*To* ELINOR.]

ELINOR: I had no idea Vedah was engaged to him. Oh, it's too—too horrible.

MRS. SEELIG: What ideas men *can* get in their heads.

ELINOR: No, I'm to blame, Mrs. Seelig. I deserve it all—I did go to his rooms—the Doctor knows.

MRS. SEELIG: Your rooms—[DE LOTA *nods.*] Together?

DE LOTA: Yes.

MRS. SEELIG: But, my dear Elinor—

ELINOR: The Doctor believes me—I was crazy—rebellious—vengeful—striking back—bitterly resentful of the deceit Frank had been newly guilty of. I went as much in the name of all women despitefully treated as I did in assertion of my own freedom. And then—I came to my senses. I'm not guilty or I wouldn't be in your home—

MRS. SEELIG: My dear! [*Takes* ELINOR *in her arms. Enter* SEELIG.]

MRS. SEELIG: [*Quietly.*] She's just told me.

SEELIG: [*To* HOOVER.] Colonel Emory called on me this afternoon.

HOOVER: Then you know?

SEELIG: Yes.

HOOVER: Naturally somewhat of a shock. [*Indicates* ELINOR.]

SEELIG: Yes.

HOOVER: We haven't any right to expect less from Clayton.

ELINOR: No right? Did I divorce him two years ago when he was *guilty*—really guilty. Did I?

HOOVER: No! You made a scene with the woman and got a rotten lot of newspaper notoriety—but the offense you condoned.

MRS. SEELIG: And a man that's been forgiven all that shouldn't talk about divorce if his poor wife loses her head for a minute. It's unbearable the privileges these men claim—and the double standard of morality they set up.

SEELIG: These men?

MRS. SEELIG: All of them. And that woman dramatist with her play was right. It is "a man's world."

SEELIG: It's a pretty wise world, my dear.

ELINOR: You think I should be made to suffer?

SEELIG: I think you do suffer.

ELINOR: That my offense is less forgivable than Frank's was?

SEELIG: [*Pause.*] You have my pity, Elinor, and shall have my help but I can't lie to you.

ELINOR: That I'm more guilty than he?

MRS. SEELIG: [*Pause.*] Don't ask that of a Jew, my dear—however liberal in his religion he pretends to be. My father was an orthodox Rabbi—I know.

SEELIG: What do you know?

MRS. SEELIG: Our ancient law—from which all your ideas come. A man's past was his own. *He* was not forbidden as many wives as he wanted, but if a poor girl had made a mistake and concealed it from these lords of creation, she was stoned to death unless she was the daughter of a priest—in which case she was to be burnt alive. It's always been a man's world.

SEELIG: Elinor. [*Pause.*] Do you hear that rattle of the railroad?

ELINOR: Yes.

SEELIG. All over this great land thousands of trains run every day starting and arriving in punctual agreement because this is *a woman's world*. The great steamships, dependable almost as the sun—a million factories in civilization—the countless looms and lathes of industry—the legions of labor that weave the riches of the world—all—all move by the mainspring of man's faith in woman—man's *faith*.

ELINOR: I want *him* to have faith in me.

SEELIG: This old world hangs together by love.

MRS. SEELIG: Not man's love for woman.

SEELIG: No—nor woman's love for man, but by the love of both—for the children.

ELINOR: Dick!

SEELIG: Men work for the children because they believe the children are—their own—*believe*. Every mother *knows* she is the mother of her son or daughter. Let her be however wicked, no power on earth can shake that knowledge. Every father believes he is a father only by his faith in the woman. Let him be however virtuous, no power on earth can strengthen in him a conviction greater than that faith. There is a double standard of morality because upon the golden basis of woman's virtue rests the welfare of the world.

ELINOR: Have I—lost *everything*?

SEELIG: Frank must be convinced of your love and your loyalty.

ELINOR: I *do* love him.

SEELIG: Of course. [*To* DE LOTA.] Why are you here?

DE LOTA: To—do any thing that is in my power—to assure Mrs. Clayton that she will have my protection if—it comes to the worst.

SEELIG: Well—that's where it would be.

DE LOTA: And there must be some things *you* want to say to me.

SEELIG: There are.

HOOVER: [*To* SEELIG.] Clayton's always had great respect for your opinion, Dr. Seelig.

SEELIG: I'll see Clayton, of course. [*To* MRS. SEELIG.] You 'phoned me that Mr. Burrill—

MRS. SEELIG: He's there. [*Indicates living room.*]

SEELIG: Have you seen your grandson, Judge Hoover?

HOOVER: No.

ELINOR: You must—Dick's asked for you—[*Rises.*] Come.

SEELIG: On your way out I'll see you again. [HOOVER *and* ELINOR *go out.*]

SEELIG: [*To* MRS. SEELIG.] You entertain Mr. Burrill a moment.

MRS. SEELIG: He doesn't lack entertainment.

SEELIG: What?

MRS. SEELIG: Vedah's with him.

SEELIG: [*Starting to door.*] I thought we'd agreed about that?

MRS. SEELIG: Doesn't this trouble make a difference?

SEELIG: It can't affect our decision concerning Burrill.

MRS. SEELIG: Not before Vedah. [SEELIG *goes to living room.*]

DE LOTA: Perhaps the trouble can be fixed, Mrs. Seelig—if the doctor talks to Clayton.

MRS. SEELIG: It can't be "fixed," as you call it, with me.

DE LOTA: You won't tell Vedah?

MRS. SEELIG: I won't have to tell Vedah, she loves this artist.

DE LOTA: But to marry a Christian!

MRS. SEELIG: When she might have you.

DE LOTA: It's taught me something.

MRS. SEELIG: No doubt. But, I won't sacrifice my girl to finish your education. [*Re-enter* SEELIG *with* BURRILL.]

SEELIG: Mr. Burrill is going. He first wishes to speak with Mr. De Lota.

MRS. SEELIG: Why?

SEELIG: Sarah!

MRS. SEELIG: Pardon.

BURRILL: A business matter, Mrs. Seelig. If you are leaving, Mr. De Lota, I'll walk with you—if you permit.

DE LOTA: I have some business with Dr. Seelig.

BURRILL: Could you spare *us* a few minutes?

SEELIG: Well? De Lota?

DE LOTA: With pleasure.

SEELIG: [*Going.*] Sarah.

MRS. SEELIG: [*In undertone.*] You told him? [SEELIG *nods. Goes out with* MRS. SEELIG.]

DE LOTA: Well?

BURRILL: I'm going to give you a chance to retire from this, Mr. De Lota, without exposure.

DE LOTA: Good of you.

BURRILL: Miss Seelig believes that you have served time in a penitentiary.

DE LOTA: You told her that?

BURRILL: I hadn't met you when I told Miss Seelig that the man who got an engagement in Antoine's Theatre for Mimi Chardenet had been in prison. Then you came into the room and told the rest yourself.

DE LOTA: Miss Seelig's belief is based on those two remarks?

BURRILL: Yes.

DE LOTA: Reinforced, I suppose, by your own opinion.

BURRILL: I have tried to conceal my opinion.

DE LOTA: What is your opinion, Mr. Burrill?

BURRILL: That I saw you sentenced in the Cour d'Assizes to a year's imprisonment.

DE LOTA: And you threaten to say so?

BURRILL: I hope I'm a little cleaner than that, I threaten nothing.

DE LOTA: What is it you're doing?

BURRILL: I foresee trouble—I inform you of it.

DE LOTA: You mean you foresee Miss Seelig asking me a question?

BURRILL: Yes! I—foresee your answer failing to satisfy. I foresee her doubt grow deeper—I foresee her going to her father with that doubt.

DE LOTA: And then?

BURRILL: I foresee Doctor Seelig asking what *I* know.

DE LOTA: Ah! Now we have it. Disguised, but still the threat. You tell Doctor Seelig your belief.

BURRILL: I shall decline to express my belief.

DE LOTA: Same thing, isn't it? Your reluctance and your shrugs being quite as convincing.

BURRILL: You can hardly ask me to lie for you.

DE LOTA: Miss Vedah may believe me.

BURRILL: No, she has asked me more than once to write to Paris.

DE LOTA: It would make this bluff of fair play very convincing if you did write to persons whose names I can furnish you—

BURRILL: You mean arrange a deception.

DE LOTA: I mean *write*—show Miss Seelig your letters. *Wait*—show her the answers.

BURRILL: You make it pretty hard to keep still, believe me.

DE LOTA: You think I'm unworthy to marry this girl.

BURRILL: I know you are.

DE LOTA: [*Pause.*] I'm going to tell you the truth about that Paris affair.

BURRILL: I don't care to hear it.

DE LOTA: You don't want the truth?

BURRILL: I don't want your confidence. I won't be bound by it.

DE LOTA: You're *a man's* man, Burrill—you fight in the open. Your part in this architect's row shows that. Now, in fair play—[*Telephone rings.*]

BURRILL: Someone will come to answer that. Our interview's at an end.

DE LOTA: Wait. [*Goes quickly to telephone and takes receiver from its hook.*] They may not come. [*Pause.*] I have served a year in a French prison. Captain Dreyfus served even longer for the same prejudice.

BURRILL: Your crime was proven.

DE LOTA: I'm as good as you, Mr. Burrill, or any bachelor that spends his several years in Paris. That imprisonment was a decoration.

BURRILL: Rot!

DE LOTA: I'm not a male *ingenue.* Doctor Seelig knows I've had my wild oats and I'll make a clean breast of it—my sufferings for my race will not be held against me. Vedah Seelig is a Jewess, remember, and—

BURRILL: Be still, she's a clean, high-minded girl—she'll forgive adultery in you no quicker than she'd forgive it anywhere.

DE LOTA: You think so?

BURRILL: I do.

DE LOTA: And that belief determines you to bring it to her knowledge?

BURRILL: It is already brought to her knowledge. You did that.

DE LOTA: And you make the consequence as sinister as if it had been planned?

BURRILL: I won't conspire to hoodwink a girl into marrying you. [*Enter* SEELIG. *Pause.*]

SEELIG: That 'phone rang?

DE LOTA: Yes—I was going to answer it.

SEELIG: I answered it—on the branch—upstairs. I heard what you were saying.

BURRILL: Through that?

SEELIG: Yes. [SEELIG *replaces receiver on 'phone.*]

DE LOTA: I was telling Mr. Burrill a story—for a magazine.

SEELIG: [*To* BURRILL.] Is that true?

BURRILL: I can't answer you.

SEELIG: In prison!

DE LOTA: The man I was quoting.

SEELIG: Why should a man in a story say: "Vedah Seelig is a Jewess, re-member." Why should Mr. Burrill interrupt you to defend her?

BURRILL: Good day, Doctor. [BURRILL *goes.*]

SEELIG: Your confession—just now—[*Indicates 'phone.*]

DE LOTA: At that time in Paris, with public hatred at a white heat, an ob-solete law was dug up to persecute a foreigner and a Jew.

SEELIG: What law?

DE LOTA: Imprisoning a man on the complaint of a woman's husband.

SEELIG: We are fortunate to learn it.

DE LOTA: There are some Jews I'd expect to condemn me—apostates, renegades, that join the wolves, but not you. That imprisonment was my share of the hatred the race sustains. You're big enough to see that and dismiss it. As for the offense itself—well—you know men, Doctor Seelig. You're a physician—not a Rabbi.

SEELIG: Clayton's home was not your first adventure?

DE LOTA: I didn't know this man in Paris.

SEELIG: You knew Clayton?

DE LOTA: Yes.

SEELIG: That's enough.

DE LOTA: And Mrs. Clayton?

SEELIG: What of her?

DE LOTA: You brought her *here*.

SEELIG: Well?

DE LOTA: You excuse her and condemn me?

SEELIG: [*Pause.*] There is a cynical maxim that every country has the kind of Jews it deserves. This generous New York deserves the best. A Jew has destroyed the home of a benefactor, a Jew intimate in my own home approved by me and mine. I shall do what I can to repair that destruction.

DE LOTA: There's some extenuation.

SEELIG: What?

DE LOTA: This engagement to Vedah is not the first time I have believed I was in love. There was one other—when I was much younger. The father of the Christian girl was Jew-baiter.

SEELIG: Well?

DE LOTA: I was thrown over—not because I wasn't a man—not because I hadn't ability—nor ambition—nor strength nor promise of success but—I was a Jew.

SEELIG: You will pay that price—the price of being a Jew—almost every day of your life.

DE LOTA: I know—in money—in opportunity—in sensibilities—yes; but that time I paid it—with all those and—more. [*Pause.*] Consider then the temptation when that woman who had thrown me over and married her Christian found that she still could listen to the Jew.

SEELIG: [*Pause.*] This would be a proud moment for me, Benjamin, if one of my own people had told me that story just as you have told it except—that his revenge had been to protect this Christian woman from herself.

[*Noise at door.* CLAYTON *enters violently.*]

CLAYTON: [*To* HOLLAND *who restrains him.*] Don't put your hand on my arm. [*Seeing* DE LOTA.] I thought so.

SEELIG: [*Interposing.*] Thought what?

CLAYTON: I called you on the 'phone—I heard that dog's voice.

SEELIG: One moment—[*To* DE LOTA, *who confronts* CLAYTON.] Go. [DE LOTA *starts out.*]

CLAYTON: He came here to see *her*.

DE LOTA: [*Angrily returning.*] Yes. To see her!

SEELIG: [*Loudly and again interposing.*] I said go. [DE LOTA *sullenly goes.*]

CLAYTON: And you stand for it. Your house.

SEELIG: Judge Hoover was with Mrs. Clayton—also Mrs. Seelig—then I.

CLAYTON: And my boy. Where was Dick?

SEELIG: In his room.

CLAYTON: Well, I *want* him. *He* shan't be corrupted by their damned assignations.

SEELIG: His first call, Frank, and his last.

CLAYTON: That part of it doesn't interest me.

SEELIG: And your threatened divorce was the reason?

CLAYTON: I thought they'd get together on that. Well—I want Dick. [*Pause.*] Send for him, please.

SEELIG: In a minute. He'll be glad to see you—but you mustn't say anything before him you'll regret.

CLAYTON: I promise. I just want him, that's all.

SEELIG: He's with his mother, you know.

CLAYTON: Well?

SEELIG: And Judge Hoover is also with Elinor.

CLAYTON: What of it?

SEELIG: Nothing—except—well, the boy. There mustn't be a dispute, Frank.

CLAYTON: Say that to *them.*

SEELIG: And you can't treat Mrs. Clayton as though she were a guilty woman.

CLAYTON: Why can't I?

SEELIG: Because in the *first* place she isn't guilty.

CLAYTON: Isn't?

SEELIG: No.

CLAYTON: She fools you, Seelig.

SEELIG: The physician who takes a woman through the sacred crises of her life—mental as well as physical—can't be deceived, Frank, and in the *second* place you have forfeited the right to judge her—you came into court yourself unclean.

CLAYTON: And therefore can't resent adultery.

SEELIG: Her defiant visit to De Lota's rooms wasn't adultery.

CLAYTON: Damnation! when a woman's gone that far, the specific degrees of her behavior aren't important.

SEELIG: They're very important, especially when they show recovery. A woman who stops at the edge of the precipice instead of taking the headlong plunge, mustn't be thrown into the gulf—and that by the man she herself had already rescued—by the man whose brutality forced her into the peril.

CLAYTON: Brutality!

SEELIG: A word ill chosen—I meant bestiality—who are you to pass sentence upon her?

CLAYTON: Unfortunately the man who married her.

SEELIG: Why! Dismiss the moral view of marriage. Consider it only as our modern and manly and commercial mind is organized to consider it—a civil covenant—no more.

CLAYTON: What then?

SEELIG: Why, even then your position is that of a thief—a confessed embezzler—complaining in his hypocrisy of what?—that his partner's books appear inaccurate. That is the proportion. On the sacred side of the relation you are doubly guilty—guilty of your immoral conduct—guilty of your base example and guilty of goading a good woman into desperate things. For God's sake, Frank Clayton, cleanse your mind of its masculine conceit, prejudice, selfishness and partiality—recognize your own destructive work—admit it—regret it, undo it, and ask a good woman's forgiveness. [CLAYTON *laughs ironically.* HOOVER *and* ELINOR *enter. Her appearance stills* CLAYTON, *as he turns and sees her.*]

ELINOR: Frank? [*Extends her hand pleadingly.*]

CLAYTON: Well?

ELINOR: I'm in the dust—forgive me.

SEELIG: [*In undertone.*] Judge—[*Starts out,* HOOVER *following.*]

CLAYTON: [*Checking them.*] No—none of that. Let's not contrive any interview of repentance.

ELINOR: You—you're not going to drag the—whole story into the courts.

CLAYTON: I'm going to—[*pause*] do only what is necessary.

ELINOR: [*Sits—speaks with effort at control.*] As we forgive—those that trespass against *us*—

CLAYTON: It's too late to adjust matters with a few appropriate quotations.

HOOVER: You won't waive any right by a reasonable delay.

SEELIG: None—so for pity's sake, Frank, tell Colonel Emory to wait.

CLAYTON: I've retained my own counsel—I don't ask other advice.

ELINOR: [*Brokenly.*] Why—why do you come to *see* me?

CLAYTON: I don't! I came because your friend Mr. De Lota was here *with* you.

ELINOR: Frank!

HOOVER: *I* brought De Lota.

CLAYTON: [*Explosively.*] I don't object. [*Then with fateful control.*] I'm just going to take Dick out of the muck, that's all.

ELINOR: Dick!

HOOVER: [*Bristling.*] The law prescribes the only way that—

ELINOR: [*Quickly interposing.*] Father—don't—don't. We mustn't talk of law and its wrangle over Dick. Frank's perfectly right. If I were meeting Mr. De Lota after the terrible mistake of that night Dick shouldn't be in my care at all. [*Turns to* CLAYTON.] It—it was on account of the suit—that's all. If you let Colonel Emory do that cruel thing without believing me. Father brought him—Dick wasn't here. I said that I wouldn't bring up my jealousy of that woman in Paris—nothing to blacken the name of Dick's *father*—didn't I? [*Turns to* HOOVER.]

HOOVER: She did.

ELINOR: [*Again to* CLAYTON.] You must see Dick—but leave him here, Frank, until you know the very truth—about—it all. You get him, father—

HOOVER: [*Going.*] Of course. I've seen fifty cases that looked worse than this smoothed out by a little patience.

ELINOR: [*Anxiously.*] Get Dick.

CLAYTON: You saw De Lota?

ELINOR: With father.

HOOVER: [*Turning.*] De Lota's statement to me, Frank, was identical with Elinor's.

CLAYTON: Never mind.

HOOVER: [*Coming back.*] I've got to mind—you're not informed. Elinor and De Lota were friends before you ever came to New York. [ELINOR *tries to silence* HOOVER.]

CLAYTON: Friends?

ELINOR: [*Pause, and as* CLAYTON *glares at her.*] Yes. [*To* HOOVER.] Get Dick. Go—don't say any more. [HOOVER *goes.*]

CLAYTON: [*Accusingly.*] I introduced De Lota to you only a year ago.

ELINOR: I know, but—

CLAYTON: Why pretend you were not acquainted?

ELINOR: I—I was considering his feelings.

CLAYTON: What do you mean by *that*?

ELINOR: Before I knew you—we were engaged.

CLAYTON: Engaged.

ELINOR: He and I. Father objected on account of De Lota's race—and—Father forbade me ever to speak of it in his hearing. When you and I met I was still over-sensitive about it and—.

CLAYTON: [*Furiously.*] No, by God! It won't do. You can't square it. I see it now. I've been a dupe for years and years.

ELINOR: I never saw him again until you brought him home.

CLAYTON: Don't, I'm through with it. [*Going.*]

ELINOR: *Frank*—don't go—wait! See Dick!

CLAYTON: [*Turning.*] Dick.

ELINOR: You must see your boy.

CLAYTON: *My* boy! How do I *know* he's my boy? [ELINOR *and* SEELIG *both exclaim.*]

ELINOR: Oh!

SEELIG: Frank!

CLAYTON: You've lived a lie about that blackguard all along until I trap you in his room.

ELINOR: But Dick—our baby Dick. For God's sake, Frank, don't say a thing like that.

CLAYTON: Why not, if it's here—here—[*Striking forehead.*] And hell itself can't burn it out.

SEELIG: [*At the door.*] Frank—it's the boy.

CLAYTON: No—no! [*Turns and goes rapidly out by the other door. Enter* DICK.]

ELINOR: [*To* SEELIG.] What have I done? I didn't know—I didn't know.

DICK: [*To* ELINOR.] Where's Papa?

ELINOR: [*With a heart-broken cry.*] Ah! [*Kneels and takes* DICK *in her arms.*] My boy—my boy—[*Brushes back his hair.*] *Our baby*—boy. [*Kisses and embraces him hysterically, sobbing.*]

ACT IV

SCENE: *Same as Act II, the lounging room at* CLAYTON*'s. A large couch is drawn up in front of fire. The room is lighted only by the lamp on the small table and a candelabrum near the telephone. The pictures on the wall are awry, and there is a look of general desolation about the place. A window is open at left side of room and the sound of church bells comes in.*

DISCOVERED: CLAYTON *on couch near fire—steamer rug over him—he in dressing gown and slippers. His shoes are on floor.*

Enter SUTTON *from dining-room carrying tray.*

SUTTON: I beg pardon, Sir.

CLAYTON: Well?

SUTTON: I've a bowl of bouillon and some toast—I thought maybe you'd try it, Sir.

CLAYTON: [*Indifferently.*] Thank you, Sutton.

SUTTON: [*Putting tray on table at head of the couch.*] Shall I put it nearer? [CLAYTON *shakes head.*] If you'd rather have a milk punch, Sir?

CLAYTON: No.

SUTTON: Or an egg-nogg—[CLAYTON *shakes head.*]

CLAYTON: You might shut that window.

SUTTON: Yes, sir. [*Going to the window.*]

CLAYTON: Those damn bells—

SUTTON: Yes, sir. [*Closes window.*]

CLAYTON: When did Doctor Seelig say he'd come?

SUTTON: As soon as possible.

CLAYTON: And it's been three hours.

SUTTON: Nearly three hours, yes, sir. There's the door—may be Doctor now. [*Goes to hall.* CLAYTON *re-arranges pillow and lies down again.* HOOVER's *voice is heard outside.*]

SUTTON: [*Also outside.*] He's lying down—in the smoking room. [*Enter* SUTTON. HOOVER *and* ELINOR *appear in hallway.*]

SUTTON: [*Leaning over the back of the couch.*] Pardon, sir—Judge Hoover!

CLAYTON: [*Shaking head.*] No—

SUTTON: And Mrs. Clayton, sir.

CLAYTON: [*Sitting up.*] Here?

HOOVER: [*Entering.*] I don't want to intrude, Frank, but it seems necessary. Come in, Elinor! [SUTTON *goes.* ELINOR *comes down to the couch.*]

CLAYTON: You'll have to see my attorney. I'm not able to talk any business.

ELINOR: [*Tenderly.*] You're ill, Frank?

CLAYTON: [*Coldly.*] Resting a minute—

ELINOR: I'm sorry to disturb you, but—it's for Dick. [*Pause.* CLAYTON *motions slightly to a chair which* HOOVER *places*—ELINOR *sits.*] You know that to-morrow is—a holiday? [CLAYTON *nods.*] Dick's eager about it—

CLAYTON: [*Complainingly to* HOOVER.] This isn't necessary, is it?

ELINOR: Dick's talked for days about his tree and hanging up his stocking by the big fireplace at home. Our difference, Frank, mustn't put a blight on the boy's Christmas.

CLAYTON: [*In undertone.*] My God! What drivel!

ELINOR: Drivel when I repeat it—if you will—but not as little Dick talks it day after day. His love for you isn't drivel.

CLAYTON: [*To* HOOVER.] You promised Emory to begin suit if I'd keep quiet.

HOOVER: Yes.

CLAYTON: Nearly a month ago.

HOOVER: I know—but—[*Turns to* ELINOR.]

ELINOR: *I* refuse. There's nothing left me to live for but my baby and his happiness. I won't—I won't bring an accusation against his father— [CLAYTON *moves away wearily to mantel*—ELINOR *rises.*] You are his father and only your wish to crush me makes you pretend to doubt it. I've forfeited your love, I know—I'm not here to plead against that—but to avoid any scar I can for the boy's heart. I want you to let Dick come here to-morrow—[CLAYTON *moves impatiently.*] Not with *me*—with Miss Doane. I want you to see him—and take him in your arms—

CLAYTON: [*Shakes head.*] No—

HOOVER: [*With some indignation.*] Whatever he is—he's a child—and for seven years this was his home.

CLAYTON: There'll be other anniversaries. He may as well learn now.

ELINOR: No—not now. When he's old enough to understand I'll *tell* him—the truth.

CLAYTON: What is the truth?

ELINOR: That his mother—was a foolish woman who thought her husband didn't understand her. That his father punished her out of all proportion to her offense, but only as *women* must expect punishment.

CLAYTON: [*Sneering.*] I know—because *men* are brutes.

ELINOR: Because—God has put into woman's keeping a trust—of which no one—neither husbands nor fathers tell them truly—about which the world in its vain disputes of equality misleads them—of which they learn only through their own suffering.

CLAYTON: [*Leaving* ELINOR *and going to* HOOVER.] This kind of thing is— what I try to escape.

ELINOR: [*Following.*] Let Dick spend his Christmas morning here. [CLAYTON *shakes head.*] You used to ask after him every day until you took this cruel pose of pretending that he's not *your* boy.

CLAYTON: [*To* HOOVER.] Please—

ELINOR: I couldn't tell you in Doctor Seelig's presence plainly enough. You know Father's insane antipathy to—[*pause*] to *those people.* Any word—the most sacred—any name—the most honored—by scornful repetition becomes a reproach, and I had grown fearful of ridicule about my former friendship for—Ben De Lota. That was my sole reason for silence.

CLAYTON: [*Wearily.*] My God!

HOOVER: Elinor, Frank! [*Indicates hall.*]

BURRILL: [*Outside.*] Is he too ill to be seen a moment?

HOOVER: [*Peering cautiously into hall.*] Woman, too. [*Enter* SUTTON.]

SUTTON: Mr. Burrill, sir.

CLAYTON: I said no one but Doctor Seelig.

SUTTON: Miss Seelig, Doctor's daughter, is with Mr. Burrill.

ELINOR: Father! [*Going quickly out by dining room door.*]

HOOVER: [*Following.*] I want a word, Frank, when they're gone.

CLAYTON: But not with *her.*

HOOVER: No—she'll go. [HOOVER *leaves.*]

CLAYTON: My coat! [SUTTON *gets* CLAYTON'*s coat and waistcoat from the table*—CLAYTON *takes them and nods for* SUTTON *to go.* SUTTON *goes.* CLAYTON *feebly unbuttons his dressing gown, pauses, wearily throws coat and waistcoat to a chair from which they slip to the floor.* CLAYTON *sits on the couch.* BURRILL *and* VEDAH *enter.*]

BURRILL: Sorry to disturb you, Mr. Clayton.

VEDAH: And your man says you're not well.

CLAYTON: Nothing! Won't you be seated? [VEDAH *takes chair* BURRILL *places for her.*]

BURRILL: I'm—[*Pause.*] That is, we're—well, I wanted to thank you for my contract on the court-house sculpture.

CLAYTON: They gave it to you, did they?

BURRILL: Yes. The finished marble must be up in a year. Material—workmen—studio—everything's cheaper on the other side—

CLAYTON: I know.

BURRILL: So I'm sailing day after to-morrow—unless you need me here in the architect's libel suit!

CLAYTON: They've withdrawn that.

BURRILL: They have? [CLAYTON *nods.* BURRILL *turns eagerly to* VEDAH.] Then we go—

VEDAH: Yes!

BURRILL: Vedah and I have been married—

CLAYTON: Married?

BURRILL: Half an hour ago.

VEDAH: Yes. [*Rises and stands by* BURRILL.]

BURRILL: [*Taking* VEDAH'*s hand.*] I'm the happiest man alive.

CLAYTON: [*Moodily.*] Half an hour? Ah, yes. [*With an effort rises and goes to them.*] Well, I congratulate you both.

VEDAH: Papa and Mama don't know it yet. [BURRILL *goes to the fireplace.*]

CLAYTON: An elopement?

VEDAH: Is it? If we didn't leave the city? [*Enter* SUTTON.]

SUTTON: Mrs. Seelig, Sir. [VEDAH *anxiously goes to* BURRILL. *Enter* MRS. SEELIG. SUTTON *goes out.*]

MRS. SEELIG: Vedah. [*Sees* BURRILL.] You know your father's wishes.

BURRILL: We've been married, Mrs. Seelig.

MRS. SEELIG: Vedah!

VEDAH: Yes, Mama.

MRS. SEELIG: When?

VEDAH: At five o'clock.

MRS. SEELIG: How? Who married you?

BURRILL: A Justice of the Peace.

MRS. SEELIG: Frank! [*Turns to* CLAYTON.]

VEDAH: [*Going to her mother.*] Remember your parents objected to Papa.

MRS. SEELIG: [*To* CLAYTON.] My father was a Rabbi—Doctor Seelig's ideas were advanced—even his own people thought so.

VEDAH: No couple could be happier than you have been.

MRS. SEELIG: Is *this* happiness—my only daughter runs away—why? To-day? Why secretly?

BURRILL: I'm sailing for Paris.

VEDAH: [*Returning to* BURRILL.] To be gone a year.

BURRILL: The separation was impossible.

MRS. SEELIG: Couldn't you have trusted Vedah that long?

VEDAH: It was *I*, Mama.

MRS. SEELIG: You?

VEDAH: To risk a sculptor in Paris? Oh no!

MRS. SEELIG: Well, go home and tell your poor father.

VEDAH: I want you with us, Mama.

BURRILL: I'm willing to tell the Doctor alone.

VEDAH: [*In alarm.*] No.

MRS. SEELIG: Very well, wait for me and we'll meet Papa together.

VEDAH: [*To* CLAYTON.] Good-bye! [*They shake hands.*]

CLAYTON: Good-bye. [*Shakes hands with* BURRILL.] *Bon voyage.*

BURRILL: Thank you. [*Starts out with* VEDAH.]

MRS. SEELIG: [*Impulsively.*] Vedah! [VEDAH *turns,* MRS. SEELIG *embraces and kisses her.*]

BURRILL: Thank you, Mrs. Seelig. [*Goes out with* VEDAH.]

MRS. SEELIG: [*Sighing and turning to* CLAYTON *who is at the fireplace.*] I left Elinor—waiting for Judge Hoover. When I go back I want to carry her some comfort.

CLAYTON: Your arrival will do that, Mrs. Seelig.

MRS. SEELIG: I hope so. This is Christmas Eve, you know.

CLAYTON: Yes.

MRS. SEELIG: Little Dick has always found his stocking—in there. [*Indicates the music room.*]

CLAYTON: Mrs. Clayton mustn't use Dick to break down my decision.

MRS. SEELIG: I bought a little tree—[*Indicates its height.*] I caught the

Christian shopkeeper smiling—but no matter. I had Sutton take it in at the tradesman's entrance. [CLAYTON *turns away.*] I know. You think that is more indelicacy characteristic of the race—but Vedah is going with that young man—my own heart is alive to the suffering around us. *Yours?*—yes! it comes soon enough to us all—but Frank!—that little boy who is—

CLAYTON: Please! Mrs. Seelig, the doctor's ordered me to avoid all excitement. [*Sits wearily on couch.*]

MRS. SEELIG: [*Sympathetically.*] He didn't tell *us.*

CLAYTON: Not Doctor Seelig.

MRS. SEELIG: Oh!

CLAYTON: A specialist—but he doesn't help me. Sutton 'phoned and I'm waiting for Doctor Seelig now.

MRS. SEELIG: Now? I can't meet him here. But that tree's in the house and you must let us bring Dick over. [*Enter* HOOVER.]

HOOVER: Pardon.

MRS. SEELIG: I'm going—Good night. [*She goes.*]

CLAYTON: [*Pause.*] Where is—?

HOOVER: Elinor? [*Clayton nods.*] She left immediately. [CLAYTON *lies down on couch.*] She's—not—a bad woman, Frank! What she said about my opposition was true—but we all learn. I didn't know the hearts those people had in 'em—[*Pause.*] And her girlish affair with De Lota was—well, you know Elinor's craze for music. That's the explanation—attraction was mostly artistic. [*Enter* SUTTON.]

SUTTON: Doctor Seelig.

CLAYTON: You'll have to excuse me, Judge.

HOOVER: Sorry to see you—ill, old man. [*Enter* SEELIG.]

SEELIG: Good evening.

HOOVER: Good evening, Doctor. [*Going, extends hand.*] I wish you— [*pause*] the compliments of the season.

SEELIG: The same to you, Judge. [HOOVER *goes.* SUTTON *takes* SEELIG*'s hat and coat.*]

SEELIG: Well, Frank—under the weather? [*Leans over back of couch.*]

CLAYTON: Pretty rotten.

SEELIG: Need a little air in here.

CLAYTON: I couldn't stand the damned bells.

SEELIG: Better stand them a minute. [*Opens window. The sound of church bells is heard.*]

CLAYTON: "Peace on earth, good will to men."

SEELIG: How long have you been this way? [*Taking* CLAYTON*'s pulse.*]

CLAYTON: Been here—since last night.

SEELIG: Drinking?

CLAYTON: Very little.

SEELIG: Pain anywhere?

CLAYTON: Some—back of my neck near the shoulders.

SEELIG: Headache? [CLAYTON *shakes head*.] No other pains? [CLAYTON *shakes head*.] What kept you in the house?

CLAYTON: I feel all in—rotten tired.

SEELIG: I'd have come earlier, Frank, but a long list. Then there was an accident to a little chap on Third Avenue—they brought him to the hospital—smaller than your boy. We operate on him at eight-thirty. [*Regards watch.*] When I got away from that the police stopped us at every cross street. Wonderful sight on the Avenue—people seem to have money. I think a prosperity Christmas. [*Picks up the coat and waistcoat from the floor—folds them. Straightens pictures on wall.*]

CLAYTON: Can't we have that window closed now? [*Pause—*SEELIG *closes the window, shutting out the sound of the bells.*] Ha! "Glad tidings of great joy."

SEELIG: Comes only once a year.

CLAYTON: You any respect for the whole business—that Christ fabrication?

SEELIG: [*Going to fireplace.*] You mean the Church idea—the creeds?

CLAYTON: Yes.

SEELIG: [*Pause.*] I've outgrown the one my own mother started me in, but I take off my hat to the man.

CLAYTON: Why!

SEELIG: Oh, He knew—He'd worked it all out.

CLAYTON: Worked what out?

SEELIG: This thing we call Life. He knew the essence of it.

CLAYTON: I don't see that.

SEELIG: "As a man thinketh"—that was His answer.

CLAYTON: What does that answer?

SEELIG: Everything. When I felt your pulse there and let go your hand you carried it back to the couch—so.

CLAYTON: Expect me to keep it out there like a hat-rack?

SEELIG: I'd hoped you would drop it a little.

CLAYTON: Why?

SEELIG: Hoped you'd relax. Let's try it now. [*Lifts* CLAYTON*'s hand.*] Don't tense those muscles—put your weight me. [*Drops hand.*] There!

CLAYTON: Well, what does that do?

SEELIG: That's the only part of your body that's relaxed—Now a deep breath and let go. Don't hold yourself up from the couch. So! [CLAYTON *does as told and perceptibly relaxes.*]

CLAYTON: Nerves, I know.

SEELIG: [*Tapping his own forehead.*] It's this. Why, I have patients—business men—who are always tied up like a wet fishing line—sleep that way. Do you know why that wrinkle is between your eyes?

CLAYTON: I'm sick, that's why.

SEELIG: Because the wrinkle's in your mind. That coat I took from the floor said mental wrinkles, "As a man thinketh," my dear Frank. [*Pause.*] What is it now—come?

CLAYTON: *You* don't have to ask, do you?

SEELIG: I do ask.

CLAYTON: Just to keep my mind on it, I suppose?

SEELIG: No—I want to hear you talk about it.

CLAYTON: My mind will be all right, I'll be all right, when that damned dog is dead in hell!

SEELIG: [*Pause.*] You hate him pretty bitterly, don't you?

CLAYTON: I hate him the best I know how.

SEELIG: You know what good hating does to the hater?

CLAYTON: You mean to me?

SEELIG: [*Nodding.*] To everybody. Kills him.

CLAYTON: Kills him? [SEELIG *nods.*]

SEELIG: [*Pause.*] Hate generates one of the deadliest poisons in nature. I've had trouble in my time saving a baby that had nursed milk from the breast of an angry woman. You've heard of the bite of a blue gum negro being poison.

CLAYTON: Knew a man who lost his thumb that way.

SEELIG: Well, it is no more poisonous than the bite of a red gum negro, or the bite of a red gum white man, if either of them gets angry enough, the blue gum negro is just a little nearer the animal and gets mad quicker, that's all. Now, you lie here with this grouch of yours and you generate constantly an internal poison. I haven't any medicines that can beat that.

CLAYTON: When I get so much of it in me that I shoot that cur, as I shall some day, they'll call it murder.

SEELIG: [*Pause.*] I used to get pretty angry when I was younger, but I think it was more to show off.

CLAYTON: You mean I do this to "show off?"

SEELIG: I mean you are influenced by public opinion. If you and he were the only creatures left in the world you'd admit he didn't do much more than you'd have done in his place.

CLAYTON: You mean I'd go into another man's home and ruin it?

SEELIG: This man didn't come into your home and ruin it. He meets an old sweetheart, meets her when she thinks she is being neglected.

CLAYTON: [*Sitting up.*] Neglected? Why, she had this house and our summer place at Newport—a forty-five horse power limousine—she
had—

SEELIG: See here, Frank, you were neglecting her. He did what nine men
out of ten would do. He knows the price that's being paid, and I
know, that he'd walk around the Belt Line to-night in the snow,
barefooted, to have the record closed.

CLAYTON: Suppose you think I ought to hunt him up and shake hands
with him?

SEELIG: No—don't think you should ever see him again, even mentally;
but it doesn't need murder to acquire that attitude. I want you to be
big enough to dismiss it. That's why I quote this carpenter-prophet
of Nazareth—a truth that took me a postgraduate course to learn
and twenty-five years to demonstrate—He found out by himself. He
said in one of his first sermons: "*Forgive,* and ye shall be forgiven;
give and it shall be given unto you, good measure pressed down,
shaken together and running over shall men give unto your bosom."

CLAYTON: Oh that religious elation—

SEELIG: It wasn't religion He was preaching, but a good working rule of
life. This precept of good-will—people regard the words "Good-
will" as interchangeable with "Peace," but will is active, good will is a
constructive force. I've seen sick people get well merely through two
or three hearty good wishers rooting for them. I've figured it out
that there's an influence circulating through all men when they'll
permit it, just as the current through that lamp goes through all
other lamps in this house. Stop it in the man by avarice or cupidity,
divert it by envy, *turn it back* by hate, and something goes wrong
with the machinery. "Give and it shall be given unto you."

CLAYTON: You take Him too literally, Doctor.

SEELIG: The mistake is not taking Him *literally enough.* I've cured many
taking that sermon literally. [*Sits beside* CLAYTON *on his couch.*] I find
what is on the patient's mind. Generally some hate or fear—sometimes regret or remorse—then I try to show the patient that yesterday is yesterday, that his past life doesn't concern him any more than
last year's snow. If I can get a man looking ahead—hopeful—anxious
to get on the job—why he's cured.

CLAYTON: [*Doggedly.*] I'll look ahead when I get even with this fellow.

SEELIG: Well, say you've got even—that you've dealt him some deadly
blow, irreparably injured him or his happiness! What then? My dear
Frank, there is nothing so disappointing as a satisfied revenge.

CLAYTON: I can't forget it.

SEELIG: Yes you can.

CLAYTON: It's here on my mind. [*Covers his eyes and forehead.*]

SEELIG: Because your mind is empty. Work is the answer to your condition.

CLAYTON: [*Shaking his head.*] Too late for that now.

SEELIG: Nonsense! Take this parable of the eleventh hour. The men in that were kicking because those who had worked one hour got as much as those who had put in a full day. Remember what the Nazarene proposed to pay.

CLAYTON: What?

SEELIG: *Peace of mind.* A sharehold in what He called the Kingdom of Heaven. The eleventh hour men worked only one hour, but they worked—*the last hour.* You get that peace of mind, whenever—you work, whenever you *do* something—and the splendid thing is, it's *never too late to do it.* [*Rises vigorously—stands at mantel.*]

CLAYTON: [*Wearily.*] Good God, Doctor, a man can't get up and work at something he doesn't care for in order to forget something he's thinking of all the time. It's well enough for you—always called in by some poor devil who thinks you can help him. Give me your job and your equipment for it and I'll talk hope and clean living myself.

SEELIG: [*Half sadly.*] I know that attitude. It's always the next pasture that seems the greenest. If I have any regret it is that instead of being a physician I wasn't a priest. I think most diseases are not physical so much as they are mental or spiritual.

CLAYTON: Well, I'd like to do that kind of thing myself.

SEELIG: You can do it.

CLAYTON: I can?

SEELIG: Yes—only you have to *begin.*

CLAYTON: You mean with myself?

SEELIG: I mean with the work that's nearest to you, Frank. If I wanted you to walk around Central Park you would have to get up, you would have to walk to the door; you would have to go down the steps; you would have to *walk* to Central Park. In other words, you would have to cover the ground that is nearest to you. Now, in the work you say you would like to do, you've also got to cover the ground that's nearest you. Suppose you *were* going to *save* somebody and you had your choice—whom would you save? Why, the people dearest to you. You would save—little Dick—eh?

CLAYTON: [*In pain.*] Don't talk of Dick.

SEELIG: I've got to talk of him. The boy isn't getting a father's care.

CLAYTON: You advised me not to take him.

SEELIG: I still advise that. He *is* getting a mother's care, but he needs a father's also. Now suppose you could save little Dick. The next dearest person to you would be his mother, wouldn't she?

CLAYTON: She's made her bed.

SEELIG: Yes, but after you've made beds there's something more to do than lie in them. After a reasonable time you are to get up and get *out* of them.

CLAYTON: She's all right—free to do as she likes.

SEELIG: No, she isn't. She's a slave to her remorse—she's looking back. *She* can't realize that yesterday is yesterday and that a dead yesterday is just as dead as Babylon. Now, you want work to do—why not do that?

CLAYTON: Overlook what she's done?

SEELIG: Yes—overlook what she's done. She wasn't perfect—nobody is. She makes one mistake—with you it's final. You don't judge anyone else that way. I've seen you throwing little Dick the baseball teaching him to hold it and not to break his chubby fingers—standing two yards from him—drop and drop and drop it. You didn't get tired— you were developing the boy. Now the assumption is that Elinor came to you with her character fully developed; but my, dear old friend, character never stops developing if we are in the right line. There's still the perfecting of a fine woman. You want something to do—do that.

CLAYTON: All right—Tell her.—[*Pause.*] I forgive her. [*Pause.*] But that I'm through with it just the same.

SEELIG: I'll not carry lies to her. If you forgive her you'll go where she is— you'll go looking forward and not backward—[CLAYTON *shakes head, pause*—SEELIG *regards watch.*] I hate to leave you in this mood, Frank.

CLAYTON: I'll—be all right.

SEELIG: Why not get in the machine and take a run through the Park— only a half hour—because I must get back to the hospital.

CLAYTON: [*Pause.*] You won't try any snap judgment on me—no driving up to your door and making a scene of it?

SEELIG: Chauffeur will take your order. [*Pause.* CLAYTON *begins to put on his shoes.* SEELIG *goes to the telephone.*]

CLAYTON: What are you doing?

SEELIG: I can't be home to dinner. [*'Phones.*] Yes—operator. Give me 319 Plaza—Plaza—yes.

CLAYTON: I think—[*Pause.*] *Mrs.* Seelig was here; just before you came—

SEELIG: Yes?

CLAYTON: [*Pause.*] They *expect* you at dinner.

SEELIG: [*'Phoning.*] Holland? [*Pause.*] This is Doctor—I'll speak to Mrs. Seelig—[*Speaks to* CLAYTON.] What did she want?

CLAYTON: Oh—Dick's Christmas principally.

SEELIG: That reminds me I told Dick I'd see *you*. [*'Phones.*] Hello?—yes Sarah? I can't get home to dinner dear—[*Pause.*] No—impossible. [*Pause.*] I'm at Frank Clayton's—[*Pause.*] Nothing—that is, nothing serious. He's going out with me—just to get the air, that's all. What's that? [*Pause.*] Yes, I'll speak to her.

CLAYTON: Speak to whom?

SEELIG: [*Speaking to* CLAYTON.] Mrs. Seelig wants to know if I won't speak to your wife. [*'Phones.*] Hello—that you, Elinor? [*'Pause.*] Yes—he's all right—perfectly. [*Pause.*] Not yet, but we're going out—in the car—I'll give it to him.

CLAYTON: Give what?

SEELIG: Just a minute. [*Turns to* CLAYTON *who is putting on his coat.*] It was a Christmas gift—from little Dick—he asked me to bring it here.

CLAYTON: What is it? [SEELIG *takes small package from his pocket and hands it to* CLAYTON. *As* CLAYTON *opens package* SEELIG *turns attention to 'phone again.*]

SEELIG: Yes, I'm still here—yes. [*Listens in silence as* CLAYTON *undoes the package which contains a photograph in a leather case.* CLAYTON *bends over it, deeply moved.*] Yes—yes—very well—thank you—good night.

CLAYTON: [*Quickly.*] Wait.

SEELIG: [*Startled by loudness of* CLAYTON'*s call.*] Wait. [*Laughs and explains.*] I said wait a minute.

CLAYTON: She at that 'phone?

SEELIG: Yes.

CLAYTON: [*Angrily.*] Let me have it—there are a few things I want to say to her.

SEELIG: [*Protesting.*] Not in that mood, Frank.

CLAYTON: It's all a frame up to torture me. [*Takes 'phone—speaks angrily.*] Hello! [*Anger goes from his face—whole manner changes—tone becomes gentle and affectionate.*] Dick, that you, Dick? [*Pause.*] Yes, I hear you—[*Pause.*] I *got* it, my boy, thank you—[*Pause.*] *You* bet I like it—[*Pause.*] The *tree*? [*Pause.*] Yes, by the big fireplace—[*Pause.*] To-night? Well—[*Pause.*] Then—[*Pause and effort.*] Tell her to come—with you! [*Drops 'phone on table, receiver hanging towards the floor. Sinks into chair face down on elbow sobbing.* SEELIG *walks to 'phone, hangs up receiver.* CLAYTON *reaches out his right hand blindly.* SEELIG *takes it—holds it reassuringly and firmly. Gives* CLAYTON *a tonic slap on back and helps him rise.* CLAYTON *walks back to chair facing the fire.*]

SEELIG: [*Solemnly.*] Frank! There is one moment in a woman's life—dazed by chloroform—wrung with pain—when her physician hears her speak the name of the man for whom she suffers. [*Pause.*] Every vestige of that doubt you uttered in my library must be effaced from your heart. [*Rings push button.*]

CLAYTON: I didn't—*invent* the doubt.

SEELIG: I know.

CLAYTON: I think—[*Pause.*] I *hope* to God I'll get rid of it—in time.

SEELIG: It mustn't mar this reunion. [*Pause.*] When I started for this house I hoped—for what has occurred. [*Indicates 'phone.*] I didn't know just how it would come about—but I knew—that doubt had to be removed.

CLAYTON: I don't want to think of it. [*Enter* SUTTON.]

SEELIG: [*To* SUTTON.] A gentleman is outside in a cab, just behind my car? Ask him to come in. [SUTTON *goes.*]

CLAYTON: [*Quickly turning.*] Who is it? [*Pause.*] Who?

SEELIG: I want you to be calm Frank.

CLAYTON: *Who??*

SEELIG: [*Calmly.*] The one you hate.

CLAYTON: No! By God, no! [*Starts toward the hall.*]

SEELIG: [*Interposing and catching him.*] Frank—if you had to go under the knife you'd trust me as a surgeon, wouldn't you?

CLAYTON: [*Struggling to free himself.*] You're bungling this job.

SEELIG: [*Still holding* CLAYTON.] I'm not bungling it. [*Enter* DE LOTA.]

CLAYTON: Don't come in here.

DE LOTA: Mr. Clayton—

SEELIG: [*Between the two men.*] Speak only when I bid you—[*Pause. To* CLAYTON.] Now listen! [*To* DE LOTA.] Before Mr. Clayton introduced you to Mrs. Clayton a year ago—when had you last seen her?

DE LOTA. About eight years before.

SEELIG: That is nine years ago.

DE LOTA: Nine years ago.

CLAYTON: What's one *lie* more or less.

SEELIG: Where were you *eight* years ago?

DE LOTA: In France.

SEELIG: [*Sternly.*] Where!

DE LOTA: [*Pause.*] The prison *de La Santé,* in Paris.

SEELIG: For how long a term?

DE LOTA: One year.

SEELIG: I asked you to bring your prison paper of discharge. [DE LOTA *hands paper to* SEELIG. SEELIG *regards paper and displays it to* CLAYTON.] You read French—numerals at least. The date is there.

CLAYTON: [*After a glance.*] Well?

SEELIG: Also Mr. Burrill was in the court-room when Mr. De Lota was sentenced. [*Pause.*] To show this paper, to admit in your hearing—this fact has not been an easy thing for Benjamin De Lota to do. He does it at my urging—the appeal of one *Jew*—to another *Jew*. He is going—he lives by writing criticism. His signature to an article has a money value—and despite these personal mistakes, I believe his influence in print is wholesome. He leaves your magazines. Of course, he can't expect their recommendation, but I have *promised* him—*your silence.*

CLAYTON: [*Pause.*] I shan't—[*Pause.*] Interfere. [SEELIG *turns*—DE LOTA *goes.*]

SEELIG: [*Hand on* CLAYTON's *shoulder.*] I'm proud of you—[*Pause.*] Now forgive an old practitioner who knew he had to cauterize quickly.

CLAYTON: You're—a friend all right. [*Pause.*] Prison!

SEELIG: That year.

CLAYTON: And I made that rotten accusation. What a brute I've been!

SEELIG: My dear Frank, that also is yesterday. [*Pause and change of manner.*] Dick is coming to-night?

CLAYTON: Yes.

SEELIG: And his mother—[CLAYTON *nods.*] I'll leave you alone.

CLAYTON: I'd rather you were here.

SEELIG: I'll wait as long as I can. [*Consults watch.*]

CLAYTON: [*Seated on couch.*] There's some troubling news for you.

SEELIG: For me?

CLAYTON: [*Nodding.*] I'd like to cushion it if I could.

SEELIG: You mean *bad* news!

CLAYTON: Depends.

SEELIG: [*Pause.*] Well—

CLAYTON: [*Carefully.*] You know that—Vedah—rather fancied Burrill, don't you?

SEELIG: Yes.

CLAYTON: Burrill is sailing in a day or two—and—

SEELIG: [*Pause.*] Well?

CLAYTON: Well—they've been—[*Pause.*]

SEELIG: [*Calmly.*] Married?

CLAYTON: To-day. [SEELIG *nods ruminatively. Enter* DICK. MRS. SEELIG *and* ELINOR *appear in arch.*]

DICK: [*Running to* CLAYTON.] Papa!

CLAYTON: Why, Dick boy! [*Embraces him.* ELINOR *goes into the music room.* MRS. SEELIG *comes down.*]

DICK: [*To* SEELIG.] Did you give it to him?

SEELIG: [*Still brooding.*] Yes.

DICK: [*To* CLAYTON.] You like it?

CLAYTON: You bet I liked it. [DICK *laughs*—CLAYTON *leading* DICK *toward the music room speaks to* MRS. SEELIG.] I told the Doctor.

MRS. SEELIG: You mean—?

CLAYTON: Vedah and Burrill. [*Goes with* DICK *into music room.*]

MRS. SEELIG: [*Coming to* SEELIG's *side.*] Samuel.

SEELIG: [*Pause.*] You knew it?

MRS. SEELIG: I had no idea of it—but he has to cross the ocean. They love each other—Vedah was almost broken-hearted. We wanted Vedah to sacrifice her life to teach the idea of one God—but Samuel—[*Pause. Puts hand on* SEELIG's *arm.*]

SEELIG: Well?

MRS. SEELIG: The one God was wiser than my father, who was a Rabbi. He may be wiser than we are. [*Pause*—SEELIG *gently lifts her hand and kisses it. Pause.*] Samuel—they're at home. Come forgive them and let's be happy at dinner. [SEELIG *shakes head.*] You mean you won't forgive them?

SEELIG: [*Pause.*] I mean *only* that I can't come to dinner. There is a surgery case at the hospital.

MRS. SEELIG: [*Pleading.*] Let someone else.

SEELIG: [*Shaking head.*] Too important.

MRS. SEELIG: Who is it?

SEELIG: A little boy from the East Side. I don't remember his name, but the appointment is for eight-thirty. [MRS. SEELIG *leaves his side.* ELINOR *enters,* CLAYTON *and* DICK *appear in doorway after her.* ELINOR *comes down to* SEELIG.]

SEELIG: It's all right? [ELINOR *nods yes—takes* SEELIG's *face in both hands and kisses him.*]

DICK: [*To* CLAYTON *in childish treble.*] She kissed him—

OVERTONES

by

Alice Gerstenberg

First performed by the Washington Square Players at the Bandbox Theater, New York City, on November 8, 1915.

CHARACTERS

HARRIET, *a cultured woman*
HETTY, *her primitive self*
MARGARET, *a cultured woman*
MAGGIE, *her primitive self*

TIME: The present.
SCENE: HARRIET'*s fashionable living-room. The door at the back leads to the hall. In the centre a tea table with a chair either side. At the back a cabinet.*
HARRIET'*s gown is a light, "jealous" green. Her counterpart,* HETTY, *wears a gown of the same design but in a darker shade.* MARGARET *wears a gown of lavender chiffon while her counterpart,* MAGGIE, *wears a gown of the same design in purple, a purple scarf veiling her face. Chiffon is used to give a sheer effect, suggesting a possibility of primitive and cultured selves merging into one woman. The primitive and cultured selves never come into actual physical contact but try to sustain the impression of mental conflict.* HARRIET *never sees* HETTY, *never talks to her but rather thinks aloud looking into space.* HETTY, *however, looks at* HARRIET, *talks intently and shadows her continually. The same is true of* MARGARET *and* MAGGIE. *The voices of the cultured women are affected and lingering, the voices of the primitive impulsive and more or less staccato.*
    When the curtain rises HARRIET *is seated right of tea table, busying herself with the tea things.*

HETTY: Harriet. [*There is no answer.*] Harriet, my other self. [*There is no answer.*] My trained self.

HARRIET: [*Listens intently.*] Yes? [*From behind* HARRIET's *chair* HETTY *rises slowly.*]

HETTY: I want to talk to you.

HARRIET: Well?

HETTY: [*Looking at* HARRIET *admiringly.*] Oh, Harriet, you are beautiful to-day.

HARRIET: Am I presentable, Hetty?

HETTY: Suits me.

HARRIET: I've tried to make the best of the good points.

HETTY: My passions are deeper than yours. I can't keep on the mask as you do. I'm crude and real, you are my appearance in the world.

HARRIET: I am what you wish the world to believe you are.

HETTY: You are the part of me that has been trained.

HARRIET: I am your educated self.

HETTY: I am the rushing river; you are the ice over the current.

HARRIET: I am your subtle overtones.

HETTY: But together we are one woman, the wife of Charles Goodrich.

HARRIET: There I disagree with you, Hetty, I alone am his wife.

HETTY: [*Indignantly.*] Harriet, how can you say such a thing!

HARRIET: Certainly. I am the one who flatters him. I have to be the one who talks to him. If I gave you a chance you would tell him at once that you dislike him.

HETTY: [*Moving away.*] I don't love him, that's certain.

HARRIET: You leave all the fibbing to me. He doesn't suspect that my calm, suave manner hides your hatred. Considering the amount of scheming it causes me it can safely be said that he is my husband.

HETTY: Oh, if you love him—

HARRIET: I? I haven't any feelings. It isn't my business to love anybody.

HETTY: Then why need you object to calling him my husband?

HARRIET: I resent your appropriation of a man who is managed only through the cleverness of my artifice.

HETTY: You may be clever enough to deceive him, Harriet, but I am still the one who suffers. I can't forget he is my husband. I can't forget that I might have married John Caldwell.

HARRIET: How foolish of you to remember John, just because we met his wife by chance.

HETTY: That's what I want to talk to you about. She may be here at any moment. I want to advise you about what to say to her this afternoon.

HARRIET: By all means tell me now and don't interrupt while she is here.

You have a most annoying habit of talking to me when people are present. Sometimes it is all I can do to keep my poise and appear *not* to be listening to you.

HETTY: Impress her.

HARRIET: Hetty, dear, is it not my custom to impress people?

HETTY: I hate her.

HARRIET: I can't let her see that.

HETTY: I hate her because she married John.

HARRIET: Only after you had refused him.

HETTY: [*Turning on* HARRIET.] Was it my fault that I refused him?

HARRIET: That's right, blame me.

HETTY: It was your fault. You told me he was too poor and never would be able to do anything in painting. Look at him now, known in Europe, just returned from eight years in Paris, famous.

HARRIET: It was too poor a gamble at the time. It was much safer to accept Charles's money and position.

HETTY: And then John married Margaret within the year.

HARRIET: Out of spite.

HETTY: Freckled, gawky-looking thing she was, too.

HARRIET: [*A little sadly.*] Europe improved her. She was stunning the other morning.

HETTY: Make her jealous to-day.

HARRIET: Shall I be haughty or cordial or caustic or—

HETTY: Above all else you must let her know that we are rich.

HARRIET: Oh, yes, I do that quite easily now.

HETTY: You must put it on a bit.

HARRIET: Never fear.

HETTY: Tell her I love my husband.

HARRIET: My husband—

HETTY: Are you going to quarrel with me?

HARRIET: [*Moves away.*] No, I have no desire to quarrel with you. It is quite too uncomfortable. I couldn't get away from you if I tried.

HETTY: [*Stamping her foot and following* HARRIET.] You were a stupid fool to make me refuse John, I'll never forgive you—never—

HARRIET: [*Stopping and holding up her hand.*] Don't get me all excited. I'll be in no condition to meet her properly this afternoon.

HETTY: [*Passionately.*] I could choke you for robbing me of John.

HARRIET: [*Retreating.*] Don't muss me!

HETTY: You don't know how you have made me suffer.

HARRIET: [*Beginning to feel the strength of* HETTY*'s emotion surge through her and trying to conquer it.*] It is not my business to have heartaches.

HETTY: You're bloodless. Nothing but sham—sham—while I—

HARRIET: [*Emotionally.*] Be quiet! I can't let her see that I have been fighting with my inner self.

HETTY: And now after all my suffering you say it has cost you more than it has cost me to be married to Charles. But it's the pain here in my heart—I've paid the price—I've paid—Charles is not your husband!

HARRIET: [*Trying to conquer emotion.*] He is.

HETTY: [*Follows* HARRIET.] He isn't.

HARRIET: [*Weakly.*] He is.

HETTY: [*Towering over* HARRIET.] He isn't! I'll kill you!

HARRIET: [*Overpowered, sinks into a chair.*] Don't—don't—you're stronger than I—you're—

HETTY: Say he's mine.

HARRIET: He's ours.

HETTY: [*The telephone rings.*] There she is now. [HETTY *hurries to 'phone but* HARRIET *regains her supremacy.*]

HARRIET: [*Authoritatively.*] Wait! I can't let the telephone girl down there hear my real self. It isn't proper. [*At 'phone.*] Show Mrs. Caldwell up.

HETTY: I'm so excited, my heart's in my mouth.

HARRIET: [*At the mirror.*] A nice state you've put my nerves into.

HETTY: Don't let her see you're nervous.

HARRIET: Quick, put the veil on, or she'll see you shining through me.
[HARRIET *takes a scarf of chiffon that has been lying over the back of a chair and drapes it on* HETTY, *covering her face. The chiffon is the same color of their gowns but paler in shade so that it pales* HETTY'S *darker gown to match* HARRIET'S *lighter one. As* HETTY *moves in the following scene the chiffon falls away revealing now and then the gown of deeper dye underneath.*]

HETTY: Tell her Charles is rich and fascinating—boast of our friends, make her feel she needs us.

HARRIET: I'll make her ask John to paint us.

HETTY: That's just my thought—if John paints our portrait—

HARRIET: We can wear an exquisite gown—

HETTY: And make him fall in love again and—

HARRIET: [*Schemingly.*] Yes. [MARGARET *parts the portières back centre and extends her hand.* MARGARET *is followed by her counterpart* MAGGIE.] Oh, Margaret, I'm so glad to see you!

HETTY: [*To* MAGGIE.] That's a lie.

MARGARET: [*In superficial voice throughout.*] It's enchanting to see you, Harriet.

MAGGIE: [*In emotional voice throughout.*] I'd bite you, if I dared.

HARRIET: [*To* MARGARET.] Wasn't our meeting a stroke of luck?

MARGARET: [*Coming down left of table.*] I've thought of you so often, Harriet; and to come back and find you living in New York.

HARRIET: [*Coming down right of table.*] Mr. Goodrich has many interests here.

MAGGIE: [*To* MARGARET.] Flatter her.

MARGARET: I know, Mr. Goodrich is so successful.

HETTY: [*To* HARRIET.] Tell her we're rich.

HARRIET: [*To* MARGARET.] Won't you sit down?

MARGARET: [*Takes a chair.*] What a beautiful cabinet!

HARRIET: Do you like it? I'm afraid Charles paid an extravagant price.

MAGGIE: [*To* HETTY.] I don't believe it.

MARGARET: [*Sitting down. To* HARRIET.] I am sure he must have.

HARRIET: [*Sitting down.*] How well you are looking, Margaret.

HETTY: Yes, you are not. There are circles under your eyes.

MAGGIE: [*To* HETTY.] I haven't eaten since breakfast and I'm hungry.

MARGARET: [*To* HARRIET.] How well you are looking, too.

MAGGIE: [*To* HETTY.] You have hard lines about your lips, are you happy?

HETTY: [*To* HARRIET.] Don't let her know that I'm unhappy.

HARRIET: [*To* MARGARET.] Why shouldn't I took well? My life is full, happy, complete—

MAGGIE: I wonder.

HETTY: [*In* HARRIET*'s ear.*] Tell her we have an automobile.

MARGARET: [*To* HARRIET.] My life is complete, too.

MAGGIE: My heart is torn with sorrow; my husband cannot make a living. He will kill himself if he does not get an order for a painting.

MARGARET: [*Laughs.*] You must come and see us in our studio. John has been doing some excellent portraits. He cannot begin to fill his orders.

HETTY: [*To* HARRIET.] Tell her we have an automobile.

HARRIET: [*To* MARGARET.] Do you take lemon in your tea?

MAGGIE: Take cream. It's more filling.

MARGARET: [*Looking nonchalantly at tea things.*] No, cream, if you please. How cozy!

MAGGIE: [*Glaring at tea things.*] Only cakes! I could eat them all!!

HARRIET: [*To* MARGARET.] How many lumps?

MAGGIE: [*To* MARGARET.] Sugar is nourishing.

MARGARET: [*To* HARRIET.] Three, please. I used to drink very sweet coffee in Turkey and ever since I've—

HETTY: I don't believe you were ever in Turkey.

MAGGIE: I wasn't, but it is none of your business.

HARRIET: [*Pouring tea.*] Have you been in Turkey, do tell me about it.

MAGGIE: [*To* MARGARET.] Change the subject.

MARGARET: [*To* HARRIET.] You must go there. You have so much taste in dress you would enjoy seeing their costumes.

MAGGIE: Isn't she going to pass the cake?

MARGARET: [*To* HARRIET.] John painted several portraits there.

HETTY: [*To* HARRIET.] Why don't you stop her bragging and tell her we have an automobile?

HARRIET: [*Offers cake across the table to* MARGARET.] Cake?

MAGGIE: [*Stands back of* MARGARET, *shadowing her as* HETTY *shadows* HARRIET. MAGGIE *reaches claws out for the cake and groans with joy.*] At last! [*But her claws do not touch the cake.*]

MARGARET: [*With a graceful, nonchalant hand places cake upon her plate and bites at it slowly and delicately.*] Thank you.

HETTY: [*To* HARRIET.] Automobile!

MAGGIE: [*To* MARGARET.] Follow up the costumes with the suggestion that she would make a good model for John. It isn't too early to begin getting what you came for.

MARGARET: [*Ignoring* MAGGIE.] What delicious cake.

HETTY: [*Excitedly to* HARRIET.] There's your chance for the auto.

HARRIET: [*Nonchalantly to* MARGARET.] Yes, it is good cake, isn't it? There are always a great many people buying it at Harper's. I sat in my automobile fifteen minutes this morning waiting for my chauffeur to get it.

MAGGIE: [*To* MARGARET.] Make her order a portrait.

MARGARET: [*To* HARRIET.] If you stopped at Harper's you must have noticed the new gowns at Henderson's. Aren't the shop windows alluring these days?

HARRIET: Even my chauffeur notices them.

MAGGIE: I know you have an automobile, I heard you the first time.

MARGARET: I notice gowns now with an artist's eye as John does. The one you have on, my dear, is very paintable.

HETTY: Don't let her see you're anxious to be painted.

HARRIET: [*Nonchalantly.*] Oh, it's just a little model.

MAGGIE: [*To* MARGARET.] Don't seem anxious to get the order.

MARGARET: [*Nonchalantly.*] Perhaps it isn't the gown itself but the way you wear it that pleases the eye. Some people can wear anything with grace.

HETTY: Yes, I'm very graceful.

HARRIET: [*To* MARGARET.] You flatter me, my dear.

MARGARET: On the contrary, Harriet, I have an intense admiration for you. I remember how beautiful you were—as a girl. In fact, I was quite jealous when John was paying you so much attention.

HETTY: She is gloating because I lost him.

HARRIET: Those were childhood days in a country town.

MAGGIE: [*To* MARGARET.] She's trying to make you feel that John was only a country boy.

MARGARET: Most great men have come from the country. There is a fair chance that John will be added to the list.

HETTY: I know it and I am bitterly jealous of you.

HARRIET: Undoubtedly he owes much of his success to you, Margaret, your experience in economy and your ability to endure hardship. Those first few years in Paris must have been a struggle.

MAGGIE: She is sneering at your poverty.

MARGARET: Yes, we did find life difficult at first, not the luxurious start a girl has who marries wealth.

HETTY: [*To* HARRIET.] Deny that you married Charles for his money.

[HARRIET *deems it wise to ignore* HETTY's *advice.*]

MARGARET: But John and I are so congenial in our tastes, that we were impervious to hardship or unhappiness.

HETTY: [*In anguish.*] Do you love each other? Is it really true?

HARRIET: [*Sweetly.*] Did you have all the romance of starving for his art?

MAGGIE: [*To* MARGARET.] She's taunting you. Get even with her.

MARGARET: Not for long. Prince Rier soon discovered John's genius, and introduced him royally to wealthy Parisians who gave him many orders.

HETTY: [*To* MAGGIE.] Are you telling the truth or are you lying?

HARRIET: If he had so many opportunities there, you must have had great inducements to come back to the States.

MAGGIE: [*To* HETTY.] We did, but not the kind you think.

MARGARET: John became the rage among Americans travelling in France, too, and they simply insisted upon his coming here.

HARRIET: Whom is he going to paint here?

MAGGIE: [*Frightened.*] What names dare I make up?

MARGARET: [*Calmly.*] Just at present Miss Dorothy Ainsworth of Oregon is posing. You may not know the name, but she is the daughter of a wealthy miner who found gold in Alaska.

HARRIET: I dare say there are many Western people we have never heard of.

MARGARET: You must have found social life in New York very interesting, Harriet, after the simplicity of our home town.

HETTY: [*To* MAGGIE.] There's no need to remind us that our beginnings were the same.

HARRIET: Of course Charles's family made everything delightful for me. They are so well connected.

MAGGIE: [*To* MARGARET.] Flatter her.

MARGARET: I heard it mentioned yesterday that you had made yourself very popular. Some one said you were very clever!

HARRIET: [*Pleased.*] Who told you that?

MAGGIE: Nobody!

MARGARET: [*Pleasantly.*] Oh, confidences should be suspected—respected, I mean. They said, too, that you are gaining some reputation as a critic of art.

HARRIET: I make no pretenses.

MARGARET: Are you and Mr. Goodrich interested in the same things, too?

HETTY: No!

HARRIET: Yes, indeed, Charles and I are inseparable.

MAGGIE: I wonder.

HARRIET: Do have another cake.

MAGGIE: [*In relief.*] Oh, yes. [*Again her claws extend but do not touch the cake.*]

MARGARET: [*Takes cake delicately.*] I really shouldn't after—my big luncheon. John took me to the Ritz and we are invited to the Bedfords' for dinner—they have such a magnificent house near the drive—I really shouldn't, but the cakes are so good.

MAGGIE: Starving!

HARRIET: [*To* MARGARET.] More tea?

MAGGIE: Yes!

MARGARET: No, thank you. How wonderfully life has arranged itself for you. Wealth, position, a happy marriage, every opportunity to enjoy all pleasures; beauty, art—how happy you must be.

HETTY: [*In anguish.*] Don't call me happy. I've never been happy since I gave up John. All these years without him—a future without him— no—no—I shall win him back—away from you—away from you—

HARRIET: [*Does not see* MAGGIE *pointing to cream and* MARGARET *stealing some.*] I sometimes think it is unfair for any one to be as happy as I am. Charles and I are just as much in love now as when we married. To me he is just the dearest man in the world.

MAGGIE: [*Passionately.*] My John is. I love him so much I could die for him. I'm going through hunger and want to make him great and he loves me. He worships me!

MARGARET: [*Leisurely to* HARRIET.] I should like to meet Mr. Goodrich. Bring him to our studio. John has some sketches to show. Not many, because all the portraits have been purchased by the subjects. He gets as much as four thousand dollars now.

HETTY: [*To* HARRIET.] Don't pay that much.

HARRIET: [*To* MARGARET.] As much as that?

MARGARET: It is not really too much when one considers that John is in the foremost rank of artists to-day. A picture painted by him now will double and treble in value.

MAGGIE: It's all a lie. He is growing weak with despair.

HARRIET: Does he paint all day long?

MAGGIE: No, he draws advertisements for our bread.

MARGARET: [*To* HARRIET.] When you and your husband come to see us, telephone first—

MAGGIE: Yes, so he can get the advertisements out of the way.

MARGARET: Otherwise you might arrive while he has a sitter, and John refuses to let me disturb him them.

HETTY: Make her ask for an order.

HARRIET: [*To* MARGARET.] Le Grange offered to paint me for a thousand.

MARGARET: Louis Le Grange's reputation isn't worth more than that.

HARRIET: Well, I've heard his work well mentioned.

MAGGIE: Yes, he is doing splendid work.

MARGARET: Oh, dear me, no. He is only praised by the masses. He is accepted not at all by artists themselves.

HETTY: [*Anxiously.*] Must I really pay the full price?

HARRIET: Le Grange thought I would make a good subject.

MAGGIE: [*To* MARGARET.] Let her fish for it.

MARGARET: Of course you would. Why don't you let Le Grange paint you, if you *trust* him?

HETTY: She doesn't seem anxious to have John do it.

HARRIET: But if Le Grange isn't accepted by artists, it would be a waste of time to pose for him, wouldn't it?

MARGARET: Yes, I think it would.

MAGGIE: [*Passionately to* HETTY *across back of table.*] Give us the order. John is so despondent he can't endure much longer. Help us! Help me! Save us!

HETTY: [*To* HARRIET.] Don't seem too eager.

HARRIET: And yet if he charges only a thousand one might consider it.

MARGARET: It you really wish to be painted, why don't you give a little more and have a portrait really worth while? John might be induced to do you for a little below his usual price considering that you used to be such good friends.

HETTY: [*In glee.*] Hurrah!

HARRIET: [*Quietly to* MARGARET.] That's very nice of you to suggest—of course I don't know—

MAGGIE: [*In fear.*] For God's sake, say yes.

MARGARET: [*Quietly to* HARRIET.] Of course, I don't know whether John would. He is very peculiar in these matters. He sets his value on his work and thinks it beneath him to discuss price.

HETTY: [*To* MAGGIE.] You needn't try to make us feel small.

MARGARET: Still, I might quite delicately mention to him that inasmuch as you have many influential friends you would be very glad to—to—

MAGGIE: [*To* HETTY.] Finish what I don't want to say.

HETTY: [*To* HARRIET.] Help her out.

HARRIET: Oh, yes. Introductions will follow the exhibition of my portrait. No doubt I—

HETTY: [*To* HARRIET.] Be patronizing.

HARRIET: No doubt I shall be able to introduce your husband to his advantage.

MAGGIE: [*Relieved.*] Saved.

MARGARET: If I find John in a propitious mood I shall take pleasure, for your sake, in telling him about your beauty. Just as you are sitting now would be a lovely pose.

MAGGIE: [*To* MARGARET.] We can go now.

HETTY: [*To* HARRIET.] Don't let her think she is doing us a favor.

HARRIET: It will give me pleasure to add my name to your husband's list of patronesses.

MAGGIE: [*Excitedly to* MARGARET.] Run home and tell John the good news.

MARGARET: [*Leisurely to* HARRIET.] I little guessed when I came for a pleasant chat about old times that it would develop into business arrangements. I had no idea, Harriet, that you had any intention of being painted. By Le Grange, too. Well, I came just in time to rescue you.

MAGGIE: [*To* MARGARET.] Run home and tell John. Hurry, hurry!

HETTY: [*To* HARRIET.] You managed the order very neatly. She doesn't suspect that you wanted it.

HARRIET: Now if I am not satisfied with my portrait I shall blame you, Margaret, dear. I am relying upon your opinion of John's talent.

MAGGIE: [*To* MARGARET.] She doesn't suspect what you came for. Run home and tell John!

HARRIET: You always had a brilliant mind, Margaret.

MARGARET: Ah, it is you who flatter, now.

MAGGIE: [*To* MARGARET.] You don't have to stay so long. Hurry home!

HARRIET: Ah, one does not flatter when one tells the truth.

MARGARET: [*Smiles.*] I must be going or you will have me completely under your spell.

HETTY: [*Looks at clock.*] Yes, do go. I have to dress for dinner.

HARRIET: [*To* MARGARET.] Oh, don't hurry.

MAGGIE: [*To* HETTY.] I hate you!

MARGARET: [*To* HARRIET.] No, really I must, but I hope we shall see each other often at the studio. I find you so stimulating.

HETTY: [*To* MAGGIE.] I hate you!

HARRIET: [*To* MARGARET.] It is indeed gratifying to find a kindred spirit.

MAGGIE: [*To* HETTY.] I came for your gold.

MARGARET: [*To* HARRIET.] How delightful it is to know you again.

HETTY: [*To* MAGGIE.] I am going to make you and your husband suffer.

HARRIET: My kind regards to John.

MAGGIE: [*To* HETTY.] He has forgotten all about you.

MARGARET: [*Rises.*] He will be so happy to receive them.

HETTY: [*To* MAGGIE.] I can hardly wait to talk to him again.

HARRIET: I shall wait, then, until you send me word?

MARGARET: [*Offering her hand.*] I'll speak to John about it as soon as I can and tell you when to come. [HARRIET *takes* MARGARET'*s hand affectionately.* HETTY *and* MAGGIE *rush at each other, throw back their veils, and fling their speeches fiercely at each other.*]

HETTY: I love him—I love him—

MAGGIE: He's starving—I'm starving.

HETTY: I'm going to take him away from you—

MAGGIE: I want your money—and your influence.

HETTIE *and* MAGGIE: I'm going to rob you—rob you.

[*There is a cymbal crash, the lights go out and come up again slowly, leaving only* MARGARET *and* HARRIET *visible.*]

MARGARET: [*Quietly to* HARRIET.] I've had such a delightful afternoon.

HARRIET: [*Offering her hand.*] It has been a joy to see you.

MARGARET: [*Sweetly to* HARRIET.] Good-bye.

HARRIET: [*Sweetly to* MARGARET *as she kisses her.*] Good-bye, my dear.

THE OUTSIDE

by

Susan Glaspell

First performed by the Provincetown Players on December 28, 1917.

CHARACTERS

CAPTAIN *of "The Bars" Life-Saving Station*
BRADFORD, *a Life-Saver*
TONY, *a Portuguese Life-Saver*
MRS. PATRICK, *who lives in the abandoned Station*
ALLIE MAYO, *who works for her*

SCENE: *A room in a house which was once a life-saving station. Since ceasing to be that it has taken on no other character, except that of a place which no one cares either to preserve or change. It is painted the life-saving gray, but has not the life-saving freshness. This is one end of what was the big boat room, and at the ceiling is seen a part of the frame work from which the boat once swung. About two thirds of the back wall is open, because of the big sliding door, of the type of barn door, and through this open door are seen the sand dunes, and beyond them the woods. At one point the line where woods and dunes meet stands out clearly and there are indicated the rude things, vines, bushes, which form the outer uneven rim of the woods—the only things that grow in the sand. At another point a sand-hill is menacing the woods. This old life-saving station is at a point where the sea curves, so through the open door the sea also is seen. [The station is located on the outside shore of Cape Cod, at the point, near the tip of the Cape, where it makes that final curve which forms the Provincetown Harbor.] The dunes are hills and strange forms of sand on which, in places, grows the stiff beach grass—struggle; dogged growing against odds. At right of the big sliding door is a drift of sand and the top of buried beach grass is seen on this. There is a door left, and at right of big sliding door is a slanting wall. Door in this is ajar at rise of curtain, and through this door* BRADFORD *and* TONY, *life-savers, are seen bending over a man's body, attempting to restore respiration. The* CAPTAIN *of the life-savers comes into view outside the big open door, at left; he appears to have been hurrying, peers in, sees the men, goes quickly to them.*

CAPTAIN: I'll take this now, boys.

BRADFORD: No need for anybody to take it, Capt'n. He was dead when we picked him up.

CAPTAIN: Dannie Sears was dead when we picked him up. But we brought him back. I'll go on awhile. [*The two men who have been bending over the body rise, stretch to relax, and come into the room.*]

BRADFORD: [*Pushing back his arms and putting his hands on his chest.*] Work,—tryin' to put life in the dead.

CAPTAIN: Where'd you find him, Joe?

BRADFORD: In front of this house. Not forty feet out.

CAPTAIN: What'd you bring him here for? [*He speaks in an abstracted way, as if the working part of his mind is on something else, and in the muffled voice of one bending over.*]

BRADFORD: [*With a sheepish little laugh.*] Force of habit, I guess. We brought so many of 'em back up here. [*Looks around room.*] And then it was kind of unfriendly down where he was—the wind spittin' the sea onto you till he'd have no way of knowin' he was ashore.

TONY: Lucky I was not sooner or later as I walk by from my watch.

BRADFORD: You have accommodating ways, Tony. Not sooner or later. I wouldn't say it of many Portagees. But the sea [*calling it in to the* CAPTAIN] is friendly as a kitten alongside the women who live *here.* Allie Mayo—they're *both* crazy—had that big door open [*moving his head toward the big sliding door*] sweepin' out, and when we come along she backs off and stands lookin' at us, *lookin'*—Lord, I just wanted to get him somewhere else. So I kicked this door open with my foot [*jerking his hand toward the room where the* CAPTAIN *is seen bending over the man*] and got him *away.* [*Under his voice.*] If he did have any notion of coming back to life, he wouldn't a come if he'd seen her. [*More genially.*] *I* wouldn't.

CAPTAIN: You know who he is, Joe?

BRADFORD: I never saw him before.

CAPTAIN: Mitchell telephoned from High Head that a dory came ashore there.

BRADFORD: Last night wasn't the best night for a dory. [*To* TONY, *boastfully.*] Not that I couldn't 'a' stayed in one. Some men can stay in a dory and some can't. [*Going to the inner door.*] That boy's dead, Capt'n.

CAPTAIN: Then I'm not doing him any harm.

BRADFORD: [*Going over and shaking the frame where the boat once swung.*] This the first time you ever been in this place, ain't it, Tony?

TONY: I never was here before.

BRADFORD: Well, *I* was here before. [*A laugh.*] And the old man—[*nodding toward the* CAPTAIN] he lived here for twenty-seven years. Lord, the things that happened *here*. There've been dead ones carried through *that* door. [*Pointing to the outside door.*] Lord—the ones *I've* carried. I carried in Bill Collins, and Lou Harvey and—huh! 'sall over now. You ain't seen no *wrecks*. Don't ever think you have. I was here the night the Jennie Snow was out there. [*Pointing to the sea.*] There was a *wreck*. We got the boat that stood here [*again shaking the frame*] down that bank. [*Goes to the door and looks out.*] Lord, how'd we ever do it? The sand has put this place on the blink all right. And then when it gets too God-forsaken for a life-savin' station, a lady takes it for a summer residence—and then spends the winter. She's a cheerful one.

TONY: A woman—she makes things pretty. This not like a place where a woman live. On the floor there is nothing—on the wall there is nothing. Things—[*trying to express it with his hands*] do not hang on other things.

BRADFORD: [*Imitating* TONY'*s gesture.*] No—things do not hang on other things. In my opinion the woman's crazy—sittin' over there on the sand—[*a gesture towards the dunes*] what's she *lookin'* at? There ain't nothin' to *see*. And I know the woman that works for her's crazy—Allie Mayo. She's a Provincetown girl. She was all right once, but—[MRS. PATRICK *comes in from the hall at the right. She is a "city woman," a sophisticated person who has been caught into something as unlike the old life as the dunes are unlike a meadow. At the moment she is excited and angry.*]

MRS. PATRICK: You have no right here. This isn't the life-saving station any more. Just because it used to be—I don't see why you should think—This is my house! And—I want my house to myself!

CAPTAIN: [*Putting his head through the door. One arm of the man he is working with is raised, and the hand reaches through the doorway.*] Well I must say, lady, I would think that any house could be a life-saving station when the sea had sent a man to it.

MRS. PATRICK: [*Who has turned away so she cannot see the hand.*] I don't want him here! I—[*defiant, yet choking*] I must have my house to myself!

CAPTAIN: You'll get your house to yourself when I've made up my mind there's no more life in this man. A good many lives have been saved in this house, Mrs. Patrick—I believe that's your name—and if there's any chance of bringing one more back from the dead, the fact that you own the house ain't goin' to make a damn bit of difference to me!

MRS. PATRICK: [*In a thin, wild way.*] I must have my house to myself.

CAPTAIN: Hell with such a woman! [*Moves the man he is working with and slams the door shut. As the* CAPTAIN *says, "And if there's any chance of bringing one more back from the dead,"* ALLIE MAYO *has appeared outside the wide door which gives on the dunes, a bleak woman, who at first seems little more than a part of the sand before which she stands. But as she listens to this conflict one suspects in her that peculiar intensity of twisted things which grow in unfavoring places.*]

MRS. PATRICK: I—I don't want them here! I must—[*But suddenly she retreats, and is gone.*]

BRADFORD: Well, I couldn't say, Allie Mayo, that you work for any too kind-hearted a lady. What's the matter with the woman? Does she want folks to die? Appears to break her all up to see somebody trying to save a life. What d' you work for such a fish for? A crazy fish— that's what I call the woman. I've seen her—day after day—settin' over there where the dunes meet the woods, just sittin' there, lookin'. [*Suddenly thinking of it.*] I believe she likes to see the sand slippin' down on the woods. Pleases her to see somethin' gettin' buried, I guess.

[ALLIE MAYO, *who has stepped inside the door and moved half across he room, toward the corridor at the right, is arrested by this last—stands a moment as if seeing through something, then slowly on, and out.*]

BRADFORD: Some coffee'd taste good. But coffee, in this house? Oh, no. It might make somebody feel better. [*Opening the door that was slammed shut.*] Want me now, Capt'n?

CAPTAIN: No.

BRADFORD: Oh, that boy's dead, Capt'n.

CAPTAIN: [*Snarling.*] Dannie Sears was dead, too. Shut that door. I don't want to hear that woman's voice again, ever. [*Closing the door and sitting on a bench built into that corner between the big sliding door and the room where the* CAPTAIN *is.*]

BRADFORD: They're a cheerful pair of women livin' in this cheerful—place a place that life savers had to turn over to the sand—huh! This Patrick woman used to be all right. She and her husband was summer folks over in town. They used to picnic over here on the outside. It was Joe Dyer—he's always talkin' to summer folks—told 'em the government was goin' to build the new station and sell this one by sealed bids. I heard them talkin' about it. They was sittin' right down there on the beach, eatin' their supper. They was goin' to put in a

fire-place and they was goin' to paint it bright colors, and have parties over here—summer folk notions. Their bid won it—who'd want
it?—a buried house you couldn't move.

TONY: I see no bright colors.

BRADFORD: Don't you? How astonishin'! You must be color blind. And I
guess *we're* the first party. [*Laughs.*] I was in Bill Joseph's grocery
store, one day last November, when in she come—Mrs. Patrick, from
New York. "I've come to take the old life-saving station," says she.
"I'm going to sleep over there tonight!" Huh! Bill is used to queer
ways—he deals with summer folks, but that got him. November—an
empty house, a buried house, you might say, off here on the outside
shore—way across the sand from man or beast. He got it out of her,
not by what she said, but by the way she looked at what he said, that
her husband had died, and she was runnin' off to hide herself, I
guess. A person'd feel sorry for her if she weren't so stand-offish, and
so doggon *mean.* But mean folks have got minds of their own. She
slept here that night. Bill had men hauling things till after dark—bed,
stove, coal. And then she wanted somebody to work for her. "Somebody," says she, "that doesn't say an unnecessary word!" Well, when
Bill come to the back of the store, I said, "Looks to me as if Allie
Mayo was the party she's lookin' for." Allie Mayo has got a prejudice
against words. Or maybe she likes 'em so well she's savin' of 'em.
She's not spoke an unnecessary word for twenty years. She's got her
reasons. Women whose men go to sea ain't always talkative.

[*The* CAPTAIN *comes out. He closes door behind him and stands there beside it. He looks tired and disappointed. Both look at him. Pause.*]

CAPTAIN: Wonder who he was.

BRADFORD: Young. Guess he's not been much at sea.

CAPTAIN: I hate to leave even the dead in this house. But we can get right
back for him. [*A look around.*] The old place used to be more
friendly. [*Moves to outer door, hesitates, hating to leave like this.*] Well,
Joe, we brought a good many of them back here.

BRADFORD: Dannie Sears is tendin' bar in Boston now.

[*The three men go; as they are going around the drift of sand* ALLIE
MAYO *comes in carrying a pot of coffee; sees them leaving, puts down the
coffee pot, looks to the door the* CAPTAIN *has closed, moves toward it, as if
drawn.* MRS. PATRICK *follows her in.*

MRS. PATRICK: They've gone? [MRS. MAYO *nods, facing the closed door.*]

MRS. PATRICK: And they're leaving—him? [*Again the other woman nods.*]
Then he's—? [MRS. MAYO *just stands there.*] They have no right—just
because it used to be their place—! I want my house to myself!

[*Snatches her coat and scarf from a hook and starts through the big door toward the dunes.*]

ALLIE MAYO: Wait. [*When she has said it she sinks into that corner seat—as if overwhelmed by what she has done. The other woman is held.*]

ALLIE MAYO: [*To herself.*] If I could say that, I can say more. [*Looking at the woman she has arrested, but speaking more to herself.*] That boy in there—his face—uncovered something—[*Her open hand on her chest. But she waits, as if she cannot go on; when she speaks it is in labored way—slow, monotonous, as if snowed in by silent years.*] For twenty years, I did what you are doing. And I can tell you—it's not the way. [*Her voice has fallen to a whisper; she stops, looking ahead at something remote and veiled.*] We had been married—two years. [*A start, as of sudden pain. Says it again, as if to make herself say it.*] Married—two years. He had a chance to go north on a whaler. Times hard. He had to go. A year and a half—it was to be. A year and a half. Two years we'd been married. [*She sits silent, moving a little back and forth.*] The day he went away. [*Not spoken, but breathed from pain.*] The days after he was gone. I heard at first. Last letter said farther north—not another chance to write till on the way home. [*A wait.*] Six months. Another. I did not hear. [*Long wait.*] Nobody ever heard. [*After it seems she is held there, and will not go on.*] I used to talk as much as any girl in Provincetown. Jim used to tease me about my talking. But they'd come in to talk to me. They'd say—"You may hear *yet*." They'd talk about what must have happened. And one day a woman who'd been my friend all my life said—"Suppose he was to walk *in*!" I got up and drove her from my kitchen—and from that time till this I've not said a word I didn't have to say. [*She has become almost wild in telling this. That passes. In a whisper.*] The ice that caught Jim—caught me. [*A moment as if held in ice. Comes from it. To* MRS. PATRICK *simply.*] It's not the way. [*A sudden change.*] You're not the only woman in the world whose husband is dead!

MRS. PATRICK: [*With the cry of the hurt.*] Dead? My husband's not dead.

ALLIE MAYO: He's not? [*Slowly understands.*] Oh. [*The woman in the door is crying. Suddenly picks up her coat which has fallen to the floor and steps outside.*]

ALLIE MAYO: [*Almost failing to do it.*] Wait.

MRS. PATRICK: Wait? Don't you think you've said enough? They told me you didn't say an unnecessary word!

ALLIE MAYO: I don't.

MRS. PATRICK: And you can see, I should think, that you've bungled into things you know nothing about! [*As she speaks, and crying under her*

*breath, she pushes the sand by the door down on the half buried grass—
though not as if knowing what she is doing.*]

ALLIE MAYO: [*Slowly.*] When you keep still for twenty years you know—
things you didn't know you knew. I know why you're doing that.
[*She looks up at her, startled.*] Don't bury the only thing that will
grow. Let it grow. [*The woman outside still crying under her breath
turns abruptly and starts toward the line where dunes and woods meet.*]

ALLIE MAYO: I know where you're going! [MRS. PATRICK *turns, but not as if
she wants to.*] What you'll try to do. Over there. [*Pointing to the line
of woods.*] Bury it. The life in you. Bury it—watching the sand bury
the woods. But I'll tell you something! *They* fight too. The woods!
They fight for life the way that Captain fought for life in there!
[*Pointing to the closed door.*]

MRS. PATRICK: [*With a strange exultation.*] And lose the way he lost in
there!

ALLIE MAYO: [*Sure, sombre.*] They don't lose.

MRS. PATRICK: Don't lose! [*Triumphant.*] I have walked on the tops of
buried trees!

ALLIE MAYO: [*Slow, sombre, yet large.*] And vines will grow over the sand
that covers the trees, and hold it. And other trees will grow above the
buried trees.

MRS. PATRICK: I've watched the sand slip down on the vines that reach out
farthest.

ALLIE MAYO: Another vine will reach that spot. [*Under her breath, tenderly.*] Strange little things that reach out farthest!

MRS. PATRICK: And will be buried soonest!

ALLIE MAYO: And hold the sand for things behind them. They save a wood
that guards a town.

MRS. PATRICK: I care nothing about a woods to guard a town. This is the
outside—these dunes where only beach grass grows, this outer shore
where men can't live. The Outside. You who were born here and
who die here have named it that.

ALLIE MAYO: Yes, we named it that, and we had reason. He died here
[*reaches her hand toward the closed door*] and many a one before him.
But many another reached the harbor! [*Slowly raises her arm, bends it
to make the form of the Cape. Touches the outside of her bent arm.*] The
Outside. But an arm that bends to make a harbor—where men are
safe.

MRS. PATRICK: I'm outside the harbor—on the dunes, land not life.

ALLIE MAYO: Dunes meet woods and woods hold dunes from a town
that's shore to a harbor.

MRS. PATRICK: This is the Outside. Sand. [*Picking some of it up in her hand*

and letting it fall on the beach grass.] Sand that *covers*—hills of sand that move and cover.

ALLIE MAYO: Woods. Woods to hold the moving hills from Provincetown. Provincetown—where they turn when boats can't live at sea. Did you ever see the sails come round here when the sky is dark? A line of them—swift to the harbor—where their children live. Go back! [*Pointing.*] Back to your edge of the woods that's the *edge of the dunes.*

MRS. PATRICK: The edge of life. Where life trails off to dwarfed things not worth a name. [*Suddenly sits down in the doorway.*]

ALLIE MAYO: Not worth a name. And—meeting the Outside! [*Big with the sense of the wonder of life.*]

MRS. PATRICK: [*Lifting sand and letting it drift through her hand.*] They're what the sand will let them be. They take strange shapes like shapes of blown sand.

ALLIE MAYO: Meeting the Outside. [*Moving nearer; speaking more personally.*] I know why you came here. To this house that had been given up; on this shore where only savers of life try to live. I know what holds you on these dunes, and draws you over there. But other things are true beside the things you want to see.

MRS. PATRICK: How do you know they are? Where have you been for twenty years?

ALLIE MAYO: Outside. Twenty years. That's why I know how brave *they* are. [*Indicating the edge of the woods. Suddenly different.*] You'll not find peace there again! Go back and watch them *fight!*

MRS. PATRICK: [*Swiftly rising.*] You're a cruel woman—a hard, insolent woman! I knew what I was doing! What do you know about it? About me? I didn't *go* to the Outside. I was left there. I'm only—trying to get along. Everything that can hurt me I want buried—buried deep. Spring is here. This morning I *knew* it. Spring—coming through the storm—to take me—take me to hurt me. That's why I couldn't bear—[*she looks at the closed door*] things that made me know I feel. You haven't felt for so long you don't know what it means! But I tell you, Spring is here! And now you'd take *that* from me—[*looking now toward the edge of the woods*] the thing that made me know they would be buried in my heart—those things I can't *live* and know I feel. You're more cruel than the sea! "But other things are true beside the things you want to see!" Outside. Springs will come when I will not know that it is spring. [*As if resentful of not more deeply believing what she says.*] What would there be for me but the Outside? What was there for you? What did you ever find after you lost the thing you wanted?

ALLIE MAYO: I found—what I find now I know. The edge of life—to hold
life behind me—[*A slight gesture toward* MRS. PATRICK.]

MRS. PATRICK: [*Stepping back.*] You call what you are life? [*Laughs.*] Bleak
as those ugly things that grow in the sand!

ALLIE MAYO: [*Under her breath, as one who speaks tenderly of beauty.*] Ugly!

MRS. PATRICK: [*Passionately.*] I have *known* life. I have known *life.* You're
like this Cape. A line of land way out to sea—land not life.

ALLIE MAYO: A harbor far at sea. [*Raises her arm, curves it in as if around
something she loves.*] Land that encloses and gives shelter from storm.

MRS. PATRICK: [*Facing the sea, as if affirming what will hold all else out.*]
Outside sea. Outer shore. Dunes—land not life.

ALLIE MAYO: Outside sea—outer shore, dark with the wood that once was
ships—dunes, strange land not life—woods, town and harbor. The
line! Stunted straggly line that meets the Outside face to face—and
fights for what itself can never be. Lonely line. Brave growing.

MRS. PATRICK: It loses.

ALLIE MAYO: It wins.

MRS. PATRICK: The farthest life is buried.

ALLIE MAYO: And life grows over buried life! [*Lifted into that; then, as one
who states a simple truth with feeling.*] It will. And Springs will come
when you will want to know that it is Spring.

[*The* CAPTAIN *and* BRADFORD *appear behind the drift of sand. They
have a stretcher. To get away from them* MRS. PATRICK *steps farther into
the room;* ALLIE MAYO *shrinks into her corner. The men come in, open
the closed door and go in the room where they left the dead man. A moment later they are seen outside the big open door, bearing the man
away.* MRS. PATRICK *watches them from sight.*]

MRS. PATRICK: [*Bitter, exultant.*] Savers of life! [*To* ALLIE MAYO.] You
savers of life! "Meeting the Outside!" Meeting—[*But she cannot say
it mockingly again; in saying it, something of what it means has broken
through, rises. Herself lost, feeling her way into the wonder of life.*]
Meeting the Outside! [*It grows in her as slowly.*]

WHY MARRY?

A Comedy in Three Acts

by

Jesse Lynch Williams

First performed at the Astor Theater, New York City, on December 25, 1917.

CHARACTERS

JEAN, *an attractive girl of twenty-five, brought up to be married but nothing else. She lives at the house.*

REX, *a good-looking young man a year or two older, not brought up to be anything but rich. He lives at a near-by house.*

LUCY, *the mistress of the house, trying to be an "old-fashioned wife" in a new-fashioned home.*

HELEN, JEAN's *elder sister, a more or less new woman who doesn't believe in marriage. She no longer lives at her brother's house.*

JOHN, LUCY's *husband, who owns the house and thinks it is womanly for women to be as men want them to be.*

THE JUDGE, *their Uncle Everett, who understands all of them and believes in divorce!*

THEODORE, *their cousin, a human clergyman.*

ERNEST, *a brilliant young scientist who makes a great discovery.*

BUTLER

FOOTMAN

A few Servants and Poor Relations also appear and disappear.

TIME: A September week-end not long ago.
PLACE: A country house not far away.
     Act I: The Terrace, Saturday afternoon.
     Act II: The Terrace, Sunday morning.
     Act III: The Terrace, Sunday evening.

ACT I

Up from the fragrant garden comes a girl, running. She takes the broad terrace steps two at a stride, laughing, breathless, fleet as a fawn, sweet as a rose. She is hotly pursued by a boy, handsome, ardent, attractively selfish, and just now blindly determined to catch the pretty creature before she gains the protecting shelter of home. She is determined to let him but not to let him know it. . . . There, she might have darted in through the open door, but it is such a cold, formal entrance; she pretends to be exhausted, dodges behind a stone tea-table, and, turning, faces him, each panting and laughing excitedly; she alluring and defiant, he merry and dominant.

She is twenty-five and he is a year or two older, but they are both children; in other words, unmarried.

REX: Think I'll let you say that to me?

JEAN: [*Making a face at him.*] Think I'm afraid of you!

REX: Take it back, I tell you.

JEAN: I won't.

REX: I'll make you.

JEAN: [*With a dance step.*] Think so, do you?

REX: I warn you.

JEAN: Booh-woo! [*He makes a feint to the right, then dashes to the left and catches her.*]

REX: [*Triumphantly.*] Now! . . . You would, would you?

JEAN: [*Struggling.*] Let me go.

REX: I couldn't think of it.

JEAN: [*Seizes his hands to free herself—can't.*] You're so strong it isn't fair.

REX: You're so sweet—it isn't fair. [*Smiling down at her struggles, rejoicing in his strength, her weakness, he gently draws her near.*]

JEAN: [*Knows what is coming.*] No, Rex.

REX: Yes.

JEAN: You mustn't.

REX: But I will. [*He laughs and kisses her lightly on the cheek. Therefore she struggles furiously. Therefore he does it again. And again. Suddenly he enfolds her completely and kisses her passionately—cheeks, mouth, eyes— until she gasps in alarm. Laughter has gone from them now.*]

JEAN: Oh, please! . . . some one will come.

REX: [*With the intoxication of such moments.*] I don't care who comes—I love you.

JEAN: No . . . let me go.

REX: Not till you kiss me, Jean. [JEAN *hesitates, brushes his cheek lightly with her lips, and in pretty confusion tries to escape.*] Not till you say you love me, Jean. [*Eyes hidden in his coat, she bobs her head. He laughs and loves it.*] Say it!

JEAN: I—er—do.

REX: Do *what*? Say it! [*She cannot. He swings her about, bringing her face close to his.*]

JEAN: I love you, Rex. Are you sure you love me?

REX: Am I sure! You irresistible little—[*Begins to kiss her. Masculine triumph.*]

JEAN: And want to marry me, Rex?

REX: [*Stops—startled—had not thought of that.*] Why—er—of course. What did you suppose! [*Drops his eyes, sobered.*]

JEAN: [*Feminine triumph.*] And me "a penniless orphing"?

REX: [*Fascinated by the way she says it, he laughs. Then, his honor touched.*] Why, what kind of a man do you take me for! [*And wants her lips again.*]

JEAN: [*Giving herself to him, head sinks upon his shoulder.*] Then, oh, Rex, love me and be nice to me and—take me away from all this! [*She covers her face with her hands and sobs. He pats her tenderly, with a manly look on his face.*]

[LUCY *comes up from the garden. She is dressed in white with a garden hat, a garden basket filled with flowers in one hand, long scissors in the other. She is* JOHN's *wife, the mistress of the house, sister-in-law to* JEAN; *conspicuously a "sweet" woman, affectedly so, a contrast with* JEAN's *more modern, less delicate charm.* JEAN *is frank and brave,* LUCY *indirect and timid, pretty but fading, forty but fighting it.*]

JEAN: [*Laughing.*] It's all right, Lucy—we're engaged!

LUCY: Well, I should hope so! [*Shoots a look at* JEAN, *"So?"*]

REX: [*Recovering himself.*] I have often tried to thank you and good old John for letting me come over here so much, but now! How can I *ever* thank you? See-what-I-mean?

LUCY: I'll tell you how. Behave yourself after you are married to John's little sister.

JEAN: Rex, have you had a fearful past? How fascinating!

REX: I'm going to have a glorious future, all right.

JEAN: Not unless you do as I tell you. Going to obey me, Rex?

REX: You bet I am.

JEAN: Then begin now. Go! . . . Get out! [*She pushes* REX, *laughing and protesting, toward the garden.*] I want to tell Lucy how nice you are. Run along over to the golf club, and by and by—if you *are* a good boy—you can take me out in your new car. [REX *kisses the hand on his arm and leaves, laughing.*] My dear, he has five cars! Thank you so much. [*Alone, they throw off the mask worn before men.*]

LUCY: Now, deary, tell me all about it. How did it happen?

JEAN: Oh, I simply followed your advice.

LUCY: Picked a quarrel with him?

JEAN: [*Laughing*] Yes. I pretended to believe in woman suffrage!

LUCY: Good! They hate that.

JEAN: I told him all men were bullying brutes!

LUCY: They are! And then you ran away?

JEAN: Of course.

LUCY: And he after you?

JEAN: Of course.

LUCY: And you let him catch you?

JEAN: Of course—well . . . he caught me. [*They both laugh.*]

LUCY: I can guess the rest.

JEAN: Why, it didn't take five minutes.

LUCY: And now it's to last through all eternity. . . . Isn't love wonderful?

JEAN: Um-hum. Wonderful. [*They begin to cull out the flowers.*]

LUCY: But you do love him, dear, don't you?

JEAN: [*Arranging flowers.*] I did then. I don't now. Why is that, Lucy?

LUCY: Oh, but you will learn to love him. [JEAN *shrugs, drops flowers, and turns away.*] Now, now! no worrying—it brings wrinkles! [*Patting* JEAN's *shoulder.*] Rex is just the sort to give the woman he adores everything in the world.

JEAN: [*Wriggling out of* LUCY's *embrace.*] I am not the woman he adores.

LUCY: Why, Jean! He's engaged to you.

JEAN: But he's in love with my sister. You know that as well as I do.

LUCY: [*Uncomfortably.*] Oh, well, he was once, but not now. Men admire these independent women, but they don't marry them. Nobody wants to marry a sexless freak with a scientific degree.

JEAN: Oh, what's the use, Lucy? He's still wild about Helen, and she still laughs at him. So you and John have trotted out the little sister. Why not be honest about it.

LUCY: Well, I may be old-fashioned, but I don't think it's nice to talk this way when you're just engaged.

JEAN: Here comes your "sexless freak"—not with a degree, either.

LUCY: [*Following* JEAN's *gaze.*] With a man!

JEAN: [*Smiling.*] With *my* man.

[HELEN, *with* REX *bending toward her eagerly, appears. She is a beautiful woman of twenty-nine, tall, strong, glorious plenty of old-fashioned charm, despite her new-fashioned ideas. She is dressed in a tennis costume and is swinging a racquet.*]

REX: But they told me you were going to stay abroad all winter.

HELEN: My work, Rex—I had to get back to work.

REX: Work! . . . You are too good to work.

JEAN: [*Amused, not jealous.*] Is this your high-powered car, Rex? Have you learned to run it yet?

REX: [*Startled.*] But . . . well . . . you see, I met Helen on the way. See-what-I-mean?

JEAN: [*Laughing.*] Oh, we see.

REX: But I hadn't seen her for so long. I thought—[*looks from* HELEN *to* JEAN] . . . wait, I'll get the car. [*He hurries off.*]

LUCY: [*To* JEAN.] Why couldn't she have stayed abroad!

JEAN: Helen, don't talk about your work before Lucy—it shocks her.

HELEN: Oh, very well; make it my "career"!

JEAN: [*Arm around* HELEN.] Sssh!—that's worse.

LUCY: Helen, dear, I deem it my duty to tell you that you are being talked about.

HELEN: Lucy, dear, do you always find your true happiness in duty?

LUCY: Well, if you think you are going back to that horrid place again . . . after what happened that night? John won't hear of it.

HELEN: If the Baker Institute of Medical Experiment is not a respectable place you should make John resign as trustee. [*She laughs it off.*]

LUCY: John is trustee of—oh, nearly everything. That makes it all the worse. It isn't as if you had to work.

HELEN: Oh, but John is so rich now, his credit can stand it. And you oughtn't to mind! Why, some of our most fashionable families now contain freaks like me. It's becoming quite smart, just as in former days one of the sons would go into the Church or the navy.

LUCY: Well, of course, I am old-fashioned, but going down-town every day with the men,—it seems so unwomanly.

HELEN: But wasn't I womanly for years ? Instead of going down-town and working with highbrows, I stayed up-town and played with low-brows—until I was bored to death.

LUCY: [*Sighs.*] Yes, that's what comes of going to college, leaving the home, getting these new ideas. All the same, Helen, the men, really nice men, don't like it.

HELEN: Well, you see, I don't like really nice men, so that makes it agreeable all around.

LUCY: If it were only art or music or something feminine, but that awful laboratory! How can a lady poison poor, innocent little monkeys?

HELEN: If I were a lady I'd *dine* with monkeys. . . . Do you know what the word means, Lucy? In Anglo-Saxon times "lady" meant "one who gives loaves"; now, one who *takes* a loaf.

LUCY: Very clever, my dear, but some day you'll be sorry. No man, Helen, likes a woman to have independent views.

JEAN: Helen can afford to have independent views; she has an independent income—she earns it.

LUCY: Independent income! Her salary wouldn't pay for your hats.

JEAN: All the same, I wish I had gone to college; I wish I had learned a profession.

LUCY: What have these New Women accomplished? Just one thing: they are destroying chivalry!

HELEN: Not entirely, Lucy, not entirely. For instance, I am the best assistant Ernest Hamilton has, but the worst paid; the others are all men. Hurray for chivalry!

LUCY: Well, I'm just an old-fashioned wife. Woman's sphere is the home. My husband says so.

HELEN: But suppose you haven't any husband! What can a spinster do in the home?

LUCY: *Stay* in it—till she gets one! That's what the old-fashioned spinster used to do.

HELEN: The old-fashioned spinster used to spin.

LUCY: At any rate, the old-fashioned spinster did not stay out of her home all night and get herself compromised, talked about, sent abroad! Or, if she did, she knew enough to remain abroad until the gossip blew over. [LUCY *turns to leave.*]

HELEN: [*Mischievously.*] Ah, that wonderful night! [LUCY *turns back, amazed.*] The night we discovered the Hamilton antitoxin, the night that made the Baker Institute famous! And, just think, I had a hand in it, Lucy, a hand in the unwomanly work of saving children's lives! But, of course, an old-fashioned spinster would have blushed and said: "Excuse me, Doctor Hamilton, but we must now let a year's work go to waste because you are a man and I am a woman, and it's dark outdoors!" . . . That's the way to preserve true chivalry.

LUCY: You think we can't see through all this? Science—fiddlesticks! The good-looking young scientist—that's why you couldn't stay abroad. We see it, John sees it, and now every one will see it. Then how will you feel?

HELEN: Ernest *is* rather good-looking, isn't he?

LUCY: Do you think your brother will let you marry a mere scientist! . . . Oh, well, Doctor Hamilton is in love with his work—fortunately. . . . Besides, he's a thoroughbred; he wouldn't even look at a girl who throws herself at his head.

HELEN: So I needn't try any longer? Too bad.

LUCY: [*Losing her temper and going.*] Oh, you New Women are quite superior, aren't you? . . . Thank heavens, little Jean didn't elbow *her* way into men's affairs; she had no unwomanly ambitions for a career! But she is engaged to Rex Baker!

HELEN: Jean, is this true?

LUCY: [*Triumphantly.*] *Marriage* is woman's only true career.

HELEN: Jean! You can't, you won't, you mustn't marry Rex!

LUCY: [*Flouncing out.*] "She who will not when she may," my dear!

JEAN: [*Avoiding* HELEN's *eyes.*] Lucy hears John coming—he'd take her head off if she weren't there to meet him. [HELEN *only looks at her.*] He bullies and brow-beats her worse than ever. I can't stand it here much longer. It's getting on my nerves.

HELEN: Jean! You care for Rex no more than I do.

JEAN: [*Still evasive.*] John's bringing out Uncle Everett and Cousin Theodore. My dear, the whole family is up in the air about you.

HELEN: Oh, I can take care of myself, but you! . . . Jean, you're not the sort to marry Rex or any other man, unless you simply can't live without him.

JEAN: [*After a little pause.*] Well . . . how can I live without him—without some man? You can support yourself. I can't.

HELEN: But you wouldn't live on a man you didn't really love!

JEAN: Why not? Lucy does; most wives live on men they don't really love. To stop doing so and get divorced is wrong, you know.

HELEN: Jean, Jean, poor little Jean!

JEAN: Well, I'd rather have domestic unhappiness of my own than watch other people's all my life.

HELEN: I don't like to hurt you, dear, but—[*Takes* JEAN's *face and raises it.*] How about that nice boy at the Harvard Law School?

JEAN: Don't! [*Controls herself, then, in a low voice.*] Bob is *still* at the Law School, Helen.

HELEN: Can't you wait, dear?

JEAN: He never asked me to, Helen.

HELEN: He would, if you let him.

JEAN: It wouldn't be fair. It takes so long to get started. Everything costs so much. Why, nowadays, men in the professions, unless they have private means, can't marry until nearly *forty*. When Bob is forty I'll be forty, Helen.

HELEN: Ah, but when a girl really cares!

JEAN: Helen, do *you* know?

HELEN: Never mind about me—you!

JEAN: Oh, we'll get over it, I suppose. . . . People do! Some day, perhaps, he'll smile and say: "Just think, I once loved *that* fat old thing!" [*Suddenly changes to sobbing.*] Helen! When Rex caught me and kissed me I shut my eyes and tried to think it was Bob.

HELEN: [*Takes* JEAN *in her arms.*] You can't keep on thinking so, dear.

JEAN: But that isn't the worst! When he held me fast and I couldn't get away, I began . . . to forget Bob . . . to forget everything . . . [*Breaks off, overcome with shame.*] But not now, not now! It's not the same thing at all. [*Buries face in* HELEN*'s breast and sobs it out.*] Oh, I feel like the devil, dear. . . . And all this time he doesn't really want me—he wants you, you! I trapped him into it; I trapped him!

HELEN: And I know Rex—he's a good sport; he'll stick to it, if you do, dear—only you won't! You've caught him by playing on his worst—don't hold him by playing on his best!

JEAN: But what shall I do? I'm nearly twenty-six. I've got to escape from home in some way.

HELEN: But what a way! [REX *returns.*]

REX: Ready, Jean? [*To* HELEN.] Lucy and John and your Cousin Theodore are in there having a fine, old-fashioned family fight with the judge.

HELEN: With Uncle Everett? What about?

REX: They shut up when they saw me. All I heard was the parson—"Marriage is a social institution." Grand old row, though. [*A* BUTLER *and* FOOTMAN *appear, wheeling a tea-wagon.*] Looks as if they were coming out here.

HELEN: Then I am going in. [*Detaining* JEAN.] You will follow my advice?

JEAN: [*Apart to* HELEN.] Oh, I don't know. Soon or late I must follow the only profession I have learned.

[JEAN *leaves with* REX. HELEN *watches them, sighs, and goes in. The* SERVANTS *arrange the tea-table and go into the house.* LUCY *comes out, followed by her husband,* JOHN, *and the* JUDGE, *who is* UNCLE EVERETT, *and* COUSIN THEODORE. JOHN, *the masterful type of successful American business man; well set up, close-cropped mustache, inclined to baldness; keen eye, vibrant voice, quick movements, quick decisions, quick temper.* UNCLE EVERETT *is a genial satirist with a cynical tolerance of the ways of the world, which he understands, laughs at, and rather likes.* COUSIN THEODORE, *a care-worn rector, who, though he buttons his collar behind, likes those who don't; a noble soul, self-sacrificing and sanctified, but he does not obtrude his profession upon others—never talks shop unless asked to do so, and prides himself upon not being a bigot. They are continuing an earnest discussion, with the intimate manner of friendly members of the same family.* JOHN, LUCY, *and* THEODORE *deeply concerned;* UNCLE EVERETT *detached and amused.*]

THEODORE: But, Uncle Everett, hasn't Aunt Julia always been a good wife to you?

JUDGE: Quite so, quite so, a good wife, Theodore, a good wife.

LUCY: And a *devoted* mother to your children, Uncle Everett?

JUDGE: Devoted, Lucy, devoted.

JOHN: She has always obeyed you, Uncle Everett.

JUDGE: Yes, John—a true, old-fashioned woman.

THEODORE: She has been a great help to me in the parish work, Uncle Everett.

JUDGE: An earnest worker in the vineyard, Theodore—in fact, I might say, a model female.

ALL: Then why, *why* do you want a divorce?

JUDGE: Because, damn it, I don't like her!

LUCY: But think of poor Aunt Julia!

JUDGE: But, damn it, she doesn't like *me*.

THEODORE: [*Wagging head sadly.*] Ah, yes, I suppose there has been fault on both sides.

JUDGE: Not at all! No fault on either side. . . . Both patterns of Christian fortitude to the end! We still are. Just listen to this telegram.

LUCY: [*Puzzled.*] From Aunt Julia?

JUDGE: Yes from Aunt Julia in Reno. Not used to travelling without me; knew I'd worry. Thoughtful of her, wasn't it? [*Puts on glasses.*] A night letter. Much cheaper; your Aunt Julia was always a frugal wife. Besides, she never could keep within ten words. [*Reads.*] "Arrived safely. Charming rooms with plenty of air and sunlight. Our case docketed for March 15th. Wish you were here to see the women in Divorcee Row—overdressed and underbred." Rather neat, eh? "Overdressed and underbred." "I should love to hear *your* comments on the various types." Now, isn't that sweet of her? Well, you know, I always *could* make her laugh—except when I made her cry. "Write soon. With love. Julia." Now [*folds telegram*], isn't that a nice message? From a wife suing for divorce? You happily married people couldn't beat that. [*Pats telegram and pockets it tenderly.*]

JOHN: [*Like a practical business man.*] But if there's no other woman, no other man—what's it all about?

JUDGE: She likes her beefsteak well done; I like mine underdone. She likes one window open—about so much [*indicates four inches*]; I like all the windows open wide! She likes to stay at home; I like to travel. She loves the opera and hates the theatre; I love the theatre and hate the opera.

THEODORE: Stop! aren't you willing to make a few little sacrifices for each other? Haven't you character enough for that?

JUDGE: We've been making sacrifices for twenty-five years, a quarter of a century! Character enough to last us now. . . . Why, I remember the first dinner we had together after we were pronounced man and wife, with a full choral service and a great many expensive flowers—quite a smart wedding, Lucy, for those simple days. "Darling," I asked my blushing bride, "do you like tutti-frutti ice-cream?" "I adore it, dearest," she murmured. I hated it, but nobly sacrificed myself and gave her tutti-frutti and gained character every evening of our honeymoon! Then when we got back and began our "new life" together in our "little home," my darling gave *me* tutti-frutti and indigestion *once a week* until I nearly died!

LUCY: But why didn't you tell her?

JUDGE: I did; I did. Got chronic dyspepsia and struck! "*You* may adore this stuff, *darling*," I said, "but I hate it." "So do I, dearest," says she. "Then why in thunder have you had it all these years, *sweetheart?*" "For your sake, *beloved!*" And that tells the whole story of our married life. We have nothing in common but a love of divorce and a mutual abhorrence of tutti-frutti. "Two souls with but a single thought, two hearts that beat as one!" It has been the dream of our lives to get apart, and each has nobly refrained for the other's sake. And all in vain!

JOHN: Bah! All a cloak to hide his real motive. And he knows it!

JUDGE: [*After a painful pause.*] I may as well confess. [*Looks around to see if overheard. Whispers.*] For over twenty years I—I have broken my marriage vow! [LUCY *drops her eyes.* THEODORE *aghast.* JOHN *wags head.*] So has your Aunt Julia!

THEODORE: No! not that!

JUDGE: Well, we solemnly promised to love each other until death did us part. We have broken that sacred vow! I don't love *her;* she doesn't love *me*—not in the least!

JOHN: Rot! A matured, middle-aged man, a distinguished member of the bar—break up his home for that? Damned rot!

JUDGE: Right again, John. That's not why I'm breaking up my home. I prefer my club. What does the modern home amount to?—Merely a place to leave your wife.

LUCY: Of course, it doesn't matter about the poor little wife left at home.

JUDGE: Wrong, Lucy, it does matter. That's why I *stayed* at home and was bored to death with her prattle about clothes and the opera, instead of dining at the club with my intellectual equals, picking up business there, getting rich like John, supplying her with *more* clothes and a whole *box* at the opera, like yours, Lucy.

LUCY: [*Shoots a glance at her husband.*] Oh, that's the way you men *always* talk. It never occurs to you that business, business, *business* is *just* as much of a bore to us!

JUDGE: Wrong again! It did occur to *me*—hence the divorce! She couldn't stand seeing *me* bored; I couldn't stand seeing *her* bored. Once we could deceive each other; but now—*too* well acquainted; our happy home—a hollow mockery!

THEODORE: You ought to be ashamed! I love my home!

JOHN: So do I. [*He glances sternly at* LUCY.]

LUCY: [*Nervously.*] So do I.

JUDGE: All right. Stick to it, if you love it. Only, don't claim credit for doing what you enjoy. I stuck to my home for a quarter of a century and disliked it the whole time. At last I'm free to say so. Just think of it, Lucy, free to utter those things about marriage we all know are true but don't dare say! Free to be honest, John! No longer a hypocrite, no longer a liar! A soul set free, Theodore—two souls, in fact. "Two souls with but a single thought—"

THEODORE: Stop! You have *children* to consider, not merely your own selfish happiness!

LUCY: Yes, think of Tom and little Julia!

JUDGE: We did . . . for a quarter of a century—sacrificed everything to them, even our self-respect—but now—what's the use? We are childless now. Tom and Julia have both left us for "little homes" of their own to love.

THEODORE: Ah, but don't you want them to have the old home to come back to?

JUDGE: "No place like home" for children, eh? You're right—can't have too much of it. Most children only have *one* home. Ours will have *two*! When they get bored with one they can try the other.

THEODORE: But, seriously, Uncle Everett—"Whom God hath joined together!"

LUCY: [*Clasping* JOHN*'s arm.*] Yes, Uncle Everett, marriages are made in heaven.

JUDGE: I see; quite so; but your Aunt Julia and I were joined together by a pink parasol made in Paris.

JOHN: What rot! Stop your fooling and speak the truth, man.

JUDGE: Just what I'm doing—that's why you think I'm fooling. A very pretty parasol—but it wasn't made in heaven. You see, God made poor, dear Julia pale, but on that fatal day, twenty-five years ago, the pink parasol, not God, made her rosy and irresistible. I did the rest— with the aid of a clergyman, whom I tipped even more liberally than the waiter who served us tutti-frutti. Blame *me* for it, blame her, the parasol, the parson, but do not, my dear Theodore, blame the Deity for our own mistakes. It's so blasphemous. [*A pause.* LUCY *takes place at the tea-table to serve tea.*]

LUCY: And to think we invited *you,* of all people, here to-day of all days! [*To* JOHN.] We mustn't let Rex know. The Bakers don't believe in divorce.

JOHN: What's this? You don't mean that Jean—?

LUCY: Yes! just in time—before he knew Helen was back.

JOHN: [*Jumps up.*] She's landed him! She's landed him! We're marrying into the Baker family! The Baker family! [*Shaking hands right and left.*] Why, she'll have more money than any of us! . . . Well, well! We'll all have to stand around before little Jean now! . . . My, my! Lucy, you're a wonder! Those pearls—I'll buy them; they're yours! Hurray for Lucy! [*Kisses* LUCY.]

LUCY: [*Feeling her importance.*] Now, if I could only get *Helen* out of this awful mess and safely married to some nice man!

JUDGE: [*Sipping his tea.*] Meaning one having money?

THEODORE: The Hamiltons are an older family than the Bakers, Lucy, older than our own.

JUDGE: Meaning they *once* had money.

JOHN: [*Still pacing to and fro.*] Waste a beauty on a bacteriologist? A crime!

THEODORE: See here, John, Ernest Hamilton is the biggest thing you've got in the Baker Institute! One of the loveliest fellows in the world, too, and if you expect me—why did you ask us here, anyway?

JUDGE: Far as I can make out, we're here to help one of John's sisters marry a man she doesn't love and prevent the other from marrying the man she does.

JOHN: Oh, look here: I've nothing against young Hamilton. . . . I *like* him—proud of all he's done for the institute. Why, Mr. Baker is tickled to death about the Hamilton antitoxin. But, Theodore, this is a practical world. Your scientific friend gets just two thousand dollars a year! . . . Lucy, send for Helen. [LUCY *goes obediently.*]

JUDGE: Well, why not give the young man a raise?

JOHN: Oh, that's not a bad salary for scientists, college professors, and that sort of thing. Why, even the head of the institute himself gets less than the superintendent of my mills. No future in science.

JUDGE: Perfectly practical, Theodore. The superintendent of John's mills saves the company thousands of dollars. These bacteriologists merely save the nation thousands of babies. All our laws, written and unwritten, value private property above human life. I'm a distinguished jurist and I always render my decisions accordingly. I'd be reversed by the United States Supreme Court if I didn't. We're all rewarded in inverse ratio to our usefulness to society, Theodore. That's why "practical men" think changes are "dangerous."

JOHN: Muck-raker!

JUDGE: It's all on a sliding scale, John, For keeping up the cost of living you and old man Baker get . . . [*Stretches arms out full length.*] Heaven only knows how much. For saving the Constitution I get a . . . good deal. [*Hands three feet apart.*] For saving in wages and operating expenses your superintendent gets so much. [*Hands two feet apart.*] For saving human life Ernest Hamilton gets that. [*Hands six inches apart.*] For saving immortal souls Theodore gets—[*Holds up two forefingers an inch apart.*] Now, if any one came along and saved the world—

THEODORE: [*Interrupts.*] They crucified Him.

JOHN: Muck-raker, muck-raker.

LUCY: [*Returning.*] Tried my best, John, but Helen says she prefers to talk with you alone some time.

JOHN: [*Furious.*] She "prefers"? See here! Am I master in my own house or not?

JUDGE: But Helen is a guest in it now. No longer under your control, John. She's the New Woman.

THEODORE: John, *you* can't stop that girl's marrying Ernest, if she wants to; he's head over heels in love with her.

LUCY: What! We thought he was in love with his work!

THEODORE: He thinks there's no hope for him, poor boy.

LUCY: [*To* JOHN.] And she is mad about him!

JOHN: [*To* LUCY.] And he is on the way out here now!

THEODORE: What! He's coming to see her?

JOHN: No, no, thinks she's still in Paris—so she was when I invited him, damn it—but something had to be done and done delicately. That's why I invited you two.

JUDGE: [*Bursts out laughing*] Beautiful! These lovers haven't met for a month, and to-night there's a moon!

THEODORE: [*Also laughs.*] You may as well give in, John. It's the simplest solution.

LUCY: [*Timidly.*] Yes, John, she's nearly thirty, and think how she treats all the *nice* men.

JOHN: Who's doing this? You go tell Helen . . . that her Uncle Everett wants to see her! [LUCY *shrugs, starts reluctantly, and lingers listening.*]

THEODORE: Now, uncle, you have more influence over her than any of us—don't let her know about . . . Aunt Julia. Helen thinks the world of you.

JUDGE: Of course not, never let the rising generation suspect the truth about marriage—if you want 'em to marry.

THEODORE: There are other truths than unpleasant truths, Uncle Everett, other marriages than unhappy marriages.

JUDGE: Want me to tell her the truth about your marriage?

LUCY: [*At the door.*] Why uncle! Even *you* must admit that Theodore and Mary are happy. [JOHN *is too much surprised to notice* LUCY'*s presence.*]

JUDGE: Happy? What's that got to do with it? Marriage is a social institution. Theodore said so. . . . Every time a boy kisses a girl she should first inquire: "A sacrifice for society?" And if he says, "I want to gain character, sweetheart," then—"Darling, do your duty!" and he'll do it.

LUCY: Well, Theodore has certainly done *his* duty by society—six children!

JUDGE: Then society hasn't done its duty by Theodore—only one salary!

JOHN: The more credit to him! He and Mary have sacrificed everything to their children and the Church—even health!

THEODORE: We don't need your pity! We don't want your praise! Poverty, suffering, even separation, have only drawn us closer together. We love each other through it all! Why, in the last letter the doctor let her write she said, she said—[*Suddenly overcome with emotion, turns abruptly.*] If you'll excuse me, Lucy . . . Sanitarium . . . the telephone. [THEODORE *goes into the house.*]

JUDGE: Not praise or pity but something more substantial and, by George, I'll get it for them! [*Turns to* JOHN, *who interrupts.*]

JOHN: See the example *he* sets to society—I honor him for it.

JUDGE: Fine! but that doesn't seem to restore Mary's radiant health, Theodore's brilliant youth.

LUCY: Ah, but they have their *children*—think how they adore those beautiful children!

JUDGE: No, don't think how they adore them, think how they *rear* those beautiful children—in the streets; one little daughter dead from contagion; one son going to the devil from other things picked up in the street! If marriage is a social institution, look at it socially. Why, a marriage like mine is worth a dozen like theirs—to Society. Look at my well-launched children; look at my useful career, as a jackal to Big Business; look at my now perfectly contented spouse!

LUCY: But if you are divorced!

JUDGE: Is the object of marriage merely to stay married?

LUCY: But character, think of the character they have gained.

JUDGE: Oh, is it to gain character at the expense of helpless offspring? Society doesn't gain by that—it loses, Lucy, it loses. . . . But simply because, God bless 'em, "they love each other through it all," you sentimental standpatters believe in lying about it, do you?

JOHN: [*Bored, whips out pocket check-book and fountain pen.*] Oh, talk, talk,

talk! Money talks for *me*. . . . But they're both so confoundedly proud!

JUDGE: Go on, write that check! [JOHN *writes.*] They must sacrifice their pride, John. Nothing else left to sacrifice, I'm afraid.

JOHN: Well, you get this to them somehow. [*Hands check to* JUDGE.]

JUDGE: Aha! Talk did it. . . . Five thousand? Generous John!

JOHN: [*Impatiently.*] Never mind about me. *That* problem is all settled; now about Helen. . . . Lucy! I thought I told you—[LUCY, *in a guilty hurry, escapes into the house.*]

JUDGE: John, charity never settles problems; it perpetuates them. You can't cure social defects by individual treatment.

JOHN: [*More impatiently.*] Does talk settle anything?

JUDGE: Everything. We may even settle the marriage problem if we talk *honestly.* [THEODORE *returns from telephoning to the sanitarium.*] Theodore, it's all right! John honestly believes in setting an example to society! Crazy to have his sisters go and do likewise!

THEODORE: Splendid, John! I knew you'd see it—an ideal match.

JUDGE: [*Overriding* JOHN.] Right, Theodore, ideal. This scientific suitor will shower everything upon her John honors and admires: A host of servants—I mean sacrifices; carriages and motors—I mean character and morals; just what her brother advocates in Sunday-school—for others. An ideal marriage.

JOHN: [*Hands in pockets.*] You think you're awfully funny, don't you? Humph! I do more for the Church, for education, art, science than all the rest of the family combined. Incidentally, I'm not divorced. . . . But this is a practical world, Theodore, I've got to protect my own.

LUCY: [*Returning.*] Helen will be here in a minute.

JOHN: [*Suddenly getting an idea.*] Ah! I have it! I know how to keep them apart!

THEODORE: Be careful, John—these two love each other.

JUDGE: Yes, young people still fall in love. Whether we make it hard or easy for them—they *will* do it. But, mark my words, unless we *reform marriage,* there is going to be a sympathetic *strike* against it—as there is already against having children. Instead of making it harder to get apart, we've got to make it easier to stay together. Otherwise the ancient bluff will soon be called!

LUCY: Sssh! Here she comes.

THEODORE: *Please* don't talk this way before her.

JUDGE: All right, I'm not divorced yet . . . still in the conspiracy of silence. [HELEN *appears at the door. A sudden silence.*]

HELEN: [*Kissing* THEODORE *and* JUDGE *affectionately.*] I'm *so* sorry to hear about dear Mary. [*To* JUDGE.] But why didn't Aunt Julia come? Is she ill, too? [*Slight panic in the family party.*]

JUDGE: She's gone to Re—Re—Rio Janeiro—I mean to Santa Barbara—wants a complete change—The Rest Cure. [*To* THEODORE *apart.*] Lie number one. [*Another silence.* LUCY *makes tea for* HELEN.]

HELEN: [*Taking the cup.*] Well, go on!

THEODORE: Go on with what?

HELEN: [*Stirring tea.*] Your discussion of marriage.

LUCY: How did you know?

HELEN: Oh, it's in the air. Everybody's talking about it nowadays. [*She sips tea, and the others look conscious.*]

THEODORE: My dear, marriage is woman's only true career.

HELEN: [*Raising her shield of flippancy.*] So Lucy tells me, Cousin Theodore. But a woman cannot pursue her career, she must be pursued by it; otherwise she is unwomanly.

JUDGE: Ahem. As we passed through the library a while ago, I think I saw your little sister being pursued by her career.

HELEN: Yes, uncle, but Jean is a true woman. I'm only a New Woman.

JUDGE: All the same, you'll be an old woman some day—if you don't watch out.

HELEN: Ah, yes, my life's a failure. I haven't trapped a man into a contract to support me.

LUCY: [*Picks up knitting bag and does her best to look like "just an old-fashioned wife."*] You ought to be ashamed! Making marriage so mercenary. Helen, dear, haven't you New Women any sentiment?

HELEN: Enough sentiment not to make a mercenary marriage, Lucy, dear.

JUDGE: Ahem! And what kind of a marriage do you expect to make?

HELEN: Not any, thank you, uncle.

JUDGE: What! You don't believe in holy matrimony?

HELEN: Only as a last extremity, uncle, like unholy divorce.

JUDGE: [*Jumps.*] What do you know about that?

HELEN: I know all about it! [*Others jump.*] I have been reading up on the subject. [*All relax, relieved, but now gather about the young woman.*]

[*TOGETHER:*] {
THEODORE: Come now, simply because many young people rush into marriage without thinking—
LUCY: Simply because these New Women—
JOHN: Simply because one marriage in a thousand ends in divorce—
}

HELEN: Wait! . . . One in a thousand? Dear me, what an idealist you are, John! In America, one marriage in every eleven now ends in divorce. And yet you wonder why I hesitate.

JOHN: One in eleven—rot! [*To* JUDGE.] All this muck-raking should be suppressed by the Government. "One in eleven!" Bah!

HELEN: [*Demurely.*] The Government's own statistics, John. [*They all turn to the* JUDGE *for denial, but he nods confirmation, with a complacent smile, murmuring: "Two souls with but a single thought."*]

LUCY: [*Sweetly knitting.*] Well, I may be old-fashioned, but it seems to me that nice girls shouldn't *think* of such things. . . . Their husbands will tell them all they ought to know about marriage—after they're married.

HELEN: Ah, I see. Nice girls mustn't think until after they rush in, but they mustn't rush in until after they think. You married people make it all so simple for us.

JUDGE: Right! The way to cure all evil is for nice people to close their minds and mouths to it. It's "unpleasant" for a pure mind, and it "leaves a bad taste in the mouth." So there you are, my dear.

JOHN: [*Coming in strong.*] Oh, talk, talk, talk! I've had enough. See here, young lady, I offered to pay all your expenses abroad for a year. You didn't seem to appreciate it—well, the trustees of the institute are now to give Doctor Hamilton a year abroad. How do you like that? [*All turn and look at* HELEN.]

HELEN: Splendid! just what he needs! Doctor Metchnikoff told me in Paris that America always kills its big men with routine. When do we start? [*She tries to look very businesslike.*]

JOHN: [*Springing to his feet.*] "We!" Do you think *you* are going?

HELEN: Of course! I'm his assistant—quite indispensable to him . . . [*To all.*] Oh, well, if you don't believe me, ask him!

JOHN: [*Pacing to and fro.*] What next! Paris! Alone, with a man!—Here's where I call a halt!

HELEN: But if my work calls me, I don't really see what you have to say about it, John.

JOHN: Better not defy me, Helen. [*He scowls.*]

HELEN: Better not bully me, John. [*She smiles.*]

JOHN: I am your brother.

HELEN: But not my owner! [*Then, instead of defiance, she turns with animated interest to the others.*] You know, all women used to be owned by men. Formerly they ruled us by physical force—now by financial force. . . . But at last they are to lose even *that* hold upon us—poor dears! [*Pats* JOHN's *shoulder playfully.*]

JOHN: [*Amused, but serious.*] That's all right in theory, but this is a practical world. My pull got you into the institute; my pull can get you out. You give up this wild idea or give up your job!

HELEN: [*Delighted.*] What did I tell you? Financial force! They still try it, you see. [*To* JOHN.] What if I refused to give up either, John?

JOHN: [*Emphatic.*] Then as a trustee of the institute I ask for your resignation—right here and now! [*Turns away.*] I guess *that* will hold her at home a while.

HELEN: I simply *must* go to Paris now. I've nothing else to do!

JOHN: [*With a confident smile.*] You will, eh? Who'll pay your expenses this time?

HELEN: [*Matter of fact.*] Doctor Hamilton.

LUCY: Helen! please! You oughtn't to say such things even in joke.

HELEN: He'll take me along as his private secretary, if I ask him. [*A pause. The others look at one another helplessly.*]

JUDGE: John, she's got you. You might as well quit.

JOHN: Nonsense. I have just begun. You'll see.

THEODORE: If you're so independent, my dear, why don't you marry your scientist and be done with it?

HELEN: [*Resents the intrusion but hides her feelings.*] Can you keep a secret? [*They all seem to think they can and gather near.*] He has never asked me! [*The family seems annoyed.*]

LUCY: [*With match-making ardor.*] No wonder, dear, he has never seen you except in that awful apron. But those stunning dinner gowns John bought you in Paris! My dear, in evening dress you are quite irresistible!

JUDGE: [*Apart to* THEODORE.] Irresistible? Pink parasols. What a system!

HELEN: But you see, I don't *want* him to ask me. I've had all I could do to keep him from it. [*The family seems perplexed.*]

JOHN: She's got *some* sense left.

LUCY: But suppose he did ask you, dear?

HELEN: Why, I'd simply refer the matter to John, of course. If John said, "Love him," I'd love him; if John said, "Don't love him," I'd turn it off like electric light. [*The family is becoming exasperated.*]

LUCY: [*Insinuating.*] Oh, you can't deceive us. We know how much you admire him, Helen.

HELEN: Oh, no you don't! [*The family is amazed.*] Not even he does. Did you ever hear how he risked his life in battle down in Cuba? Why, he's a perfect hero of romance!

JOHN: [*Mutters.*] Never even saw a war—mollycoddle germ killer!

HELEN: Not in the war with Spain—the war against yellow fever, John. . . . No drums to make him brave, no correspondents to make him famous—he merely rolled up his sleeve and let an innocent-looking mosquito bite him. Then took notes on his symptoms till he became delirious. . . . He happened to be among those who recovered. [*The family is impressed.*]

THEODORE: Old-fashioned maidens used to marry their heroes, Helen.

HELEN: [*Arising, briskly.*] But this new-fashioned hero only gets two thousand a year, Theodore. [*She turns to escape.*]

JOHN: [*Nodding.*] I told you she had sense.

THEODORE: Helen! You selfish, too? Why, Mary and I married on half that, didn't we, John? [*He looks around. The family looks away.*]

HELEN: [*With unintended emphasis.*] Doctor Hamilton needs every cent of that enormous salary—books, travel, scientific conferences—all the advantages he simply must have if he's to keep at the top and do his best work for the world. The most selfish thing a girl can do is to marry a poor man. [*With that she hurries up the steps.*]

THEODORE: [*Following her.*] All the same, deep down under it all, she has a true woman's yearning for a home to care for and a mate to love. [*She is silently crying.*] Why, Helen, dear, what's the matter?

HELEN: [*Hiding her emotion.*] Oh, why can't they let me *alone!* They make what ought to be the holiest and most beautiful thing in life the most horrible and dishonest. They make me hate marriage—hate it!

[*Unseen by* HELEN, *the* BUTLER *steps out.*]

THEODORE: [*Patting her shoulder.*] Just you wait till the right one comes along.

BUTLER: [*To* LUCY.] Doctor Hamilton has come, ma'am.

HELEN: [*With an old-fashioned gasp.*] Good heavens! [*And runs to the family.*]

LUCY: Show Doctor Hamilton out. [*The* BUTLER *goes.*]

HELEN: A plot to entrap him! [*Running to and fro wildly.*] But it's no use! I'm going . . . until he's gone! [HELEN *runs into the garden.*]

JUDGE: Fighting hard, poor child.

THEODORE: But what'll we do?

JUDGE: Don't worry—she can't stay away—the sweet thing!

JOHN: Now listen, we must all jolly him up—he'll be shy in these surroundings.

JUDGE: Going to surrender, John?

JOHN: What I am going to do requires finesse.

LUCY: [*In a flutter, seeing* HAMILTON *approach.*] Oh, dear! how does one talk to highbrows?

JUDGE: Talk to him about himself! Highbrows, lowbrows, all men love it. [ERNEST HAMILTON, *discoverer of the Hamilton antitoxin, is a fine-looking fellow of about thirty-five, without the spectacles or absent-*

mindedness somehow expected of scientific genius. He talks little but very rapidly and sees everything. It does not occur to him to be shy or embarrassed "in these surroundings"—not because he is habituated to so much luxury, on two thousand a year, nor because he despises it; he likes it; but he likes other things even more. That is why he works for two thousand a year, instead of working for fat, fashionable fees in private practice. JOHN *meets his distinguished guest at the door—effusively, yet with that smiling condescension which wealthy trustees sometimes show to "scientists, college professors, and that sort of thing."*]

JOHN: Ah, Doctor Hamilton! Delighted to see you on my little farm at last. Out here I'm just a plain, old-fashioned farmer.

[ERNEST *glances about at the magnificence and smiles imperceptibly. He makes no audible replies to the glad welcome, but bows urbanely, master of himself and the situation.*]

LUCY: Doctor Hamilton! So good of you to come.

THEODORE: How are you, Ernest? Glad to see you.

LUCY: I don't think you've met our uncle, Judge Grey.

JUDGE: [*Humorously adopting their manner.*] Charmed! I've heard so much about you!—from my niece.

LUCY: [*To* ERNEST'*s rescue, like a tactful hostess.*] A cup of tea, Doctor Hamilton?

ERNEST: [*Unperturbed by the reference to* HELEN.] Thanks.

JOHN: [*While* LUCY *makes tea. Trustee manner.*] I have often desired to express my admiration of your heroism in the war against yellow fever in er—ah—*Cuba,* when you let an innocent-looking mosquito bite you—

LUCY: [*Nodding and poising sugar-tongs.*] And then took notes on your symptoms till you became delirious!

ERNEST: No sugar, thanks. [*He looks from one to another with considerable interest.*]

JUDGE: No drums to make you famous, no war correspondents to make you brave—I mean the other way round.

ERNEST: [*To* LUCY *poising cream pitcher.*] No cream, please.

JOHN: Senator Root says this one triumph alone saves *twenty million dollars a year* to the business interests of the United States! I call that true patriotism.

ERNEST: [*With a nod of assent to* LUCY.] Lemon.

THEODORE: [*With sincerity.*] General Wood says it saves more *human lives* a year than were lost in the whole Spanish War! I call it service.

JUDGE: Colonel Goethals says the Panama Canal could not have been built if it hadn't been for you self-sacrificing scientists. Not only that, but you have abolished forever from the United States a scourge which for more than a century had through periodic outbreaks spread terror, devastation, and death. [*A pause.*]

ERNEST: [*Bored, but trying to hide it.*] Dear me! you are all very kind, I'm sure. . . . You know about the four who *died* to prove that theory? One of them was a woman. [*He looks at* JOHN, *who looks at* JUDGE, *who looks at* LUCY, *who looks at* THEODORE. *He takes up his cup.*] Delicious tea.

THEODORE: Ah, but they didn't do it for fame, for money—that's the beauty of the sacrifice.

ERNEST: [*With a smile.*] Quite so. . . . That's what Congress told us when we suggested a pension for the widow of the first victim.

ALL: What! Did Congress refuse the pension?

ERNEST: [*Finishes his tea.*] They finally voted the sum of seventeen dollars a month for the widow and no less than two dollars a month extra for each of his children. . . .

LUCY: Is that all?

ERNEST: No. . . . We pestered Congress to death until, a few years ago, they replaced the pension with an annuity of one hundred and twenty-five dollars a month—though some of them said it was a very bad precedent to establish. [*Returns cup to* LUCY.] No more, thanks, delicious. [*And turns to admire the wide-sweeping view of the farm, hands in pockets.*]

JOHN: [*After a pause.*] And yet think how we taxpayers are held up for *war* pensions!

JUDGE: The sliding scale, John. If these fellows would only destroy as many lives as they save, we'd call 'em generals and admirals, dress 'em up in gold lace, like elevator boys, and give 'em a house in Washington. After death a life-sized statue, waving a sword. . . . At least, we'd know their names, John. [JOHN *approaches and joins his guest.*]

ERNEST: Charming little farm you have here.

JOHN: Doctor Hamilton, America kills its big men with routine. You are too valuable to the nation to lose—the trustees think you need a year abroad.

ERNEST: That's strange, I came out here to suggest that very thing. . . . Somebody has been saying kind things about me in Paris. Just had a letter from the great Metchnikoff—wants me to come over and work in the Pasteur! Chance of a lifetime! . . . You didn't have to jolly me up to consent to that!

JOHN: [*Pacing terrace with his guest, arm in arm.*] By the by, my sister is rather keen on science.

ERNEST: Best assistant I ever had. You can pile an awful lot of routine on a woman. The female of the species is more faithful than the male. . . . She's over there already. We can get right to work.

JOHN: She'll be back before you start.

ERNEST: [*Stops short.*] I didn't know that. . . . Well, what is it? [JOHN *hesitates, turns to the family, all watching with breathless interest.*]

THEODORE: Don't you see, old chap, under the circumstances it would hardly do for her to go back to Paris with you.

ERNEST: Why not?

LUCY: You're a man.

ERNEST: [*Smiling.*] You mean I'm dangerous?

LUCY: But she's a woman.

JUDGE: They mean *she's* dangerous.

JOHN: My dear fellow, we are going to ask you quite frankly to decline to take her.

ERNEST: [*Looks about at the circle of anxious faces. He won't let them read him.*] So that's it, eh? . . . But it's the chance of a lifetime for her, too. She needs it more than I do. She's had so little chance to do original work.

JOHN: But she's a woman.

ERNEST: Just what has that to do with it?

JOHN: Everything. We have the highest respect for you, Doctor Hamilton, but also . . . one must respect the opinions of the world, you know.

ERNEST: [*Thinks it over.*] That's right. One must. I forgot to think of that. . . . It's curious, but when working with women of ability one learns to respect them so much that one quite loses the habit of insulting them. Too bad how new conditions spoil fine old customs. . . . Suppose you let her go and let me stay. I can find plenty to do here, I fancy.

JOHN: I fear it would offend our generous benefactor, Mr. Baker. He has set his heart on your going abroad, meeting other big men, getting new ideas for our great humanitarian work. [*The family exchange glances while* JOHN *lies on.*] Besides, my sister would only go to accommodate you. She particularly desires to stay here this winter. That's why she is returning so soon, you see.

ERNEST: [*Believes it.*] Oh, I see. . . . I'm sure I have no desire to *drag* her over with me. . . . [*Smiles at himself.*] I rather thought the opportunity to continue our experiments together . . . but that's all right.

JOHN: Then it's all settled—you agree to go alone?

ERNEST: [*A slight pause.*] Yes, alone. It's quite settled.

JOHN: How soon could you start?

ERNEST: [*Absently.*] How soon? Why, just as soon as I get some one to run my department.

JOHN: Could my sister run it?

ERNEST: [*Smiles*] Could she run it? It can't run without her! She's as systematic as [*to* LUCY]—as a good housekeeper.

JOHN: [*With a satisfied look at the others.*] Then *that's* all fixed! She'll stay when I tell her that you want her to. Could you arrange to start at once?

ERNEST: [*Hesitates.*] By leaving here to-night, I could.

JOHN: [*With a triumphant look at the family.*] Then I'll telephone for your passage—I have a pull with all the steamship lines. [*Going.*] Of course I hate to cut short your week-end, but I don't want to spoil any scientific careers. [JOHN *hurries in to telephone.* ERNEST *starts too, as if to stop him, but restrains the impulse. He stands alone by the door gazing out over the landscape while* LUCY, THEODORE, *and the* JUDGE *discuss him in low tones by the tea-table.*]

LUCY: Can't you see, you stupid men! He's crazy about her—but thinks there's no hope.

THEODORE: When she finds he's leaving for a year . . . she'll change her mind about marriage! [ERNEST *comes back to earth and to the house-party.*]

JUDGE: [*To* ERNEST, *joining them.*] Ahem! We were just discussing the marriage danger—I mean the marriage problem.

ERNEST: [*With a smile.*] Go right on—don't mind me.

THEODORE: [*Old-friend manner.*] See here! When are *you* ever going to marry?

ERNEST: [*Modern bachelor's laugh.*] When am I ever going to get more than two thousand a year?

THEODORE: Bah! what has money got to do with it! Just you wait till the right one comes along. [HELEN *comes along, stealing up the steps from the garden on tiptoe with the grave, absorbed look of a hunter stalking game. She catches sight of the man she wants and stops short, as motionless as if frozen. But not so! Her lovely hands were poised; one of them now goes to her bosom and presses there. There is nothing icy about this New Woman now.*]

ERNEST: [*As unconscious of danger as a mountain-lion on an inaccessible height, smiles easily at his sentimental old friend* THEODORE.] How do you know "the right one" hasn't come already? [THEODORE *catches sight of Helen. She shakes her head in silent pleading, taps a finger on her lips, and in a panic flees noiselessly across toward the door.*]

THEODORE: [*Suppressing a laugh.*] Then don't let her go by! [HELEN *stops at the door and makes a face at* THEODORE.]

ERNEST: [*Affecting indifference.*] Oh, I couldn't stop her, even if I wanted to.

THEODORE: [*Turning to wink at* HELEN.] How do you know? Did you ever ask her?

ERNEST: To marry me? Oh, no! She hasn't any money.

THEODORE: [HELEN *is dumfounded.*] Money! You wouldn't marry for money! [HELEN *draws near to hear the answer.*]

ERNEST: You don't suppose I'd marry a woman who hadn't any? Most selfish thing a poor man can do. [HELEN *is interested.*]

THEODORE: Oh, fiddlesticks! You modern young people—

ERNEST: [*Interrupts.*] Make her a sort of superior servant in an inferior home—not that girl! [HELEN *is pleased.*]

THEODORE: Feministic nonsense! The old-fashioned womanly woman—

ERNEST: Sentimental twaddle! What makes it more "womanly" to do menial work *for* men than intellectual work with them? [HELEN *delighted, applauds noiselessly.*]

THEODORE: All the same, I'll bet you wouldn't let a little thing like that stand in your way if you really cared for a woman enough to marry her.

ERNEST: [*Benign and secure.*] But, as it happens, I don't. Nothing could induce me to marry. [HELEN *raises her chin, her eyes glitter dangerously.*]

THEODORE: So you are going to run away to Europe like a coward?

ERNEST: [*Smiles patronizingly.*] Theodore, you are such an incorrigible idealist! I have nothing to be afraid of—I simply do not care to *marry!*

HELEN: That's just what *I* said! [*All turn and behold* HELEN.]

ERNEST: My heavens! [*He steps back like a coward.*]

HELEN: But I agree with you perfectly. [*She holds out her hand to him.*] I was *so* afraid you believed in marriage. [*He rushes to her eagerly.*]

JUDGE: [*As the lovers shake hands.*] You wronged him. Apologize.

ERNEST: Why—why—all this time, I thought *you* had the usual attitude.

JUDGE: Wronged *her*. Both apologize.

HELEN: Why didn't you ever tell me you had such enlightened views?

ERNEST: Why didn't you ever tell me?

JUDGE: Each understands the other now. Everything lovely!

HELEN: Think of the discussions we might have had!

JUDGE: Not too late yet. Julia and I had discussions for a quarter of a century.

HELEN: Don't think I had any hand in this. [*Laughs.*] I was going to warn you, but now—it is unnecessary now.

ERNEST: Warn me? What do you mean?

HELEN: Can't you see? It was all a plot! [LUCY *draws near noiselessly.*] A plot to entrap you in marriage! They had about given me up as a bad job. *You* were my last hope. They were going to throw me at your head. [*Louder but without turning.*] Weren't you, Lucy dear?

LUCY: [*Caught listening, turns abruptly to the others.*] These New Women are utterly shameless.

HELEN: [*To* ERNEST.] These old-fashioned women are utterly shameless. After a decent interval, they will all with one accord make excuses to leave us here alone, so that I can—[*she comes nearer*] ensnare you! [ERNEST *laughs nervously.*] Lucy is going to say—[*imitates* LUCY's *sweet tones:*] "If you'll excuse me, I always take forty winks before dressing." Dressing is the hardest work Lucy has to do. Cousin Theodore will find that he must write to his wife, and Uncle Everett will feel a yearning for the billiard room. [ERNEST *is nodding and chuckling.*] They're hanging on longer than usual to-day, and I simply must have a talk with you.

ERNEST: Our shop-talk would scandalize 'em!

HELEN: Wait, I'll get rid of them! [*She sits and begins to make tea.*]

ERNEST: I've had my tea, thanks.

HELEN: Stupid! Sit down. [*Indicates a chair close to hers. He takes it cautiously.*] We'll have a little fun with them in a minute. [*She is busy now making tea.*]

THEODORE: [*To* LUCY *and the* JUDGE *apart.*] You may be right, Uncle Everett, but upon my word it is the strangest courtship I ever witnessed.

LUCY: They ought to be spanked.

JUDGE: Don't worry, old Mother Nature will attend to that.

LUCY: Well, I may be old-fashioned, but—

JUDGE: [*Interrupting.*] But this is merely a new fashion, my dear Lucy. Nature her ancient custom holds, let science say what it will.

HELEN: [*Handing cup to* ERNEST *with a glance at the others.*] Now, then, be attentive to me. [*He leans toward her rather shyly, abashed by her nearness. She makes eyes at him reproachfully.*] Oh, can't you be more attentive than *that*? [*She acts like a coquette and he looks into her beautiful eyes and while he is doing so she says with a fascinating drawl.*] Now tell me a-all about anterior poliomyclitis!

ERNEST: [*Suddenly taken aback, he laughs.*] Nothing doing since you left. [*And bends close to explain.*]

LUCY: If you'll excuse me, Doctor Hamilton, I always take forty winks before dressing. We dine at eight. [*Going, she signals to the others.* ERNEST *and* HELEN *exchange smiles.*]

THEODORE: [*Laughing, to* LUCY.] Ss't! Don't tell John what's going on!

Keep him busy telephoning. [LUCY *nods excitedly and almost runs to obey the Church.*] Helen, if you and Ernest will excuse me, I really must write to Mary. [*Their shoulders are close together and they seem too absorbed to reply.* THEODORE *smiles down upon them and signals the* JUDGE *to come along. The* JUDGE, *however, shakes his head but waves* THEODORE *into the house.* UNCLE EVERETT *looks at the lovers with quizzical interest. He draws near and eavesdrops shamelessly.*]

HELEN: You oughtn't to have dropped the polio experiments.

ERNEST: You oughtn't to have dropped me—right in the *midst* of the experiments. Those agar plates you were incubating dried up and spoiled. You played the very devil with my data.

JUDGE: God bless my soul! what are we coming to?

HELEN: [*Without turning.*] It's perfectly proper for your little ears, uncle, only you can't understand a word of it. Won't *any* one play billiards with you?

JUDGE: But I'm fascinated. It's so idyllic. Makes me feel young again.

HELEN: [*To* ERNEST.] Oh, you have plenty of men assistants who can estimate antitoxin units.

ERNEST: Men assistants lose interest. They are all so confoundedly ambitious to do original work. Why is it women can stand day after day of monotonous detail better than men?

HELEN: Because men always made them tend the home!

JUDGE: Ah, nothing like a good old-fashioned love scene—in the scientific spirit.

HELEN: Uncle, dear! *Can't* you see that he is paying me wonderful compliments? Haven't you any tact? Go and play Canfield in the library.

JUDGE: [*Lighting cigar.*] Very well, I'll leave you to your own devices and may God, *your* God, have mercy on your scientific souls.

HELEN: [*With sudden animation and camaraderie, thinking they are alone.*] Now I must tell you what Doctor Metchnikoff said about you and your future!

JUDGE: Sst! [HELEN *and* ERNEST *turn.*] My children—[*Pause—raises his hand.*] Don't forget the scientific spirit! [*The* JUDGE *saunters off into the garden, smoking.*]

ERNEST: How did you ever meet Metchnikoff?

HELEN: [*Chaffing.*] I had worked under Hamilton! They *all* wanted to meet me.

ERNEST: [*With an unmistakable look.*] U'm . . . was that why? [*Fleeing danger.*] Didn't you let them know your part in that discovery? Why, if it hadn't been for you, I should never have stumbled upon the thing at all.

HELEN: Oh, I know my place too well for that! Talk about *artistic* temperament, you scientists are worse than prima donnas.

ERNEST: [*Takes printers' proofs out of pocket, hands them to her in silence.*] Some proofs of a monograph I was correcting on the train. Mind hammering those loose sentences of mine into decent English? You can write—I can't.

HELEN: [*Reading innocently.*] "Recent Experiments in Anterior Poliomyelitis by Ernest Hamilton, M.D., Ph.D., and Helen"—what! why, you've put *my* name with yours! [*Much excited and delighted.*]

ERNEST: Well, if you object—like a prima donna—[*Takes out pencil to mark on proof.*]

HELEN: [*Snatching proofs away.*] Object? Why, this makes my reputation in the scientific world.

ERNEST: Well, didn't you make mine?

HELEN: [*Still glowing with pride, but touched by his unexpected generosity.*] You can't imagine what this means to me. It's so hard for a woman to get any recognition. Most men have but one use for us. If we get interested in anything but *them* it is "unwomanly"—they call it "a fad." But they've *got* to take me seriously now. My name with Ernest Hamilton's! [*Points to her name and swaggers back and forth.*]

ERNEST: [*Bantering.*] But then, you see, you are a very exceptional woman. Why, you have a mind like a man.

HELEN: Like a man? [*Coming close to him, tempting him.*] If you had a mind like a woman you would know better than to say that to me! [*Re-enter* JUDGE *from garden. He smiles and glances at them. The lovers keep quiet as he crosses to the door. Then they look at each other and smile.* JUDGE *has gone into the house. It is nearly dark. The moon is rising.*]

ERNEST: [*Raises eyebrows.*] They all take for granted that I want to make love to you. [*Smiles but avoids her eyes.*]

HELEN: [*Avoids his.*] Well, you took for granted that I wanted you to! . . . You are about the most conceited man I ever knew.

ERNEST: How can I help it when you admire me so?

HELEN: I? Admire you?

ERNEST: You're always telling me what great things I'm going to do—stimulating me, pushing me along. Why, after you left, everything went slump. Tell me, why did you leave? Was I rude to you? Did I hurt your feelings?

HELEN: Not in the least. It was entirely out of respect for your feelings.

ERNEST: *My* feelings? [*Laughing.*] Oh, I see. You got it into your head that *I* wanted to marry *you!*

HELEN: Men sometimes do.

ERNEST: [*Looks away.*] I suppose they do.

HELEN: It's been known to happen.

ERNEST: Talk about conceit! Well, you needn't be afraid! I'll never ask you to marry *me*.

HELEN: [*Turns and looks at him a moment.*] You can't imagine what a weight this takes off my mind. [*She looks away and sighs.*]

ERNEST: [*Enthusiastically.*] Yes! I feel as if a veil between us had been lifted. [*He looks away and sighs too. Some one begins "Tristan and Isolde" on the piano within. The moon is up.*]

HELEN: [*After a pause.*] Suppose we talk about—our work.

ERNEST: Yes! Our work. Let's drop the other subject. Look at the moon! [*Music and the moonlight flooding them.*]

HELEN: Seriously, you promise never to *mention* the subject again? [*She keeps her eyes averted.*]

ERNEST: I promise. [*He keeps his eyes averted.*]

HELEN: [*Turning to him with a sudden change to girlish enthusiasm.*] Then I'll go to Paris with you!

ERNEST: [*Recoils.*] What's that?

HELEN: Why, Doctor Metchnikoff—he promised me he would invite you.

ERNEST: Yes, but—

HELEN: Don't miss the chance of a lifetime!

ERNEST: No, but you—*you* can't come!

HELEN: If you need me I can, and you just said—

ERNEST: But you mustn't come to Paris with me!

HELEN: Don't you want me with you?

ERNEST: You are to stay at home and run the department for me.

HELEN: [*Stepping back.*] Don't you want me with you?

ERNEST: [*Stepping forward, with his heart in voice.*] Do I *want* you! [*Stops.*] But I am a man—you are a woman.

HELEN: What of it? Are you one of those small men who care what people say? No! That's not your reason! [*She sees that it is not.*] What is it? You must tell me.

ERNEST: [*Hesitates.*] It's only for your sake.

HELEN: [*With feeling.*] Think of all I've done for *your* sake. You wouldn't be going yourself but for me! I was the one to see you needed it, I proposed it to Metchnikoff—I urged him—*made* him ask you—for *your sake!* And now am I to be left at home like a child because you don't care to be embarrassed with me?

ERNEST: Oh, please! This is so unfair. But I simply can't take you now.

HELEN: [*With growing scorn.*] Oh! You are all alike. You pile work upon me until I nearly drop, you play upon my interest, my sympathy— you get all you can out of me—my youth, my strength, my best! And then, just as I, too, have a chance to arrive in my profession, you, of all men, throw me over! I hate men. I hate you!

ERNEST: And I love you! [*They stare at each other in silence, the moonlight flooding* HELEN'*s face, the music coming clear.*]

HELEN: [*In an awed whisper, stepping back slowly.*] I've done it! I've done it! I *knew* I'd do it!

ERNEST: No. I did it. Forgive me. I had to do it.

HELEN: Oh, and this spoils everything!

ERNEST: [*Comes closer.*] No! It glorifies everything! [*He breaks loose.*] I have loved you from the first day you came and looked up at me for orders. I didn't want you there; I didn't want any woman there. I tried to tire you out with overwork but couldn't. I tried to drive you out by rudeness, but you stayed. And that made me love you more. Oh, I love you! I love you! I love you!

HELEN: Don't; oh, don't love me!

ERNEST: [*Still closer.*] Why, I never knew there could be women like you. I thought women were merely something to be wanted and worshipped, petted and patronized. But now—why, I love everything about you: your wonderful, brave eyes that face the naked facts of life and are not ashamed; those beautiful hands that toiled so long, so well, so close to mine and not afraid, not afraid!

HELEN: You mustn't! I *am* afraid now! I made you say it. [*Smiling and crying.*] I have always wanted to make you say it. I have always sworn you shouldn't.

ERNEST: [*Pained.*] Because you cannot trust me, you fear me?

HELEN: Because I love you!

ERNEST: [*Overwhelmed.*] You—love—me! [*He takes her in his arms, a silent embrace with only the bland blasé moon looking on.*]

HELEN: It is because I love you that I didn't want you to say it—only I did. It is because I love you that I went abroad—to stay, only I couldn't! I couldn't stay away! [*She holds his face in her hands.*] Oh, do you know how I love you? No! . . . you're only a *man!*

ERNEST: [*Kissing her rapturously.*] Every day there in the laboratory, when you in your apron—that dear apron which I stole from your locker when you left me—when you asked for orders—did you know that I wanted to say: "Love me"! Every day when you took up your work, did you never guess that I wanted to take you up in my arms?

HELEN: [*Smiling up into his face.*] Why didn't you?

ERNEST: Thank God I didn't! For while we worked there together I came to know you as few men ever know the women they desire. Woman can be more than sex, as man is more than sex. And all this makes man and woman not less but more *overwhelmingly* desirable and necessary to each other, and makes both things last not for a few years, but forever! [*Sound of voices approaching from the garden. The lovers separate. It is* JEAN *and* REX, REX *laughing,* JEAN *dodging until caught and kissed.*]

JEAN: No, no—it's time to dress. . . . Be good, Rex—don't! [*Without seeing* HELEN *and* ERNEST, *they disappear into the house.* HELEN *is suddenly changed, as if awakened from a spell of enchantment.*]

HELEN: What have we done! This is all moonlight and madness. To-morrow comes the clear light of day.

ERNEST: Ah, but we'll love each other to-morrow!

HELEN: But we cannot marry—then or any other to-morrow.

ERNEST: Can't? What nonsense!

HELEN: [*Shaking her head and restraining him.*] I have slaved for you all these months—not because I wanted to win you from your work but to help you in it. And now—after all—shall I destroy you? No! No!

ERNEST: I *love* you—you love *me*—nothing else matters.

HELEN: Everything else matters. I'm not a little débutante to be persuaded that I am needed because I am wanted! I haven't *played* with you; I have *worked* with you, and I *know!* Think of Theodore! Think of Lucy! And now poor little Jean. Marry you? Never!

ERNEST: You mean your career?

HELEN: [*With supreme scorn.*] *My* career? No! yours—always yours!

ERNEST: [*With the same scorn and a snap of the fingers.*] Then *that* for my career. I'll go back into private practice and make a million.

HELEN: That's just what I said you'd do. Just what you must not do! Your work is needed by the world.

ERNEST: [*Wooing.*] You are my world and I need you. . . . But there is no love without marriage, no marriage without money. . . . We can take it or leave it. Can we leave it? No! I can't—you can't! Come! [*She steps back slowly.*] Why should we sacrifice the best! Come!

HELEN: So *this* is what marriage means! Then I *cannot* marry you, Ernest!

ERNEST: You cannot do without me, Helen! [*Holds out his arms.*] Come! You have been in my arms once. You and I can never forget that now. We can never go back now. It's all—or nothing now. Come! [*She is struggling against her passion. He stands still, with arms held out.*] I shall not woo you against your will, but you are coming to me! Because, by all the powers of earth and heaven, you are mine and I am yours! Come!

[*Like a homing pigeon she darts into his arms with a gasp of joy. A rapturous embrace in silence with the moonlight streaming down upon them. The music has stopped.* JOHN, *dressed for dinner, strolls out upon*]

*the terrace. He stops abruptly upon discovering them. The lovers are too
absorbed to be aware of his presence.*]

ACT II

It is the next morning, Sunday. It appears that at JOHN*'s country place
they have breakfast at small tables out upon the broad, shaded terrace over-
looking the glorious view of his little farm.*

*   ERNEST and* THEODORE, *the scientist and the clergyman, are breakfasting together. The others are either breakfasting in their rooms or are not yet
down, it being Sunday.*

*   The man of God is enjoying his material blessings heartily. Also he seems
to be enjoying his view of the man of science, who eats little and says less.*

THEODORE: [*With coffee-cup poised.*] What's the matter with your appetite
   this morning, Ernest? [ERNEST, *gazing up at one of the second-story
   windows, does not hear. The door opens. He starts. Then, seeing it's only
   a servant with food, he sighs.*] Expecting something? The codfish
   balls? Well, here they are. [ERNEST *refuses the proffered codfish balls,
   scowls, brings out cigar case, lights cigar, looks at watch, and fidgets.*]
   Oh, I know—you're crazy to go with me—to church! [ERNEST
   doesn't hear. Creates a cloud of smoke.] Their regular rector is ill. So I
   agreed to take the service this morning. . . . Always the way when off
   for a rest . . . isn't it? [*No answer.* THEODORE *gets up, walks around the
   table, and shouts in* ERNEST*'s face.*] Isn't it?
ERNEST: [*Startled.*] I beg your pardon?
THEODORE: [*Laughs,* ERNEST *wondering what's the joke.*] Oh, you're hope-
   less! [*Going.*] I can't stand people who talk so much at breakfast.
ERNEST: [*Suddenly wakes up.*] Wait a minute. Sit down. Have a cigar. Let's
   talk about God. [THEODORE *stops smiling.*] But I mean it. I'd like to
   have a religion myself.
THEODORE: I had an idea you took no stock in religion. [*Takes the cigar.*
   ERNEST *holds a match for him.*]
ERNEST: [*Enthusiastically.*] Just what I thought, until . . . well, I've made a
   discovery, a great discovery!
THEODORE: A scientific discovery?
ERNEST: [*With a wave of the hand.*] It makes all science look like a . . .
   mere machine.
THEODORE: Well, if you feel so strongly about it . . . better come to
   church after all!

ERNEST: I'm not talking about the Church—I'm talking about *religion*.

THEODORE: You're not talking about religion; you're talking about—love.

ERNEST: [*Quietly.*] Certainly; the same thing, isn't it? I'm talking about the divine fire that glorifies life and perpetuates it—the one eternal thing we mortals share with God. . . . If *that* isn't religious, what is? [THEODORE *smiles indulgently.*] Tell me, Theodore—you know I wasn't allowed to go to church when young, and since then I've always worked on the holy Sabbath day, like yourself—does the Church still let innocent human beings think there's something inherently wrong about sex? [THEODORE *drops his eyes.* ERNEST *disgusted with him.*] I see! Good people should drop their eyes even at the mention of the word.

THEODORE: Sex is a necessary evil, I admit, but—

ERNEST: [*Laughs.*] Evil! The God-given impulse which accounts for you sitting there, for me sitting here? The splendid instinct which writes our poetry, builds our civilizations, founds our churches—the very heart and soul of life is evil. Really, Theodore, I don't know much about religion, but that strikes me as blasphemy against the Creator.

THEODORE: Very scientific, my boy, very modern; but the Church believed in marriage before Science was born.

ERNEST: As a compromise with evil?

THEODORE: As a sacrament of religion—and so do you!

ERNEST: Good! Then why practise and preach marriage as a sacrament of property? "Who giveth this woman to be married to this man—" Women are still goods and chattels to be given or sold, are they?

THEODORE: Oh, nonsense!

ERNEST: Then why keep on making them promise to "serve and obey"? Why marry them with a ring—the link of the ancient chain? [*He smiles.*] In the days of physical force it was made of iron—now of gold. But it's still a chain, isn't it?

THEODORE: Symbols, my dear fellow, not to be taken in a literal sense— time-honored and beautiful symbols.

ERNEST: But why insult a woman you respect—even symbolically?

THEODORE: [*With a laugh.*] Oh, you scientists!

ERNEST: [*Joining in the laugh.*] We try to find the truth—and you try to hide it, eh? Well, there's one thing we have in common, anyway— one faith I'll never doubt again; I believe in Heaven now. I always shall.

THEODORE: Do you mind telling me why, my boy?

ERNEST: Not in the least. I've been there. [JOHN *comes out to breakfast. He is scowling.*] Good morning; could you spare me five minutes?

JOHN: [*Ringing bell.*] Haven't had breakfast yet.

ERNEST: After breakfast?

JOHN: I've an appointment with young Baker.

ERNEST: [*Smiles.*] I'll wait my turn.

JOHN: Going to be pretty busy to-day—you, too, I suppose, if you're sailing to-morrow.

ERNEST: I can postpone sailing. This is more important.

JOHN: I should hate to see *anything* interfere with your career. [LUCY *also arrives for breakfast. She "always pours her husband's coffee."*]

ERNEST: I appreciate your interest, but I'll look out for my "career." [*To* LUCY.] Could you tell me when your sister will be down?

JOHN: [*Overriding* LUCY.] My sister is ill and won't be down at all . . . until *after* you *leave.* [LUCY *pretends not to hear.* THEODORE *walks away.*]

ERNEST: [*Aroused, but calm.*] I don't believe you quite understand. It is a matter of indifference to me whether we have a talk or not. Entirely out of courtesy to you that I suggest it.

JOHN: Don't inconvenience yourself on my account.

ERNEST: [*Shrugs shoulders and turns to* THEODORE.] Wait, I think I'll sit in church till train time.

THEODORE: [*Smoothing it over.*] Come along. I'm going to preach about marriage! [THEODORE *starts off.*]

ERNEST: [*Going, turns to* LUCY.] Thanks for your kindness. Will you ask the valet to pack my things, please? I'll call for them on the way to the station. [*To* JOHN.] Do you understand? I have no favors to ask of you. You don't own your sister—she owns herself. [*The scientist goes to church.*]

JOHN: [*With a loud laugh, turns to* LUCY.] Rather impertinent for a two-thousand-dollar man, I think. [*Resumes breakfast, picks up newspaper.* LUCY *says nothing, attending to his wants solicitously.*] Bah! what does this highbrow know about the power men of my sort can use . . . when we have to. [LUCY *cringes dutifully in silence.* JOHN, *paper in one hand, brusquely passes cup to* LUCY *with other.*] Helen got her own way about college, about work, about living in her own apartment— but if she thinks she can put *this* across! Humph! These modern women must learn their place. [LUCY, *smiling timidly, returns cup.* JOHN *takes it without thanks, busied in newspapers. A look of resentment creeps over* LUCY'*s pretty face, now that he can't see her.*] Ah! I've got something up my sleeve for that young woman. [LUCY *says nothing, looks of contempt while he reads.*] Well, why don't you say something?

LUCY: [*Startled.*] I thought you didn't like me to talk at breakfast, dear.

JOHN: Think I like you to sit there like a mummy? [*No reply.*] Haven't you *any*thing to say? [*Apparently not.*] You never have any more, nothing interesting. . . . Does it ever occur to you that I'd like to be diverted? . . . No!

LUCY: Yes. . . . Would you mind very much if . . . if I left you, John?

JOHN: Left me? When—where—how long?

LUCY: [*Gathering courage.*] Now—any place—entirely.

JOHN: [*Bursts out laughing.*] What suddenly put *this* notion in your head?

LUCY: I'm sorry—John, but I've had it—oh, for years. I never dared ask you till now.

JOHN: [*Still glancing over paper.*] Like to leave me, would you? . . . You have no grounds for divorce, my dear.

LUCY: But *you* will have—after I leave you.

JOHN: [*Yawns.*] You have no lover to leave with.

LUCY: [*Daintily.*] But couldn't I just desert you—without anything horrid?

JOHN: [*Reads.*] No money to desert with.

LUCY: [*Springs up—at bay.*] You won't let me escape decently when I tell you I don't want to stay? When I tell you I can't stand being under your roof any longer? When I tell you I'm sick of this life?

JOHN: [*Gets up calmly.*] But, you see, I can stand it. I want you to stay. I'm not sick of it. You belong to me.

LUCY: [*Shrinking away as he approaches.*] Don't touch me! Every time you come near me I have to nerve myself to stand it.

JOHN: What's got into you? Don't I give you everything money can buy? My God, if I only gave you something to worry about—if I ran after other women like old man Baker—

LUCY: If you only would!—Then you'd let *me* alone. To me you are repulsive.

JOHN: [*Taking hold of her.*] Lucy! You are my wife.

LUCY: [*Looking him straight in the eye.*] But you don't respect me, and I— I hate you—oh, how I hate you!

JOHN: [*Holds her fast.*] I am your husband, your lawful husband.

LUCY: [*Stops struggling.*] Yes, this is lawful—but, oh, what laws you men have made for women! [*The* JUDGE *comes out, carrying a telegram.*]

JUDGE: Rather early in the day for conjugal embraces, if you should ask me. [JOHN *and* LUCY *separate.*] Makes me quite sentimental and homesick. [JUDGE *raises telegram and kisses it.*]

LUCY: [*Calming herself.*] From Aunt Julia again? Do you get telegrams every day from Reno?

JUDGE: No, but she caught cold. Went to the theatre last night and caught a cold. So she wired me—naturally; got the habit of telling me her troubles, can't break it, even in Reno.

JOHN: I thought she hated the theatre!

JUDGE: So she does, but I'm fond of it; she went for my sake. She's got the habit of sacrificing herself for me. Just as hard to break good habits as bad.

JOHN: True women enjoy sacrificing themselves.

JUDGE: Yes, that's what we tell them. Well, we ought to know. We make 'em do it. [*Brings out a fountain pen and sits abruptly.*] That's what I'll tell her. I can hear her laugh. You know her laugh.

LUCY: [*Rings for a servant.*] A telegraph blank?

JUDGE: [*With a humorous expression he brings a whole pad of telegraph blanks out of another pocket.*] Carry them with me nowadays. [*Begins to write.*] Wish I hadn't sold my Western Union, John.

JOHN: I don't believe you want that divorce very much.

JUDGE: It doesn't matter what *I* want—what she wants is the point. You must give the woman you marry tutti-frutti, divorces—everything. . . . Why, I've got the habit myself, and God knows I don't enjoy sacrifice—I'm a man! The superior sex!

JOHN: I don't believe you appreciate that wife of yours.

JUDGE: [*Between the words he's writing.*] Don't I? It isn't every wife that'd travel away out to Reno—you know how she hates travelling—and go to a theatre—and catch a cold—and get a divorce—all for the sake of an uncongenial husband. [*Suddenly getting an idea, strikes table.*] I know what gave her a cold. She raised all the windows in her bedroom—for *my* sake!—I always kept them down for *her* sake. I'll have to scold her. [*Bends to his writing again.*] Poor little thing! She doesn't know how to take care of herself without me. I doubt if she ever will. [*Looks over telegram. A* SERVANT *comes, takes telegram, and goes.*]

JOHN: Uncle Everett, I want your advice.

JUDGE: John! do *you* want a divorce?

JOHN: No, we are not that sort, are we, Lucy? [*No answer.*] Are we, dear?

LUCY: [*After a pause.*] No, we are not that sort!

JOHN: We believe in the sanctity of the home, the holiness of marriage.

LUCY: Yes, we believe in—"the holiness of marriage!" [*Turns away, covering her face with her hands and shuddering.*]

JOHN: Lucy, tell Helen and Jean to come here. [LUCY *goes.*] Well, young Baker spoke to me about Jean last night. I told him I'd think it over and give him my decision this morning.

JUDGE: That's right. Mustn't seem too anxious, John. When the properly qualified male offers one of our dependent females a chance at woman's only true career, of course it's up to us to look disappointed.

JOHN: But I didn't bring up the little matter you spoke of.

JUDGE: About that chorus girl? . . . Afraid of scaring him off?

JOHN: Not at all, but—well, it's all over and it's all fixed. No scandal, no blackmail.

JUDGE: Hum! By the way, got anything on Hamilton?

JOHN: I don't believe in saints myself.

JUDGE: I see. . . . Good thing, for Rex isn't a saint. I suppose you'd break off the match. [REX, *in riding clothes, comes out.* JOHN *salutes him warmly. The* JUDGE *is reading the paper.*]

REX: [*Not eagerly.*] Well?

JOHN: Well, of course, you realize that you're asking a great deal of me, Rex, but—[*Offers hand to* REX *warmly.*] Be good to her, my boy, be good to her.

REX: [*Shaking hands, forced warmth.*] Thanks awfully. See-what-I-mean? [*To* JUDGE.] Congratulate me, Judge; I'm the happiest of men.

JUDGE: [*Looking up from newspaper.*] So I see. Don't let it worry you. [JEAN, *in riding costume, comes from the house.*]

JOHN: [*Signalling* JUDGE *to leave.*] If Helen asks for me, I'm in the garden.

JUDGE: If any telegrams come for me, I'm writing to *my wife!* [JEAN *and* REX *alone, they look at each other, not very loverlike.*]

JEAN: [*Impulsively.*] You weren't in love with me yesterday. You aren't now. You would get out of it if you honorably could. But you honorably *can't!* So you have spoken to John; you are going to see it through, because you're a good sport. . . . I admire you for that, Rex, too much to hold you to it. You are released.

REX: [*Amazed.*] Why—why—you you don't suppose I want to be released?

JEAN: Well, I do! . . . Yesterday I let you propose to me when I cared for some one else. That's not fair to you, to me, to him!

REX: [*In a sudden fury.*] Who is he? What do you mean by this? Why didn't you tell me?

JEAN: I am telling you now. What have you ever told me about yourself?

REX: [*Blinking.*] You had no right to play fast and loose with me.

JEAN: I'm making the only amends I can. You are free, I tell you.

REX: I don't want to be free! He can't have you! You are mine! If you think you can make me stop loving you—

JEAN: [*Interrupting.*] Love, Rex? Only jealousy. You've never been in love with me—you've always been in love with Helen. But you couldn't get her, so you took me. Isn't that true, Rex?

REX: [*After an uncomfortable pause.*] I'll be honest with you, too. Yesterday I wasn't really serious. I felt like a brute afterward. You tried your best to prevent what happened and ran away from me. But now—

JEAN: Don't you know why I ran away? To make you follow. I made you catch me. I made you kiss me. Then you realized that we had been thrown together constantly—deliberately thrown together, if you care to know it—and, well, that's how many marriages are made. But I shan't marry on such terms. It's indecent!

REX: [*Another pause.*] I never thought a *woman* could be capable of such honesty! . . . Oh, what a bully sport you are! You aren't like the rest that have been shoved at me. Why, I can respect you. You are the one for me. [*He tries to take her.*]

JEAN: [*Restraining him with dignity.*] I am sorry, Rex, but I am not for you.

REX: Jean! without you . . . don't you see—I'll go straight to the devil!

JEAN: That old, cowardly dodge? Any man who has no more backbone than that—why, I wouldn't marry you if you were the last man in the world.

REX: [*Frantic to possess what he cannot have.*] You won't, eh? We'll see about that. I want you now as I never wanted anything in my life, and I'll win you from him yet. You'll see! [HELEN *now appears.*]

HELEN: Oh, I beg your pardon. Lucy said John was out here.

JEAN: I'll call him. [*She runs down into the garden.*]

REX: I'll call him. [*He runs after* JEAN. HELEN *helplessly watches them go, sighs, standing by the garden steps until* JOHN *ascends. He looks at* HELEN *a moment, wondering how to begin. She looks so capable and unafraid of him.*]

JOHN: If you hadn't gone to college, you could have done what Jean is doing.

HELEN: [*With a shrug and a smile.*] But how proud you must be, John, to have a sister who isn't compelled to marry one man while in love with another. *Now*, aren't you glad I went to college? [*She laughs good-naturedly at him.*]

JOHN: Humph! If you think I'd let a sister of mine marry one of old man Baker's two-thousand-dollar employees—

HELEN: Why, John, didn't Ernest tell you? Doctor Hawksbee has offered him a partnership. Just think of that!

JOHN: What! Going back into private practice?

HELEN: But it's such a fashionable practice. Hawksbee's made a million at it.

JOHN: But the institute needs Hamilton.

HELEN: Ah, but we need the money!

JOHN: [*Disconcerted.*] So you are going to spoil a noble career, are you? That's selfish. I didn't think it of you. There are thousands of successful physicians, but there is only one Ernest Hamilton.

HELEN: [*Laughs.*] Oh, don't worry, John, he has promised me to keep his two-thousand-dollar job.

JOHN: Ah, I'm glad. You must let nothing interfere with his great humanitarian work. Think what it means to the lives of little children! Think what it means to the future of the race! Why, every one says his greatest usefulness has hardly begun!

HELEN: Oh, I know all that, I've thought of all that.

JOHN: Now, such men should be kept free from cares and anxiety. What was it you said yesterday? "He needs every cent of his salary for books, travel, all the advantages he simply must have for efficiency." To marry a poor man—most selfish thing a girl could do!

HELEN: Yes, John, that's what I said yesterday.

JOHN: [*Scoring.*] But that was before he asked you! [HELEN *smiles. He sneers.*] Rather pleased with yourself now, aren't you? "Just a woman after all"—heroine of cheap magazine story! Sacrifices career for love! . . . All very pretty and romantic, my dear—but how about the man you love! Want to sacrifice his career, too?

HELEN: But I'm not going to sacrifice what you are pleased to call my career. . . . Therefore he won't have to sacrifice his.

JOHN: What! going to keep on working? Will he let the woman he loves work!

HELEN: [*Demure.*] Well, you see, he says I'm "too good" to loaf.

JOHN: Humph! who'll take care of your home when you're at work? Who'll take care of your work when you're at home? Look at it practically. To maintain such a home as he needs on such a salary as he has—why, it would take all your time, all your energy. To keep him in his class you'll have to drop out of your own, become a household drudge, a servant.

HELEN: And if I am willing?

JOHN: Then where's your intellectual companionship? How'll you help his work? Expense for him, disillusionment for both. If you're the woman you pretend to be, you won't marry that man!

HELEN: [*Strong.*] The world needs his work, but he needs mine, and we both need each other.

JOHN: [*Stronger.*] And marriage would only handicap his work, ruin yours, and put you apart. You know that's true. You've seen it happen with others. You have told me so yourself!

HELEN: Then that settles it! We must not, cannot, shall not marry. We have no right to marry. I agree with all you say—it would not join us together; it would put us asunder.

JOHN: And you'll give him up? Good! Good!

HELEN: Give him up? Never! The right to work, the right to love—those rights are inalienable. No, we'll give up marriage but not each other.

JOHN: But—but—I don't understand.

HELEN: [*Straight in his eyes.*] We need each other—in our work and in our life—and we're to have each other—until life is ended and our work is done. Now, do you understand?

JOHN: [*Recoiling.*] Are you in your right mind? Think what you're saying.

HELEN: I have thought all night, John. You have shown me how to say it.

JOHN: But, but—why, this is utterly unbelievable! Why I'm not even shocked. Do you notice? I'm not even shocked? Because everything you have said, everything you have done—it all proves that you are a good woman.

HELEN: If I were a bad woman, I'd inveigle him into marriage, John.

JOHN: Inveigle! Marriage! Are you crazy? . . . Oh, this is all one of your highbrow jokes!

HELEN: John, weren't you serious when you said marriage would destroy him?

JOHN: But this would destroy *you!*

HELEN: Well, even if that were so, which is more important to the world? Which is more important to your "great humanitarian work"?

JOHN: Ah, very clever! A bluff to gain my consent to marrying him—a trick to get his salary raised.

HELEN: [*With force.*] John, nothing you can do, nothing you can say, will ever gain my consent to marrying him. I've not told you half my reasons.

JOHN: My God! my own sister! And did you, for one moment, dream that I would consent to that!

HELEN: Not for one moment. I'm not asking your consent. I'm just telling you.

JOHN: [*After scrutinizing her.*] Ridiculous! If you really meant to run away with this fellow, would you come and tell *me*, your own brother?

HELEN: Do you suppose I'd *run* away without telling, even my own brother?

JOHN: [*Looks at her a moment; she returns his gaze.*] Bah!—all pose and poppycock! [*He abruptly touches bell.*] I'll soon put a stop to this nonsense. [*Muttering.*] Damnedest thing I ever heard of.

HELEN: John, I understand exactly what I'm doing. You never will. But nothing you can do can stop me now.

JOHN: We'll see about that. [*The* BUTLER *appears.*] Ask the others to step out here at once; all except Miss Jean and Mr. Baker, I don't want them. Is Doctor Hamilton about?

BUTLER: No, sir, he went to church.

JOHN: All right. [*The* BUTLER *disappears.*] To church! My God! [HELEN *pays no attention. She gazes straight out into the future, head high, eyes clear and wide open.*]

JOHN: First of all, when the others come out, I'm going to ask them to look you in the face. Then you can make this statement to them, if you wish, and—look them in the face.

HELEN: [*With quiet scorn.*] If I were being forced into such a marriage as poor little Jean's, I would kill myself. But in the eyes of God, who made love, no matter how I may appear in the eyes of man, who made marriage, I know that I am doing right. [LUCY *comes out, followed by the* JUDGE.]

JOHN: [*Not seeing them. He is loud.*] Say that to Uncle Everett and Cousin Theodore! Say that to my wife, stand up and say that to the world, if you dare.

LUCY: [*To* JUDGE.] She has told him!

JOHN: [*Wheeling about.*] What! did she tell you? Why didn't you come to me at once?

LUCY: [*Tremulous.*] She said she wanted to tell you herself. I didn't think she'd dare! [*They all turn to look at* HELEN. THEODORE *comes back from church alone.*]

HELEN: It had to be announced, of course.

THEODORE: [*Advancing, beaming.*] Announced? What is announced? [*All turn to him in a panic.*]

LUCY: [*Hurriedly.*] Their engagement, Theodore!

JUDGE: [*Overriding* HELEN.] Yes, John has given his consent at last—example to society. [*Prods* JOHN.]

JOHN: [*Also overrides* HELEN.] Of course! One of the finest fellows in the world.

THEODORE: [*Delighted.*] And withal he has a deep religious nature. Congratulations. My dear, he'll make an ideal husband. [*Takes both* HELEN's *hands, about to kiss her.*]

HELEN: [*Can't help smiling.*] Thank you, cousin, but I don't want a husband. [*A sudden silence.*]

THEODORE: [*Looks from one to the other.*] A lover's quarrel?—already!

JUDGE: [*Enjoying it.*] No, Theodore, these lovers are in perfect accord. They both have conscientious scruples against marriage.

JOHN: Conscientious!

JUDGE: So they are simply going to set up housekeeping without the mere formality of a wedding ceremony. [THEODORE *drops* HELEN*'s hands.*]

HELEN: [*Quietly.*] We are going to do nothing of the sort.

THEODORE: Uncle Everett! [*Takes her hands again.*]

HELEN: We are not going to set up housekeeping at all. He will keep his present quarters and I mine.

JOHN: But they are going to belong to each other.

THEODORE: [*Drops* HELEN*'s hands—aghast.*] I don't believe it.

JUDGE: [*Apart to* THEODORE.] The strike against marriage. It was bound to come.

THEODORE: [*To* JUDGE.] But Church and State—[*indicates self and* JUDGE] must break this strike.

HELEN: John is a practical man. He will prove to you that such a home as we could afford would only be a stumbling-block to Ernest's usefulness, a hollow sphere for mine. You can't fill it with mere happiness, Lucy, not for long, not for long.

JUDGE: [*Restrains* THEODORE *about to reply.*] Oh, let her get it all nicely talked out, then she'll take a nap and wake up feeling better. [*Whispering.*] We've driven her to this ourselves, but she really doesn't mean a word of it. Come, dear child, tell us all about this nightmare.

HELEN: [*Smiles at the* JUDGE.] Why, think what would happen to an eager intellect like Ernest Hamilton's if he had to come back to a narrow-minded apartment or a dreary suburb every evening and eat morbid meals opposite a housewife regaling him with the social ambitions of the other commuters. Ugh! It has ruined enough brilliant men already. [JUDGE *restrains* THEODORE *and others who want to interrupt.*] Now at the University Club he dines, at slight expense compared with keeping up a home, upon the best food in the city with some of the best scientists in the country. . . . Marriage would divorce him from all that, would transplant him from an atmosphere of ideas into an atmosphere of worries. We should be forced into the same deadly ruts as the rest of you, uncle. Do you want me to destroy a great career, Theodore?

THEODORE: Do you want to be a blot upon that career?

HELEN: [*Lightly.*] I'd rather be a blot than a blight, and that's what I'd be if I became his bride. Ask John.

LUCY: Do you want to be disgraced, despised, ostracize!

HELEN: [*Smiles at* LUCY.] A choice of evils, dear; of course, none of those costly well-kept wives on your visiting list will call upon me. But instead of one day at home, instead of making a tired husband work for me, I'll have all my days free to work with him, like the old-fashioned woman you admire! Instead of being an expense, I'll be a help to him; instead of being separated by marriage and divergent interests, we'll be united by love and common peril. . . . Isn't that the orthodox way to gain character, Theodore?

JOHN: Oh, this is all damned nonsense! Look here, You've either got to marry this fellow now or else go away and never see him again; never, never!

HELEN: Just what I thought, John. I intended never to see him again. That was why I let you send me abroad. But I'll never, never do it again. [*Smiling like an engaged girl.*] It was perfectly dreadful! Ernest couldn't get along without me at all, poor thing. And I, why, I nearly died.

JOHN: Then you'll have to be married, that's all.

THE OTHERS: Why, of course you'll have to, that's all.

HELEN: [*Nodding.*] Oh, I know just how you feel about it. I thought so, too. at first, but I can't marry Ernest Hamilton. I love him.

THEODORE: But if you love him truly—marriage, my dear, brings together those who love each other truly.

HELEN: But those who love each other truly don't need anything to bring them together. The difficulty is to keep apart. [*A reminiscent shudder.*]

JOHN: That's all romantic rot! Every one feels that way at first.

HELEN: At first! Then the practical object of marriage is not to bring together those who love each other, but to keep together those who do not? [*To* LUCY.] What a dreadful thing marriage must be! [JUDGE *chokes down a chuckle.*]

JUDGE: Ah, so you wish to be free to separate. Now we have it.

HELEN: To separate? What an idea! On the contrary, we wish to be free to keep together! In the old days when they had interests in common marriage used to make man and woman one, but now it puts them apart. Can't you see it all about you? He goes down-town and works; she stays up-town and plays. He belongs to the laboring class; she belongs to the leisure class. At best, they seldom work at the same or similar trades. Legally it may be a union, but socially it's a *mésalliance*—in the eyes of God it's often worse. . . . No wonder that one in eleven ends in divorce. The only way to avoid spiritual separation is to shun legal union like a contagious disease. Modern marriage *is* divorce. [*She turns to go, defiantly.*] I've found my work, I've found my mate, and so has he! What more can any human being ask? [*The* BUTLER *appears.*]

BUTLER: [*To* JOHN.] Doctor Hamilton is outside in a taxicab, sir.

JOHN: Show him here at once!

BUTLER: He says he does not care to come in, sir, unless you are ready to talk to him now.

JOHN: Well, of all the nerve! You bet I'm ready! [*Starts off.* HELEN *starts, too.*]

JUDGE: [*Intercepting them calmly.*] Wait a minute—wait a minute. [*To* SERVANT.] Ask Doctor Hamilton kindly to wait in the library. [*The* BUTLER *goes.*] Now, we're all a bit overwrought. [*Soothes* HELEN, *pats her hand, puts arm about her, gradually leads her back.*] I still believe in you, Helen, I still believe in him. [*To all.*] It's simply that he's so deeply absorbed in his great work for mankind that he doesn't realize what he is asking Helen to do.

HELEN: [*Quietly.*] So I told him . . . when he asked me to marry him.

ALL: What! He *asked* you to *marry* him?

HELEN: Of course! *Implored* me to marry him. [*She adds, smiling.*] So absorbed—not in mankind, but in me—that he "didn't realize what he was asking me to do."

LUCY: [*Utterly amazed.*] And you refused him! The man who loves you honorably?

HELEN: [*Demurely.*] Of course! You don't suppose I'd take advantage of the poor fellow's weakness. Women often do, I admit—even when not in love, sometimes. . . . Not because they're depraved but dependent.

JOHN: [*To all.*] And then he proposed this wicked substitute! Poisoned her innocent mind—the bounder!

HELEN: But he did nothing of the sort.

JOHN: Oh, your own idea, was it?

HELEN: Of course!

JOHN: [*To all.*] And he is willing to take advantage of the poor child's ignorance—the cad! [*To* THEODORE.] "Deep religious nature," eh?

THEODORE: I can't believe it of him.

HELEN: He knows nothing about it yet. I haven't even seen him since I made my decision. [*All exchange bewildered glances.*]

JOHN: [*Apart to* JUDGE.] We've got to get him off to Paris. It's our only hope.

JUDGE: [*Apart to* JOHN.] You can't stop her following. She's on the edge of the precipice—do you want to shove her over? You are dealing with big people here and a big passion. [*The* BUTLER *returns.*]

BUTLER: Doctor Hamilton asks to see Miss Helen while waiting.

JUDGE: [*Calmly to* BUTLER.] Tell Doctor Hamilton that Miss Helen will see him here. [*The* BUTLER *leaves.*]

JOHN: Are you crazy! We've got to keep 'em apart—our one chance to save her.

JUDGE: No, bring them together. *That* is our one chance. Come, we'll go
down into the garden and they'll have a nice little talk. Nothing like
talk, John, honest talk, to clear these marriage problems. [*Going.*]

JOHN: And let them elope? In that taxicab?—not on your life! [*Runs to
and fro.*]

JUDGE: Come, John, girls never notify the family in advance when they
plan elopements. It's not done.

THEODORE: [*Going.*] Uncle Everett is right. Ernest will bring her to her
senses. He *has* a deep religious nature. [JUDGE *leads* JOHN *away to the
garden.*]

LUCY: [*Lingering—to* HELEN.] If you offer yourself on such terms to the
man who loves you honorably, he'll never look at you again.

THEODORE: [*Leading* LUCY *off to garden.*] Don't worry! She won't.
[ERNEST *rushes out to* HELEN.]

HELEN: Ernest!

ERNEST: At last! [*He takes her in his arms; she clings to him and gazes into
his eyes; a long embrace.*] Tell me that you're all right again.

HELEN: [*Smiling with love and trust.*] Except that you deserted me, dear,
just when I needed you most. Ernest, Ernest! never leave me again.

ERNEST: Deserted you? Why, your brother said you were ill.

HELEN: Ah, I see . . . he was mistaken.

ERNEST: [*Jubilant and boyish.*] But never mind now, I've got you at last,
and I'll never, never let you go. You've got to sail with me to-
morrow. Together! Oh, think! Together. [*Another embrace.*]

HELEN: Are you *sure* you love me?

ERNEST: [*Laughs from sheer joy of her nearness.*] Am I sure? Ten million
times more to-day than yesterday.

HELEN: Even so . . . it is not, and can never be, as I love you.

ERNEST: [*With her hands in his, gayly.*] Then you can apologize.

HELEN: Apologize?

ERNEST: For saying, years and years ago—in other words, last night—that
you didn't think you'd marry me after all. [*She starts.*] Why, what's
the matter? You're trembling like a leaf. You *are* ill!

HELEN: No; oh, no.

ERNEST: [*Tenderly.*] Still a few lingering doubts? I had hoped a good
night's rest would put those little prejudices to sleep forever.

HELEN: Sleep? [*She shakes her head, gazing at him soberly.*]

ERNEST: So you could not sleep? Neither could I; I was too happy to
sleep. I was afraid I'd miss some wondrous throbbing thought of
your loveliness. [*Takes her passive hand, puts a kiss in it, and closes it
reverently while she looks into his eyes without moving.*] Do you know,
I'm disappointed in love. I always thought it meant soft sighs and

pretty speeches. It means an agony of longing, delicious agony, but, oh, terrific. [*She says nothing.*] Dear, dear girl, it may be easy for you, but I can't stand much more of this.

HELEN: Nor I.

ERNEST: You must come to Paris with me or I'll stay home. All through the night I had waking visions of our being parted. Just when we had found each other at last. Some terrible impersonal monster stepped in between us and said: "No. Now that you have had your glimpse of heaven—away! Ye twain shall not enter here . . ." Silly, wasn't it? But I couldn't get the horror of it out of my head.

HELEN: [*Nodding.*] Do you know why, Ernest? Because it was in mine. It came from my thought to yours. You and I are attuned like wireless instruments. Even in the old blind days, there in the laboratory I used to read your mind. Shall I tell you the name of the monster that would put us asunder? . . . Its name is Marriage.

ERNEST: But I need you. You know that. And you need me. It's too late. We are helpless now—in the clutch of forces more potent than our little selves—forces that brought us into the world—forces that have made the world. Whether you will or no, this beautiful binding power is sweeping you and me together. And you must yield.

HELEN: [*Reaching for his hand.*] Ah, my dear, could anything make it more beautiful, more binding than it is now?

ERNEST: It is perfect. The one divine thing we share with God. The Church is right in that respect. I used to look upon marriage as a mere contract. It's a religious sacrament.

HELEN: Does the wedding ceremony make it sacred?

ERNEST: That mediæval incantation! No, love, which is given by God, not the artificial form made by man.

HELEN: I knew it! I knew you'd see it—the mistake of all the ages. They've tried to make love fit marriage. It can't be done. Marriage must be changed to fit love. [*Impulsively.*] Yes, I'll go to Paris with you.

ERNEST: [*About to take her in his arms.*] You darling!

HELEN: [*Steps back.*] But not as your wife.

ERNEST: [*Stops—perplexed.*] You mean . . . without marriage?

HELEN: I mean without marriage. [*They look into each other's eyes.*]

ERNEST: A moment ago I thought I loved you as much as man could love woman. I was mistaken in you—I was mistaken in myself. For now I love you as man never loved before. You superb, you wonderful woman!

HELEN: [*Holds out her hand to be shaken, not caressed.*] Then you agree?

ERNEST: [*Kneels, kisses her hand, and arises.*] Of course not! You blessed girl, don't you suppose I understand? It's all for my sake. Therefore for your sake—no.

HELEN: Then for my sake—for the sake of everything our love stands for!

ERNEST: [*Laughing fondly.*] Do you think I'd let you do anything for anybody's sake you're sure, later, to regret?

HELEN: Then don't ask me to marry you, Ernest. We'd both regret that later. It would destroy the two things that have brought us together, love and work.

ERNEST: Nonsense. Nothing could do that. . . . And besides, think of our poor horrified families! Think of the world's view!

HELEN: Aren't we sacrificing enough for the world—money, comforts, even children? Must we also sacrifice each other to the world? Must we be hypocrites because others are? Must we, too, be cowards and take on the protective coloring of our species?

ERNEST: Our ideas may be higher than society's, but society rewards and punishes its members according to its own ideas, not ours.

HELEN: Do you want society's rewards? Do you fear society's punishment?

ERNEST: [*Jubilantly enfolding her.*] With you in my arms, I want nothing from heaven, I fear nothing from hell; but, my dear [*shrugs and comes down to earth with a smile and releases her*], consider the price, consider the price.

HELEN: Aren't you willing to pay the price?

ERNEST: I? Yes! But it's the woman, always the woman, who pays.

HELEN: I am willing to pay.

ERNEST: I am not willing to let you.

HELEN: You'll have to be, dear. I shall go with you on my terms or not at all.

ERNEST: [*With decision.*] You will come with me as my wife or stay at home.

HELEN: [*Gasping.*] Now? After all I've said, all I've done? Ernest: I've told the family! I relied upon you. I took for granted—Ernest, you wouldn't—you couldn't leave me behind now.

ERNEST: Thanks to you and what you've made of me, I must and will.

HELEN: Ernest! [*Opens her arms to him to take her.*]

ERNEST: [*About to enfold her—resists.*] No! If you love me enough for that [*points to her pleading hands*]—I love you enough for this. [*He turns to go.*] Come when you're ready to marry me.

HELEN: [*Shrill, excited, angered.*] Do you think this has been easy for me? Do you think I'd offer myself again on any terms? Never!

ERNEST: You must marry me—and you will.

HELEN: You don't know me. Good-by!

ERNEST: Very well! [ERNEST, *afraid to stay, goes at once. She waits motionless until she hears the automobile carrying him away. She immediately turns from stone to tears, with a low wail. In utter despair, hands outstretched, she sinks down upon a bench and buries her face in her hands.*]

HELEN: Oh, Ernest! . . . How could you? [LUCY, THEODORE, JUDGE *and* JOHN *all hurry back, all excited.*

THEODORE: Did you see his horrified look?

LUCY: Fairly running away—revolted. Ah! [*Points at* HELEN. HELEN *arises, defiant, confident, calm.*]

JOHN: [*To* HELEN.] What did I tell you!

LUCY: You have thrown away the love of an honorable man.

THEODORE: Trampled upon the finest feelings of a deep nature.

JOHN: Let this be a lesson to you. You've lost your chance to marry, your chance to work, and now, by heavens! you will cut out "independence" and stay at home, *where women belong,* and live down this disgrace . . . if you can.

LUCY: With one excuse or another—he'll stay away. He'll never come back.

HELEN: [*Clear and confident as if clairvoyant.*] He will! He is coming now. . . . He is crossing the hall. . . . He is passing through the library. . . . He's here! [*But she doesn't turn.* ERNEST *reappears at the door and takes in the situation at a glance.*]

JOHN: [*Still turned toward* HELEN.] He'll never look at you again, and I don't blame him! I'm a man; I know. We don't respect women who sell out so cheap.

ERNEST: You lie! [*All turn, astounded.* HELEN *runs toward* ERNEST *with a cry of joy.* JOHN *starts to block her. To* JOHN.] Stop! You're not fit to touch her. No man is.

JOHN: [*With a sarcastic laugh.*] Humph! I suppose that's why you ran away.

ERNEST: Yes. To protect her from myself.

JOHN: Then why come back?

ERNEST: To protect her from you! You cowards, you hypocrites! [*He rushes down to* HELEN, *puts his strong arm about her shoulder and whispers rapidly.*] Just as I started, something stopped me. In a flash I saw . . . all this.

HELEN: [*Clasping his arm with both hands.*] I made you come! I made you see!

JOHN: [*Advances menacingly.*] By what right are you here in my home? By what right do you take my sister in your arms?

ERNEST: By a right more ancient than man-made law! I have come to the cry of my mate. I'm here to fight for the woman I love! [*Arm about*

HELEN, *defies the world. To all.*] My trip to Paris is postponed. One week from to-day gather all your family here, and in your home we'll make our declaration to the world.

JOHN: In my home! Ha! Not if I know it.

JUDGE: [*Restraining* JOHN.] Play for time, John—he'll bring her around.

JOHN: [*To* ERNEST.] Do you mean to marry her or not? Speak my language! [ERNEST *releases* HELEN *and steps across to* JOHN.]

ERNEST: *She* decides that—not you. [*All turn to* HELEN.]

HELEN: Never!

JOHN: [*Shaking off* JUDGE. *To* HELEN.] You'll go with this damned fanatic only over my dead body.

HELEN: [*High.*] And that will only cry aloud the thing you wish to hide from the world you fear. [*Just now* JEAN *is seen slowly returning from the garden without* REX. *Her pretty head is bent and, busy with her own sad thoughts, she is startled by the following:*]

ERNEST: There are laws to prevent marriage in some cases but none to enforce marriage on women—unless they will it.

JOHN: [*Beside himself with rage.*] Enforce! Do you think I'll ever *allow* a sister of mine to marry a libertine?

JEAN: [*Thinks they are discussing her, and is outraged.*] But I'm not going to marry him! My engagement is broken. [*General consternation. Sobbing,* JEAN *runs into house.*]

JOHN: My God, what next? Lucy, don't let Rex get away! You know what he'll do—and when he sobers up, it may be too late. [*To* ERNEST.] As for you, you snake, you get right out of here.

JUDGE: [*In the sudden silence.*] Now you've done it, John.

ERNEST: Oh, very well, this is your property.

HELEN: But *I* am not! I go, too! [*She runs to* ERNEST.]

THEODORE: Don't commit this sin!

JOHN: Let her go! She's no sister of mine.

JUDGE: [*The only calm one.*] If she leaves this house now, it's all up.

JOHN: A woman who will give herself to a man without marriage is no sister of mine.

HELEN: [*About to go, turns, leaning on* ERNEST. *To all.*] Give! . . . But if I *sold* myself, as you are forcing poor little Jean to do, to a libertine she does not love, who does not love her—that is not sin! That is respectability! To urge and aid her to entrap a man into marriage by playing the shameless tricks of the only trade men want women to learn—that is holy matrimony. But to give yourself of your own free will to the man you love and trust and can help, the man who loves and needs and has won the right to have you—oh, if this is sin, then let me live and die a sinner! [*She turns to* ERNEST, *gives him a look of complete love and trust, then bursts into tears upon his shoulder, his arms enfolding her protectingly.*]

ACT III

It is well along in the afternoon of the same busy day of rest. Most unaccountably—until the JUDGE *accounts for it later—the terrace has been decked out with festoons and flowers since the excitement of the morning. Japanese lanterns have been hung, though it is not yet time to light them and though it is Sunday in a pious household.*

Most incongruously and lugubriously, LUCY *is pacing to and fro in silent concern.*

THEODORE *now comes out of the house, also looking harassed.* LUCY *turns to him inquiringly. He shakes his head sadly.*

LUCY: No word from Uncle Everett?

THEODORE: No word. He must have reached town long ago, unless he had tire trouble. . . . It's a bad sign, Lucy, a bad sign. He would surely telephone us.

LUCY: Oh, if he *only* hadn't missed their train!

THEODORE: [*Hopelessly.*] Uncle Everett is the only one who could have brought them to their senses.

LUCY: It may not be too late. He took our fastest car, our best chauffeur.

THEODORE: Detectives are to watch all the steamers to-morrow. John telephoned at once.

LUCY: But to-morrow will be too late! And, oh! when it all comes out in the newspapers! The ghastly head-lines—"well-known scientist, beautiful daughter of a prominent family!" Oh! What will people say? [JOHN, *hurried and worried, rushes out shouting for* LUCY.]

JOHN: Any news? Any news? [THEODORE *and* LUCY *give him gestures of despair.*] Then it's too late. [*He, too, paces to and fro in fury. Then bracing up.*] Well, I found Rex, over at the Golf Club. Terribly cut up. But listen; not a drink, not one! . . . Where's Jean? Got to see her at once.

THEODORE: Locked herself up in her room, John, crying her little heart out!

JOHN: Rex is a changed man, I tell you. We've got to patch it up, and we've got to do it *quick!*

LUCY: But, John! When the Bakers hear about Helen . . . Rex marry into our family? Never! We're disgraced, John, disgraced!

JOHN: [*Impatiently.*] But they're not *going* to hear about Helen. No one knows, and no one *will*. Helen has simply returned to Paris to complete her scientific research. My press-agent—he's attending to all that.

THEODORE: But questions, gossip, rumor—it's bound to come out in time!

JOHN: In time; but meanwhile, if Jean marries Rex, the Bakers will *have* to stand for it. What's more, they'll make *other* people stand for it. Backed by the Bakers, no one will *dare* turn us down. . . . Our position in the world, my business relations with the old man—*everything hangs on little Jean* now. Tell her I've simply got to see her. [LUCY *hesitates.*] Hurry! Rex is coming over later. [*He catches sight of the table, festoons, etc.*] Heavens! What's all this tomfoolery?

LUCY: [*Going.*] Uncle Everett's orders—he wouldn't stop to explain. He left word to summon the whole family for dinner. [LUCY *goes.*]

JOHN: [*Shrilly.*] The whole family! . . . To-day of all days!

THEODORE: John! You must not, shall not, force Jean to marry this man.

JOHN: [*Unappreciated.*] Haven't I done everything for my sisters? Can't they even *marry* for *me*?

THEODORE: The man she loves or none at all.

JOHN: That cub at the law school? No money to keep a wife, no prospects of any. His father's a college professor.

THEODORE: [*Shaking head sadly.*] "No love without marriage, no marriage without—money!" Ernest Hamilton's words this morning, when we walked to church.

JOHN: [*Watching house expectantly.*] Survival of the fittest, Theodore, survival of the fittest.

THEODORE: The fittest for what?—for making money! the only kind of fitness encouraged to survive, to reproduce its species.

JOHN: If the ability to make money is not the test of fitness, what is?

THEODORE: Then you are more fit than a hundred Hamiltons, are you? And Rex? How fit is he? Rex never made a cent in his life.

JOHN: He's got it, all the same. . . . See here! Haven't I enough to worry me without your butting in? Jean's got to marry *some*body, *some*time, hasn't she?

THEODORE: But not Rex, not if I can prevent it.

JOHN: But you can't—you have nothing to do with it . . . except to perform the ceremony and get a big, fat fee for it.

THEODORE: I—marry Jean and Rex? Never! [JEAN *comes out. She is frightened and turns timidly to* THEODORE *for protection.*]

JOHN: Jean, don't detain Theodore. He has an important business letter to write. [THEODORE *turns to* JOHN *indignantly.*] Your wife's sanitarium bills—better settle up before they dun you again.

THEODORE: With your money? [*Takes* JOHN*'s check out of pocket, about to tear it.*]

JOHN: [*Catching* THEODORE*'s hand.*] For Mary's sake, for the children's— don't give way to selfish pride. . . . Want to kill your wife? Then take her out of the sanitarium. Want to ruin your children? Then take them out of school! . . . Cash your check, I tell you, and pay your debts! [THEODORE *glances at* JEAN, *at check. A struggle. At bay, he finally pockets check and dejectedly goes into the house.*]

JEAN: [*With a wet handkerchief in hand.*] Well? If I refuse to marry Rex? . . . Cut off my allowance or merely bully me to death?

JOHN: [*Kindly.*] Oh, come! You've filled your romantic little head full of novels. I never force *any*body to do *any*thing. [*Suddenly breaks out.*] My heavens! what's the matter with all of you? I only want to give you and Lucy and Helen and Theodore and the whole family the best of everything in life! And what do I get for it? I'm a brutal husband, a bullying brother, and a malefactor of wealth. Lord! I guess I have some rights, even if I have got money!

JEAN: Rex has money, too. Should that give him the right to women? I, too, have some rights—even though I *am* a woman.

JOHN: Any woman who can't care enough for a Baker to marry him—Rex is the sort who would do everything in the world for the woman he loves, everything. All the Bakers are like that.

JEAN: But what would he do for the woman he no longer loves?

JOHN: He wasn't fool enough to tell you about that?

JEAN: About what?

JOHN: [*Halting.*] Nothing—I thought—I tell you, Rex has reformed.

JEAN: You thought I meant his "past." I meant his future . . . and my own.

JOHN: Well, if you expect to find a saint, you'll never get married at all.

JEAN: And if I never married at all?

JOHN: *Then* what will you do?

JEAN: [*With a wail of despair.*] That's it—then what *should* I do—what *could* I do? Oh, it's so unfair, so unfair to train girls only for this! What chance, what choice have I? To live on the bounty of a disapproving brother or a man I do not love! Oh, how I envy Helen! If I only had a chance, a decent chance!

JOHN: Any sensible girl would envy your chance. You'll never have another like it. You'll never have another at all! Grab it, I tell you, grab it. [REX *comes quietly, a determined look on his face,* JOHN *sees him.*] Now, think, before too late, think hard. Think what it means to be an old maid. [*And leaves them abruptly.* JEAN *stands alone, looking very pretty in girlish distress.* REX *gazes at her a moment and then with sudden passion he silently rushes over, seizes her in his arms, kisses her furiously.*]

JEAN: [*Indignant, struggles, frees herself, and rubs her cheek.*] Ugh! How could you!

REX: Because I love you!

JEAN: Love! It isn't even respect now.

REX: Has that fellow ever kissed you?

JEAN: I have begged you never to refer to him again.

REX: He has! He has held you in his arms. He has kissed your lips, your cheeks, your eyes!

JEAN: How many women have you held in your arms? Have I ever tried to find out?

REX: Ah! You don't deny it, you can't.

JEAN: I can! *He* respects me. I don't deserve it, but he does.

REX: Thank heavens! Oh, you don't know how this has tormented me, little Jean. The thought of any other man's coming near you—why, I couldn't have felt the same toward you again, I just couldn't.

JEAN: [*Bites her lips then deliberately.*] Well, then . . . other men have come near me . . . other men have kissed me, Rex.

REX: [*Getting wild again.*] What! When? Where?

JEAN: [*Laughing cynically.*] Oh, in conservatories in town, John's camp in the North Woods, motor rides in the country—once or twice out here on this very terrace, when I've felt sentimental in the moonlight.

REX: [*Recoiling.*] Oh! Jean! I never supposed *you* were that sort!

JEAN: [*With distaste.*] Oh, I don't make a habit of it! I'm not *that* sort. But . . . well, this isn't all I could tell you about myself, Rex.

REX: Don't! . . . Oh, what do you mean—quick.

JEAN: Oh, I've merely been handled, not hurt. Slightly shopworn but as good as new.

REX: [*After a pause, quietly.*] Jean, what makes you say such horribly honest things to me?

JEAN: Yesterday I did you a great unkindness, Rex. I deserve to suffer for it. . . . You don't suppose I enjoy talking this way about myself?

REX: I never heard a girl—a nice girl—talk like this before.

JEAN: Naturally not. Usually "nice" girls hide it. It's an instinct in women—to keep up their value. . . . Often I've had thoughts and feelings which "nice" girls of your artificial ideal are supposed never to have at all. Perfectly natural, too, especially girls of my sort. We have so little to occupy our minds, except men! To have a useful, absorbing occupation—it rubs off the bloom, lowers our price in the market, you see.

REX: Oh, stop! . . . If you're not going to marry me, say so, but—

JEAN: But I am! I am not going to be a dependent old maid. [REX, *bewildered, only gazes at her.*] But, first, I want you to know exactly what you're getting for your money. That seems only businesslike.

REX: [*Recoils.*] Would you only marry me for that?

JEAN: I told you I loved another man. Do you want me?

REX: [*With jealousy returning.*] Do I want you! He shan't have you. [*He comes close.*]

JEAN: Then take me.

REX: [*Seizes her passionately.*] I'll make you love *me!* [*Kisses her triumphantly.*] I'll bring a different light into those cold eyes of yours. Wait until you're married! Wait until you're awakened. I'll make you forget that man, all other men. You are to be mine—all mine, all mine! [*During this embrace* JEAN *is quite passive, holds up her cheek to be kissed, and when he seeks her lips she shuts her eyes and gives him her lips. He suddenly stops, chilled; holding her at arm's length.*] But I don't care to marry an iceberg. Can't you love me a little? Haven't you any sentiment in your cynical little soul . . . you irresistible darling!

JEAN: In my soul? Yes! It's only my body I'm selling, you know. [*Then deliberately—clearly without passion—throws her arms about his neck, clinging close and kissing him repeatedly until* REX *responds.*]

REX: Look out, here comes the parson. [THEODORE *comes out of the house.*]

JEAN: Oh, Theodore! Rex and I have come to an understanding. . . . Will you solemnize our blessed union?

THEODORE: Not unless you truly love each other. Marriage is sacred.

JEAN: [*Rapidly.*] A large church wedding—that will make it sacred. A full choral service—many expensive flowers—all the smartest people invited—that always makes the union of two souls sacred.

THEODORE: Those who truly love—their friends should witness the solemn rite, but—

JEAN: [*Interrupts. To* REX.] And my wedding gown will be white satin with a point-lace veil caught up with orange-blossoms and a diamond tiara—"the gift of the groom"—that ought to make it solemn.

THEODORE: The white veil is the symbol of purity, Jean.

JEAN: [*Rattling on wildly.*] Of purity, Rex, do you hear? Whenever you see a bride in the white symbol of purity she is pure—that proves it. That makes it all so beautiful! so sacred! so holy! holy! holy! [*Hysterically turns and runs into the house as* JOHN *comes out.*]

THEODORE: [*Following.*] Jean, you must not, you shall not—[JOHN *blocks*

THEODORE. REX *runs in after* JEAN. *To* JOHN.] John, I warn you! I'll prevent this marriage. I'll tell every clergyman in the diocese. I'll inform the bishop himself. This marriage would be a sacrilege.

JOHN: You dare threaten me—after all I've done for you!

THEODORE: Your five thousand was a loan—not a bribe—every cent of it will be returned.

JOHN: You can't return it. I wouldn't let you if you could. Come, it's all in the family. [THEODORE *shakes his head.*] You know that beautiful Gothic chapel old man Baker is building on his estate? He likes you. I'll tell him you're just the man he's looking for—safe and sane—no socialistic tendencies.

THEODORE: Don't trouble yourself—he offered me the place this morning.

JOHN: You didn't refuse it!

THEODORE: I did—this morning. But since my last talk with you I've reconsidered, I've telephoned my acceptance.

JOHN: [*Genuinely glad.*] Bully! Great! Why, now you're fixed for life. "Only one kind of fitness encouraged," eh? . . . Right always triumphs in the end. Never lose your faith again, Theodore.

THEODORE: Right? That whited sepulchre! his mill hands dying like flies, his private life a public scandal!

JOHN: [*With a cynical grin.*] Then why accept his tainted money?

THEODORE: [*From his soul.*] To keep my wife alive. To keep my children out of the streets. To keep myself out of deeper debt to you. That's why I accept it—that's why many a man sells his soul to the devil. . . . If I had only myself to consider—why, to me a little thing like death would be a blessed luxury. But I, why, John, I cannot afford—even to die. I must compromise and live—live for those dependent on me. . . . Your five thousand will be returned with interest, but your little sister will not be married to a man she does not want.

JOHN: But Rex wants *her* and money talks in this world, louder than the Church. Refuse to marry Baker's son and how long will you keep Baker's chapel? Think it over, Theodore, think it over. [*Suddenly the* JUDGE *in motor garments covered with dust comes out panting, followed by* LUCY *calling.*]

LUCY: Uncle Everett! Uncle Everett!

JUDGE: John! Oh, John!

JOHN: Where is she!

THEODORE: You were too late!

JUDGE: Wait! Give me time to get my breath. [*Fans himself with his cap and mops brow.*]

JOHN: My detective—didn't he meet their train? [JUDGE *nods yes.*]

LUCY: But they saw him first? [JUDGE *shakes head no.*]

THEODORE: Didn't he follow them? [JUDGE *nods yes.*]

JOHN: Where'd they go? Where are they? Speak, man, speak!

JUDGE: [*Raises cap and handkerchief.*] Now, just give me a chance and I'll tell the whole story. . . . The detective was waiting at the station. He saw them step out of the train. He followed them to the cab-stand. He watched them get into a taxi—jumped into another himself—and away they went, pursued by the detective and blissfully ignorant of his existence. . . . Even now they don't know they were being watched—or else . . . well, they might have taken another course.

LUCY: Quick! Tell us the worst.

JUDGE: [*Hesitates.*] Well . . . they drove straight to Helen's apartment.

LUCY: And you were too late. I thought so.

JOHN: But my detective?

JUDGE: He followed and reported to me when I reached town.

LUCY: Reported what? Tell us all.

JUDGE: First he saw Ernest help Helen out of the taxi—very tenderly, like this. Little they realized then how every detail was to be reported to you now!

JOHN: Go on! Go on!

JUDGE: Then the detective saw Ernest deliberately—

LUCY: Yes, go on.

JUDGE: Deliberately lift his hat like this, say "good afternoon" just like that, and drive on to his own apartment a mile away. [*There is a sudden silence; the others waiting, the* JUDGE *now sits down.*]

LUCY: Oh, is that all?

THEODORE: Why, it's exactly as if they were engaged!

JUDGE: No, Theodore, not *exactly* as if engaged.

JOHN: You're keeping something back from us! Speak!

JUDGE: [*Gets up from chair.*] Must I tell you? It's rather delicate. . . . Well, he didn't even step into the vestibule to kiss her good-by. [*All look at each other.*]

JOHN: But where are they now? Quick!

LUCY: They met later! I knew it.

JUDGE: Yes, it's true. They are alone together at this very moment.

ALL: Where! Where!

JUDGE: [*Pointing to house.*] There.

JOHN: What! What are they doing here?

JUDGE: [*Resumes fanning.*] Discussing the marriage problem. [*General rejoicing and relief.*] Sssh! Not so loud, you might interrupt them.

JOHN: [*Nodding knowingly.*] Cold feet! Knew he'd lose his job.

LUCY: The disgrace. She couldn't face it.

THEODORE: No, conscience. A deep religious nature. [*They all think it over a moment, each sure of his own diagnosis.*]

JOHN: [*Turning to* JUDGE *with amusement.*] So! Decided the soul-mate theory wouldn't work in practice, eh?

THEODORE *and* LUCY: And they agree to marry?

JUDGE: [*Stops fanning.*] Marry? My, no! Nothing like that. They think less of marriage than ever now! Helen is using woman's sweet indirect influence on Ernest in there at this moment! [*All start toward the house impulsively, but on second thoughts they all stop.*]

JOHN: Then how on earth did you get them back!

JUDGE: [*Lighting cigar.*] Oh, perfectly simple, I promised Helen you'd apologize to Ernest; promised Ernest you'd apologize to Helen. [*To* LUCY.] Promised both you'd arrange a nice little family party for 'em. They bear no grudge. They're too happy.

LUCY: [*Horrified. Indicates table.*] The family party—for *them?* Horrors!

JUDGE: [*Tossing away match.*] Yes, here in your happy home. [*The others turn on the* JUDGE *indignantly.*] Well, don't jump on *me.* I tell you they positively decline to elope until after they tell the whole damn family. Considerate of them, I say. You don't deserve it, if you ask me.

JOHN: [*Incredulous.*] Tell the whole . . . see here, are they crazy? Are *you* crazy? Do you think *I'm* crazy? [*Impetuously turns toward the house, a man of action.*]

JUDGE: [*Stopping* JOHN.] Wait! . . . You've already done your best to destroy your sister—but you've utterly failed. They have done nothing wrong—*as yet.* Why, they are the finest, truest, noblest pair of lovers I ever met! Now, aren't they, Theodore?

THEODORE: I can't say that I call Helen's ideas of marriage "noble," exactly!

JUDGE: [*Grandiloquent.*] She is willing to sacrifice even marriage for his career. Isn't that noble? And he! willing to sacrifice even his career for marriage. Both noble, if you ask me.

JOHN: [*Loud.*] Noble tommy-rot!—a pair of pig-headed, highbrow fools! They don't have to sacrifice anything for anybody. Can't they work together just as well married as unmarried?

JUDGE: [*Slyly.*] That's what I said to her, but you had already convinced her that it was impractical. Work and marriage—"combine the two, and you'll fail at both"—your own warning, John.

JOHN: [*Angry.*] B'r'r—you think you're very funny, don't you! But that's my sister in there, planning to be that fellow's mistress—right here in my own house! Anything funny about that!

JUDGE: [*Stepping aside.*] All right, go put a stop to it then! [JOHN *starts to-*

ward house.] It's your own house—turn her out again. [JOHN *stops short.*] What are you going to do about it, John? [JOHN *has no answer.*] Drive little Jean into marriage with a man she does not love— she is an old-fashioned girl. But your other sister—you can't make her marry even the man she does love, unless she sees fit. She is the New Woman! Society can no longer force females into wedlock—so it is forcing them out . . . by the thousands! Approve of it? Of course not. But what good will our disapproval do? They will only laugh at you. The strike is on. Few of the strikers will let you see it. Few of the strikers have Helen's courage. But, believe it or not, the strike will spread. It cannot be crushed by law or force. Unless society wakes up and reforms its rules and regulations of marriage, marriage is doomed. . . . What are you going to do about it? [*Silence.*] I thought so—nothing. Call them bad women and let it go at that. Blame it all on human nature, made by God, and leave untouched our human institutions, made by man. You poor little pessimists! Human nature to-day is better than it ever was, but our most important institution is worse—the most sacred relationship in life has become a jest in the market-place. . . . You funny little cowards, you're afraid of life, afraid of love, afraid of truth. You worship lies, and call it God!

JOHN: [*Interrupts.*] All right, all right—but we can't change marriage overnight just to suit Helen. What are *you* going to do about it?

JUDGE: There's just one thing to do. Will you back me up in everything I say?

JOHN: [*Acknowledging his own defeat.*] Anything—everything.

JUDGE: Then tell Helen she doesn't have to marry, that, with the best intentions, the Church has made a muddle of monogamy.

THEODORE: Uncle Everett, I protest.

JUDGE: That we all admire their consecrated courage and advise their trying this conscientious experiment.

JOHN: Not if I have anything to say about it!

JUDGE: But you haven't. Do please get that through your head. . . . Theodore, they've talked enough, ask them to step out here and receive John's blessing. [*Impatiently.*] Go on—I'll fix John. [THEODORE *goes. To* JOHN, *who is about to burst forth.*] Oh, see here, did you ever pull a dog into the house against his will? . . . Let him alone and he'll follow you in, wag his tail, and lick your hand.

JOHN: You mean, they'll come in, be respectable?

JUDGE: Admit that marriage has numerous drawbacks—and they'll see its advantages. Deny it and they'll see nothing but each other. Marriage is in a bad way, but it's the less of two evils. Marriage *must* adjust itself to the New Woman—*but* the New Woman must meanwhile adjust herself to marriage. [*Briskly to* LUCY.] Now, then, did you send out that hurry call for the family this evening?

LUCY: Yes, they're on their way here now, but Uncle Everett, Doctor Hamilton said, next week.

JUDGE: Yes, I know—it'll be a little surprise party for Helen. . . . Did you order some music?

LUCY: Yes, the musicians are to be stationed in the library.

JUDGE: Excellent—excellent. [*Indicates tables and festoons.*] All that junk will help, too. A good Sunday supper this evening, Lucy; your best champagne, John—gay spirits, family affection, warm approval, toasts to the future. Why, all we'll have to do is—[*Breaks off.*] Here they come. Now follow my lead. They've done a lot of thinking since you saw them last, but—make one misstep and it's all off.

LUCY: Be nice to her, John. It was just a girlish impulse. [JOHN *opens arms to receive* HELEN.]

JOHN: My sister! All is forgiven.

HELEN: [*Stops short, her lip curls.*] *You* forgive *me?* [*Before* JOHN *can reply,* THEODORE *and* ERNEST *follow, talking.*]

ERNEST: But I tell you he had a perfect right to put me off his property. The thing I can't overlook—[*Sees* JOHN *and* LUCY. *Points finger at them accusingly.*] Theodore has told me what you thought. Please don't judge us by yourselves again—you licentious-minded married people! [*He shrugs his shoulders with fastidious disgust and turns his back upon them.*]

JOHN: [*Gasping.*] Well, I'll be damned.

JUDGE: [*Whispers.*] Stand for it—he's right.

THEODORE: But Ernest . . . I'm bound to say when two people run away together—

ERNEST: Ah, Theodore! you, too? Are all married people alike? Did we want to "run away" as you call it? Did we not ask for a week to think it over? Did we not stipulate that in any case we must frankly face the family first? But this person—what did he do? He ordered us off his property, like trespassers! What could we do? Sit down in the road and wait a week? Bah! we went home—you suspicious married people, you hypocritical, unspeakable married people! [JUDGE *has difficulty in restraining* JOHN.] Why, I believe our good friend the Judge here is the only decent-minded, properly married person on your property.

JOHN: [*Bursting out.*] Decent-minded—why, he's div—[LUCY *stops him.*]

JUDGE: [*Steps in.*] Dev-oted to his wife. Lucy is jealous of what I'm doing for my wife. [*Controls laughter.*] Now come, we must all just let bygones be bygones. We know your intentions are honorable, your courage admirable; and for whatever was amiss in word, deed, or thought, we all humbly apologize—don't we, John? [JOHN *bows uncomfortably.*] Lucy? Theodore? And now I want you all to tell Ernest and Helen what you told me—that their arguments against marriage are unanswerable, their logic unimpeachable, and we no longer have the slightest intention or desire to get them divorced by matrimony. [JOHN, THEODORE, *and* LUCY *look dubious.* JUDGE *crosses over and pinches them.* HELEN *and* ERNEST *are utterly bewildered.*] Why, we wouldn't let a little thing like marriage come between them for the world, would we, John? would we, Lucy? would we, Theodore?

JOHN: [*With an effort.*] I agree with Uncle Everett entirely.

JUDGE: And you, Theodore?

THEODORE: [*In a low voice.*] Perfectly.

JUDGE: And you, Lucy?

LUCY: [*With a nervous glance at* JOHN.] Absolutely.

JUDGE: [*To the lovers.*] There. You see?

[ERNEST *looks from one to the other in amazement.*]

HELEN: [*Laughing.*] I don't believe a word of it!

JUDGE: Why not? why not?

HELEN: Very well, then. Invite the whole family here next Sunday!

JUDGE: They'll be here in an hour. [*Points to tables.*]

HELEN *and* ERNEST: [*Recoiling.*] In an hour!

JUDGE: Yes, you are to begin your new life together this evening! Isn't it lovely?

HELEN: [*Gasping.*] But that's so sudden. Why, we—we aren't ready.

THEODORE: Just as ready as you'll ever be.

JUDGE: Ernest's vacation begins to-morrow—your honeymoon.

HELEN: But, don't you see—

LUCY: Those new Paris clothes John gave you—your trousseau.

ERNEST: Well, but—

JUDGE: And this family gathering this evening, your—in a manner of speaking—wedding party. [*Waving aside all the lovers' objections.*] Now, it's all fixed, let's go and dress for the—as it were—ceremony.

ERNEST: [*Blocks the way. Serious.*] Wait! Did I ever say I would not marry this woman? [*All stop, turn, exchange glances.*]

JUDGE: [*Apart.*] Ah! a broad-minded chap.

JOHN: [*With a wink at* JUDGE.] Ah! so you think you'd like to marry my sister after all?

ERNEST: Oh, you're an ass! What have I been doing for the past twenty-four hours? Begging her to marry me. What have you been doing? Preventing it. Why did I postpone sailing for a week? Why did I insist upon the family party? [*Comes nearer to* JOHN.] You're an idiot.

JUDGE: [*Pinching* JOHN.] Stand for it, John. You've got to stand for it. Tell him you love him like a brother . . . in-law.

JOHN: [*Controls himself.*] Well, I . . . I—you have my consent, Doctor Hamilton, I'm sure.

ERNEST: *Your* consent! What's that got to do with it? [*They all turn toward* HELEN. ERNEST *steps between them.*] Now wait! . . . This morning you tried bullying. Did it work? This afternoon bluffing. Think *that* will work? [*Hand on* HELEN'*s shoulder.*] You can't frighten her into marriage. I've tried that myself. We've got to appeal to some higher motive than self-interest or superstition with *this* woman, racial motives, unselfish motives. [*With force.*] But don't talk to me about her being "immoral." I won't stand for it. If you want her to marry, prove the morality of marriage.

THEODORE: The "morality of marriage"! What next?

ERNEST: [*To* THEODORE.] That's what I said—the morality of *marriage!* This woman is not on trial before you. Marriage is on trial before her, and thus far I'm bound to say you've not made out a good case for it. But simply *justify* her marrying me, and—I give you my word—you can perform the ceremony this very evening. No license is required in this State, you know. [*This creates a sensation.*]

JUDGE: Now, what could be fairer than that! [*To* HELEN.] Do you agree to this?

HELEN: [*She nods.*] We agree in everything.

JUDGE: *Both* broad-minded!

HELEN: [*Quietly.*] I never said I did not believe in a legal wedding—[*others surprised*] for those who can afford the luxury of children. . . . But for those who have to take it out in working for other people's children all their lives—a ceremony seems like a subterfuge. Without children I don't see how any marriage is ever consummated—socially.

THEODORE: Ah, but this relationship—it's a sacred thing in itself.

HELEN: [*Sincerely.*] I know it. I want to do right, Theodore, please believe that I do! But the kind of marriage preached by the Church and practised by the world—does that cherish the real sacredness of this relationship? Of course, I can only judge from appearances, but so often marriage seems to destroy the sacredness—yes, and also the usefulness—of this relationship!

ERNEST: But, my dear girl—

HELEN: [*Smiles.*] He thinks so, too. Only he has a quaint, mannish notion that he must "protect me." [*To* ERNEST, *patting his arm.*] Haven't you, dear! [*Again she has raised the shield of flippancy.*]

JUDGE: What did I tell you, Theodore? The old marriage doesn't fit the New Woman. A self-supporting girl like Helen objects to obeying a mere man—like Ernest.

HELEN: [*Patting the* JUDGE's *arm affectionately, too.*] Uncle Everett, you know nothing about it! You think you understand the new generation. The only generation you understand is the one which clamored for "Woman's Rights." [*To* ERNEST.] I obey you already—every day of my life, do I not, dear? [*Looking up into his face.*] You're my "boss," aren't you, Ernest? [*To* JUDGE.] But I do object to contracting by law for what is better done by love.

JUDGE: [*Laughs fondly.*] But suppose the promise to obey were left out?

HELEN: But the contract to love—[*To* THEODORE.] that's so much worse, it seems to me. Obedience is a mere matter of will, is it not? But when a man promises to love until death

THEODORE: Are you so cold, so scientific, so *unsexed,* that you cannot trust the man you love?

HELEN: Why, Theodore, if I didn't trust him I'd *marry* him! Contracts are not for those who trust—they're for those who don't.

LUCY: [*Takes* HELEN *apart.*] Now, I may be old-fashioned, Helen, but I'm a married woman, and I know men. You never can tell, my dear, you never can tell.

HELEN: Do you think I'd live with a man who did not love me? Do you think I'd live on a man I did not love? [LUCY *blinks.*] Why, what kind of a woman should I be then! The name wife—would that change it? Calling it holy—would that hallow it? . . . Every woman, married or not, knows the truth about this! In her soul woman has always known. But until to-day has never dared to tell.

ERNEST: [*Approaching* HELEN.] Oh, come now—those vows—they aren't intended in a literal sense. Ask Theodore. Why, no sane person means half of that gibberish. "With all my worldly goods I thee endow"—millions of men have said it—how many ever did it? How many clergymen ever expect them to! . . . It's all a polite fiction in beautiful, sonorous English.

HELEN: The most sacred relationship in life! Ernest, shall you and I enter it unadvisedly, lightly, and with LIES on our lips? . . . Simply because others do?

ERNEST: [*A little impatient.*] But the whole world stands for this. And the world won't stand for that.

HELEN: Is that reverently, soberly, and in the fear of God? No, cynically, selfishly, and in the fear of man. I don't want to be obstinate, I don't like to set myself up as "holier than thou," but, Ernest, unless we begin honestly, we'll end dishonestly. Somehow marriage seems wicked to me.

JUDGE: [*Nudging* THEODORE.] How do you like that?

THEODORE: John is right—they've gone mad.

ERNEST: All the same, you've got to marry me—you've simply *got* to.

HELEN: You are mistaken. I do *not* have to marry *any one*. I can support myself.

ERNEST: Then I'm disappointed in you.

HELEN: And I in you.

ERNEST: I thought you were sensible.

HELEN: I thought you were honest.

ERNEST: Honest! You accuse me of dishonesty?

HELEN: You don't believe in "half of that gibberish." Yet you are willing to work the Church for our own worldly advantage! You are willing to prostitute the most sacred thing in life! If that is not dishonest, what is!

ERNEST: And you are the woman I love and want to marry! In all my life I was never accused of dishonesty before.

HELEN: You never tried to marry before. No one is honest about marriage.

ERNEST: I never shall try again. I'm going to Paris to-morrow and I'm going alone.

HELEN: Then do it. Don't threaten it so often—do it.

ERNEST: I shall. And I'll never come back.

HELEN: Nobody asked you to.

ERNEST: Helen—for the last time—just for my sake—marry me.

HELEN: For the last time—no! no! NO!! I won't be a hypocrite even for your sake. [*She turns away, he starts off, then stops, rushes over to her.*]

ERNEST: [*Holds out arms.*] I can't. You know it. Without you I'm nothing.

HELEN: [*Taking both his hands.*] Without you. . . . Oh, my dear, my dear.

ERNEST: Forgive me, forgive me.

HELEN: It was all my fault.

ERNEST: No, I was a brute. I'm not worthy of you.

HELEN: [*Covering his lips with her hand.*] Sssh—I can't stand it—I was perfectly horrid to you. And you were doing it all for my sake. [*Laughing and crying.*] You dear old thing—I knew it all the time. [*They seem about to embrace.*]

JUDGE: [*Shaking with laughter.*] Was there ever in the world anything like it! . . . Well, children, see here. He's willing to lie for your sake. She's willing to die for your sake. Now, why not just split the difference and have a civil ceremony for *our* sake.

THEODORE: No, they will marry for a better reason. Think of the *sin* of it! [*To* HELEN.] Have you no sense of sin?

JUDGE: If not, think of the humor of it! Have you no sense of humor?

HELEN: [*Still drying eyes and smiling to* JUDGE.] Not a scrap. Neither has Ernest. Have you, dear?

ERNEST: I *hope* not—judging from those who always say they have.

THEODORE: [*Solemnly.*] Helen, look at Ernest—Ernest look at Helen. [*The lovers do so.*] Look into each other's very souls! . . . You know, you *must* know, that in the eyes of God this thing would be a sin, a heinous sin. [*The lovers gaze deep into each other's eyes in silence.*]

ERNEST: [*Tremulous from the emotion he has just been through.*] The glory and the gladness I see in this woman's eyes a sin? Her trust in me, my worship of her, our new-found belief in a future life, our greater usefulness together in this—bah! don't talk to me about sin! Such women cannot sin—they love.

JOHN: [*Tired out.*] Oh, you can talk all night, but this is a practical world. How long could you keep your job in the institute? Then how'll you live! Private practice? No respectable home will let you inside the door.

ERNEST: I've seen the inside of respectable homes. I want no more. [*Taking from his pocket a piece of paper.*] This morning I came to ask for your sister's hand in marriage. Your manners did not please me. So I cabled over to Metchnikoff. [*Hands cablegram to* JOHN.] His answer. Positions await us both at the Pasteur Institute in Paris. That luxurious suite on to-morrow's steamer still waits in my name.

THEODORE: Ernest! Stop! Think! This woman's soul is in your hands. [ERNEST *seems to hesitate.* HELEN *crosses to him.* JUDGE *seizes* JOHN, *whispers, and shoves him across.*]

JOHN: Doctor Hamilton! I apologize! . . . You're a man of the world. You know what this means—she doesn't. She is in your power—for God's sake go to Paris without her. [JOHN *tries to lead* HELEN *away from* ERNEST. *She shudders at* JOHN's *masterful touch and clings to her lover.*]

ERNEST: And leave her here in *your* power? Never again! You've forced her out of her work—you'd force her into legalized prostitution, if you could, like her innocent little sister. [*Snatches* HELEN *away from* JOHN.] No, married or not, she sails with me in the morning. That's final. [*The lovers turn away together.*]

JUDGE: Where are you going?

HELEN: To ask Marie to pack my trunk.

ERNEST: To telephone for a motor.

JUDGE: But you won't start until after the family party?

ERNEST: Of course not. [*In a sudden silence* HELEN *and* ERNEST *walk into the house, leaving the family in despair.*]

JUDGE: [*After a long sigh, to* JOHN.] I knew you'd bungle it, I knew it— but there's still a chance, just one more card to play.

[*The* BUTLER *comes out.*]

LUCY: Good heavens! Already?

BUTLER: Mr. and Mrs. Willoughby, Doctor and Mrs. Grey, and the Misses Grey.

LUCY: [*Flurried.*] And we're not even dressed!

JUDGE: No matter. It's Sunday—many orthodox people . . . why, Mr. Baker won't even dine out on Sunday. [*Enter the persons announced. Greetings. "How warm it is for September."* . . . *"And how's the baby, Margaret?"* etc. JOHN *and* JUDGE *apart are planning excitedly.* JEAN *and* REX *come out, and finally* HELEN, *followed by* ERNEST.]

BUTLER: Dinner is served, ma'am. [*The* SECOND MAN *touches button. Japanese lanterns glow, silver shines, and all move toward the tables, a happy, united family.*]

LUCY: [*Going-to-dinner manner as she leads the way.*] We can hardly go out formally because we're already out, you know. Aunt Susan, will you sit over there on John's right? Doctor Hamilton by me? Rex on the other side?

JOHN: Here, Helen. No, Jean, you are beside Rex, you know.

JUDGE: Until married, then you're separated.

LUCY: Cousin Charlie—that's it. [*All take their places.*] Most extraordinary weather for September, isn't it?

JUDGE: [*He slaps his cheek.*] Isn't it?

LUCY: [*Shocked and hurt.*] That's the first mosquito I have ever known on our place.

JOHN: [*Indignantly.*] We never have mosquitoes here. You must have been mistaken. [*The* SERVANTS *are passing in and out of house with courses. The* BUTLER *now brings a telegram to* JUDGE.]

JUDGE: From Julia! [*Tears it open eagerly, reads, and then shouts.*] She's coming back to me, she's coming back! Look at that, look at that! [*Jumps up and shows telegram to John. Then taking it around to Lucy he sings to tune of "Merrily we roll along":*]

> Aunt Julia is coming back
> Coming back—coming back
> Aunt Julia is coming back
> Coming back from Reno.

HELEN: [*Laughing.*] From Reno? That sounds like divorce, Uncle Everett.

JUDGE: Like divorce? Does that sound like divorce? [*Takes telegram from* LUCY *and hands it to* HELEN.] Read it aloud.

HELEN: [*Reading.*] "Dear boy, I can't stand it, either. Come to me or I go to you."

JUDGE: [*Sings during the reading.*] Coming back from Reno. [*Breaks off—* to HELEN.] So you thought we wanted a divorce, did you?

HELEN: I never dreamed of such a thing.

JUDGE: [*Looks at her a moment, then in a burst.*] Well, *I* did. The dream of my life—your Aunt Julia's, too. We thought we believed in trial marriage, but we don't—we believe in trial *separation!*

THEODORE: [*Uncomfortably.*] They thought they didn't love each other, but they do, you see.

JUDGE: We don't, we don't, but we can't get along without each other . . . got the habit of having each other around and can't break it. . . . This morning I telegraphed: "Are you doing this just for my sake?" She replied, "Tutti-frutti." [*Sings.*] Aunt Julia's coming back. Oh, I'm too happy to eat. [*Singing, while others eat and drink:*]
Coming back, coming back,
Aunt Julia is coming back
Coming back from Reno.
And I don't care who knows it. The more the better for marriage. The truth—give me more truth, give me more—champagne. [BUT-LER *fills glass as* JUDGE *raises it.*] Here's to your Aunt Julia, the best wife—I ever had. [*All rise, drink, laugh, and sit down.*] And I'll never, never get another. . . . You know I thought maybe I might. Oh, Everett, Everett, you sly dog, you old idiot you!

JOHN: [*Arises, clearing throat, tapping on glasses for silence.*] And now, speaking of divorce, I have an engagement to announce. [*Some laughter but all quiet down. He smiles at* JEAN.] Of course, you can't guess whose. Friends, it is my privilege to announce the engagement of my good friend Rex Baker to my dear sister Jean. [*Gentle applause and congratulations. Music begins.*] And so I will now ask all to arise and drink to the health and prosperity of my little sister and my brother-in-law to be! And my best wish is that they will be as happy as my better half and me. [*All cheer and drink health standing.*] Speech, Rex! [*Some of them playfully try to put him on his feet.*]

REX: [*Shaking his head and maintaining his seat.*] I can't make a speech. I'm too happy for words—See-what-I-mean?

HELEN: [*In a low, significant tone.*] Jean, aren't you going to say something?

JEAN: [*Arises, all silent, she looks at* LUCY, REX, JOHN.] Words cannot describe my happiness, either. [*She resumes her seat, and all gather round to congratulate* JEAN *and* REX.]

JOHN: [*Rapping for quiet.*] One moment, one moment. Another toast, another toast! [*Others quiet down.*] We have with us to-night one who, in honoring whom we honor ourselves, one who with capital back of him would soon become the greatest scientist in America! [JUDGE *leads applause,* "*hear, hear!*" *etc.* JOHN *raises glass.*] To the distinguished guest whom I am proud to welcome to my humble board, to the noble humanitarian whom Mr. Baker delights to honor, to the good friend whom we all admire and trust, Doctor Ernest Hamilton! [*All applaud and about to drink health,* JUDGE *jumps up.*]

JUDGE: And to his fair collaborator! the brave woman who at this modern warrior's side daily risks her life for others, handling death and disease in those mighty but unsung battles for the common weal! [*Applause.*] A New Woman? No, friends, look behind the stupid names the mob would cast, like stones to destroy, look and you will see your true conservative—willing to appear radical in order to conserve woman's work in the world! willing to appear ridiculous to right ancient wrongs! willing even to appear *wrong*—for those she loves! Ah, the same old-fashioned woman we all adore, in a form so new we blindly fail to understand her glorious advent before our very eyes! To Helen, the gracious embodiment of all that is sweetest, noblest, and best in womanhood—to Helen! Our lovely Helen!

JOHN: [*Up again at once.*] Family approval, social esteem, and an honored career—all this is theirs for the asking! To-day to me they have confessed their love—to-night to you I now announce . . . their engagement! Long life and happiness to Helen and Ernest! [*Great enthusiasm—even pounding on the table.* ERNEST *arises, looking surprised.* JOHN *signalling to rest of family to join in.*]

THE FAMILY: [*Glasses raised, drowning out* ERNEST.] Long life and happiness, long life and happiness!

ERNEST: [*Raises hand.*] Wait! Before you drink this toast. . . . [*The glasses stop midway. Sudden silence.*] Your congratulations we appreciate, your kind wishes we desire—but not on false pretences. We are not engaged to be married. [*In the tense silence a shudder ripples the family joy.*]

REX: [*Apart to* JEAN.] Gee! They had a scrap, too?

JOHN: [*Up, nervously.* ERNEST *still standing.*] If I may interrupt. . . . He has financial reasons—I respect him for it. But this very day the Baker Institute in recognition of Doctor Hamilton's distinguished services to humanity has doubled his salary—doubled it! It's all right now—it's all right.

REX: [*Apart to* JEAN.] Four thousand, eh? . . . get a very decent touring car for that.

ERNEST: [*To all.*] That is very kind, but that is not the point. True, our mutual needs are such that we cannot live or work apart, but our convictions are such that we cannot live and work *together*—in what you have the humor to call "holy wedlock." Now, Helen, the motor is waiting. [*Sensation. Gasps of amazement and horror. Some jump up from table. A chair is upset.* ERNEST *holds* HELEN'*s wrap. General movement and murmurs.*]

JOHN: [*Barring way.*] You leave this house only over my dead body. [*Others gather around lovers.*]

JUDGE: [*To all.*] Stand back! . . . Let him among you who has a purer ideal of love, a higher conception of duty, cast the first stone. [*All stop. Silenced.*]

THEODORE: But this man and this woman would destroy marriage!

JUDGE: [*Standing beside lovers.*] No! Such as they will not destroy marriage—they will save it! They restore the vital substance while we preserve the empty shell. Everything they have said, everything they have done, proves it. The promise to love—they could not help it—they took it—I heard them. The instinct for secrecy—they felt it—we all do—but straightway they told the next of kin. [*Points to* JOHN.] Even when insulted and driven forth from the tribe, they indignantly refused to be driven into each other's arms until you of the same blood could hear them plight their troth! Believe in marriage? Why, there never was, there never will be a more perfect tribute to true marriage than from this fearless pair you now accuse of seeking to destroy it! [JOHN *tries to interrupt, but the* JUDGE *waves him down.*] They have been not only honorable but old-fashioned, save in the one orthodox detail of accepting the authority constituted by society for *its* protection and for *theirs.* [*To* HELEN *and* ERNEST.] But now, I'm sure, before starting on their wedding journey—another old-fashioned convention they believe in—that, just to please us if not themselves, they will consent to be united in the bonds of holy wedlock by Cousin Theodore who stands ready and waiting with prayer-book in hand. [*Family subsides. Everybody happy.* THEODORE *steps up, opens prayer-book.*]

THEODORE: "Dearly beloved, we are gathered together here in the sight of God—"

HELEN: [*Suddenly loud and clear.*] Theodore! are you going to marry Rex and Jean?

JOHN: [*Impatiently.*] Of course, of course, Mr. Baker's chaplain.

ERNEST: [*Recoiling.*] Theodore! You! Are you going to stand up and tell the world that God has joined those two together—GOD? [THEODORE *looks at* JOHN *but does not deny it and says nothing.*]

HELEN: Then you will be blaspheming love—and God who made it. No, you shall not marry us.

ERNEST: [*Agreeing with* HELEN.] Some things are too sacred to be profaned.

THEODORE: [*Overwhelmed.*] Profaned? . . . By the Church?

JOHN: Your love too sacred for the Church? The Church has a name for such love! The world a name for such women!

ERNEST: [*About to strike* JOHN, *then shrugs.*] A rotten world! A kept Church! Come, let's get away from it all! Come! [HELEN *offers her hand in farewell to* LUCY, *but* JOHN *shields her from* HELEN'*s touch, then to* JEAN. REX *shields* JEAN *from contamination, but* JEAN *weeps.*]

JUDGE: [*Barring the way. To* ERNEST.] Stop! You cannot! The very tie that binds you to this woman binds you to us and to the whole world with hooks of steel! [*The lovers are still going,* JUDGE *ascends steps, facing them.*] For the last time! before too late! *Ernest!* You *know* that in the eyes of God you *are* taking this woman to be your wife.

ERNEST: In the eyes of *God*, I *do* take Helen to be my wife—but—

JUDGE: You, Helen! Speak, woman, speak!

HELEN: I take Ernest to be my husband in the eyes of God, but—

JUDGE: [*Raises his hand augustly and in a voice of authority.*] Then, since you, Ernest, and you, Helen, have made this solemn declaration before God and in the presence of witnesses, I, by the authority vested in me by the laws of this State do now pronounce you man and wife! [MR. *and* MRS. HAMILTON *look at each other bewildered. Meanwhile the silence has been pierced, first by a little hysterical scream from* JEAN, *then the others all wake up and crowd about the happy pair, congratulating them. The women who had snubbed* HELEN *before cover her with kisses, for now she is fit for their embraces.*]

JOHN: [*To* THEODORE.] Saved! Saved! Respectable at last, thank God. [*Raising his glass and hammering for attention.*] Here's to the bride and groom. [*All cheer, raise glasses, and drink.*]

ERNEST: [*When the noise dies down. As the others kiss* HELEN.] A moment ago you were a bad woman. Now [*To all.*] behold! she is a good woman. Marriage is wonderful. [JOHN *and* LUCY *run to* JUDGE *and shake hands.*]

JUDGE: [*To* JOHN *and* LUCY, *his wife.*] Yes, Respectability has triumphed this time, but let Society take warning and beware! beware! beware!

A NOTE ON THE EDITOR

Keith Newlin is associate professor of English at the University of North Carolina at Wilmington, where he teaches courses in late nineteenth- and early twentieth-century American fiction and drama. He is co-editor of the *Selected Letters of Hamlin Garland* (1998) and *The Collected Plays of Theodore Dreiser* (2000).